Chickamauga:

BLOODY BATTLE
IN THE WEST

Two days they fought, and evermore
those days shall stand apart,
Keynotes of epic chivalry
within the nation's heart.

MAURICE THOMPSON
"The Ballad of Chickamauga"

Books by Glenn Tucker

POLTROONS AND PATRIOTS, 2 vols.
  (A History of the War of 1812)

TECUMSEH
  Vision of Glory

HIGH TIDE AT GETTYSBURG
  The Campaign in Pennsylvania

HANCOCK THE SUPERB

CHICKAMAUGA:
  Bloody Battle in the West

Chickamauga:

BLOODY BATTLE
IN THE WEST

by GLENN TUCKER

Maps by Dorothy Thomas Tucker

Morningside

1992

The author acknowledges with appreciation the permission of these publishers to quote from their copyrighted material:

Appleton-Century-Crofts, Inc., to quote from Mary Boykin Chesnut, *A Diary from Dixie*. Copyright, 1905, D. Appleton & Company.

The University of Pennsylvania Press, to quote from *Soldier in the West: The Civil War Letters of Alfred Lacey Hough*, edited by Robert G. Athearn. Copyright 1957 by the Trustees of the University of Pennsylvania.

The Norwegian-American Historical Association, Northfield, Minnesota, to quote from Hans Christian Heg, *Civil War Letters of Colonel Heg*. Copyright, 1936, Norwegian-American Historical Association.

To the Memory

OF THE MANY STUDENTS and former students of DePauw University and DePauw Preparatory School at Greencastle, Indiana, who fought in the great battle of the western armies at Chickamauga, among them Colonel James Frazer Jaquess, commanding the 73rd Illinois, the first "Preachers' Regiment," Laiboldt's brigade; Captain Eli Lilly, commanding the 18th Indiana Light Artillery, Wilder's brigade; Lieutenant Colonel William D. Ward, commanding the 37th Indiana, Sirwell's brigade; Lieutenant Colonel James T. Embree, commanding the 58th Indiana, Buell's brigade; Colonel John T. Smith, commanding the 31st Indiana, Cruft's brigade; Lieutenant Colonel Marsh B. Taylor, commanding the 10th Indiana, Croxton's brigade; Lieutenant James W. L. Slavens of Major General George H. Thomas' staff; Adjutant Eli F. Ritter, 79th Indiana, brigade of Samuel Beatty (father of Mary R. Beard, the historian); and numerous company officers and enlisted men, including Captain Josiah B. Gathright of the 8th Kentucky Confederate Cavalry, serving in Bragg's army.

Introduction—Revised Edition

For more than thirty years since its original publication in 1961, Glenn Tucker's *Chickamauga: Bloody Battle in the West* has been the sole modern account of the bloodiest two days of fighting in our American Civil War. Tucker combined a general outline of battle action with a colorful narrative of the human interest background and drama involved from the perspective of the generals down through the enlisted ranks.

The publication of this revised edition must necessarily be accompanied by a few words of explanation as to the scope of these revisions. Since Tucker is deceased, his final approval of the additions and corrections made by interlineation in the text could not be obtained. However, in the spring and summer of 1973, it was my great privilege to actually work with him in revising his *High Tide at Gettysburg* for publication of a new edition by the Press of Morningside Bookshop. During that time I became familiar with the types of amendments and changes he wanted made for the revised edition of that book. His concerns dealt with the correction of matters of fact and record, such as officers' proper names and ranks, place names, regimental and brigade identities, numbers and dates, and a few additional words to improve clarity. These matters, when revised, strengthened the text without changing his descriptions of events and his interpretation of them. In making the revisions to this book, I have conscientiously tried to adhere to Tucker's desires and proofed the text for those types of matters of fact while not modifying any of his descriptions or interpretations in the text or accompanying maps, even where my interpretation of those facts might not concur. Thus I believe that this revised edition will strengthen yet remain true to the spirit and content of Glenn Tucker's original account.

Finally, this revised edition is the culmination of a friendship formed twenty years ago with Robert J. Younger of Morningside when I first visited his shop in 1972 to acquire a copy of his initial reprint of this book. We both shared a special interest in this battle and maintained a desire over the years that someday this Tucker book would also be revised and made available to new students of this greatest battle of the western armies, so that they too might better understand the passion behind and in the name—CHICKAMAUGA!

Ken Bandy
Beloit, Ohio, May 20, 1992

FOREWORD

THIS IS A STORY about an extraordinary and perhaps the most stubbornly contested battle of American history. Two armies of approximately the same strength met in the deep woods of north Georgia and fought with a determined fury rarely approached in the desperate war between the states.

While this book undertakes to give an account of the battle, it is quite as much a story of the officers and men of both armies who left there a heritage of courage that can stir the present generation. Never has it been surpassed in the wars of western civilization.

Among the Chickamauga people were characters as fresh, vivid and often as peculiar as any encountered in the pages of the American story. As studies, some of them are even more fascinating than the complex evolutions of the armies which met by chance on this field.

It was a battle of inconsistencies. The outcome turned on an assault by a Northerner in Southern gray—Bushrod Johnson, an émigré to Tennessee from Ohio, who with his division clove through the center of the Union army. One of his stellar regiments, the 25th Tennessee, was led by the Broadway-born Lieutenant Colonel Bogardus Snowden. Another, the 1st Arkansas Rifles, came during this assault under the command of Lieutenant Colonel Daniel H. Reynolds, an Ohioan who had attended Ohio Wesleyan University in Rosecrans' home county. A fellow Ohioan, Otho French Strahl, led a gray-clad Tennessee brigade in Cheatham's division. One of the last dogged attacks against the Federal position on Snodgrass Hill was directed by a second native of New York City, the Alabama general, Archibald Gracie.

The hill was defended and the Union army was saved from complete disaster by a rugged Virginian in blue, a noble fighter and great tactician, George H. Thomas, Bushrod Johnson's classmate at West Point.

A St. Louis newspaperman called it "a soldier's battle," and so it was, because it was more a series of desperate struggles between groups in the thickets than grand sweeps over which generals of corps or divisions had control. A chronological recital of how small units clashed again and again, surging back and forth, retreating and rallying, dying and inflicting death, presents the danger of becoming humdrum. Such has sometimes seemed the case with accounts of this battle, which had no long, cleared valley and looming heights for a Pickett-Pettigrew assault; no magnetic figure of a Robert E. Lee; no missing Jeb Stuart; no toss of dice for the high stakes of Washington, Philadelphia and New York. But it did have drama in abundance and hard fighting in full measure.

In order to break and relieve the sequence of brigade clashes, personality sketches and stories about the participants have been introduced frequently. These are offered to relieve the tumultuous haste with which this complicated battle spilled through the tangled woods. There is leisure here for an anecdote.

A reason for this book is that no earlier account of Chickamauga has been discovered written with anything approaching full detail and giving room to the general atmosphere and less weighty incidents of the dogged, bloody fray. Many of these facts, assembled from state archives, regimental histories and personal manuscripts, as well as from the published memoirs and histories, have not before been brought together. A complete account of the battle would, of course, require volumes.

In his early years the writer knew Chickamauga above all other battles. It was the battle of the uncle of the wooden leg, the battle of the uncle with the deaf ear, the battle of the men who sat under the shade trees of the courthouse in a little Indiana town and talked of times so vast and consequential that nothing else ever seemed quite worth while. An effort has been made to tell the story dispassionately but with full credit to the strong characters in both armies who appeared on this field, and with full recognition also of the weaknesses that were at times glaringly exposed.

G. T.

ACKNOWLEDGMENTS

MANY PERSONS have given help during my work on this book and to them I express gratitude. Especially do I thank Ray D. Smith, Chicago, and his secretary, Helen Reynolds, for providing me with numerous references from Mr. Smith's extensive, personally-prepared index of the *Confederate Veteran* Magazine; and Mrs. Jenny Hallman, Secretary to the Librarian of Furman University, Greenville, South Carolina, for making at nominal charge photostats of articles from the *Confederate Veteran*, Southern Historical Society Papers and other publications.

Rock Comstock, Park Historian, Chickamauga-Chattanooga National Military Park, Fort Oglethorpe, Georgia, for accompanying the Tuckers on tours of the Chickamauga battlefield area, and for making available manuscripts, newspaper clippings, books and other headquarters information. He read the manuscript of this book and made informed and valuable suggestions, though he should not be held accountable for material used or conclusions reached. Appreciation is expressed also to Charles S. Dunn, Superintendent, and Edgar M. Carden, Administrative Assistant, of the Chickamauga Park, for their pleasant assistance.

Peter A. Brannan, Director, and Alma Hall Pate, Military Archivist, Alabama State Department of Archives and History, Montgomery. Hazel W. Hopper, head of the Indiana Division, and members of her staff, Indiana State Library, Indianapolis.

Colonel Willard Webb, Chief of the Stack and Reader Division, Library of Congress, Washington. Mary R. Davis and Evelyn Kline, Special Collections Department, Emory University Library, Atlanta. Mary Bryan, Archivist, State of Georgia, Atlanta. Margaret Ligon, Librarian, and Elizabeth Shepard, Reference Librarian, Pack Memorial Library, Asheville, North Carolina. Mary Seagle, Librarian, Henderson County Public Library, Hendersonville, North Carolina, for obtaining books on inter-library loan.

James W. Patton and his staff, Southern Historical Collection, University of North Carolina Library, Chapel Hill, North Carolina. S. A. Wetherbee, Reference Librarian, Illinois State Library, Springfield, Illinois. Frank M. Stubblefield, Brighton, Illinois, and Phoebe E. Andrews, La Jolla, California, for information about General Bushrod R. Johnson.

For providing information, lending books, making suggestions or giving other help I thank also Eleanore Cammack, Archivist, DePauw University, Greencastle, Indiana; John R. Peacock, High Point, North Carolina; James Ripley Jacobs, Easley, South Carolina; Stanley P. Barnett, Columbus, North Carolina; E. Merton Coulter, University of Georgia, Athens, Georgia; Bell I. Wiley, Emory University, Atlanta, Georgia; R. Gerald McMurtry, Director, Lincoln National Life Foundation, Fort Wayne, Indiana; Rodney C. Loehr, University of Minnesota, Minneapolis, Minnesota; George W. McCoy, Editor, Asheville *Citizen-Times*, Asheville, North Carolina; Brigadier General Eric S. Molitor, U.S.A. Retired, Hendersonville, North Carolina; George B. Manhart, DePauw University; and D. Laurance Chambers for reading the manuscript and giving much help.

For drawing the maps and assisting in the research I am indebted, as in other instances, to Dorothy Thomas Tucker, my wife.

Contents

PART IV—THOMAS: ROCK OF CHICKAMAUGA

PART I

ROSECRANS:

Gifted Eccentric

CHAPTER ONE

A Hoosier Horseman
Opens the Gate

ELEMENTS of Rosecrans' Army of the Cumberland entered Chattanooga, Tennessee, on the morning of September 9, 1863, without the loss of a man.

Much as the American people of a later generation would dread the ghastly sacrifice of life they believed would inevitably be exacted at the crossing of the Rhine, or in storming the Japanese mainland, so had the North come to look with terror toward the impending battle for the heart city of the South, protected by its lofty mountains and great, bridgeless river.

But Rosecrans, by skillful maneuvers heralded to the North as comparable to those of Napoleon or Marlborough at their best, had dislodged Bragg, first from Tullahoma, where the Southern army had rested through the spring months while the Northern general leisurely collected horses and prepared his forward movement, and then, as the corn ripened and provisions were promised ahead, from Chattanooga itself.

This railroad communication center, which alone of all the Southern cities tied the Confederacy into a fairly compact nation, had been thus won speedily, artfully, by strategy instead of lead.

Rosecrans had bypassed the fort-girdled city by a feint to his left, then a wide swing to his right, and like overripened fruit it fell at the mere tread of the approacher. Colonel John T. Wilder, the Greensburg, Indiana, ironmaster whose brigade of mounted infantry had equipped itself out of its own pocketbooks with the sensational new Spencer repeating rifle, had ridden down the right bank of the Tennessee as early as August 21, at a time when Bragg intended to fight it out for the town. Young Captain Eli Lilly, the Greencastle, Indiana, druggist who had become as proficient with the guns as any artillery instructor in the old army, had set up his battery on the close reaches of Stringer's Ridge. In compliance with orders from Major General Thomas L. Crittenden, who commanded the 21st Corps that made up the left wing of Rosecrans' army, he had tossed some shells across the Tennessee River to advise the Southern general that the season for evacuation of the city was at hand.

Wilder gave plausibility to Rosecrans' feint to the left by operating ingeniously along the north bank of the river so as to suggest a movement in force above Chattanooga. He with his mounted infantry and Colonel Robert H. G. Minty with a mixed cavalry brigade of Michigan, Indiana, Pennsylvania and United States regular troops, guarded every ford and patrolled every mile of waterfront from Washington to Williams Island, a distance of about fifty miles.

The resourceful Hoosier occupied the attention of an entire Confederate army corps by threatening suddenly and haphazardly to attack at the different crossings. Every night he sent out details to build large campfires behind the fords, thus indicating the presence of sizable forces: divisions or army corps. To give the impression of large-scale pontoon building, he had his men saw boards and throw the end pieces into the creeks feeding the Tennessee River. To enhance the illusion he had them pound on barrels, and even a sailor might mistake the sound for hammering on the sides of boats. Brigadier General William B. Hazen, who commanded a brigade of Major General John M. Palmer's division, Crittenden's corps, operated upstream with Wilder and added to Bragg's uncertainty by making diversions and pretenses at crossings. Because of these stratagems, Bragg kept his men busy fortifying the upstream fords, when all the while Rosecrans was shifting his army and covertly crossing behind the mountains downstream.[1]

Wilder had come up in front of Chattanooga so rapidly and unexpectedly that he captured artillerymen and animals of a Confederate battery on the north shore, then bagged a part of the picket,

while Captain Lilly was unlimbering his guns. The Federals looked
down from their heights and saw soldiers and civilians running
about in what they called "great consternation." Soon a Confederate battery west of the town opened. Lilly replied accurately
and the fire was quickly silenced. A 32-pounder in the town was
handled more effectively, but a Federal shell hit inside the em-
brasure from which the gun was being fired, and it too was
silenced. Lilly pounded and sank a steamboat, the *Paint Rock*,
disabled another, the *Dunbar*, at the Chattanooga wharf, and tore
apart and splintered the pontoons which Bragg had been holding
in readiness to be thrown across the river should he decide to
recross and operate against Rosecrans' flank or rear. The Northerner already was giving a hint that he was moving impetuously.

Meantime Colonel Smith D. Atkins, the youthful Freeport,
Illinois, lawyer who commanded the 92nd Illinois mounted infantry of Wilder's brigade, had crossed downstream at Battle
Creek, after annoying the enemy upstream at Harrison, being protected by two rifled 10-pounders of the 5th Wisconsin battery.
The brush at Harrison gave the battery opportunity to test its
marksmanship in some of the first firing along the river. As Atkins
had approached the riverbank he had seen a Confederate officer
with a sash across his shoulder come down to the opposite bank
and kneel under a box elder.

"What is he doing?" Atkins inquired of his adjutant, but
a little puff of blue smoke gave the answer before the rifle ball
sang over their heads. The Confederate was getting in a first shot
at the approaching enemy. Colonel Atkins observed, "If you see
a man shooting a rifle at you a mile away you have plenty of time
to dodge . . . but you may as well stand still." He knew that
one is as likely to dodge into as away from the path of the bullet.
The evidence of Confederate resistance caused the lieutenant commanding the Wisconsin battery to take the range on the Confederate gun emplacements—a fort with a brass gun in the center
and two steel guns on the flanks. The lieutenant had a novel device,
"a flat piece of brass full of holes of different sizes," by which, if
a man stood up on the opposite shore, he could determine the
range and begin what Atkins called "scientific firing."

No range-finder could have been more exact. When the Federals entered Chattanooga they learned that their first shot had dismantled the brass gun inside the Confederate fort and killed four men.

Once over the river, Atkins was ordered by Major General Joseph J. Reynolds to move toward Chattanooga. He marched at 3 A.M. on the morning of September 9, drove in the enemy pickets, passed over and around the head of Lookout Mountain where it is skirted by the river, and at 9:30 A.M. pushed his advance scouts down the Chattanooga streets.

The only obstacle to Atkins' entry was that Wilder and other units still had the city under desultory fire from across the river and it was difficult to inform them that friends, not enemies, were approaching from the southwest. Patiently a lad with a semaphore spelled out the words "Ninety-second Illinois." By the time three letters of the last word had been signaled, a great shout went up from Wilder's men on the opposite bank. A short time later the Stars and Stripes flew from the roof of the Crutchfield House, three stories high on the Chattanooga skyline. It had been Bragg's headquarters.[2]

Bragg had at length detected the progress of Rosecrans' two corps under Major Generals George H. Thomas and Alexander McD. McCook toward his left and rear, but he made no effort to retard them at the river. He had, in fact, withdrawn the brigade he had earlier stationed on outpost duty opposite Bridgeport, where he had burned the railroad bridge. He had begun on September 8 to move his army toward Ringgold and La Fayette, Georgia, across the parched land. The 33rd Alabama found the dust "half way up to our knees" and thought they must look like "a low line of dusty creatures without feet" as the regiment passed down the Chattanooga street, and, a little later, headed in Indian file through the mountain passes.

As he came around Lookout Mountain, Atkins could witness the withdrawal of Bragg's rear guard. He directed one of his companies to follow toward Rossville, five miles out on the roads to the south, then moved with the balance of the regiment to the Chattanooga railroad depot.

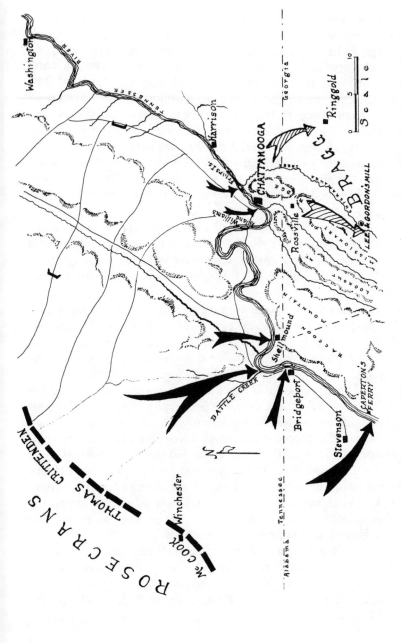

Rosecrans crossing the Tennessee River. Small units demonstrate above and opposite Chattanooga while the main Federal army crosses below.

While the initial bombardment was in progress George D. Wagner, commanding a brigade of Wood's division, Crittenden's corps, had reinforced Wilder on the north bank and set up additional batteries. They joined for several days in the random firing that preceded the evacuation. Though Wilder's men insisted they bombed not the town but only the fortifications, someone's shell fired from Stringer's Ridge on Saturday, August 21, the day the bombardment opened, hit in front of the First Presbyterian Church on Market Street. President Davis had requested a "fast day" for the Southern cause and it was being observed faithfully in the town. A visiting minister, the Reverend B. M. Palmer of New Orleans, was delivering his prayer before the crowded congregation.

Sudden and frightening as was the explosion, the cool, gritty minister did not break the even tenor of his supplication; nor did the larger part of the congregation leave its place, including Major C. W. Heiskell and Dr. W. J. Worsham, both of the 19th Tennessee Infantry.

The main injury was to a little girl, whose leg was broken. Her parents, rushing her from the city, halted at the home of Lieutenant Colonel Beriah F. Moore's father. The officer was absent, and his elderly father declined to admit the distressed family, maintaining that his house was already packed with fugitives from the bombardment. The refusal kindled anger among onlookers. Witnessing the incident was Brigadier General Preston Smith, the gallant Memphis militia officer who had been grievously wounded at Shiloh and had commanded Cleburne's celebrated division on part of the Kentucky campaign. He severely upbraided the old man for barring his door to the wounded child. This so incensed Lieutenant Colonel Moore when he heard the facts that he in turn denounced Smith in writing as a coward and bully. Such heat was not infrequent among the high-spirited officers of Bragg's army, even when an enemy was knocking at the Confederacy's inner door.

General Smith accepted the challenge, though dueling was supposed to be suspended for the war. But neither the general nor the lieutenant colonel was in a position to give or receive much satisfaction, for General Smith had an appointment he had to keep with

death a few days later in the deep woods at Chickamauga, and Lieutenant Colonel Moore had a like rendezvous within sight of his
father's home on Missionary Ridge. Major Heiskell interceded to
give each a brief, additional span of life.

About the only other result of the bombardment was that
twenty-three-year-old Henry Watterson, who sat in the congregation, gained a bride. The young newspaperman had returned to
his native Tennessee after a short term as music critic on the New
York *Times* and was editing and printing the daily Chattanooga
Rebel on wallpaper, while serving also on the staffs of some of the
Confederate generals. He admired the young lady who sat com-
posedly in the choir during the bombardment, escorted her home,
and soon made her Mrs. Watterson.[3]

Brigadier General Wagner sent the first foot soldiers into the
town. The 97th Ohio of Colonel John Q. Lane crossed the river
in boats which the Northerners had secreted in coves and protected with artillery along the riverbank. Wilder went up the
river and crossed at Friar's Island, fighting off a Confederate rear
guard. By this time Crittenden's forces were converging on Chattanooga from three directions. The mixed Ohio, Indiana and Kentucky brigade of Samuel Beatty moved in from the Tennessee
River crossing at Shellmound, worked its way up Nickajack Trace
and reached the summit of Lookout Mountain on the early morning of September 9, where it looked down on Chattanooga, empty
of everything except Confederate rear-guard cavalry. Dust clouds
were visible to the south. Beatty hurried word to Rosecrans that
Bragg had vacated the town, confirming intelligence already dispatched to army headquarters by Wagner; then he moved toward
Rossville to maintain contact and report on the enemy's retreat.

Colonel William Grose's brigade followed Samuel Beatty. It
scaled Lookout Mountain near the Hawkins farm nine miles southwest of Chattanooga and drove off Bragg's left-wing skirmishers
in a neat little action that probably involved about as much severe
fighting as Hooker's more extensive occupation of Lookout Mountain a few weeks later in the widely-heralded "battle above the
clouds." Now the 24th Ohio, a regiment which had fought at Cheat
Mountain in West Virginia, had been a part of Buell's succoring

force that rushed to Grant's aid at Shiloh, and had stood faithfully at Stone's River, distinguished itself by its impetuous assault. Grose gave especial praise to Captain Isaac N. Dryden "for daring bravery in ascending the mountain and driving and punishing the enemy." He too would live until he entered the woods at Chickamauga.[4]

CHAPTER TWO

Over the River and Ranges

FEW MORE spectacular feats had occurred during the war than Rosecrans' crossing of the Tennessee River in late August and early September 1863.

The army collected a sufficient number of boats for the construction of a single pontoon, which was thrown over the river at Caperton's Ferry, the crossing for the town of Stevenson, the important railroad junction of the area. Major General Philip H. Sheridan, a division commander of McCook's corps, meantime began building a trestle bridge at Bridgeport. It was not very satisfactory because a substantial portion of it collapsed while under construction, but fortunately for the army, no troops were on it when the timbers plunged into the river. By September 2, when a good part of the army was already over the river, it was repaired and serviceable, and Sheridan crossed.

The divisions of Richard W. Johnson and Jefferson C. Davis, both of McCook's corps, marched across the pontoon bridge during the three days of August 29, 30, and 31. Brigadier General John M. Brannan's division of Thomas' corps made a more resourceful and exciting crossing at the mouth of Battle Creek, which enters the river between Shellmound and Bridgeport, about twenty-five air miles below Chattanooga. The locality was shielded from Bragg's army, then still in the town, not only by the great bends of the winding river, but also by the parallel ridges of Raccoon and Lookout mountains.

Brannan's division crossed mainly in the most primitive of craft, pirogues such as were used by the Indians and the early French settlers. They were hollowed out from the huge Tennessee poplars and would hold a small company, or up to fifty men. The poplars were cut and shaped behind the protecting forests along Battle Creek and floated down to the river when Rosecrans signaled the moment for crossing. From other timbers the soldiers built barges large enough to float the artillery, while the good swimmers fastened fence rails into small rafts that would hold their guns, ammunition, equipment and clothing. These they pushed ahead of them as they breasted the current. The odd-looking flotilla swept out of the mouth of Battle Creek on August 29, covered by Federal sharp-shooters along the north bank. Brannan easily effected a landing and drove off the Confederate pickets on the southern shore.[1]

Reynolds' division crossed mainly in small boats that had been collected up and down the river. Soon the bulk of Thomas' infantry was south of the Tennessee. Then began the movement of the artillery and baggage of both corps across the river—great trains of supplies that would be sufficient for twenty-five days, should the army be severed that long from its base; enough ammunition for two large battles; horses and mules, herds of cattle, guns and caissons, blacksmith shops, ambulances—everything a great army would require operating footloose in an enemy country.

For seven days the corps of Thomas and McCook—roughly 40,000 infantry and artillery—passed the river, until on September 4, while part of Crittenden's corps was still facing Chattanooga north of the river and creating diversions upstream, Rosecrans had the larger part of his force on the south side.

Brigadier General John Beatty, one of the warm, sincere officers of Rosecrans' army, who commanded a brigade of Major General James S. Negley's division, rode down to the pontoons at Stevenson with Lieutenant Colonel Harrison C. Hobart of the 21st Wisconsin and Colonel Timothy R. Stanley, commanding another of Negley's brigades. As they approached the river they joined another group of mounted officers—Rosecrans, McCook, Negley, commander of the second of Thomas' divisions, and Brigadier General James A. Garfield, Rosecrans' chief of staff.

Rosecrans drew up his horse and shook hands with the newcomers, giving a somewhat formal greeting which Beatty recorded as "How d'ye do?" The others followed the commanding general's lead and shook hands, Negley with a friendly smile, Garfield with what was regarded a politician's grip. Then the party rode to the pontoons, around which a goodly part of a regiment was swimming, the men diving, splashing, ducking one another, taking full advantage of the clear blue mountain water that filled the broad river. The officers seemed to enjoy the good spirits of the soldiers, who were frisking when they should have been marching. In his diary entry that night Beatty dwelt on the beauties of the Tennessee country where the new, ribbonlike pontoon bridge spanned the river: "The island below, the heavily-wooded banks, the bluffs and mountain, present a scene that would delight the soul of the artist."[2]

Bragg, who all the while had received reports—often partial and unsatisfactory—in Chattanooga, had held tenaciously to the belief that the Federal movement downstream was a feint and that the main crossing would be upstream. He understandably adhered to this opinion, not only because of Wilder's deceptions, but also because Major General Ambrose E. Burnside had come down from Cincinnati and was operating against Knoxville, which he captured on September 6. Rosecrans normally might be expected to move toward rather than away from Burnside. Good judgment would seem to dictate that he merge his own Army of the Cumberland with Burnside's Army of the Ohio and then confront Bragg with a vastly superior and united force. That, indeed, was his ultimate intention.

But there were other considerations. Rosecrans' base was Nashville, not Knoxville. If he went upstream in order to keep closer contact with Burnside, he would be moving away from his railroad supply line which ran from Nashville to Stevenson, about thirty-five air miles downstream from Chattanooga. Stevenson was a proper depot for a flanking movement to the right. If he should move upstream toward Burnside he would be entering a barren, unproductive, and, at that time, almost a desolate country having few good roads and presenting aggravated supply problems. His army was not of a size for him to detach the heavy details which would be necessary to guard the mountainous routes, nor did he have enough mules for hauling. Moreover, he did not need Burn-

side to win Chattanooga. He needed Burnside to protect his left
from any encircling movement by Bragg's army after it had been
forced out of Chattanooga and a battle impended.

Downstream he had also the benefits of two mountain ranges,
Raccoon and Lookout, to screen his movements and keep Bragg
baffled as to where he intended to strike. Bragg's miserable intelligence during these early stages of the Chickamauga campaign
was a failure of his methods and not of his cavalrymen. He concentrated his horsemen on his flanks and neglected his front.
Nathan B. Forrest's cavalry was far on his right and thus the
services of the best of his subordinates were lost to him in the
immediate Chattanooga area.

Harmful also to his army had been the murder in May 1863
of Major General Earl Van Dorn, whose fondness for a woman
and indifference to her jealous husband had deprived the Confederacy of his able leadership at this critical time. Rated by no
less an authority than Major General Dabney H. Maury as "the
greatest cavalry soldier of his time" and "the most remarkable
man . . . Mississippi has ever known," Van Dorn could have supplied the Confederate army with some of the dash so wanting
in the two top commanders, Bragg and Leonidas Polk, the bishop.
Coming up from Mississippi to assist Bragg and operate in Rosecrans' rear, he was shot just before the opening of the summer
campaign.[3]

Bragg learned of Rosecrans' crossing downstream not from any
vigilant screen of headquarters scouts, but from a citizen of the
Caperton's Ferry area who brought him the intelligence on August
31. Still, information from such an untrained observer could not
reassure him whether this was the main crossing or simply a diversion to cover the crossing expected at any moment upstream.
Thus it was partly due to Bragg's lamentable intelligence methods
that Rosecrans was able to get his army to the south bank without
fighting a major battle and to effect his well-nigh bloodless capture
of Chattanooga—one of the great strategic achievements of the
war.

For three days after September 4, Rosecrans' army was laboriously engaged in crossing Raccoon Mountain, which, as it ex-

tended to the southwest, became Sand Mountain. The trails zig-zagged and the ascents were severe.

Baird's division of Thomas' corps stationed details with long ropes at the difficult curves and steep climbs, and when the mules faltered—though, as a Hoosier soldier explained, they were "stimulated by the most fiery language known to an army teamster"—the ropes were attached to the heavily loaded wagons. The men, straining to the cadence of "a long pull, a strong pull, and a pull altogether," heaved the wagons to the summit. The top of the range was reached September 5, but this was by no means the end of the army's mountain climbing.

Crossing Raccoon and Sand Mountain took Rosecrans into Wills Valley. Ahead of him, separating him from Bragg's army and, as he supposed, Bragg's line of flight to Rome and Atlanta, was the long, steep Lookout Mountain range, over which there were but three usable passes. The first was immediately at the Tennessee River, where a poorly engineered road and a single-track railroad afforded connection with Chattanooga from the west and north. The railroad had crossed the Tennessee River at Bridgeport before the bridge was burned; then ran southwest to Stevenson, where it divided, one route going to Murfreesboro and Nashville and the other through north Alabama to Huntsville and thence west. This was the pass that was used by Colonel Atkins.

The second pass was Stevens Gap, which gave entry twenty-six miles south of Chattanooga into a pleasant farm and pastureland called McLemore's Cove. The third gap was Winston's, forty-two miles south of Chattanooga. Bragg had made no effort to defend Raccoon or Sand Mountain and now he left unguarded these Lookout Mountain defiles. Although it meant a dispersal of his army over a wide area, Rosecrans determined at this juncture to send one of his corps through each of the three Lookout Mountain gaps.

The reason had its origin as much with the War Department as with army headquarters. For Rosecrans, who was never reluctant to take chances but was not disposed to rashness, was being goaded by Halleck. The pressure was being applied in much the same manner that the commander in chief had, from his Washington desk, prodded Meade after Gettysburg, though he had had no actual knowledge of the field situation or of the condition of Meade's army after the ordeal of three days on Cemetery Ridge.

Meantime the balance of Crittenden's corps made the passage at Bridgeport, Shellmound and Battle Creek. Crittenden accompanied Wood's division into Chattanooga, arriving at 12:30 P.M. on September 9, three hours after the entry of Colonel Atkins. That afternoon the divisions of Palmer and VanCleve marched around the point of Lookout Mountain with their artillery and ammunition trains, and by nightfall Crittenden's Twenty-first Corps was well concentrated around Chattanooga—Wood in the city and Palmer and VanCleve at Rossville. That night Crittenden ordered Palmer and VanCleve to pursue Bragg vigorously on the morning of September 10, moving to Ringgold and on to Dalton, Georgia. Wood was to leave Wagner's brigade as a garrison for Chattanooga and follow with his other two brigades, those of Buell and Harker, down the La Fayette road.

Rosecrans had been anything but the War Department's darling since he had contemptuously turned down Halleck's preposterous offer that the next permanent rank of major general in the regular army would be given to the general who won the first victory. Where Grant merely ignored the auction, Rosecrans denounced it with all his fiery vigor, and by doing so not only deeply offended Halleck, whose chagrin must have been acute after he read Rosecrans' reply, but also the covert originator of the unsavory transaction, Secretary of War Stanton. Rosecrans had made it clear that he was serving not his personal interest, as Halleck seemed to imply, but his country.

Halleck had carried on his harassing ever since Rosecrans settled down in his campaign of what became scoffingly termed "masterly inactivity" after Stone's River. The general had so inured himself to complaint that when President Lincoln wrote him a suggestion, he gave no more satisfaction in reply than that he would "attend to it." Even the patient President would have to wait his turn.[4]

But Rosecrans now began to heed Halleck at exactly the wrong moment. The commander in Washington had an impression that the Confederacy was breaking up and that Bragg was heavily involved in the disintegration. Lee had been forced back from Pennsylvania, Vicksburg had capitulated and Chattanooga had been evacuated without a battle. A substantial body of opinion in Washington was that Bragg was in headlong flight to Rome and Atlanta and should be followed in haste, just as Lee, in the judgment of the President and the War Department, should have been pressed relentlessly and attacked vigorously after his withdrawal from Seminary Ridge. Halleck, without being on the ground, did not hesitate to urge upon Rosecrans a hot pursuit of Bragg. But as the mountain ranges shielded Rosecrans' movements from Bragg, so did they also screen Bragg's movements from Rosecrans.

At this time Bragg made some substantial contributions to his enemy's false impressions. He sent back scouts to pose as deserters. They passed over the mountains or filtered into Chattanooga by the scores, carrying sensational disclosures of how the Confederate army, demoralized by the loss of its stronghold, was in full flight, unlikely to put up any serious resistance this side of Rome and probably nowhere along the 119-mile route between Chattanooga and Atlanta.

Rosecrans had achieved the great object of his campaigning with the capture of Chattanooga. His movement to the right had forced Bragg to retire or face the likelihood that his communications would be cut and that he would be isolated from his depots and workshops. The Southerner was not to be trapped into another Vicksburg, so he accepted retreat. Rosecrans might at this stage have reversed the march of Thomas and McCook and concentrated these two corps with that of Crittenden in Chattanooga. Then, with Chattanooga as a base, he might have faced to the south and begun a more orderly campaign against Bragg's army and Atlanta. That was Thomas' recommendation.

But the misleading reports of Bragg's demoralization, added to the War Department clamorings, persuaded Rosecrans to the more venturesome course of advancing on a wide front through the mountains in the hope that he might interpose his army between the enemy and Atlanta, or possibly strike Bragg a flank blow as he marched south, and bag or annihilate his entire army. At this stage Rosecrans did not have the information that Bragg was being heavily reinforced, though Halleck might have told him. He thought he had to deal only with the 35,000 to 40,000 Confederates who had confronted him at the outset of the campaign back at Tullahoma.

Bragg could have no certainty about which of the lower passes Rosecrans would debouch from and could only await a revelation of the Federal general's intentions. Clusters of Georgia and Tennessee countryfolk stood at vantage points on the ridges, watched the march of the Federal corps, and then sent off messengers to Bragg at night to tell him of the day's developments. To one delegation of these volunteer scouts the restrained Southern commander grew emphatic enough to slam his fist on the table and declare that Rosecrans would soon be driven north of the Tennessee again.

Far from flying pell-mell toward Rome, Bragg had retired toward La Fayette as a strategic necessity, but he had kept his army fairly well concentrated at a time when Rosecrans was inviting disaster by extending his front abnormally and advancing through gaps approximately forty miles apart. With his left in La Fayette, twenty-six miles south of Chattanooga, and his right resting on Chickamauga Creek at a point where it was crossed by the La Fayette-Chattanooga road, Bragg awaited both reinforcements and a clarification of the enemy's purposes.[5]

CHAPTER THREE

The General Relishes
Midnight Talkfests

Up to this point in his campaign Rosecrans had revealed all of the strategical ability for which he had become distinguished in his earlier campaigns in West Virginia and Mississippi.

The North was electrified by the intelligence that he had maneuvered Bragg out of the mountain citadel. Southern Negroes rejoiced.

> Ole Rosey's down in Tennessee
> Bobbin' around, bobbin' around;
> And settin' all the darkies free
> As he goes bobbin' 'round.
> The big Secesh no more will be
> "Bobbin' around," "bobbin' around,"
> For Rosey's down in Tennessee
> An' he am "bobbin' around."[1]

The eyes of the nation were on the Army of the Cumberland. Neither Meade's victory in Pennsylvania nor Grant's capture of Vicksburg had been the occasion for greater applause or more general relief. It did seem that the months of the Confederacy might be numbered on a single hand. The death thrust could soon be delivered. If Rosecrans could defeat Bragg in Georgia and thereby sever Virginia and the Carolinas from the Gulf states, the war might readily be finished before the coming of the Georgia winter.

31

Rosecrans was gifted, lovable, irritable, peculiar. No doubt he was the closest approach to genius among the Federal generals. The South—and the enemy is usually a fair judge—rated him at this stage the ablest. The Atlanta *Commonwealth* called him "a wily strategist," "a brave and prudent leader." The newspaper found an explanation: "He is different from the native Yankee, being bold, frank, outspoken, and possessing the dash and manner of the Western people."

Henry M. Cist, the newspaperman-general who was with him at Stone's River and Chickamauga and in later years served long as secretary of the Society of the Army of the Cumberland, declared that Rosecrans' fame as "the greatest strategist of the war" was secure despite the hammerings of an overabundance of enemies with an underabundance of scruples. The Ohio correspondent, Whitelaw Reid, tended to agree, saying "competent critics, after surveying the whole field," placed Rosecrans at the head of the Northern strategists. Numerous others supported this view, both before and after the Chickamauga campaign.[2]

The Rosecrans family had come from Brandenburg via Amsterdam, settled with the Dutch in New York, then moved to Pennsylvania. The German name means "wreath of roses." The immediate family, consisting of physician Daniel Rosecrans and his four sons, had emigrated to Kingston Township, Delaware County, Ohio, from the Wyoming Valley in Pennsylvania in 1809. One of the four émigré sons, Crandell, was the general's father.

During the War of 1812 Crandell Rosecrans enlisted under William Henry Harrison and became a captain and adjutant of a company of light horse. After peace he farmed, ran a country store, sold real estate and acquired a fair competence.

William's mother, Jane Hopkins, was granddaughter of Stephen Hopkins of Scituate, Rhode Island, colonial governor and aged Signer of the Declaration of Independence, who resolutely remarked when he saw his wavering script on the document, "My hand may tremble but my heart does not."

As a lad Rosecrans was gifted, versatile, precocious. Although opportunities for schooling were meager in the Delaware County farm country, he studied so eagerly that at fifteen he had exhausted the possibilities of his neighborhood. He had mastered retail business methods so well by the time he was fourteen that he was sent to liquidate a store nearby which he did with credit. He worked as bookkeeper, debt collector and clothing store clerk. Like Lincoln, he had his first view of slavery when he made a boat trip down the Mississippi, a journey on which he sickened at Vicksburg and came near death. He detested slavery: "Of all the aristrocracies upon earth, that of the slaveholder is the most . . . contemptible, the most damnable."

Adept at mathematics and fascinated with scientific subjects, he yearned so strongly to go to West Point that without confiding in his family he wrote a letter of application to Secretary of War Joel R. Poinsett, a letter which must have excited the curiosity of the Secretary because he set the appointment machinery into motion. But time was required, and the impatient Rosecrans received no prompt reply. Instead of being disheartened he now went to his father, drew up a formal petition with parental approval and supporting documents from his Congressman, and took the bulky package to the post office. As he was about to mail it he was handed a letter from the War Department. It was his appointment to the Military Academy.[3]

His hard study made him almost a recluse. He stood fifth in a class of fifty-six and was third in mathematics. His roommate was James Longstreet, not much of a help with the books. The two were distinguished at the academy. Longstreet was voted the most handsome; Rosecrans was regarded the most studious. Earl Van Dorn, whom he would oppose in Mississippi and Tennessee, was a classmate. Other classmates were Lafayette McLaws, John Pope, Abner Doubleday.

After graduation he joined the engineer corps at Fortress Monroe, returned to West Point to instruct in engineering and philosophy, served as post commissary and quartermaster, built the new cadet barracks, and then went to the Washington Navy Yard on loan by the army to the Bureau of Docks and Yards. He missed field duty in the war with Mexico, the practical training ground of so many of his Civil War associates, but his behind-the-lines service was outstanding. In Washington he worked so tirelessly his health gave way. Pressed as he was, he found time to teach a Sunday school class of 700 Negro children. Jefferson Davis, Secretary of War, liked his work and declined to accept his resignation, but gave him a leave for three months to reconsider.

Rosecrans quitted the service April 1, 1854, to become an architect and consulting engineer in Cincinnati. During the next seven years his rise in business was astonishingly rapid. He took over direction of extensive mining interests in West Virginia, where he conducted geological surveys and pointed with striking accuracy to profitable new veins of coal to be exploited. He became president of a navigation company formed to transport coal to the market. Turning to coal oil, he built a production plant of large capacity, then began experiments to develop a pure, odorless, readily marketable oil.

He had been working in the laboratory for sixteen days when a safety lamp exploded, burning him terribly. His clothes were ignited and his flesh seared and blistered but he struggled first to put out the flames and save the plant. Then he walked the mile and a half to his home, went to bed and remained on his back for eighteen months. His life was often despaired of but his resolution pulled him through the terrible ordeal. His business languished but his partners, though possessing no background in engineering and chemistry, managed to keep it solvent while he was recovering.

Industrious, resourceful, possessing ample scientific learning to put him in the forefront of his times, he worked hard on experiments and inventions. Among his inventions were the odorless oil, a round lamp wick, a short, practical lamp chimney and a new and economical method of manufacturing soap. War came just as he recovered from his burns. Even before he could put his business into shape, the people of Cincinnati and, in turn, the Ohio state government, pressed army duties on him, first as drillmaster of the "Marion Rifles" in his own Fourteenth Ward, then as the engineer officer to lay out Camp Dennison where the volunteers were assembling. In the eastern cities he became an efficient procurer of arms for Ohio troops. Governor Dennison appointed him Chief Engineer of Ohio. Finally he won the field service he desired as colonel of the 23rd Ohio Volunteer Infantry.

The 23rd Ohio was undoubtedly the most unusual regiment of the war, measured by the great names included in its original roster. Aside from Colonel Rosecrans, who rose to command an army, two future Presidents, Rutherford B. Hayes and William McKinley, marched in its ranks. A well-remembered brigade commander, Eliakim Parker Scammon, who led the Kanawha Division at Second Manassas and at Antietam, was on its rolls, as was also Stanley Matthews, later United States Senator and Associate Justice of the United States Supreme Court.[4]

Soon Rosecrans was appointed a brigadier general in the regular army, an unusual promotion at that time for one who had been so long out of the service. He reported to McClellan in Cincinnati and was off to spectacular battles in West Virginia.

Rosecrans had embraced Catholicism—after long introspection rather than through sudden emotional agitation. Unlike the Southern Lieutenant General Leonidas Polk, the Episcopal bishop second in rank in Bragg's army, who was won suddenly from a military to an ecclesiastical career by the forensic power of a West Point chaplain, Rosecrans moved by slow degrees toward his new faith. He accepted it over strong parental objection before his graduation from West Point.

His sincerity and devoutness were so marked that they led his youngest brother, Sylvester Horton Rosecrans, to accept Catholicism. The family had been stanchly Methodist, and to this denomination the second son, Wesley, as his name might imply, adhered. Sylvester Horton rose to distinction in the Catholic Church while Wesley went to Iowa and devoted his life to farming.

William's affection for Sylvester, whose character throws light on the attitude of the general, was expressed in attentiveness to the younger man's education. Sylvester idolized his older brother and was guided to St. John's at Fordham, New York, where he was graduated with high honors. Through his brother's auspices he came under the tutelage of the Reverend John B. Purcell, Catholic Bishop of Cincinnati and later Archbishop and Patriarch of the West and a close friend and supporter of President Lincoln. Purcell won the censure of Southern Catholics and strict Constitutionalists by keeping the American flag flying over his Cathedral during the Civil War. Sent by Bishop Purcell to Rome for theological studies, Sylvester was ordained there and returned to Cincinnati to be one of the pastors of the Cathedral. He rose to become the first Bishop of the See of Columbus.

Testimony is abundant as to the inspiring character of this contrite, simple man, who endeared himself to his generation in Ohio. He wrote much, presided over a Cincinnati college, visited the Army of the Cumberland, promoted athletics, and devoted literally every cent he could obtain to charity. Frequently it was noted that he walked long distances simply because he did not have the money for carfare. When he died it was discovered that his entire worldly wealth consisted of only two silver half dollars.[5]

Though no less intense in his purpose, William was more worldly in his aim. Both brothers learned with alacrity. But lessons in human relationships were much more perplexing to the general than were mathematical theorems, and he was anything but conventional in his transactions with his soldiers.

One of his irritating habits was to prowl through the camp at night and see a lot of things which some of the other generals thought it would be better for the commanding officer to be ignorant of. If he heard talk or singing, or if a tent showed a light after taps, he would strike with his sword on the canvas and command silence and darkness. In retaliation the men would sometimes pretend that he was merely an inebriated wagoneer or a practical joker and would shout rough banter at him, then offer profound apologies when he would put his head through the tent door. His chief subordinate in West Virginia felt it would have been wiser to avoid "unnecessary collision with the privates" and concluded that "an impulsive man is too apt to meddle with details."

Still, the soldiers loved him. His personal courage was known to every officer or private who had served with him in West Virginia, at Iuka or at Stone's River. It had been demonstrated in his business well before the war on the occasion when he was burned almost fatally by the explosion of benzole gas. The scars caused by the accident, especially the large one across his forehead, were clearly visible during the war, and were apparent in photographs.

He was in the middle of the battles in West Virginia, at Iuka and at Corinth. "He is truly a hero on the battlefield," an onlooker said. When his chief of staff was killed by his side at Stone's River —his head shot off by a cannon ball—Rosecrans' remark was: "Brave men die in battle. Let us push on." In such instances men flinch instinctively, but not Rosecrans. He might be excitable, even emotionally unstable, as some said, but from anger, not from fear.

His division commander John M. Palmer noted that he never blanched, and termed his courage "magnificent." "I made up my mind then," said Palmer, "that if I was about to fight a battle for the dominion of the universe, I would give Rosecrans the command of as many men as he could see and who could see him."[6]

His measures were thorough. When he required horses, he seized every animal in Nashville that could stand on its feet, making only three exceptions. These were the carriage horse of Mrs. James K. Polk, widow of the eleventh President; the team of the manager of the State Insane Asylum, and the saddle horse of Major William B. Lewis, who had served as aide and quartermaster for General Andrew Jackson during the Creek War. Lewis had been such a frequent resident at the White House that he was part of the Jackson family entourage. Being above eighty years of age, he lived and rode in another era. When importuned to spare other mounts for private use, Rosecrans replied that he would not even leave one for his friend Bishop James Whalen, the Catholic Bishop of Nashville.

Nearly any Federal general could have studied with benefit Rosecrans' methods of camp sanitation, which had a sharp bearing on the good health of his command. A special correspondent of the Philadelphia *Inquirer* was delighted to note that the ground was swept as clean as a Cincinnati parlor. Old Rosey was intolerant of litter.

As to his innate military ability and leadership qualities, there were those who doubted his excellence. The New York *Herald* correspondent W. F. G. Shanks, who came to know the Army of the Cumberland and its generals as intimately as he understood James Gordon Bennett's eccentricities, regarded Rosecrans as weak, theatrical, excitable, at times vehement and incoherent—

about all a general should not be. The newspaperman could not discern in him one single attribute of good generalship. He was neither a strategist nor a tactician, but "tricky like an Indian."

The correspondent did reveal his bias when he charged the general with being a demagogue. The evidence cited was that Rosecrans chatted with the men jocularly during his inspections and always spoke pleasantly to them, reserving for the officers any censures for faults in equipment or appearance. In earlier correspondence to the *Herald*, Shanks did not regard the contact between general and soldier so reprehensible. He had told of the soldiers' pride in their commander and of how one boasted, "The General spoke to me today." Even to prisoners, Rosecrans talked not unfeelingly, in such words as "By George, old fellow, you fight well, you can't whip this army!"

His habit of putting the blame on the officers instead of the men was noticed when he inspected his troops back in Bowling Green earlier in the war. He seemed impatient of soldiers who complained they could not get shoes, blankets or canteens.

"Go to your captain and demand what you need!" he exclaimed vehemently. "Go to him every day till you get it. Bore him for it! Bore him in his quarters! Bore him at mealtime! Bore him in bed! Bore him, bore him, bore him! Don't let him rest."

Then he told the captains to do the same thing with the colonels. An officer who observed the reaction said, "The men came to like 'Rosey.' "[7]

John Beatty, who commanded a brigade of Negley's division, had an unhappy experience with Rosecrans' temper. While the army was in camp during the spring preparations, he had been confused about an order. He thought it was intended for Brigadier General Samuel Beatty, who commanded the first brigade of Van-Cleve's division, and had not executed it as Rosecrans desired. When he explained the mixup of names the commanding general exploded.

"Why in hell and damnation didn't you mount your horse and come to headquarters to inquire?" Rosecrans shouted. Then, in a white frenzy, he stormed in language that Beatty regarded as "ungentlemanly, abusive and insulting."

Chief of Staff James A. Garfield and a group of other officers were there, and Beatty's humiliation was extreme. "For an instant I was tempted to strike him," the subordinate wrote that night in his diary. But his good judgment restrained him, and he about-faced and stalked out of the room.

When they met next on the drill field Rosecrans greeted him cheerfully and the incident was closed. But was there not remaining a hint that the general lacked full balance under stress? Were not such emotional rages too severe? Some of the other generals thought so. Major General Jacob Cox had noticed back in the West Virginia campaigns that his speech, ordinarily rapid, became hurried to the point of stammering when he was excited.

W. D. Bickham, an observer who spent three months with him, gave a description of army headquarters at Murfreesboro. There the commanding general occupied the Keeble residence with its charming garden, and utilized as well the town house of the former Congressman, Charles Ready. Three weeks before Rosecrans' arrival the elegant Ready mansion had been the scene of the marriage of the Confederate cavalryman John Hunt Morgan to the bewitching Martha Ready, known as the girl who set a new style in Washington society by wearing a curl dangling down her forehead. Lieutenant General Leonidas Polk had officiated. Jefferson Davis was a wedding guest. The Northerners seemed exultant to find that in the rich aristocratic Southern setting "the sofas and tables and stands and what-nots"—almost everything in fact—"were manufactured by low plebeians in the greasy town of Cincinnati."[8]

Amid these surroundings Rosecrans conducted his army business with speed and efficiency. He rose regularly at eight and always had morning devotions with his priest. He ate breakfast, went to his office and worked until two in the afternoon, reading the morning reports, issuing orders, meeting callers. At two he mounted with his staff and rode through camps and fortifications. A careful dresser himself, he exacted neatness, military posture, and close attentiveness from his aides. Since he insisted that all have handsome mounts, the party made a striking picture of military trimness as he led it through the regimental streets and across the drill fields. Everywhere and always he was cheered vociferously—possibly because on these inspections the general was preceded by outriders who signaled his coming, and the flag was borne at the head of his small escort column.

About the only defect in his military appearance was that he nearly always had a cigar in his mouth. Even though it might go out in a period of stress, as in battle, he would hold the stump in his teeth for hours. Completely absorbed, he would take it out of his mouth when giving orders, then put it back mechanically.

He wore a black felt hat ordinarily tipped back sharply on his head so that the rear brim covered his neck and the back collar of his coat. His horses were magnificent and spirited: "Boney," a handsome bay, and "Robey," a slim-angled gray.

A combination dinner and supper was served at headquarters at four. As the general ate but two meals daily, so it had to be with the staff. After a companionable meal where the talk was lively, he lighted a fresh cigar, read the newspapers, and idled until darkness. Then, as if his inventions with the kerosene lamp had won him to night work, he began the main business at headquarters, handling it rapidly and with sureness, rarely hesitating in making a decision. He dictated letters—"hundreds of letters," one observer said—passed on court martial verdicts, read reports, did what was necessary to run the army. Map study was almost an obsession with him, and he personally invented a method of making copies of maps available to subordinates by photographic duplication. In the matter of night hours he was a pitiless tyrant with his staff.

All of this ended at midnight, when the hours of conversation and relaxation commenced. At these night chats that were not unlike college "bull sessions" the commanding general was blithe, facetious, happy, almost charming. At times he would ramble on until daylight. He never retired before 2 A.M. The matter of creeds and faiths appears to have been discussed in good spirit, with nobody yielding much or becoming provoked, either.

He enjoyed literary and historical topics quite as much as religion and was thoroughly at home in the classics. The soldier-scribe Bickham, who seems to have tried to give a fair picture of these nighttime confabs, said he "charmed" the other officers—

the juniors of his staff, to be sure—by his illustrations and the "pungent and comprehensive character of his crictism." That observer scoffed at a newspaper story saying that McClellan and Buell, two of the best-read Northern generals, surpassed Rosecrans in their grasp of both science and literature. Few in the country were ahead of Rosecrans in science. He excelled in geology and mineralogy and kept abreast of general scientific investigation. Most of his staff must have become excellent amateur geologists by the time they reached the rock mountains encircling Chattanooga.

He was an excellent student of military history, but one of his most capable subordinates thought he relied too heavily on military precedents, knew the answers to problems before they arose, and therefore did not approach each one on its own merits. His tendency was more to salute than to augment the judgment of history.

The love of fellowship, late hours and philosophical discussion had been passed down to him no doubt by his great-grandfather, the Signer Stephen Hopkins, whom John Adams discovered a fountain of learning when they were working together on the committee to draft the Articles of Confederation. The sedate Adams recorded that Hopkins kept them up "until eleven and sometimes twelve o'clock!" with his erudite ramblings. Like Hopkins the Signer, learned in classical lore and ancient and British history, and eager discourser on the great events of the past, Rosecrans the general talked the night hours away.

Some looked questioningly at Rosecrans' proclivity toward night councils of war. Possibly it was an unconscious clutching for a captive audience. More likely it was a wholehearted respect for the opinions of the army's second ranking officer, Major General George H. Thomas, and a desire to have Thomas' views placed from time to time before the other high officers. One of the evidences of Rosecrans' ability was that he never underrated Thomas.

The headquarters attitude, as one attentive scribe observed it, was strikingly harmonious. There was "no shouting, no loud talking, nor rude, boisterous laughter." "An oath is rarely heard—a loud one, never." Liquor was used sparingly when at all. "Due respect is paid for the Sabbath day." Rosecrans attended his church invariably in the morning. "We have not heard an angry word pass between members of this household in many months."[9]

Still, with all his lively good humor, John Beatty judged that Rosecrans' laugh was not a "free, hearty kind." While a winning conversationalist in quarters, where the words came easily and he sparkled with ideas, he surprised his staff by almost funking out when addressing a gathering of troops. He did learn public speaking later in life, when he served in Congress, but in Tennessee in 1863, "he hesitated and stammered upon attempting to address even a line of soldiers at review."

The Georgia correspondent who introduced Rosecrans to Atlanta readers called him "modest, refined, polite, and affable," and said "he would command respect in any community." How the Southern writer obtained so clear an impression of an enemy general was not explained, but he wrote of Rosecrans' erect posture, mild features, clear gray eyes. "His complexion is florid, hair slightly tinged with gray, and his features and person would be called handsome." His nose was his most prominent feature—a "Roman" nose, big, long and arched.

The whispered charge that he was partial to Catholic officers was patently false. On his original staff were members of a variety of creeds. But the only Catholic was his chief of staff, Lieutenant Colonel Julius P. Garesche, who was killed at Stone's River, one of the best-known officers in the army and long a fixture under Cooper and Buell in the adjutant general's office in Washington before the war. None could remotely have believed he had been appointed for religious reasons.

The most frequently related story of how Rosecrans reconciled his profanity with his strict religious code was told by a Presbyterian minister, the Reverend Dr. Morris of Lane Theological Seminary of Cincinnati, who visited the army as a member of a commission caring for wounded soldiers. At headquarters he met the general and, among others, Father Tracy, the general's chaplain. Just then a staff officer entered with information that a spy had been caught inside the lines. The aroused general grew agitated, then highly profane. When the excitement passed, he recalled that clergymen were present. He turned back to them, asked their pardon and exclaimed, "Gentlemen, I sometimes *swear*, but I never *blaspheme!*"[10]

Now operating far in the enemy country and possessing no water transportation, Rosecrans had been hard pressed all along for supplies. The vigilant Confederate cavalry continually interrupted his railroad communication with Nashville and Louisville. During the year ended July 1, 1863, his railroad was open only a little more than seven months. There was not a single bridge or trestle but that was destroyed and had to be rebuilt, some four times, within this year. Tunnels were repeatedly clogged with debris. Often the army was on half rations.

Apparently indifferent to obstacles, Halleck all the while had been demanding an advance by the Army of the Cumberland. He did not recognize that the Barrens between Murfreesboro and Chattanooga were destitute even of vegetables, and could not or did not produce enough fresh food to prevent scurvy, which became a threat in this stepchild army. In one instance a regiment saw a planting of potatoes and broke ranks to dash into the field and devour them raw, without taking time to knock off or wash off the clinging bits of dirt.

Colonel Donn Piatt, a newspaper writer and the confidant and worshiper of Thomas, attributed to that general both a tenacity to the Union cause and an influence over Rosecrans that held the irritable commanding general in restraint and prevented him from what he was often inclined to do: tear his commission into shreds and heap on Stanton, whom he regarded a mere clerk, the contempt and scorn he heartily felt toward the domineering Secretary of War. Thomas told Piatt: "We must take it for granted that they are doing all in their powers to meet our demands." And again, defending his chief from War Department censure over Rosecrans' delays after Stone's River, he said to Piatt, "We cannot move from our base of supplies until this place is rendered secure. It would not only be the loss of millions in money, but the loss of our army."

Thomas felt that Stanton did not take into consideration the fact that Bragg could choose his defenses so as to double the value of his numbers; but Thomas credited the Washington authorities with acting on their best judgment, a concession Rosecrans was by no means prepared to make. Stanton's personal vindictiveness against him, he was confident, was what had deprived the army of horses and mules.

Stanton, while a director of armies, was at heart a politician. Nothing would have given him more personal pleasure than to relieve Rosecrans as commander of the Army of the Cumberland just as he had previously relieved Buell. But the situations were different. Buell had been anything except an abolitionist. He had aroused the political animosity of Governor Oliver P. Morton of Indiana, who had taken on the role of volunteer commander in chief of Union armies in the West, and of Governor Andrew Johnson of Tennessee, both of whom wanted him out. Buell lacked political influence in Washington—a good thing to have in this war.

On the other hand, Rosecrans had protection, even beyond that offered by Secretary Salmon P. Chase, if the findings and opinions of Colonel Piatt are to be given credence. His security was that Stanton feared his removal would alienate the large Catholic war party in Cincinnati, which was giving the administration the most faithful support at a time when there was much Vallandigham-ism and Copperhead-ism in southern Ohio, southern Indiana and southern Illinois. Whether or not any basis existed for such apprehension is beside the point, but it seems clear that Stanton was again attributing to others his own devious methods and purposeful judgments, and believing that supporters of the administration were in it for what they could get. In any event, he smarted under Rosecrans' contempt but feared to raise a finger to rid himself of the irritation.

During the season of wrangling, Rosecrans also had not hesitated to challenge the reasoning of the canny Lincoln. He contended that the best time to attack Bragg was not prior to but after Vicksburg, should it fall. Lincoln pointed out that Bragg could be fought better before Johnston was free to support him. But Rosecrans wondered why Grant, after Vicksburg had capitulated, would not be better able to keep Johnston from reinforcing Bragg than when he had Pemberton also on his hands. The question was pertinent because, as Rosecrans pointed out to Lincoln, Grant had "a better base of supplies and more favorable country; a better railroad and more rolling stock" than the Army of the Cumberland had in operating over the Barrens.[11]

CHAPTER FOUR

Politician and "Bird of Ill Omen"

ROSECRANS' relations with Washington and his future in the service were tied closely to his chief of staff, the politically minded Brigadier General James A. Garfield, an Ohio schoolteacher and lawyer, whose handshake seemed to say, according to the observant John Beatty, "Vote early, vote right."

Garfield had been a member of the court martial that tried Fitz John Porter on the charge of disobeying five of General John Pope's orders at the Second Manassas. During the trial his closely reasoned and concisely expressed opinions as to Porter's guilt won the respect of the presiding officer of the court, the radical Major General David Hunter, who seemed to delight in guilty verdicts. Hunter, then about to head an expedition to the South Carolina coast, requested that Garfield be made his chief of staff, to which Secretary of War Stanton readily assented and announced the appointment.

But before Garfield could leave Washington, word came that Garesche, the Cuban-born Frenchman who had served Rosecrans with the highest efficiency as chief of staff, had been killed at Stone's River. Secretary Chase, always alert to opportunities to advance his own political prosperity along with his country's military fortunes through an indirect control over key army positions, prevailed on Stanton to appoint Garfield to the more important post in the west, then induced Rosecrans to accept and even to put in a request for Garfield. Chase's influence was at high tide. At almost the same instant he was landing for his protégé Hooker the command of the Army of the Potomac.

Rosecrans appears to have been caught off guard by the appointment of Garfield, who was to have a profound bearing not only on his own future usefulness but also on his standing as a soldier in history. Rosecrans was by no means among those of the old regular army most ready to impose confidence in volunteer officers. His own diligent studies had persuaded him that the military was an exacting profession mastered only by long effort, for which forensic talents or advancement in legal or literary pursuits offered no substitutes. The intrepid Garesche, whose blood and brains had been scattered over his chief's face and shoulders, had been one of the most competent West Point graduates, though as in many other cases, circumstances had not awarded him rank commensurate with his abilities.

Rosecrans' reactions toward Garfield were of a personal rather than a military nature. Preceding the arrival of the new chief of staff were reports that he was pedagogical by nature and was a Campbellite preacher addicted to theological debate. Garfield had indeed preached, as he had taught. But he had worked as a carpenter and had walked the canal towpaths in his rise from an impoverished orphan boy to a college professorship and a position of political influence in Ohio before he entered the military service. When he appeared at Murfreesboro the officers, many of whom had known him under Buell, were again impressed by the warmth of his strong personality, while Rosecrans soon found he was anything except the "pious wrangler" or "religious fraud" some had reported him to be.[1]

Garfield, then thirty-three, was a man of powerful build, massive features and convincing words. His blue eyes were sharp and expressive. His forehead, high and wide, had, just above the eyes, a ridge so prominent that, as has been said, it seemed almost to have been turned up with a plowshare. His dome was so huge that his black slouch hat would easily have encircled the head of Daniel Webster.

After some trial conversations Rosecrans was entranced with him. Well educated in the law and liberal arts, and an honor student at Williams College, Garfield possessed a striking vocabulary gained from his assiduous study of the Greek and Latin classics.

Fervid, imaginative, industrious and of large capacities, he was precisely the man to win the gifted Rosecrans, who responded to a scintillating intellect with the rapture of a mineralogist who discovers an unsuspected vein of rich ore.

Garfield, an able speaker, was called on occasionally to preside before army groups, as when he introduced the popular Cincinnati entertainer and reciter, T. Buchanan Reid, at an assemblage of soldiers in the Murfreesboro Court House. Regarding this appearance, the able John Beatty considered that Garfield's words did not have their customary felicity. Beatty acknowledged, however, that he was distracted by Garfield's buttons: too many buttons—a splendid double row of buttons that glistened above the brilliance of the speaker's introductory remarks.

Still, there was a natural question in the army of where Garfield reposed his first loyalty. Major General John M. Palmer, ardent in his devotion to Lincoln though he had been reared a Jacksonian Democrat and had been a stanch Douglas man, looked on Garfield as an agent of the Chase-Ben Wade faction of radicals whose covert purpose even at that early date was to unseat Lincoln. He judged that the budding Ohio politician had been placed in the position of chief of staff in order that he might size up Rosecrans as a potential candidate on the Republican ticket in 1864. On his calls at headquarters Palmer talked with Garfield but held him at arm's length and, being suspicious of his views, never sought to elicit them.

Palmer was able to give Chase and Wade credit for wholesome motives. They believed, he conceded, that the rebellion could be stamped out only by severity such as their own stern personalities were prepared to impose, and would never yield to the compassionate policies Lincoln appeared to espouse. But Palmer sensed Lincoln's greatness, shunned association with hostile cliques, and doubted Garfield.

Rosecrans was indeed at that period being appraised as a possible candidate for the Presidency, but Garfield was not an active factor in any plan to deprive Lincoln of the nomination. Horace Greeley, who was applying the axle grease to any anti-Lincoln vehicles he could set in motion, looked inquiringly at Rosecrans, then sent

James R. Gilmore to Murfreesboro. Gilmore was a successful busi-
nessman who retired at an early age to take on the more exacting
but less remunerative occupation of newspaper writing. He was to
look over Rosecrans, judge his capacity and, if he appeared to be
good political merchandise the New York *Tribune* might offer to
the country, sound him out on the proposition of running for high
office.

Through Gilmore, Greeley opened negotiations with Garfield
on the question of Rosecrans' availability, but Garfield immediately
rebuffed the suggestion, declaring it would "destroy both a wonderful President and an excellent soldier." Garfield's opinion
proved unimportant, for Rosecrans himself entertained no political
ambitions. To the contrary, he was "refreshingly hearty" in his
contempt for politicians. This aversion extended to the heads of
political caucuses and clubs, and "the connivers of election tricks
and the winkers at ballot-box frauds." He opposed strict party
adherence and attributed the Civil War to "partyism." Manifestly
he would not have been a docile candidate for Greeley and the
anti-Lincolnites. To those about him he made it clear that he had
dismissed the subject of politics until after the war.

Gilmore, incidentally, interviewed President Lincoln a little
later at the White House, was captivated by the President's common-sense remarks, and became one of his most energetic supporters for a second term.[2]

Garfield's relationship as chief of staff to Rosecrans called for
close personal loyalty. He was the medium through which the
commander's will was exerted on the army, and the channel
through which communication flowed to the government in
Washington. The affinity between commanding general and chief
of staff was well described by Marshal Foch in World War I when
he said, "Weygand is I."

Rosecrans was not aware of the question of Garfield's first
loyalty. Garfield committed the indiscretion of writing in a highly
critical vein about his commander to his own sponsor, Secretary
Chase—a letter which was to rise and plague him in later years and
bring into focus other phases of his conduct while he was serving
Rosecrans in this confidential post.

Chase was an admirer of his fellow Ohioan, Rosecrans, and made no use of this Garfield letter (though he was unable to repress a subsequent letter). One interpretation placed on Chase's pigeon-holing of the letter was that the Cabinet officer thought Garfield himself aspired to command of the Army of the Cumberland. Chase knew there was no likelihood of such an important assignment going to a citizen soldier, who had no West Point training. He could scarcely have believed that Garfield thought it possible. Still another explanation was that Garfield wanted Thomas to command in place of Rosecrans and was operating behind the scenes to that end. But a reading of the letter suggests that Garfield wanted no more than to impress the Secretary of the Treasury, at that time regarded a possible presidential nominee in 1864, with his own military perspicacity for any later benefits that might accrue.

Garfield wrote first at a time when the War Department long had been expressing its impatience over Rosecrans' reluctance to move against Bragg's army after the battle of Stone's River. That battle was fought on December 31, 1862, and January 2, 1863, and it was not until June 23 that Rosecrans began his advance against Bragg. By July 4 he had maneuvered the Southern general out of Tullahoma and Shelbyville. Again he halted and again the War Department began its insistence that he move. During this second delay Garfield wrote his unsolicited opinion, dated July 27, 1863.

Garfield's letter bristled with complaint: "I cannot conceal from you the fact that I have been greatly tried and dissatisfied with the slow progress we have made in this department since the battle of Stone's River." Again: "I have no words to tell you with how restive and unsatisfied a spirit I waited and plead for striking a sturdy blow. . . . The army had grown anxious, with the exception of its leading generals, who seemed blind to the advantages of the hour." And still: "I was the only one who urged upon the General the imperative necessity of striking a blow at once, while Bragg was weaker and we stronger than ever before." And: "I shall never cease to regret the sad delay which lost us so great an opportunity to inflict a mortal blow upon the center of the rebellion."

Another self-satisfying remark was: "Pleasant as are my relations here I would rather command a battalion that would follow and follow and strike and strike than to hang back while such golden moments are passing."[3] He took the precaution to mark the letter "confidential."

While Garfield did at different times during and after the campaign find much about Rosecrans to commend, the critical attitude seemed to prevail, despite the fact that Rosecrans had reasons against a hasty advance which a more sympathetic subordinate might have regarded as sound. The three main considerations were to wait until Burnside's army moved down from Cincinnati into east Tennessee and gave him protection on his left flank; to get some of Grant's troops that were idle after Vicksburg to give him protection on his right; and finally, to wait until the corn ripened in southeast Tennessee and upper Georgia.

Unmoved by these prerequisites, Halleck on August 5 sent him a peremptory order to advance. Rosecrans still took his time and it was not until August 16 that he felt sufficiently prepared to begin his skillful maneuvers over the Cumberland Mountains against Chattanooga.

In order to protect himself from Halleck's urgency, Rosecrans had in early June submitted the question of an advance to his leading generals. Of the eighteen consulted, all, including Thomas, but with the exception of Garfield, had recommended against it. Garfield drew up a written demurrer from the majority opinion on June 8 and appeared to take some credit for the fact that the army finally did move late that month.[4]

Efforts to excuse Garfield's letter to Chase have been made on the ground that he was saying to the Secretary the same thing he had been telling Rosecrans himself; but advising his chief was a vastly different matter from writing a secret complaint to one of the ranking officers of the government, who was then aspiring to even higher place.

During the campaign Rosecrans had no knowledge of Garfield's confidential correspondence and the relationship between the two appeared sincere and cordial. The letter was published after the war in the New York *Sun* by Charles A. Dana, then the editor. As Assistant Secretary of War he was sent by Stanton to be at Rosecrans' elbow in Chattanooga and at Chickamauga.

Had Stanton combed the country it is doubtful if he could have chosen one less suited than Dana by training and temperament to give a balanced estimate of the abilities of the commander of a great army in action. Dana had paid a visit to the front at Vicksburg, where he found Grant's methods to his liking; then had reached Rosecrans' army on September 11, at a time when it was sprawled over the north Georgia countryside.

As Dana explained his duties later, they were to observe and report the movements of Rosecrans against Bragg. Stanton, therefore, was scarcely frank about the nature of the assignment in the letter of introduction he gave to Dana and which Dana handed to Rosecrans on his arrival. It said his visit was "for the purpose of conferring with you upon any subject which you may desire to have brought to the notice of the department."

Rosecrans was perfectly capable of bringing things to the attention of the department himself. But with characteristic bluntness he took advantage of Dana's remarks and plunged into a diatribe against the War Department for ignoring his requisitions and thwarting his plans, identifying by name his two superiors, Halleck and Stanton. Dana stopped him with an explanation that he had no authority to listen to complaints: "I was sent here for the purpose of finding out what the Government could do to aid you, and have no right to confer with you on other matters."[5]

Giving Rosecrans aid, of course, was not Dana's main function. Much as the distrusting Commune liked to have its own agents travel with generals commanding armies of the French Revolution, or as the council of Venice was more placid when a kinsman of the Doge kept personal attendance on a *condottiere* in the service of the Serene Republic, or as the Senate of Carthage had a deputy with a Punic force, so Stanton wanted his own confidential reporter with the Army of the Cumberland, whose commander he doubted wholeheartedly.

Even a less touchy general might have found the presence of Dana intolerable. His dispatches, written daily, were not submitted to the army commander, and there must have been curiosity about their content. Rosecrans would be the individual best advised on the moves of the army and therefore able to give more accurate information than anything Dana was sending in. Dana's status consequently was that of an informer, whom Andrew Jackson probably would have put in irons or drummed out of the camp before sundown. Rosecrans, however, curbed his temper and took the time to explain the situation of the different elements of his army to Dana, a man who had no command of logistics or strategy and was of little value in the all-important matter of defeating the enemy.

Dana had reached the high responsibility of Assistant Secretary of War because Stanton had liked one of his newspaper articles in the New York *Tribune*, though his military discernment might have been judged from his authorship for the *Tribune* of the notorious "Forward to Richmond" campaign which led to the hasty and disastrous battle of Bull Run. Horace Greeley had opposed the campaign and was so sickened by Bull Run that he could not go to the *Tribune* office for two weeks; nevertheless, he accepted the responsibility before the public and history. But he fired Dana, his managing editor, and announced that the paper would refrain from criticizing army movements thereafter. Stanton, mindful of Dana's pleasing editorial on another subject, called him to Washington, made him a War Department clerk and after the Vicksburg campaign advanced him to the Assistant Secretaryship.

Dana had been an upstate New York farm boy who studied diligently in the Buffalo public library, learned Latin and Greek, lectured on English poetry, attended Harvard, and eventually turned up as one of the managing trustees of the Brook Farm, where for five years he was associated with Nathaniel Hawthorne, George Ripley, Margaret Fuller and others of that celebrated group who made the experiment notable, though it was a failure. Dana did appear among the most practical of the lot, for he won the assignment of business manager, but he was usually called "Professor," being the Greek and German teacher. He was rated a consistent skeptic and a lively conversationalist. He had written for the magazines, and when the farm broke up he went into newspaper reporting and editing, the only foundation for his War Department service.

Attentive soldiers immediately sensed the singular nature of his assignment and treated him "as if he were a bird of ill omen." Most of the men adored old Rosey, and looked on Dana as a spy. They ridiculed him openly when they would see him riding behind Rosecrans. Pretending to confuse him with a sutler, they would call out, "Hey, old sutler! When are you going to open out?" Possibly this downgrading by the men was what made him more assertive about his War Department rank, and led him to the indiscretion—of which only one other high civilian official of the government is known to have been guilty—of issuing orders to military personnel on the battlefield. Another scribe called him "officious." As to his reports, it has been said with some justice that "parts of his information and all of his opinions" were wrong. For the balance of the campaign he was as much a fixture as Garfield at headquarters. Neither appeared to feel that he owed his first loyalty to the army commander.[6]

CHAPTER FIVE

Burnside Dallies Around Knoxville

BURNSIDE'S capture of Knoxville on September 6 was a fulfillment of President Lincoln's cherished ambition to relieve the east Tennesseans, who had remained loyal to the Federal government in what was truly a civil war, often an intrafamily war. Two Confederate forces guarded the region. A corps of fluctuating size, with a maximum strength of about 10,000, under Major General Simon B. Buckner occupied Knoxville and environs. Another force of about 2,500 men under Brigadier General John W. Frazer held Cumberland Gap.

Burnside was the Northern odd-jobs general who had commanded on the North Carolina coast, led a corps in the Army of the Potomac and later the entire army during the unfortunate Fredericksburg campaign, then had taken over the command in Cincinnati, where he had directed the capture of Morgan's Raiders. He had collected the troops and planned the Knoxville expedition, on which he was to co-operate with Rosecrans' Army of the Cumberland.

Burnside had been appointed to West Point by Caleb B. Smith, Secretary of the Interior in Lincoln's cabinet. Smith, then a Congressman from Indiana, had been attracted to him when he was a lad working on a tailor's bench at Liberty, Indiana.

Though Burnside had been given unusual opportunity in the early stages of the war, his performance was rarely up to expectations, and Lincoln did not appear to be sanguine about his success at Knoxville. When handed a dispatch that said firing had been heard in the direction of Knoxville, the President made the enigmatic remark that he was "glad of it." Asked to explain, he went on: "Why, you see, it reminds me of Mrs. Sallie Ward, a neighbor of mine, who had a large family. Occasionally . . . one would be heard crying in some out-of-the-way place, upon which Mrs. Sallie would exclaim, 'There's one of my children that isn't dead yet.' "[1]

The success of Rosecrans' thrust into the heart of the Confederacy depended in large measure on the co-operation that could be maintained between him and Burnside. Burnside had been delayed for a month by Morgan's raid into Indiana and Ohio. An earlier delay had been occasioned by the necessity in mid-June of lending two of his divisions—Potter's and Welsh's—under the command of Major General John G. Parke, a force of about 8,000 men, to help Grant in front of Vicksburg. The corps was returned, greatly wasted by dysentery and other diseases of the miasmal banks of the Mississippi, at a time when Burnside already had begun his movement, but he had moved in anticipation of its arrival.

Before Burnside left Kentucky, Halleck advised him that he was to connect with Rosecrans' left. These instructions, as Halleck explained it, were "repeated five or six times, and he has answered that he is moving with that object."

When Burnside approached Knoxville, Bragg directed Simon Buckner to retire to Loudon, south of the Tennessee River, and, a little later, to join him south of Chattanooga. Seeing the abandonment of Knoxville, the Raleigh, N. C., *Weekly Standard* reiterated a complaint heard earlier in Richmond, that "we are losing ground inch by inch and acre by acre." Bragg's continual tendency to retire gave rise to the story of the conversation between two elderly ladies:

"I wish," said one, "as General Bragg is a Christian man, that he were dead and in heaven; I think it would be a godsend to the Confederacy."

"Why, my dear," responded the other, "if the general were near the gates of heaven, and invited in, at that moment he would fall back."[2]

Buckner's retirement left exposed the Confederate force under Frazer at Cumberland Gap and it was ordered to retreat into Virginia. But Frazer, a West Point graduate, had rations for forty days and insisted that he could hold the well-fortified mountain citadel, called "the Gibraltar of America," and the order for him to evacuate it was withdrawn. When the gap was invested by the Federals on three sides, prospects did not appear so bright to Frazer.

Colonel John F. De Courcy brought down a brigade of Ohio and Unionist Tennessee troops from Crab Orchard, Kentucky. Brigadier General James M. Shackelford appeared with cavalry on the Tennessee approaches. Then Burnside, having Knoxville well secured, advanced with a brigade, making the march of sixty miles from Knoxville in fifty-two hours.

He advised Frazer, whose surrender already had been demanded by De Courcy and Shackelford, to communicate only with him, but when Burnside reached the Confederate camp at the head of his staff he found the American flag flying and learned that the gap had been occupied for an hour by De Courcy's 86th Ohio regiment under Lieutenant Colonel R. W. McFarland. Incensed, the commanding general placed De Courcy under arrest and ordered him back to Lexington, Kentucky, to the anger of his men. They credited him with the capture by a brilliant coup, thus saving many lives that would have been wasted had the heights been stormed.

McFarland drew up a remonstrance against the arrest and sent it to President Lincoln, but he never learned whether it was received. Said McFarland: "I believe it was the unanimous opinion of the twenty-eight officers of De Courcy's brigade that this trouble actually grew out of jealousy caused by the brilliant result of De Courcy's tactics."[3]

What the Cumberland Gap expedition demonstrated was that Burnside could cover sixty miles in fifty-two hours. He was under orders to close on Rosecrans and support his left. His army appeared before Knoxville on September 3 and entered the city on September 6 with 10,000 of the 21,630 men on his August 30 returns. Knoxville is 114 miles from Chattanooga. If Burnside had moved with anything like the speed of his march to Cumberland Gap, he could have joined Rosecrans—or could have sent part of his command to reinforce Rosecrans—easily in seven or eight days, allowing for the bad terrain; that is, by September 14 or 15, well in advance of the battle of Chickamauga. When he entered Knoxville he captured five locomotives and more than twenty cars which might have been employed in part of this movement.

Instead, Burnside engaged in side expeditions that had no relationship to the main movement against Bragg's army, but all the while he reassured Halleck that he had in mind the proposed union with Rosecrans as promptly as it was possible. When Halleck learned at length that Bragg's army was being heavily reinforced, he sent Burnside urgent dispatches on September 13 and 14, the latter saying: "There are reasons why you should re-enforce General Rosecrans with all possible dispatch. It is believed the enemy will concentrate to give him battle. You must be there to help him."

President Lincoln, who was anxiously watching the messages reaching the War Department telegraph office, was provoked by Burnside's faltering into one of his few outbursts of profanity during the war. When the critical message came from Burnside saying, "I shall go on to Jonesboro," a town in exactly the opposite direction from Rosecrans' army, Lincoln exclaimed, "Damn Jonesboro!"

Burnside appears to have felt that his occupation of east Tennessee was the more important part of the campaign and that Rosecrans' movements were of secondary value. An explanation of his actions might be found in his conversation with one of his corps commanders, Major General George L. Hartsuff. Before leaving Ohio, Burnside had said that if the armies came together he would waive his rank and serve under Rosecrans. Now he told Hartsuff he could not go to Chattanooga because he was Rosecrans' senior by three days and there might be confusion about who commanded. Hartsuff's response was prompt: "Let me go. I don't rank him."

Burnside claimed there was not time to send Hartsuff. In his later explanation he alleged that he was "averse to doing what would in any way weaken our hold in east Tennessee."[4]

One by one the conditions Rosecrans had laid down before beginning his campaign were falling. Burnside would not safeguard his left. Grant's army had been dispersed on different tasks after the capture of Vicksburg, none of which included detachment of a corps to give Rosecrans protection on his right, the direction from which Bragg might be reinforced from Joseph E. Johnston's army in Mississippi. Of the three conditions, only one was being met, and that by the bountiful hand of nature. The corn was ripening in east Tennessee and north Georgia.

CHAPTER SIX

Frustration in McLemore's Cove

WHILE Negley's division was advancing up Lookout Valley on September 5, the 78th Pennsylvania Infantry, which had played an important part in turning the tide at Stone's River, learned that Rosecrans had been well advised to delay his campaign until the harvest season.

They found luscious watermelons and corn still green enough for roasting ears, and, more important, a mill on Lookout Creek heaped full of corn, wheat and rye. They ground everything in the mill, scoured the valley for more grain, and handed out the abundant supplies to the rest of the army as it passed.

The flour was left unbolted because the soldiers, according to the regimental commander, Lieutenant Colonel Archibald Blakeley, could bake it better that way. They delighted Old Pap Thomas by sending him a bag of unbolted wheat flour which he later said "made the sweetest and best bread he had ever tasted."

There at the mill in Lookout Valley began a series of incidents that were to have a profound bearing on the war and influence the Northern cause perhaps as much as a battle victory. The ground was low and damp and while the Pennsylvanians were grinding flour and rounding up beef a number grew ill. Sixteen were unable to march when the division moved toward Stevens Gap. Since there were no ambulances, an improvised hospital was set up in tents on a hillside. Food and medicine were provided and a private of Company G who happened to be a physician, Dr. W. S. Hosack, was left in charge. The regiment went on in what was believed to be hot pursuit of Bragg; they became involved in the battle of

Chickamauga and never got back to Lookout Valley to pick up Dr. Hosack and his hospital. Bragg's army overran the territory and made them all prisoners. Hosack was sent to Libby Prison.

In the prison he met a fellow Pennsylvanian, Major Henry White, who had been captured in Virginia, and to whom the prison command and guards were devoting the most solicitous attention. While he was serving in the army Major White had been elected to the Pennsylvania state senate. That body was so closely divided between war and peace factions that Major White's absence allowed the anti-war party to deadlock the senate on war votes. Thus the state of Pennsylvania was rendered impotent at a critical moment in the struggle when it should have been appropriating money, raising troops and making provisions for the vigorous prosecution of the war. Major White could not be replaced in the Senate because there was no way by which his resignation could be obtained from Libby Prison. The Confederate officials, knowing the situation, took especial pains to prevent him from communicating with anyone outside.

Then Hosack was exchanged. This seems to have been because he was a surgeon. Major White wrote his resignation from the Pennsylvania senate on tissue paper; Hosack cut a back button from his coat, took out the stuffing and inserted the resignation in its place, then sewed the button on again. When exchanged, Hosack made for his home in Dayton, Pennsylvania, but stopped at Indiana, Pennsylvania, to hand over the button to Thomas White, the major's father. The father hurried it to Governor Curtin. The Governor was thus enabled to declare the seat vacant and order a special election; a candidate stanch in his support of the war and the Union was elected and the deadlock that had rendered the state government of Pennsylvania powerless was broken.

"How ignorant we were," said regimental commander Blakeley, "of the important results that followed the detail of Dr. Hosack to remain and care for our sick comrades under the shadow of the mountains and dark forests in Dade County, Georgia, in the early days of September, 1863!"[1]

One reason Rosecrans had remained stationary around Murfreesboro for months after the battle of Stone's River was the inadequacy of his cavalry. He received little help from Washington in building this arm, though he had written that with 6,000 more horsemen he could advance within three days; nor were his requests that his troopers be armed with revolving rifles honored. Now, as the campaign began to culminate, the absence of a cavalry that could compete with the seasoned Confederate horse led by Major General Joseph Wheeler and even more skillfully by Brigadier General Nathan B. Forrest began to be felt severely. Forrest patrolled Bragg's right and Wheeler his left.

Rosecrans' lack of an enterprising cavalry deprived him of information about Bragg's dispositions and led him at this stage into a blunder that was well-nigh fatal to two divisions of his army. The threatened disaster was the near pocketing of Negley's and Baird's divisions of Thomas' corps in McLemore's Cove, about twenty-five miles south of Chattanooga.

Thomas had not favored the impetuous march or the wide dispersal of Rosecrans' three corps, and had pushed Negley ahead into the Cove only at the insistence of the commanding general. Thomas had recommended that upon the capture of Chattanooga, Rosecrans should strengthen his line of communications with Nashville via Bridgeport, secure what had already been gained, reprovision the army, then resume the offensive with more deliberation and certainty. His point was sound that the army was not carrying supplies sufficient for it to follow up a victory even should it gain one in the rapid pursuit of Bragg.

But Rosecrans believed the preponderance of the evidence was that Bragg was retreating on Rome and he consequently overrode Thomas' advice. Thus the army continued its advance through the widely separated passes of Lookout Mountain. The chill of the early autumn of 1863 in north Georgia was beginning to be felt. On the night of September 8 the soldiers slept under their blankets.

Crittenden to the north had moved around the end of Lookout Mountain into Chattanooga and Rossville, then had marched south on the roads toward Ringgold and La Fayette, separated about fifteen miles from Thomas. Thomas, with Negley's division in advance, began passing through Stevens Gap on September 9, while McCook was moving through Winston's Gap forty-two miles

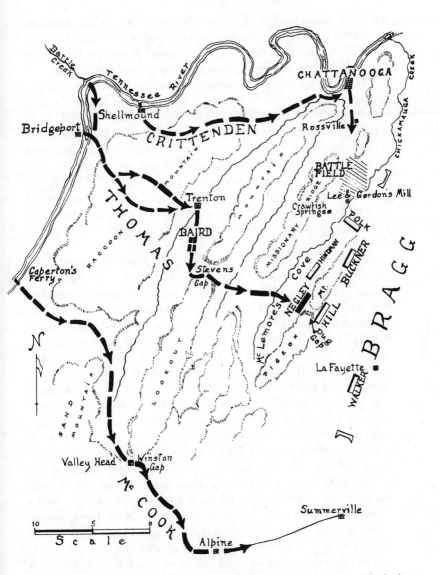

Rosecrans' hazardous dispersal of his corps crossing Lookout Mountain. Negley's exposed position is shown in McLemore's Cove.

south of Chattanooga. But by the mountain roads McCook would have to follow to gain contact with Crittenden through Rossville, he was fully fifty miles away, or, considering the mountains and his heavy baggage, four to five days' marching time.

Negley advanced into McLemore's Cove without much caution, having assurances that there was no enemy in his front. He rode ahead with his staff, followed by Colonel William Sirwell, commanding his 3rd Brigade, and the brigade staff. Then came the 78th Pennsylvania, which threw out no skirmishers, Lieutenant Colonel Blakeley having been informed that none was needed. The morning of September 10 was crisp, clear, beautiful. "I rode out with most thankful heart that Chattanooga had been surrendered to us without the great battle we expected," Blakeley later reflected. His regiment was the advance unit of Sirwell's brigade of Negley's division.

They moved across the Cove, six to nine miles wide, approached the cedar thickets along Chickamauga Creek near its headwaters, and looked into Dug Gap, the Pigeon Mountain pass by which they intended to move into La Fayette and pounce on whatever Confederates they could find there. They were altogether uninformed that La Fayette was held by the greater part of Bragg's army.[2]

Suddenly from in front of Dug Gap, Confederate skirmishers opened fire on the mounted group of division and brigade commanders and staffs who were riding in front of their commands. The general wheeled and galloped in furious haste to the 78th Pennsylvania, shouting, "Into line, Colonel! Into line!" The regiment was brought quickly into line, though the ground was rough and strewn with rocks, the dead lower limbs of the cedar trees were sharp as needles, and the road over which they were marching was narrow. When deployed, the regiment crossed Chickamauga Creek, passed a large cornfield, gained more open country and reached a point near the Widow Davis' house called Davis' Cross Roads. There the road from Stevens Gap to Dug Gap crossed a road leading up the valley from Crawfish Springs.

The regiment advanced to a knob from which it could overlook the Cove, and drove the Confederate pickets back into Dug Gap.

But it gained a sufficient view ahead to appall it with the knowledge that Bragg was not retreating; instead, he had Negley's division all but surrounded with a vastly superior force. At that moment not a single body of Federal troops was in supporting distance of Negley, who stood alone near the western mouth of Dug Gap, an easy prey for Bragg's army.

Negley, a huge, handsome man who radiated good will without losing firmness, enjoyed the confidence both of Thomas and his men, just as he had that of General Buell earlier, all recommendations of the highest order. He was one of the leading horticulturalists of western Pennsylvania, a graduate of what is now the University of Pittsburgh, and a leader of a commanding attitude that would send him to Congress many terms after the war. He had served in the Mexican War, pushed forward in the Pennsylvania militia and, when disunion threatened, was elected brigadier general and given command of the Pennsylvania militia in Pittsburgh.

Along with Thomas, he was a part of Major General Robert Patterson's division in the Shenandoah Valley during the Bull Run campaign. When the three-months men went home he raised his own Pittsburgh brigade, went into the western armies and held Nashville very capably while Bragg was bypassing him and invading Kentucky.

He was known as a good drillmaster. When Rosecrans reviewed the Army of the Cumberland, the staff rated Negley's division among the very best in appearance and discipline. As one of the four division commanders in Thomas' hard-fighting Fourteenth Corps, he enjoyed high prestige as the army dipped into Georgia.

From the knob commanding a view of Dug Gap and Pigeon Mountain the Pennsylvanians saw heavy bodies of Confederates poised to advance on both flanks. These troops were Major General Thomas C. Hindman's division on the Federal left, supported by Buckner's corps, and the forward elements of D. H. Hill's corps in their front and on their right.

Negley already had been alerted to his danger by an indiscreet and boastful Confederate lieutenant he had captured during the exchange with the pickets, and by a lad who guilelessly disclosed that Confederates were at his house only a mile away, on the flank of the Federal division.

Negley withdrew to a woods west of the north-south road and adjoining the Widow Davis' house and called on Thomas for assistance. After darkness he shifted his position twice, changing front and facing to the north so as to confront Hindman, who was in force to attack up the Cove.[3]

To save Negley from being gobbled up by the greater part of Bragg's army, Baird's division began on the late afternoon of September 10 one of the most rapid marches of its history. All night the soldiers marched along the mountain road, through clouds of thick, stifling dust. On the morning of September 11, sleepless, grimy, exhausted, the division bivouacked in McLemore's Cove, at the foot of Lookout Mountain. After a short halt it hastened down and across the Cove another nine miles to where it could see Negley deployed for battle, ready to fight it out with the superior enemy force if he had to. Baird deployed on Negley's left and threw out skirmishers. Negley's emergency appeared eased, though it was by no means certain that the two divisions were not in as critical a situation as Negley alone had been before Baird's rapid march. Thomas' other two divisions, those of Reynolds and Brannan, were still west of Lookout Mountain.

But events were not developing happily in Bragg's army. As soon as the commanding general was advised that Negley was coming through Stevens Gap and was alone entering McLemore's Cove, he ordered D. H. Hill to move on Davis' Cross Roads from La Fayette through Cove Gap and Catlett's Gap, a short distance to the north. He ordered Hindman to converge on the crossroads from the north, moving along the road that leads from Crawfish Springs. Bragg issued his attack orders on the night of September 9, then on the morning of the tenth took a position on Pigeon Mountain overlooking the Cove to await the development of his plans. It was, as one of his officers described it, an opportunity "which comes to most generals only in their dreams."

Perhaps there is nothing more pathetic than a general waiting vainly for the sound of the guns of an attack he has ordered—waiting hour after hour in the silence and at length recognizing that the plan he has devised so carefully has miscarried or that his orders have been ignored. Bragg dismounted, paced back and forth in his anxiety, dug his spurs into the ground, smote the air, hoped and despaired. Meantime Negley was advancing across the Cove, reaching the mouth of Dug Gap, falling back after his contact with the Confederate pickets, then, upon detecting the presence of enemy troops on his left, changing front in the darkness and facing north while Baird's division rushed to his help.

On September 10 Bragg was poorly served not only by Hindman but by Hill. Why neither attacked has never been very well explained, though the literature on the failure has been plentiful. Hill contended that Cleburne, who commanded his advanced division, was ill, but Cleburne himself pleaded no illness and seemed to go about in good condition. None knowing him could attribute a failure to personal reluctance.

Hill pleaded also that Bragg had not given the plan his personal supervision, and that he was ignorant of the roads, the enemy's position and the barricades in Dug Gap. These obstructions made passage into McLemore's Cove difficult.

Hindman's indisposition to attack, for which Bragg later placed him under arrest, resulted partly from Negley's prompt deployment and bold show of strength, which caused the Confederate general to believe he faced much heavier odds.

Hindman of course had other ready explanations, which suggest that Bragg did not make everything unmistakably clear, or at least that there was sufficient leeway for the generals to exercise their independent judgment, which so often ran counter to that of their chief.

Hindman's view was that he should not attack until D. H. Hill had opened communication with him and until his and Cleburne's division united at Davis' Cross Roads. When he had no word from Hill he halted five miles down the Cove, sent scouting parties forward toward both the crossroads and the base of Lookout Mountain, and waited. A civilian brought him a report that the Federals held Dug and Catlett's gaps, and it was through these Pigeon Mountain passes that Hill was expected to advance with the divisions of Cleburne and Breckinridge. Hindman's scouts gave information that the gaps were so filled with debris as to be impassable, so he sent a messenger to Bragg asking further instructions.

All of the early part of the tenth his troops rested in the Cove, filling their canteens from Chickamauga Creek; then, apparently more concerned about water than assaulting Negley, Hindman advanced them a mile to a good spring and again waited. Here he heard from other civilians that a heavy Federal force was approaching Stevens Gap. Apparently this was Baird's division marching in haste to Negley's support. Then he learned from one of Hill's brigade commanders how Negley's men—Sirwell's brigade, as we have seen—had at 12:30 P.M. attacked less than a mile in front of Dug Gap, and had charged and broken the Confederate cavalry.

Hill sent a note dated 1:30 P.M., informing Hindman that Cleburne had been ordered to Dug Gap, and, if the enemy attacked there, Hindman should attack in their rear. Since the copy of the order was sent for Hindman's "information and guidance" and gave him no positive instructions, Hindman took it to mean that he should engage the enemy after Hill did. Thus the day passed with each general waiting for the other, and the opportunity was wasted away.[4]

Thomas C. Hindman had been an enterprising soldier in the trans-Mississippi department, and his conduct in the later phases of the Chickamauga campaign was in sharp contrast with his lethargy in McLemore's Cove. He had been an outstanding resident of Arkansas when the war broke and had played one of the leading roles with his stump speeches to take Arkansas out of the Union.

Born in Knoxville, Tennessee, he had been educated in Lawrenceville, New Jersey, had been cited for conspicuous bravery in the Mexican War, had served in the Mississippi legislature as a stanch Jefferson Davis man, then had moved across the Mississippi River to Helena, Arkansas. A lawyer and a gifted speaker, he was sent by the Helena district to Congress in 1858. Hindman's great vitality and enthusiasm helped to inflame his state with war sentiment, and everyone—including the Negroes, who gave a benefit

ball for the "Suddern 'Fed'cy"—was put to work making muni-
tions and medical supplies and performing numerous tasks for the
cause.

Like George Pickett, he wore his hair in long curling locks and
was something of a dandy in his civilian dress with his pink gloves
and rattan cane. He was small and tended to be tyrannical.

After secession, Hindman raised a regiment, commanded a brigade at Shiloh, where he was wounded, and because of his good
fighting there was made a major general. In command of the Confederate army at Prairie Grove, Hindman was at first aggressive
and appeared to be winning, but he lost the battle by suddenly
taking a defensive position and awaiting attack, thereby allowing
his opponent, Brigadier General James G. Blunt, to unite his forces
on the field. Hindman has been called a "man of genius," a man
who would have been a good Secretary of War but was unable to
command an army or plan a battle. However, he was to prove at
Chickamauga that he could strike hard under competent leadership.

Bragg said Hill "failed, in a querulous, insubordinate spirit,"
to send in Cleburne's division to join Hindman, using Cleburne's
alleged illness as a pretext. Bragg, who never spared himself from
extreme exertions, rode half the night to reach Hill's headquarters; there he found Cleburne thoroughly surprised that anyone
should have reported him incapacitated. Suppressing his anger
after the failure of the tenth, Bragg ordered an attack on the
morning of September 11.

During the early part of the eleventh there was still great opportunity and still unaccountable confusion and reluctance. Cleburne was well prepared for battle. Between midnight and dawn
his first brigade, Wood's, cleared Dug Gap of its obstructions,
and even before daylight he had two brigades on the west side of
Pigeon Mountain. He stationed couriers along the crest to hasten
the word when Hindman began firing. But time passed, the morning advanced, and no rattle came from down the Cove. The officer
in charge of the detail finally returned to Dug Gap, where Bragg
and Hill had arrived to consult with Cleburne. Bragg again engaged in his restless walking.[5]

But Negley and Baird, and Thomas and eventually Rosecrans,

were by this time fully alert to their danger. The two Federal divisions, aggregating about 10,000 men, were confronted by 30,000 Confederates of Hill's and Buckner's corps. They were allowed to withdraw from the Cove as they had entered it, through Stevens Gap. Beginning at 8 A.M., the withdrawal of the Federals was orderly but it required the better part of the day.

Cleburne made an effort to cut them off, with Wood's brigade in the lead. Graphic was the description of a soldier of the 18th Alabama of the race to catch Thomas' men at Stevens Gap. The Alabama regiment had just dragged itself over Pigeon Mountain. "The horses could not pull the guns and wagons over . . . so men were used instead. I was one of a team of forty men put to a wagon. . . . The quartermasters and wagonmasters talked to us as if we were horses sure enough . . . I remember how an old colonel of artillery did curse."

Skirmishing and advancing, Cleburne's men plunged through Chickamauga Creek, here only waist-deep, and reached the base of Lookout Mountain after dark. "Thomas' corps had barely passed by the road. We distinctly heard the racket and confusion incident to getting the artillery and wagons up the mountain."

Negley received an abundance of applause for escaping. Said Lieutenant Colonel Blakeley, commander of his advance guard: "The extrication of our division from the environment of Dug Gap by General Negley was to my mind the most masterly piece of generalship I saw during the war."[6]

But it was applause that would not be heard much after the greater stresses of Chickamauga.

Rosecrans and his companion Dana were not alarmed over Bragg's activity in McLemore's Cove and judged it was merely a display of force to check their pursuit. When Dana reached Thomas' headquarters at Stevens Gap on the night of September 12, in company with Rosecrans, he "found everything progressing favorably there," and despite the fact that two of Thomas' divisions had almost been overcome, he related that scouts were still bringing in reports that the enemy was "evacuating La Fayette and moving toward Rome." To this Dana added optimistically, "It seemed as if at last the Army of the Cumberland had practically gained a position from which it could effectively advance on Rome and Atlanta, and deliver there the finishing blow of the war."

Thomas had no such optimism. He was saying to his staff: "Nothing but stupendous blunders on the part of Bragg can save our army from total defeat. I have ordered Negley to fall back from McLemore's Cove, and I believe we may be able to save this corps. But Bragg is also in a position to strike McCook and Crittenden before they have a chance to extricate themselves."

Had Thomas' corps, or a sizable portion of it, been captured in McLemore's Cove, Crittenden's corps, isolated by fifty miles from McCook, could scarcely have escaped, and with Crittenden captured or driven back beyond the Tennessee River, McCook would have been an easy prey. Rosecrans had erred badly in not continuing to heed Thomas.

In McLemore's Cove one of the Confederacy's greatest opportunities was cast away. When Bragg placed Hindman under arrest after the battle of Chickamauga, the subordinate was able to produce Bragg's order concerning the Cove, showing it was permissive instead of peremptory. Bragg did not submit the matter to a court of inquiry. Whether Bragg should have gone to Hindman and taken personal charge of the attack—a question at times raised in the subordinate's defense—was answered by Bragg's insistence that he repeatedly sent couriers to Hindman with a reiteration of his orders.

The next disappointment was with Lieutenant General Leonidas Polk. Though Bragg failed to bag half of Thomas' corps, he had at least learned the position of the elements of Rosecrans' army, and it was clear that on the night of September 12 Crittenden was almost as exposed as Negley had been on September 10. Crittenden had pulled back from Ringgold and was concentrated across the Chattanooga-La Fayette road just north of Lee and Gordon's mill, about twelve miles removed from Thomas.

That night Bragg directed Polk to attack Crittenden. He followed his original order with three others and prepared Walker's and Buckner's corps as supports, but even the reiteration failed to induce Polk to attack. Polk wrote that he desired an additional force in order to "make failure impossible"![7]

PART II

BRAGG:

Brusque, Prickly
But "Will Fight"

CHAPTER SEVEN

Servant of the Regulations

BRAGG's standing as a general turned on the question of getting co-operation from his subordinates. Usually it was wanting. No other Southern general has been written of with such disparagement, some merited, much unjustified. If his subordinates had reason for complaint against him, he in turn had much greater cause against some of them. His army seethed with discord so persistent that it brought into question President Davis' ability to maintain respect for one of his highest ranking officers and therefore challenged the power of the Confederate government itself.

Bragg's main characteristic was an austere sense of duty that caused him to respect the army code inflexibly. He never indulged in personal weaknesses and endured none in others. Reputations often are based on incidents, and Bragg's was founded largely on one in the old army and one in the early days of the Confederacy.

The old army incident occurred when he denied his own requisition for quartermaster supplies. As temporary post commander he submitted the request, then as post quartermaster refused to honor it, thereby causing his superior to observe that he had quarreled with everyone else in the service and now was quarreling with himself.

The incident that stamped him as a stern and forbidding disciplinarian occurred on the stealthy retreat from Corinth, after the Shiloh campaign. He gave orders that no gun be discharged; death was the penalty for disobedience. The order was imperious, but one inebriated man gleefully shot at will and at length fired prankishly at a chicken. The chicken escaped but a small Negro child was wounded. The soldier who had been so indifferent about betraying the retreat route was tried by court martial, sentenced to be shot, and was shot with no further formality when Bragg approved the finding of the trial.

The event was related in many forms, perhaps the one gaining greatest credence being that Bragg had had a soldier executed for shooting a chicken. Mrs. Chesnut heard that version and in her diary recorded that the general did not understand citizen soldiers. "In the retreat from Shiloh he ordered that not a gun should be fired. A soldier shot a chicken, and then the soldier was shot." Then her informant, as she recorded it, exclaimed, "For a chicken! A Confederate soldier for a chicken!"

The story grew and was twisted. Another version of apparently the same incident was that he had a man shot for stealing apples from an orchard. An Alabama soldier wrote that he heard Bragg had hanged sixteen men on a single tree a mile from where he was "at the gap."[1] Bragg, who was really a mild-mannered man of gentle inclinations even under his lowering brow, came to be called a "porcupine," "tigerish," "bloodthirsty," and whatever else implied intolerant severity.

Dr. L. H. Stout, medical director of hospitals of the Army of Tennessee, had much business with Bragg and was impressed not with his sternness but with his amazing industry and remarkable grasp of history—"an animated thesaurus of historical facts" was his wording. Those who ate at his mess and observed his great efforts—physical and mental—feared he did not eat enough to stay alive. He did take on a haggard, almost cadaverous appearance. Sometimes his staff would send food to his desk to suggest it was mealtime. "No one in the army was more temperate in eating and drinking than he was." Dr. Stout termed him a "sphinx" to thousands who sought him. Obviously he was a clear, sharp thinker, because his orders—always brief—were dictated with dispatch, and "an erasure or interlineation in a manuscript of his would have been a curiosity."

A little later in the Chattanooga campaign Stout talked to one of the chaplains about Bragg. The chaplain had been through the camps, and he heard the commanding general denounced on all sides. But always these officers were talking about their own

chances for promotion while Bragg was at headquarters laboring
night and day, indifferent to his personal fortunes in his zeal for
the cause. He was in no sense a sphinx to the chaplain, but "his
manner indicates that you must be brief and speak to the point."
He did not mull over questions but decided instantly.

Still, it was all business and no light informalities. One left his
presence without any warmth—sometimes with a touch of ill-
humor. "Ah! if he only had a suavity of manner commensurate
with his self-denying patriotism and untiring industry, what a
success he would be!"

Bragg's name had become familiar to the entire country in the
accounts of Buena Vista, in the Mexican War, more because of
his commander's words than his own. General Zachary Taylor
had ordered him to "Give them a little more grape, Captain
Bragg!" Bragg had complied gloriously and had held his ground
even when his infantry support left him. Next to "Old Rough and
Ready" he was the hero of the battle. Here his brother-in-arms
Jefferson Davis came to admire him.

Thereafter he was looked on as the leading artillery officer of
the army: peculiar, never giving or receiving flattery, possessing
few friends, and living almost like an army Javert in his devotion
to red tape and regulations.

Sherman was one of his confidants in the old army. As war
loomed Bragg wrote his friend, then superintendent of the Louisiana State Military Academy, that duty might throw them into
different camps and into "an apparent hostile attitude; but it is
too terrible to contemplate and I will not discuss it." Sherman
thought Bragg never truly wanted to leave the Union.[2]

But Bragg was a thorough Southerner, and never had doubts
about his course. He had been born in 1817 in Warrenton, in
northeastern North Carolina, near the Virginia line, into an enterprising family of leaders. His father, Thomas, was a capable con-
tractor, who in 1830 built the North Carolina state capitol at
Raleigh after the old capitol had been destroyed by fire. His
mother, Margaret Crossland, was a woman of education and great
vitality who by her own ambition sharply influenced her six
sons and six daughters.

John, the eldest, was graduated from the University of North Carolina, studied law, served in the North Carolina legislature, then moved to Mobile, Alabama, where he became judge, state legislator, and, before the war, a States' Rights Democrat in Congress. Another brother, Thomas, attended Partridge's Military Academy in Middletown, Connecticut, then studied law, entered the North Carolina legislature, became Governor, United States Senator, and Attorney General in the Confederate cabinet.

Braxton entered West Point shortly after his sixteenth birthday. Only two classmates were younger. He was a "tall, ungainly plebe almost uncouth in manner but bright and engaging in conversation." Out of the fifty at graduation, he was fifth in this large class that included Hooker, Jubal Early, Sedgwick, and the unfortunate Pennsylvanian John C. Pemberton. His inflexible integrity was noted at the Academy, along with an unusual frankness of expression, extending even to harshness, brusqueness, rudeness. The quality that impaired his service as army commander already had become established in his student days.

After graduation he went to Fortress Monroe and then to a round of army posts. His acquaintance with Sherman, perhaps his closest, was strengthened when they served at Fort Moultrie in the 3rd Artillery—Bragg as first lieutenant in Company E and Sherman as second lieutenant in Company G. Two of Bragg's lieutenants who gained fame with him in Mexico were there— George H. Thomas and John F. Reynolds.

While they were all together at Fort Moultrie the young officers watched the ships plying to and from Charleston in the cotton trade. They went out loaded with bales and returned with rock ballast. And they always dumped their ballast in one place in Charleston harbor. Finally the dump site reared itself above the water and ultimately became the foundation on which engineers built Fort Sumter. Who the fort belonged to would become a vital question. Long treatises would be written about whether it was United States property or a part of South Carolina—whether it followed the palmetto flag out of the Union or properly adhered to the Stars and Stripes. But Bragg and Thomas could not possibly suspect that this dump would someday touch off a frightful civil war that would bring them face to face as adversaries, one as commander and the other as almost the leader *de facto* in the most desperate battle in that conflict.

In the old army Bragg acquired a reputation as a stickler, alert to detect the slightest dereliction by his post commander, or infringement on his own prerogatives. His attitude caused Grant to describe him as having an "irascible temper" and being "naturally disputatious." Nothing in his conduct was calculated to make him popular with either superiors or subordinates.

The blunt and often opinionated editor of the Richmond *Examiner*, John M. Daniel, described him as having "an iron hand and wooden head." Again, when President Davis later elevated Bragg to top military adviser, the *Examiner* said the appointment came "like a bucket of water on a newly kindled grate."

Davis, looking for something less evident to explain Bragg's difficulties, attributed them to his own admiration of the general. Somehow the rumor had spread that they were brothers-in-law. "You have the misfortune," Davis wrote him, "of being regarded as my personal friend, and are pursued therefore with malign censure by men regardless of truth."[3]

More than from Davis' friendship, Bragg's unpopularity must have grown out of his own bad health, notably his dysentery, a heritage from the old army days, which tended to sour him mentally while it weakened him physically. His headaches were severe; the impression is gained he may have suffered from stomach ulcers.

But there were good points, mainly his ability to maintain in fighting trim an army composed of divergent elements from the gulf and western states of the Confederacy, containing a great many fiery, hard-riding, some of them hard-drinking individualists among the officers and in the ranks. When he brought his troops up from Pensacola, where he commanded in the early stages of the war, they were the best-drilled soldiers in the army with which Albert Sidney Johnston set out for Shiloh, especially since many of the men drilled by Hardee had been lost at Fort Donelson.

Bragg was a specialist in logistics, saw to it that his army was well provisioned, and was so attentive to his medical corps as to show a surprising humanity beneath his coldness.

Bragg's popularity with the soldiers was not enhanced when he abolished liquor, maintaining that it was the cause of most of the army's ills. The high power of the green whisky common throughout the Confederacy in war days can be appreciated by the numerous stories about it, one being that when a drop fell on the pavement it rent the air like a peal of thunder. Another was that when one examined a drop through the microscope he could see a whole medley of stabbings and shootings and twice as many brawls. Bragg seemed to nurse grievances against drinking officers, however understanding he may have seemed of their imprudence at the time. In one of his recapitulations after the war he complained that Cheatham had been so drunk on the field at Stone's River that a staff officer had had to hold him on his horse. Breckinridge was charged with a similar offense in the Chattanooga campaign—that Brigadier General S. R. Gist had to be set as a watch over him to restrain him from giving an order. Bragg thought Breckinridge was "as gallant and true a man as ever lived" and appeared to be more sympathetic than angered by the incident, which must have been a rarity. But Lincoln was not the only one who had trouble with drinking generals. Bragg forgave Cheatham because his work had been so meritorious but he had Polk warn him that another offense would not be tolerated.[4]

The Northern actress and spy, the beautiful and talented Miss Major Pauline Cushman, was interviewed by John Morgan and Nathan Bedford Forrest after she was caught behind the Confederate lines, then was turned over to the "bony, angular, sharp-pointed" Bragg who was "without kindness or humanity, or any of the milder parts of human nature in his composition." His gestures were impatient, his address acrid and his physiognomy heartless.

In their colloquy Bragg was quoted as claiming that he sent out no spies but knew, nevertheless, "what goes on at the Yankee headquarters better than the clerks there know." He told her that she had important papers in her possession and "if they prove you to be a spy, nothing can save you from a little hemp." She found his talk "not so spicy, nor so cheerful" as that of the two cavalry leaders, who seemed greater admirers than Bragg of feminine pulchritude, even in a spy. Bragg had her tried and sentenced to the noose, but she feigned illness until she was rescued by the advance of Rosecrans' army into Murfreesboro. Whether Bragg would have gone through with the sentence is anyone's guess, but his conversation with Pauline did not have a ray of sunshine in it.

His medical director, Dr. A. J. Ford, told how Bragg called him to an interview at midnight, just before the retreat from Murfreesboro after the battle of Stone's River. Bragg walked back and forth—his habit under stress—with tears in his eyes.

"Doctor," he said, "I intend evacuating Murfreesboro and have sent for you to advise me as to what can be done with my poor wounded men who cannot be moved."

The doctor had a suggestion. They could be left under the care of a competent local doctor, B. W. Avent, who was good in hospital management as well as medicine. Bragg agreed. It seemed to lift the weight of responsibility off his shoulders. The medical director wondered if many in the army would ever realize that the general had enough sympathy to weep.[5]

Bragg's difficulties with his subordinate generals began directly after his retreat from Stone's River and were partly the result of that retreat, and partly of the failure of the Kentucky campaign. Neither side had won much advantage on the field but Bragg's withdrawal signalized that it was a Northern victory. Bragg's generals had, in fact, counseled the retreat, but it was from their staffs that the undercurrent of criticism began to seep through the army and reach the Southern newspapers.

On January 11, 1863, nine days after the battle, Bragg wrote a challenging note to Generals Polk, Hardee, Cleburne and a number of others, pointing out these facts, saying that if he had misunderstood the advice he had received it should be clarified, but if not, then an end should be put to "the malignant slanders being propagated by men who have felt the sting of discipline." The correspondence and recriminations are not properly a part of the Chickamauga story except that they disclosed a unanimous feeling among the higher officers that the Confederate cause would be benefited by Bragg's retirement from the army command.

Cleburne's reply after consulting others was a model of forthrightness: "They unite with me in personal regard for yourself, in a high appreciation of your patriotism and gallantry, and in appreciation of your great capacity for organization, but at the same time they see with regret, and it also has met my observation, that you do not possess the confidence of the army in other respects in that degree necessary to secure success."

Polk, after receiving an elucidation of Bragg's letter, sent the correspondence to President Davis and urged that Bragg be relieved. ". . . If he were Napoleon or the great Frederick, he could serve our cause at some other points better than here." Polk recommended that command of the Army of Tennessee be given to Joseph E. Johnston.

Breckinridge concurred in the feeling that Bragg did not have the army's confidence. He had himself been so deeply offended by Bragg that he had been tempted to challenge the general to a duel, to which his troops urged him. The division had performed nobly at Stone's River and in less than half an hour had lost 36 per cent of its numbers, yet Bragg mistakenly had sent an unjustifiably critical dispatch about it to Richmond, which deeply incensed the rank and file of the division and caused it to call on its commander for redress. The gifted Kentuckian, former Vice President of the United States and a candidate for the highest office in the last election, addressed his soldiers and mollified them with the thought that they must endure personal wrong for the cause, but he also promised that if he and Bragg survived the war he would respond to their request and call the commanding general to account.[6]

Thus was Bragg's army seething beneath the surface as it faced the talented strategist Rosecrans who was believed about to begin an advance. The agitation was far too violent for President Davis to ignore it, but neither was he disposed to permit subordinates to depose one of the highest ranking officers of the Confederacy by a round-robin complaint. He was rightfully puzzled as to why Bragg had written to his officers and invited their criticism. That question was uppermost when he directed General Joseph E. Johnston, the department commander, to go to Bragg's army at Tullahoma and report on conditions there.

Said Davis: "Why General Bragg should have selected that tribunal [of his own officers], and have invited its judgment upon him, is to me unexplained; it manifests, however, a condition of things which seems to me to require your presence."

Johnston went and discovered wholehearted dissatisfaction among the generals—with Cheatham, for one, saying he would never go into battle under Bragg again. But Johnston found the army unshaken, and the troops were reported by their field officers as in high spirits. The dissatisfaction, it developed, resulted more from Bragg's abortive Kentucky campaign than from the retreat after Stone's River. There were indications that it was subsiding. Johnston made the sensible recommendation that if Bragg were to be replaced, his successor should not be selected from among the officers of the Army of Tennessee. He disqualified himself also, since he was the one engaged in the investigation; and he held firm to that decision, though put under pressure by Secretary of War James A. Seddon to take the assignment.

When Johnston had completed his fact-gathering he wrote Davis again, saying he had inspected the entire army, that its appearance was encouraging, and that it "gives positive evidence of General Bragg's capacity to command." He went on to say that the army was healthy, well clothed, and in good spirits, and that the return of absentees after Stone's River had strengthened the brigades. Johnston thought operations had been admirably conducted and said he could find "no record of more effective fighting in modern battles than that of this army in December." It showed "skill in the commander and courage in the troops."

About the only reform Johnston suggested was that the army stop eating so much fresh pork. But diet could not have caused the cross tempers. In view of such stanch support of Bragg no further action from President Davis could be expected. The matter was closed for the Chattanooga-Chickamauga campaign.

But it was quite apparent that Bragg did not have the warmhearted co-operation of his corps and division commanders that had been attained by Lee in the eastern theater of the war. Whether it was the fault of the general or of his subordinates, Bragg did not get quick responses to his orders. Back in Richmond Mrs. Chesnut noted in her diary: "Bragg and his generals do not agree. I think a general worthless whose subalterns quarrel with him. Something is wrong about the man. Good generals are adored by their soldiers. See Napoleon, Caesar, Stonewall, Lee."

Another incident during his early army days may have bearing on Bragg's certain severity. An attempt was made to assassinate him. His escape was nothing short of a miracle. Someone had placed a heavily charged twelve-pound shell outside his tent, within two feet of his head, and had exploded it with a slow fuse. It blew his bed, bedding and tent to bits. Shell fragments passed above and below him, pierced his blanket, but did not touch him. "I was not aware that I had an enemy in the world," he said guilelessly.[7]

CHAPTER EIGHT

"Old Pete" Hears Distant Guns

JAMES LONGSTREET's First Corps of the Army of Northern Virginia was back in the rolling hill country behind the Rapidan River, recuperating after its desperate fights in the Wheat Field, the Peach Orchard, on Little Round Top, and on Cemetery Ridge at Gettysburg.

The Pennsylvania campaign had been a failure. The affairs of the Confederacy had been brought to a jarring crisis by the loss of Pemberton's army and Vicksburg at the moment Lee was being repulsed beyond the Potomac.

As if to relieve itself from further anguish over the companions missing after Gettysburg, the First Corps soldiers plunged into a round of dances and festivities and of feasting on the plentiful Virginia harvest of 1863.

"Ah! those were lovely days," mused Longstreet's efficient chief of staff, G. Moxley Sorrel, in later reflections. The corps headquarters was fixed in the pleasant country seat of Erasmus Taylor, owner of a large, back-country plantation, whose spacious house on the social occasions was "crowded with joyous, happy Virginia girls." Before these "lovely eyes and true Virginia hearts" the young officers who had been spared in the hardest fighting of the war to that date assumed their most gallant behavior. Dances in the daytime, dances at night; riding parties on the fresh-spirited horses that seemed to be plentiful even after two and a half years of war; picnics, occasional leaves of absence, excursions from camp and to Richmond. "Hard, brave work had earned the guerdon and it was no niggard hand that gave it."

85

His own mounts having been lost at Gettysburg, Sorrel bought two new horses at a cost of $2,500 in Confederate money, which at the current rate would have been about $250 in gold.

But perhaps the most elating development for the corps was that Zebulon Vance, the energetic North Carolina governor who was emerging as one of the dominant civilian figures in the Southern struggle for independence, sent up, especially for Longstreet's men, 14,000 new uniforms made from the ample stocks of cloth he had accumulated from the new textile mills he had helped establish in North Carolina, and from blockade runners that plied with impunity into and out of the Cape Fear River at Wilmington. The gift was indeed generous, for there was not one North Carolina soldier in Longstreet's corps and, apart from the remnants of Pickett's division resting near Richmond, none who was not from the deep South or Arkansas and Texas. "The ranks looked decidedly better" said Sorrel, who inspected them after the tattered garments worn into Pennsylvania had been cast aside.

Longstreet, always restive in camp and fertile with suggestions about the grand strategy of the war, reflected on the plan he had proposed to Secretary of War James A. Seddon when he had passed through Richmond in May, before the Gettysburg campaign, and which, with his customary stubbornness—now fortified by hindsight, he believed would have been the best counteroffensive against the Northern armies pressing at that time into middle Tennessee, Virginia and down the Mississippi.

Conditions had grown much worse since May. Vicksburg had capitulated. Rosecrans had maneuvered Bragg out of Tullahoma and was advancing by a series of adroit flanking movements toward Chattanooga.

Longstreet's recommendation before the Gettysburg campaign was that Bragg be reinforced by a corps from Lee's army and by union with Joseph E. Johnston's army, which would move up from Mississippi. This combined force could overwhelm Rosecrans, march to the Ohio River and force Lincoln to call Grant back from Vicksburg to save Ohio and Indiana from invasion.[1]

Now that the emergency in the West had grown more acute, and as Rosecrans was commanding the greatest respect in the

South, "Old Peter" Longstreet was keenly disturbed. He was impatient with the other Southern armies—none sizable, to be sure—which were "apparently spectators, viewing these tremendous threatenings without thought of turning minds or forces to arrest the march of Rosecrans." Though Old Peter has been commended more as a tactician than a strategist, he could readily see, as did President Jefferson Davis, the paramount importance of holding Chattanooga. Its loss would cut the Confederacy through the middle.

Without consulting Lee, who had vetoed his earlier proposal and had preferred to make a toss at ending the war in Pennsylvania, Longstreet wrote directly to Secretary Seddon on August 15. Strict military formality—never a fetish in the Southern army —would have necessitated forwarding the letter through Lee. Longstreet eased his conscience by recalling that Seddon at their earlier interview had invited his suggestions on military matters. He knew Lee would oppose a division of the Army of Northern Virginia, even though Meade was showing no enterprise after his success at Gettysburg and it was a fair gamble that he would remain docile even if confronted with something less than Lee's entire force.

Longstreet told Seddon that if Rosecrans were allowed to march through Georgia it would be the death stroke to the Confederacy. The lungs had been lost at Vicksburg, and the impending Georgia campaign would be a blade through the heart. Dissolution would set in quickly. The only hope was to utilize the interior lines possessed by the South. A part of Lee's army could go on the defensive and still give ample security to Richmond; elements of it could be detached and sent to help Bragg. Bragg's army should be reinforced also from elsewhere in the South and Rosecrans should be dealt a crushing blow before aid could be rushed to him from other Northern armies. The hopes of the South were languishing. Only by utilizing the advantages of a quick concentration could they be revived. Longstreet had not consulted Lee, he explained, because, like other generals, Lee did not like to have large elements of his army beyond his easy reach.

Once the letter had been dispatched, Longstreet did not hesitate to talk with Lee about it. The commanding general had a strong affection for the Old War Horse and did not appear to resent his subordinate's act in going over his head and dealing directly with the War Department. When he inquired if Longstreet would be willing to go west himself "and take charge there," Old Peter assented conditionally, his requirements being that he be given time before a battle to win the confidence of the western soldiers and that he be allowed to follow up a victory with an aggressive march against the North.

Just at that time Lee was called to Richmond for consultations with President Davis—which grew protracted, because the President's poor health required that he rest often. The War Department scribe J. B. Jones noticed that when Lee rode out with Davis on August 29 there was no cheering for either. "I suppose," he observed, "General Lee has lost some popularity among idle street walkers by his retreat from Pennsylvania."

The meeting of the two top figures of the Confederacy stirred up a host of rumors. One was that Lee would take most of his army to recapture the territory lost by Pemberton, Bragg and Loring in the West. This was doubted because it might involve the loss of all Virginia. While diarist Jones felt such might be a fitting retribution to the "extortionate farmers" demanding preposterous prices for food, he doubted it would be beneficial "to lose the whole country and sacrifice the cause, to punish the speculators."

After Gettysburg, punishing deserters was a more pressing problem than speculators, and when inducements for their return did not serve, more severe measures had to be adopted.

Another rumor was that plans to reinforce the West were a ruse and that Lee was preparing another northern campaign. A still later report was that Lee would take two corps west and leave one to defend Richmond, aided by militia and conscripts which might swell the force to 50,000, an army large enough to sustain a protracted siege.

Lee wrote to Longstreet, who held command on the Rapidan during his absence, asking that the army be prepared for offensive operations against Meade, which did not indicate he was taking kindly to the idea of sending detachments to Bragg. Longstreet responded that the preparations were being made, but he did not regard prospects for an offensive inviting unless the army were strong enough to cross the Potomac again, as the enemy would merely fortify and hold in Virginia. Then he restated his proposition that "our best opportunity for great results is in Tennessee." He said that if two corps could hold the situation in Virginia and one sent to Tennessee, more could be accomplished than by resuming the offensive in the East.

The next word from Richmond was that Longstreet and two of his divisions, Hood's and McLaw's, would go to reinforce Bragg's army. President Davis, always conscious of the high value of Chattanooga, had so decided.[2]

Everything in Longstreet's attitude suggests he would have preferred that Lee himself head the reinforcements and take command in the West. That had been requested by President Davis, but Lee had rejected it on the ground that he had no acquaintance with the western theater. He did not want to leave Virginia; quite obviously he thought the main front was still in the East.

That Lee did not go west as Longstreet and Davis urged was probably the greatest mistake of his career. The Confederacy was in the October of its power. This was the one instance in the later stages of the war when the North was caught off guard. By the prompt use of interior lines, Rosecrans could be faced with a superior veteran force that would give every promise of putting to flight the audacious Federal general who had ventured deep into the Southern territory, and of crushing as well Burnside's Army of the Ohio coming down against Knoxville.

On such quick shifts of troops have great campaigns and great victories been built: Washington's rapid march from the New York highlands to Virginia to join the French and bag Cornwallis at Yorktown; Napoleon's crossing of the Alps to the Austrian rear; Marlborough's surprise transfer of his army from Flanders to join Prince Eugene and destroy the French Marshal Tallard at Blenheim.

Grant, and Halleck too, were caught off guard. The splendid army with which Grant had taken Vicksburg had been broken up rather recklessly and assigned to side ventures. Grant himself was out of action, lying incapacitated in a New Orleans hospital. For once the South could bring ample manpower to bear on a battle-field. If Rosecrans could be hurled back to the Ohio River most of the territory that had been lost by the South in two and a half years of struggle could be regained. Lee, who ranked Bragg, would command on the field, and would possess the audacity and in-tuitive genius to wring the most from any battle victory.

Although all reasonable prospects for the South to win the war outright and dictate a favorable peace, or gain recognition by leading European powers, had vanished at Gettysburg, where the Confederacy was at its high tide, there was still the possibility of a stalemate. Much of the later-day thinking that the outcome of the war had long since been decided at Antietam, or by the repulse of Bragg and Kirby Smith in Kentucky, or by the issuance of the Emancipation Proclamation, or even by the dual Gettysburg-Vicksburg blow, does not take into consideration the large and increasing body of sentiment in the North which favored peace and was willing to grant the South the right of self-de-termination. Lincoln's resolution was the main factor impelling the North to unremitting effort. The loss in late 1863 of the terri-tory that had been won in Tennessee and Mississippi at such a vast expenditure of life and money would have tended to demon-strate that the Confederacy sprawled over too much territory to be conquered and held by the resources the North could array against it, superior as was its wealth and manpower.

At this stage the Southerners clearly did not consider the odds against a stand-off war hopeless. The situation of the Confederacy in September 1863 was not nearly so desperate as was that of Washington and the colonies at Valley Forge in 1777. Frederick of Prussia had been confronted by adversaries more powerful and numerous and had at length won. Peter the Great was not more favorably situated before Pultowa. France before the appearance of the Maid of Orleans was in equally desperate straits. Earlier history was replete with instances of nations and heroes triumph-ing at last over great odds—Rome after Cannae or Heraclea, the Greek States after Thermopylae, Robert Bruce as he watched the spider, William of Orange at low ebb, Alfred the Great after assuming the disguise of a peasant and hiding in a cowherd's cottage. Even the great loss at Gettysburg might be nullified if the invitation to overwhelm Rosecrans could be seized and followed up. Surely it was not yet time for the South to despair.

How difficult it was proving to subjugate the South might be seen from the calculation that by the summer of 1863 every Southern soldier killed had cost the lives of two Federal soldiers, either in battle or from disease, plus $100,000.

The realist Lafayette McLaws, writing to his wife from the camp on the Rapidan, thought, "The taking of Vicksburg will release our armys [sic]" and require that the enemy devote a considerable force to holding the Mississippi. "We are back again concentrated in the interior and are increasing daily in strength and efficiency." The army had regained "all the old spirit and self-confidence" and knew it had not fallen back from "any fear of the Yankees." He was as full of zest and hopeful as ever, and he had done some of the toughest fighting at Gettysburg.

G. Moxley Sorrel said the plan to reinforce Bragg was made with the assumption that the Federal government would respond by detaching troops from Meade's army in Lee's front, but since these troops would have to travel by exterior lines, Longstreet would be ahead of them. Reliance was placed on Meade's deliberation. Said Sorrel: "His well-known prudence and lack of imagination might be trusted to keep him quiet during our great strategic coup."[3]

The first calculation, and it woefully inaccurate, was that Longstreet's divisions could be transferred from the Rapidan to Chattanooga in two days. That would be by the direct route of the Virginia & Tennessee Railroad via Bristol and Knoxville to Chattanooga, but the lapse of time after Longstreet made his original suggestion was such that both Chattanooga and Knoxville had fallen to the Northern armies.

Because the direct line through Knoxville was closed, indirect routes had to be employed through the Carolinas and north Georgia, mainly the line from Richmond via Petersburg, Virginia; Weldon and Wilmington, North Carolina; and Augusta and Atlanta,

Georgia. The distance from the Rapidan camp to Chattanooga by
the direct route through Bristol and Knoxville was 540 miles; the
route mainly employed through Wilmington and Augusta was
925 miles.

To Brigadier General A. R. Lawton, who had been one of
Stonewall Jackson's brilliant lieutenants in the Shenandoah Valley,
was assigned the task of transporting the largest body of men—
approximately 12,000—that had yet been moved by railroad such
a distance in the history of war. Lawton, a West Point graduate
whose home was Savannah, Georgia, had been critically wounded
at Antietam. Being disabled for further field duties, he had been
appointed Quartermaster General of the Confederate army. In his
later years President Grover Cleveland made him U. S. Minister
to Austria.

One surprising element about this strategic movement of troops
was pointed out by the able artilleryman, E. P. Alexander. It was
the "dilatory consideration and slow acceptance" of a plan that
ought to have been decided on even before Lee's army had regained the south bank of the Potomac after the repulse at Gettysburg. Orderly preparations might then have been made, and the
shorter route employed. The War Department imperatively
needed a plans board. It is unlikely, except for Longstreet's suggestion, that the troop movement which was to give the Confederacy
life and opportunity for an additional year and a half would ever
have been undertaken. Alexander rated even Longstreet slow in
urging the proposal.

It was not until September 9, the day on which Colonel Atkins
rode into Chattanooga and Frazer was surrendering Cumberland
Gap to De Courcy, that the first of the trains appeared at Orange
Court House and Louisa Court House to begin loading John B.
Hood's and Lafayette McLaws' divisions and Alexander's artillery: nine infantry brigades and six batteries, all strengthened to
some extent after the depletions of Gettysburg, and representing
perhaps the best striking power of Lee's army. Lee's staff officer,
Major Walter H. Taylor, looked at them and concluded: "No
better troops could be found anywhere . . ."

In the loading, preference was given to the infantry. Alexander's artillery marched overland to Petersburg and finally at 4 P.M. on September 17 the guns which had prepared the way for Pickett's and Pettigrew's assault at Gettysburg were loaded on flat cars and the men began their trip to the western front. They covered 225 miles to Wilmington in fifty-eight hours, were ferried across the Cape Fear River and at 2 P.M. resumed their movement toward Chickamauga, not knowing that at that hour the battle was raging in its full fury and by nightfall would have passed into history. Longstreet's artillery had been started too late on its journey, but artillery was not an important factor in this battle in the woods.

One difficulty in the roundabout route was that the railroads did not have uniform gauge. The entire line was single track of light construction and it was nothing short of a marvel that five infantry brigades got through in time for the battle.

When Alexander with his guns reached Augusta they found transfer necessary to a railroad of different gauge. But the cars on the new railroad were crowded with infantry so Alexander put some of his guns and horses on the highway and marched the remaining distance to Bragg's army. None arrived in time for the battle.

Another problem was that most of the railroads of that day ran from city to city and did not have junctions. The troops had to be marched across town or conveyed in drays. This would not appear to be a major difficulty except that all of the men of the two divisions were from south of North Carolina and many were touching their home country in South Carolina and Georgia for the first time after long absence and hard fighting. The temptation to steal a few days off with their families was indeed severe, and every precaution had to be taken against straggling. Sorrel insisted that there were no desertions at the stops, but the statement was too inclusive.

The rolling stock of the South was in even more miserable condition than the right-of-way. A hodgepodge collection of cars was made rapidly and nearly everything in the southeast that could roll on tracks was hurried to the railheads south of the Rapidan. The army regarded the work a supreme achievement by General Lawton and the Quartermaster Department. The long trains presented a singular sight as the engines puffed toward Richmond and the South: never before were "such crazy cars—passenger, baggage, mail, coal, box, platform"—employed to haul good soldiers, but away they went "wobbling and jumping" along the rails. Day after day the loading continued, Hood's division first, then McLaws'.[4]

Longstreet went to General Lee's tent to take his farewell. There is no record of their conversation inside, but Lee then followed Old Peter to his horse and as the corps commander put his foot into the stirrup said: "Now, General, you must beat those people out in the West." Longstreet withdrew his foot. The careful soldier wanted to assume a position of respect before replying. "If I live," he answered, standing erect. Then he continued: "But I would not give a single man of my command for a fruitless victory."

Longstreet's parting letter written a little later from Richmond showed more clearly the deep respect and love he bore his chief. He said that if he could accomplish nothing quickly he would ask to be recalled. He would be distressed at departing, just as his officers and men were distressed, did he not think it necessary.

"All that we have to be proud of," he added, "has been accomplished under your eye and under your orders. Our affections for you are stronger, if it is possible for them to be stronger, than our admiration of you."

When Hood's troops reached Richmond they were met at the tracks by a familiar figure. Major General Hood was under his surgeon's care for the severe arm wound he had received at Gettysburg, but when the men saw him put his horse on the train they knew he was going to Georgia with them. Years later he explained to Longstreet that though he had not recovered and had the use of only one arm, because "my old troops—with whom I had served so long—were thus to be sent forth to another army—quasi, I may say, among strangers" and because a number of his brigade and regimental commanders requested it, he decided to resume the command he had turned over to Brigadier General E. McIver Law in front of Little Round Top.

Longstreet's passage through Richmond and the South was a

series of ovations. Though in later war literature he was to be made the scapegoat of Gettysburg, he was then the hero of the battle. Crowds met the trains at every depot bringing food and cheering the troops on to victory. Sorrel made it clear that the men received something even more desirable than food and cheer. "Kisses and tokens of love and admiration for these war worn heroes were ungrudgingly passed around." Many companies went through the towns where they had been recruited and there they were surrounded by kinsfolk and neighbors.

Mrs. Mary Boykin Chesnut saw them when they were in Kingville, South Carolina. "God bless the gallant fellows!" She was impressed with their conduct—no intoxication, no profanity, not a rude word from all that mass of men. Miles of platform cars passed her, the soldiers sleeping in rows and looking like mummies, their gray blankets pulled over their heads. The journey must have had its discomforts, with eight days spent on hard flatcars in the open weather. The boxcars had as many on top as inside.

"A feeling of awful depression laid hold of me," Mary Chesnut wrote that night in her diary. "All these fine fellows were going to kill or be killed. Why? . . . When a knot of boyish, laughing young creatures passed me, a queer thrill of sympathy shook me."

But all of Longstreet's men were not so gentle. In Raleigh, North Carolina, Benning's Georgians wrecked the office of William W. Holden's *Standard*, of uncertain war sentiments. In Wilmington some of Hood's Texans had a melee with the town guard in which the unoffending guard came out second best. Eleven members of Robertson's brigade made their way to the Wilmington waterfront in a section between the Weldon railroad station and the Farmer's Hotel known as "Paddy's Hollow." Liquor was followed by "considerable noise and disturbance." The elderly, stay-at-home men who comprised the night police force were summoned. Strong drink must have made the constables look like Yankee soldiers, for one guard in his fifties was badly beaten, another received a severe blow on his head from a club, while the third got two knife wounds in his side, neither of them, fortunately, penetrating between the ribs. It need not be added that there were no arrests.

"Rock" Benning was in Raleigh when his soldiers gutted Holden's newspaper plant and was charged by the Raleigh *Progress* with being privy to the sacking, an accusation with which the *Standard* tended to agree. But the Atlanta *Intelligencer* looked into the matter, apparently talked with Benning, and denounced the *Progress* charge as "base falsehood." The general had been seen on the Raleigh streets an hour before the mob appeared, but when the men reached the newspaper office, he was nowhere in sight. A policeman was rushed to the railroad station, but the soldiers crowded around and held him off and he was unable to see Benning, who was alleged to be asleep. The *Standard* maintained that the mob was led by officers.[5]

McIver Law's Alabama brigade that had fought with such determination on the slopes of Little Round Top found food awaiting it in abundance, prepared by the women of the towns. The trains were stopped as each community had a festive occasion.

In Atlanta a day's delay was caused by troops who were going to Bragg from Joseph E. Johnston's army in Mississippi. Colonel Oates of the 15th Alabama in Longstreet's command looked on as McNair's mixed brigade of Arkansas and North and South Carolina troops, who would play one of the key roles in the impending battle, went through Atlanta ahead of his men.

Benning's Georgia brigade reached Atlanta first of Hood's soldiers, followed by Hood's old Texas brigade under the command of Brigadier General Jerome Bonaparte Robertson, the humane Washington County, Texas, physician who had been lured into warfare (possibly the name Bonaparte was a factor) by Sam Houston's struggle for Texan independence.

Lafayette McLaws rented a room in the Trout House in Atlanta to get a sound night's sleep and was disturbed only once. It was not an orderly with army messages but a large rat. He went back to sleep and next morning found the rat snug under his pillow.

Everyone seemed to know about Longstreet's departure except Rosecrans and his army, who were busily engaged in capturing Chattanooga and moving up the valleys of northern Georgia. Apparently it did not occur to Halleck that they would be interested. War Clerk Jones in Richmond recorded on September 12 that a deserter had gone to the enemy with intelligence that a large force had been detached from Lee's encampments. Expectations of some in Richmond were that Meade would seize the opportunity and advance. A day earlier it was known in Richmond that Washington had information about the transfer. Halleck learned on September 13 that the railroad south of Richmond was extremely busy. The next day Meade informed him that Longstreet's corps had disappeared from his front. Somebody might have put two and two together and deduced Longstreet's objective.

Eventually it did begin to dawn on the War Department that Bragg, far from fleeing toward Rome and Atlanta, was concentrated around La Fayette and would very shortly be able to face Rosecrans with a greatly augmented army. Other units were coming in. The great Federal army which had won the resounding triumph on the Mississippi appeared unable to contain Johnston and prevent him from reinforcing Bragg. Lincoln had been correct in his earlier apprehension, and Rosecrans wrong in his reassurance that Grant could cope with Johnston better after he had captured Pemberton than before. Bushrod Johnson's division, which would deliver the coup de grace to McCook's corps at Chickamauga, plus Breckinridge's veteran division of Alabama, Georgia, Louisiana, Florida, North Carolina and Kentucky troops, regarded by many as the flower of the Western armies, were now being rushed to Bragg during the idleness of much of Grant's army, and while Grant himself was laid up in New Orleans with a leg injury suffered in a fall when his horse had shied at a streetcar.

Gregg's brigade (which was to be merged into Bushrod Johnson's division) was elated when it learned at Enterprise, Mississippi, on September 11, that it had been ordered north. Said John T. Goodrich of Fayetteville, Tennessee: "With buoyant expectancy we Tennesseans were hoping that General Bragg would be sufficiently reinforced to recover our State and that we might see our home folks again after an absence of nearly two years."[6]

Johnston was able to send another important addition, consisting of Major General W. H. T. Walker's reserve corps, which Bragg had called for on the day Wilder's Federal brigade had dropped its shells around Chattanooga. With some additions, Gist's and Ector's and Liddell's and Walthall's brigades were built into two divisions, to be commanded respectively by Brigadier General S. R. Gist and Brigadier General St. John R. Liddell, and these comprised Walker's corps.

One void remained in the Southern army as it reassembled. Lieutenant General William J. Hardee, known as "Old Reliable" to the troops and undoubtedly Bragg's ablest subordinate in earlier campaigns, had been sent by President Davis to hold southern Alabama, threatened after the fall of Vicksburg. Known widely because of his authorship of Hardee's *Tactics*, a West Point graduate who had distinguished himself in the Mexican War and the old army, he had ordinarily commanded the corps made up of Breckinridge's and Major General Patrick R. Cleburne's divisions. Upon Breckinridge's return the corps was assigned to the North Carolinian Daniel Harvey Hill, who had done hard fighting in the Virginia army in the early battles and had held the "Bloody Lane" at Antietam.

Hill, testy and outspoken, had worked well with his brother-in-law Stonewall Jackson but had not preserved the best relationship with Lee. Blame was attached to him in Lee's staff for the loss of the general order at Frederick, Maryland, that gave McClellan knowledge of how Lee had divided his army in the face of the enemy in the Maryland campaign. Though he defended himself stanchly, there was no apparent regret when President Davis assigned him to command Confederate forces in North Carolina. He had been in ill health and had talked of resigning, but he accepted the North Carolina post, missed the Chancellorsville and Gettysburg campaigns, and now that his health and spirits were improved and affairs had quieted in North Carolina, he was called to Richmond by President Davis for consultation. When he told Davis that he could not command Hardee's old corps because one of Bragg's generals, Alexander P. Stewart, then with the army, ranked him, the President replied, "I can cure that," and made him a lieutenant general. He left Richmond the next day and on July 19 in Chattanooga reported to Bragg, whom he had not seen since he had served in Bragg's battery at Corpus Christi, Texas, in 1845.

Buckner had brought in his corps from Knoxville. Burnside's capture of that city had merely served to strengthen Bragg, without giving Rosecrans a single compensating advantage. Buckner, a Kentuckian and West Point graduate, whose father had fought with William Henry Harrison at the Battle of the Thames in the War of 1812, had served in the Mexican War but had resigned from the army in 1855 and gone to Chicago to make a neat fortune in real estate and become a colonel in an Illinois militia regiment. He had worked for neutrality in Kentucky and other border states but when Federal forces came down from Cairo, Illinois, he had sided with the South. His most conspicuous appearance had been as the officer left behind to surrender Fort Donelson.

The Confederates were gradually assembling their scattered forces. One of the small commands that seemed likely to be left behind was the 24th South Carolina, commanded by Colonel C. H. Stevens, who fell as a brigadier general a little later in front of Atlanta. When Beauregard had his troops facing Fort Sumter in April 1861, Stevens as a civilian had, along with Captain John Randolph Hamilton, formerly of the United States Navy, made developments which Beauregard contended signaled the revolution in naval warfare that led to the century-long era of the ironclads. Hamilton had experimented with an ironclad floating battery and Stevens had set up an ironclad land battery. Their work apparently antedated John Ericsson's *Monitor*, though Ericsson had designed something of the same nature earlier during the Crimean War.

Now Colonel Stevens was at Rome, Georgia, where he had been sent with the rest of Gist's brigade to construct fortifications and guard the rear of Bragg's army. Meantime, when Walker assumed command of the corps, Gist took charge of the division and his brigade passed to Colonel P. H. Colquitt, commander of the 46th Georgia Infantry. Colquitt likewise was at Rome. He moved the partial brigade over to Kingston to get the railroad to Dalton. But they had to watch train after train pass through Kingston, packed with Longstreet's men being rushed up from Atlanta. Their own cars that had carried them from Rome were shunted to a siding. As darkness came the situation grew worse, for when

they went to examine the locomotive they discovered that the fire
was dead under the boiler and the engineer was missing.

Colquitt, Stevens and Lieutenant Colonel Ellison Capers, who
survived to tell the story, combed the town and finally found the
house where the engineer was asleep. Such had been the demands
on the train crews that they were exhausted. The engineer, roused
from his slumber, first claimed the engine was out of order. He
did not appear concerned even when Stevens put a pistol to his
head and said he would blow his brains out if he did not return to
the train. He pleaded exhaustion. He could not take the responsibility for the lives of so many soldiers in his spent condition.
Stevens learned at about this time that he had a railroad man in
his Company A, under whose direction they got together a detail
of soldiers to fire the engine. They all but dragged the engineer
to his cab to give directions. Then when the steam was up they
blew the whistle and the long train pulled out of Kingston for
the Catoosa Woodshed, carrying the 24th South Carolina and
parts of the 8th Bn. and 46th Georgia regiments toward the banks
of Chickamauga Creek.

Colonel Colquitt had been compelling in his demands that the
engineer and the volunteer crew get the train under way. He, too,
had an appointment he would have to keep with death in the
woods next day.

Halleck, now in hot haste, was trying to get reinforcements sent
to Rosecrans. He speeded his calls for Burnside to march down
from Knoxville. Fearing that Bragg might intend to move against
Grant to recover Vicksburg, he requested Grant to transport
troops to Tuscumbia on the Tennessee River in north Alabama,
so as to anticipate and thwart Bragg's movement. He alerted Major
Generals Stephen A. Hurlburt at Memphis, John M. Schofield in
Missouri and John Pope in far off Minnesota and called on them to
send men. But all of this was late indeed, for the hostile forces
were already drawing together. Rosecrans would have to fight
with the army he had brought down from Murfreesboro and with
not one man more.[7]

CHAPTER NINE

Rosecrans Collects His Scattered Forces

For several days Crittenden's peril south of Chattanooga had been more acute than had Thomas' in McLemore's Cove. When he marched south from Chattanooga he had sent Palmer's and Van-Cleve's divisions to near Ringgold, twenty miles southeast on the Dalton road, and Wood's division to near Lee and Gordon's mill, twelve miles south on the La Fayette road. The two main elements of Crittenden's corps were therefore eight miles apart, and Wood's little division of two brigades—Wagner's brigade having been left in Chattanooga—was the only force between Bragg's army and that city, which held also only Granger's small reserve corps.

Readily Bragg might have attacked Wood, then Palmer and VanCleve, with substantially his full army, and neither Thomas nor McCook could have helped their fellow corps commander isolated by miles of marching and the mountains. Had Bragg possessed the enterprise and daring of Lee or Stonewall Jackson or the ability to enforce his concepts on his obstinate subordinates, he might have moved into Chattanooga with scarcely a halt, then passed around the point of Lookout Mountain, seized the Tennessee River crossing at Bridgeport, and made matters most uncomfortable if not calamitous for Rosecrans' army.

Meantime McCook had moved into Alpine and was headed for Summerville. When Crittenden had the greater part of his corps at Ringgold, McCook at Alpine was approximately sixty miles distant via the pass around the point of Lookout Mountain and

Chattanooga. Surely Rosecrans in his reliance on Washington and the tales fed to him by Bragg's pretended deserters had grown reckless! About the only explanation that could be offered for Bragg—and that a strained one—was that he knew heavy reinforcements were en route and was disposed to await them before initiating a battle.

Though he was soon to be overtaken by overwhelming adversity, Major General Thomas L. Crittenden had been one of the ablest of the civilian soldiers brought into high command in the Federal armies. His 21st Corps was composed of veterans seasoned in some of the most stubborn battles of the war.

Of his three divisions, two were commanded by West Point graduates—Brigadier Generals Thomas J. Wood and H. P. Van-Cleve. The other was commanded by Major General John M. Palmer, who would have a long and distinguished career in public office after the war. Palmer's had been Major General William Nelson's famous "man of war" division, so named because its huge former commander—Nelson was six feet four and three hundred pounds—was a graduate of Annapolis and a former navy officer.

When Grant was on the ropes on the first day at Shiloh, this division, the advance element of Buell's army, had brought him succor by its hurried overland march from Savannah when the guns began to sound upstream. Crittenden had commanded one of Buell's divisions alongside Nelson and with him had given splendid service on the second day at Shiloh. Crittenden fought at the "Hornet's Nest," and Nelson in front of the Peach Orchard where Albert Sidney Johnston had fallen.

Crittenden had been eating breakfast in the Galt House in Louisville when Brigadier General Jefferson C. Davis deliberately shot down the unarmed Nelson in what was perhaps the most sensational unpunished crime of the war. Crittenden had hurried to his friend's side, taken his hand and asked if he were hurt seriously, and had caught his reply, "Tom, I am murdered." Now, in the Chickamauga campaign, Davis commanded a division of Mc-Cook's 20th Corps, while Crittenden led three of the divisions that had fought with Buell at Shiloh and Perryville.

Crittenden's father, John J. Crittenden, had been Representative, Senator for four terms, Governor of Kentucky, Attorney General in the cabinets of Presidents Harrison and Fillmore. stanch Unionist and author of the "Crittenden Compromise" by which he and many others hoped to avert the war. He died at his home in Frankfort, Kentucky, July 26, 1863, while his son Thomas was engaged in the early phases of the Chattanooga campaign.

As the father had served on the staff of Governor Isaac Shelby, who accompanied the Kentucky soldiers in the War of 1812, so the son had become an aide-de-camp to his kinsman General Zachary Taylor in the Mexican War. After being at Taylor's side during the battle of Buena Vista, he had been appointed colonel of the newly organized 3rd Kentucky regiment, his major being John C. Breckinridge, later Vice President and now commander of a division in Bragg's army.

The Crittendens, father and son, were leaders in Kentucky affairs at the outbreak of hostilities. The hesitant Kentucky state government, having neither the resolution to remain in the Union nor the audacity to follow the other slave states and go out, undertook a sort of make-believe neutrality, with Simon B. Buckner, a state major general, in charge of the militia. After Buckner went into the Confederate army, September 18, 1861, Thomas L. Crittenden was placed in command of the Kentucky Unionists, and on October 27 Lincoln appointed him a brigadier general. Though his close friends of the Kentucky bluegrass section, including part of his own family, were going into the Southern army, he never wavered in his loyalty to the old government. His hard fighting and splendid conduct with Buell's army on the second day at Shiloh won him a major general's commission.

His elder brother, George B. Crittenden, became a major general in the Confederate army, but resigned after being censured for the loss of the Battle of Mill Springs to then Brigadier General George H. Thomas.

Crittenden was slim, spare and "straight as a ramrod." He had a dark complexion and black hair. More retiring than many of the volunteer officers, he carried himself with an obvious pride and dignity. He was forty-eight years old at the time of Chickamauga.

Despite his lack of professional military training, he was clearly a more accomplished soldier than his fellow corps commander McCook.

"Crittenden's corps almost worship him but McCook has always been looked on by the troops as incompetent to command," said Captain Lemark Duvall of the 90th Ohio, Palmer's division.[1]

In those September days an impression, at first almost imperceptible but growing into a whispered rumor, then swelling into a conviction, passed through the Southern camps that Longstreet's celebrated corps was coming to help Bragg. First the report was laughed at, but still it persisted.

"I well remember the tumultuous joy when the astonishing portent grew into fact," said Lieutenant Colonel Archer Anderson. "Men came who had talked with Kershaw and Hood, not ten miles off, and the most skeptical could no longer doubt that on the great day of battle now at hand soldiers of the unconquerable Army of Northern Virginia were to stand side by side with the men of Shiloh and Murfreesboro."

Though Bragg's army was well advised, Rosecrans appears to have had still no intelligence of this extraordinary transfer of troops, even after Longstreet's men were in the cars and their departure was known to Washington. Sheridan, at Alpine on September 10 on the far-away right of Rosecrans' army, happened to stumble onto the information. Uneasy, he sent out a scout to ascertain the truth about whether Bragg was falling back on Rome. The scout disappeared over the mountains, was captured, escaped, and made his way back to Sheridan's tent with the startling intelligence that Bragg's army was expecting the arrival within a very few days of Longstreet's corps from Virginia. Sheridan rushed the information to Rosecrans, and perhaps this report more than the affair at McLemore's Cove caused the commanding general to order a concentration. Even as late as the fourteenth, Rosecrans was inquiring of Halleck in Washington if Bragg had been reinforced from Lee's army![2]

But the commander of the Northern army was in no position to take chances. More by gradual acknowledgment than sudden revelation, the light of truth began to break for Rosecrans across the north Georgia hills. The gifted and adroit general, whose achievements were at that very moment being celebrated throughout the North, recognized on the night of September 12 that he had been hoodwinked; that his army stood in jeopardy of being chewed up in three big, separate bites; that the enemy was composed and concentrated in close proximity to his center, and was anything but disorganized and degenerated and in flight across north Georgia.

There was but one answer—to concentrate on his center. This Rosecrans undertook instantly.

McCook, spread out in the region of Alpine, was to close on Thomas. Thomas' and then McCook's corps would pour out of Stevens Gap to occupy McLemore's Cove, then move north to make contact with Crittenden at Crawfish Springs and at Lee and Gordon's mill.

The four days while Rosecrans was concentrating were spent in idleness by Bragg, who pulled back toward La Fayette and appeared to be content with the defensive. After the failures of Hindman, Hill and Polk, he seemed indisposed to further effort.

McCook had laboriously climbed the mountains going to Alpine and now his return march was one of much greater punishment to the troops. Often the artillery had to be hauled up the mountain trails and lowered into the valleys by the men. For four days— from the thirteenth to the seventeenth—McCook brought his corps back by forced marches, all the while being impeded by Wheeler's cavalry and exposed to attack by Bragg with overwhelming forces. But Bragg allowed him to make his way with the divisions of Richard Johnson and Davis up the road through Valley Head, and thence through Stevens Gap to Davis' Cross Roads. This route proved something of a detour and although Rosecrans censured McCook for having taken the longer route, it did, in fact, offer greater security. To Brigadier General William Lytle, commanding a brigade of Sheridan's division, was assigned the task of moving the heavy corps baggage over the mountains. Sheridan's division advanced by the less direct route through Trenton. By the night of September 17 Rosecrans' three corps were in supporting distance of one another and the great emergency to his army caused as much by the prodding from Washington as by Bragg's deceptiveness or by Rosecrans' eagerness was at an end.[3]

As rear guard was the fourth, or Reserve Corps of the Army of the Cumberland, consisting of no more than Brigadier General James B. Steedman's division and Colonel Daniel McCook's brigade, the whole commanded by Major General Gordon Granger. Rosecrans ordered it to Rossville, just over the Georgia line, to protect the Missionary Ridge gap there and make Chattanooga secure. At Rossville, reached on the thirteenth, the corps threatened for a time to explode from internal heat generated by Granger's severity, which some of the men attributed to his "West Point ideas" and others to his diminutive stature.

Granger, then forty-one years old, had a rough, brusque manner that made him disliked in the Western armies despite competent service in battles from Wilson's Creek to Chickamauga, as well as under Winfield Scott in the Mexican War. As might be expected in a corps with only one division, there was lack of warmth between him and his only division commander, Steedman. Granger seemed the antithesis of Joy, the name of his home town in Wayne County of upstate New York.

But the coolness between the generals was as nothing compared with the estrangement that was about to occur between Granger and some of his men, notably those of the 115th Illinois Volunteers, sometimes called the "Second Methodist Regiment." Like its earlier model, the 73rd Illinois, known as the "Preachers' Regiment," it was composed largely of Methodist ministers—and ministers apparently accustomed to good chicken. Those who were not ministers were mainly farmers from downstate counties of Wabash, Macon, Shelby, Christian and Schuyler, with enough scattering of German and Irish immigrants to give stubbornness, wit and the spice of variety to the different companies.

When Granger's corps reached Rossville the wagons were far behind and the men were hungry enough to give credence to a rumor started in the 115th Illinois that they were expected to live off the country now that they were in the Deep South. Foragers scattered and soon were returning with the harvesttime yield of well-cultivated farms—"large quantities of fresh beef, veal, pork and poultry, potatoes, honey" and whatever the recording soldier would mean by "etc." Each party of foragers was cordially welcomed by the regiment on its return, and matters went well until the slaughterers, dubbed the "cattle brigade," began to shoot the beef in such quantities that it "sounded like heavy skirmishing." The firing interested Granger. When the cause became known his interest turned to excitement.

Such foraging did not fit into his "regular army ideas." He decreed that those who had brought in the victuals should be arrested and disciplined. Before attending to that, he sent out a cavalry patrol to bring in the foragers still outside the camp. Somehow the men got word of the orders. They were cautioned to avoid the roads and were helped to slip into the rear of the camp. Granger, further angered, sent out additional patrols, now under the command of officers. The cavalrymen thus led proved efficient and arrested more than a hundred members of the regiment and took them to headquarters. Meantime the others had been enjoying a hearty meal of beef and chicken, putting the food where it could no longer be detected.

The provisions that had been gathered by the hundred arrested foragers were piled in front of the corps headquarters, and the men were tied to fences and trees. Quite obviously they were to be whipped. Word spread like wildfire along the company streets, and a great crowd of Methodist ministers, downstate farmers and Dutch and Irish newcomers, plus members of a nearby Michigan regiment, gathered at the big spring in front of Granger's office in the Ross house, the old home of John Ross, the Cherokee chief. Nobody could object to the men coming to get water. But Granger, looking out from his window, could sense trouble in the wind. A soldier with a blacksnake whip in his hand would have had as much chance of reaching the fence and the tied men as Bragg himself would have had of riding alone through Rossville that night into Chattanooga.

Granger knew it was a good time to duck. He learned that all of those arrested belonged to Whitaker's brigade of Steedman's division, so he discreetly withdrew from the situation, turned the men over to Steedman and directed that those guilty be punished severely. Steedman—"Old Steady" to the troops—issued an order that was far from what Granger had in mind. He released the foragers with a soft reprimand, which was no more than telling them not to pounce on the countryside for supplies so obviously again.

That would have ended the affair except that intelligence about the arrests reached the fiery Colonel Jesse H. Moore, commander of the 115th Illinois, just as he was finishing a nice mess of mutton brought in by the foragers. The colonel had been pastor of the First Methodist Church at Decatur, Illinois. His eloquence had helped to raise this and one other regiment at a spirited patriotic rally in Decatur in July 1862, following Lincoln's call for more volunteers. The colonel, a righteous man, had no intention of allowing his soldiers to suffer punishment for bringing in food he himself had eaten with relish, so, "with fire in his eyes," he rushed to Steedman's headquarters. He was appeased somewhat when he learned of Old Steady's substitution of a reprimand for a lashing, but his anger had not cooled. He asked Steedman if he thought General Granger had actually intended to have the rawhide put to the men's backs. Old Steady avowed that it was true. Colonel Moore's wrath rose up again, boiled over and seethed all around the division headquarters.

"General," he declared, "it would not have been permitted! I had made up my mind I would die before one of my men would be whipped!"

"Stop that! Stop that!" roared Steedman, seeing how close the words were to mutiny, or at least insubordination. "Go to your quarters!"

"I will obey you, General," said the colonel, "but I mean what I said."

He stalked out of Steedman's tent and regarded the matter as closed. But soldiers have a way of knowing what occurs in camp and one of them must have been at the tent flap. As the colonel walked back to his regiment the information went there before him. The band of the 22nd Michigan, of Whitaker's brigade, was already on hand, along with a great crowd of soldiers. They gave him a hearty, uproarious serenade. The preacher-colonel was a speaker of great ability, and after the music and songs he spoke mainly on the theme (what soldier could have guessed it!) of discipline and obeying the orders of superiors. He made no mention of the arrest of the foragers but dwelt on the difficulties of the long march over the mountains, then on the great battle that might be expected very soon. He could not have known that his 115th Illinois, and its neighbors the 22nd Michigan, and all the rest of Steedman's division would play a heroic role in that oncoming battle and leave nearly half their numbers on Horseshoe Ridge.

Then the band played a patriotic air and the men went to their quarters. Granger may have been nursing his wrath back in the Ross house but the Illinois soldiers, with plenty of ham and honey still hidden in their tents, were happy that night. On the next morning each man was given sixty rounds of fresh ammunition. Most surely a battle was in the air.[4]

CHAPTER TEN

The Repeaters Delay the Crossing

THE general plan of battle—if ever there was one in such confused fighting—began to take shape. Rosecrans, largely concentrated, still was not safe. Bragg was bringing his army north from La Fayette and quite clearly meant to interpose between Rosecrans, whose left was at Lee and Gordon's mill, and Chattanooga, his reserve center and base.

Rosecrans set up his headquarters at Crawfish Springs, a village grown around a heavy gushing of water from a subterranean creek. A road ran to Chattanooga from Crawfish Springs, passing through McFarland's Gap in Missionary Ridge. Approximately parallel to it was the La Fayette-Chattanooga road, called the La Fayette road in battle literature, which ran past Lee and Gordon's mill to Rossville. Both of these roads were essential to Rosecrans. He needed them to keep contact with his reserve under Granger in Rossville, and with Chattanooga.

Chickamauga Creek (technically West Chickamauga Creek) meandered northward to the Tennessee River, its general course being substantially parallel to the La Fayette road. Rosecrans was on the west side of Chickamauga Creek. Consequently Bragg's plan was to move down the eastern side, cross below Lee and Gordon's mill and turn Rosecrans' left, which he knew on September 17 to be situated at the mill. Bragg's attack was originally planned for the eighteenth but the troops could not be moved in time and he was compelled to defer it until the nineteenth. It was a costly delay because it gave Rosecrans a chance to adjust his army and better protect the routes to Chattanooga.

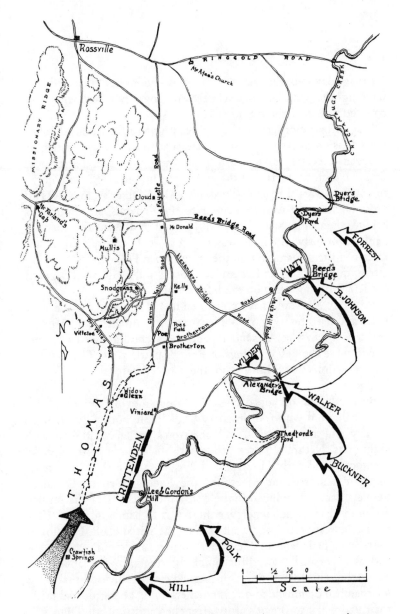

Bragg assumes the offensive. He is shown here trying to interpose between
Rosecrans and Chattanooga by crossing Chickamauga Creek below Rosecrans' left. Thomas is shown in his night march across the rear of Crittenden
to hold the road to Rossville and Chattanooga.

Bragg devoted the eighteenth to preliminaries, especially to winning the Chickamauga Creek crossings, not ordinarily accounted a part of the main battle.

Bragg's battle orders on the eighteenth were for Bushrod Johnson's division to cross the Chickamauga at Reed's bridge, which he believed to be far downstream from where the Federal army was situated, then turn left (south) and sweep up the creek from north to south toward Lee and Gordon's mill. Walker's corps was to cross farther upstream and closer to the Federals, at Alexander's bridge, then unite with Bushrod Johnson and assail the enemy's flank vigorously. Buckner was to cross at Thedford's ford, still farther upstream and join in the attack, then Polk was to assist by attempting to cross at Lee and Gordon's mill. Hill would guard the left flank upstream on the left of Polk.

Probably all would have gone well had it not been for the vigilance and hard fighting of Wilder's mounted infantry and Minty's cavalry, the first at Alexander's and the second at Reed's bridge, which were the key crossings in Bragg's battle plan. The first delaying action was Minty's on the Confederate side of Reed's bridge.

Bushrod Johnson approached the bridge moving along the road from Ringgold with four infantry brigades supported by Forrest's cavalry and accompanied by Robertson's artillery battalion with eight guns. Naturally Forrest rode with the column personally. As his doctor and early biographer John Allen Wyeth said of both him and his frequent adversary, the Federal General David S. Stanley, each "convinced himself that the interests of the service required his presence wherever there was a chance to fight." Certainly Forrest would not want to miss the initial clash. He moved upstream a little later to Alexander's bridge, a promising point. He had as a personal escort for quick-fighting purposes about 300 men—the remnants of the high-mettled cavalry division that John Morgan had commanded on his northern raid. These 300 had made their way back to Bragg's army after the catastrophe in Ohio.

On his right, Bushrod Johnson was well protected from any force Granger might send out of Rossville by Pegram's cavalry division of Forrest's corps.

Dr. Wyeth wondered what thoughts must have filled the minds of Forrest and Bushrod Johnson as they rode along together, for it was they who had broken Grant's right wing at Fort Donelson. Of all the Confederate high officers penned up by Grant in February 1862, Forrest had been the most unwilling to be captured. He had refused in advance to be bound by any surrender terms and had ridden through Grant's army to safety.

At 7:30 A.M. Forrest began skirmishing with Minty along Pea Vine Creek about a mile east of Reed's bridge, and all the way back to the bridge the fighting continued stubbornly. Minty confronted the strong Confederate column with three regiments and one battalion of cavalry and a section of the Chicago Board of Trade artillery. The cavalry battalion was part of the 3rd Indiana regiment. Another battalion of this regiment had found its way into the Army of the Potomac and had served with Major General John Buford's cavalry division in the Gettysburg campaign. Company C of the 3rd Indiana cavalry had led Buford's advance on June 30, 1863; had made the first contact with Pettigrew's Confederate brigade and had picked up the first Confederate prisoners at Gettysburg. It was a coincidence that the other section of the same regiment was now to engage in the opening clash at Chickamauga, the comparable great battle of the western armies.[1]

Long lines of Confederate infantry flying their regimental colors came into sight, overlapping Minty to the north and forcing him back toward Reed's bridge. Dust clouds on the road to Dyer's ford to the north, announcing the presence of another column, caused him to call on Wilder, who sent seven companies of the 72nd Indiana Mounted, the 123rd Illinois Mounted and a section of Lilly's battery. Pushed back step by step, Minty was still fighting at Reed's bridge at noon. By a quick onrush, the Confederates drove him across it so rapidly he could only damage and not destroy it. His delaying action continued, but when Forrest's cavalry began to ford the creek downstream, Minty at about 3:30 P.M. called in his guard at Dyer's ford and retired. Bushrod Johnson began marching his division of about 3,600 across Reed's bridge at 4:30 P.M.

Meantime, upstream, Walker with his corps of two divisions, plus Forrest personally with some guns, approached Alexander's bridge at noon and drove back Wilder's skirmishers on the east side. They were arrested before reaching the crossing by four guns of Lilly's well-stationed 18th Indiana battery, which fired long-range canister and shell effectively at from 600 to 1,200 yards. So stubbornly did Wilder guard the bridge with his infantry fire that two charges by Walthall's brigade of Liddell's division failed to carry it. The Northerners had taken off the planking and built a lunette commanding the roadway.

Forrest's chief of artillery was youthful Captain John Watson Morton. He would be twenty-one years old on September 19, the next day, but he got no birthday present in front of Alexander's bridge. Instead, his brand new artillery uniform neatly packed in a wagon came under the scrutiny of a hungry mule and the animal considered it a nice morsel. Then his frightened Negro servant Bob left him, taking all his rations. His three horses were killed or disabled. By the time he was twenty-one and across Alexander's bridge he had no horses, no food, not one dollar in cash, and only the old faded uniform. He was nevertheless a good enough officer to be termed "one of the military jewels which cluster in [Forrest's] diadem."

As Morton approached the bridge on the eighteenth he put his guns on a bluff and blazed away at Wilder and Lilly across the creek. He was compelled to corrct one of his artillerists, who was holding the spare cartridges too close to the friction primer, where they might be ignited. The lad took the criticism blithely, and responded, "All right, Captain. We'll whip this fight, or Molly Stark's a widow."[2]

Forrest was continually in the heat of the action, issuing orders, directing the fire of his cavalrymen and artillery. He wore a linen duster but had his pistol belt buckled on the outside. Early in the fighting his beautiful horse was shot from under him. A gift of the citizens of Rome, Georgia, the mount had been a reward for the capture of the Federal cavalry raider Streight.

Walker's men, like Bushrod Johnson's, forded upstream and downstream about 3:30 P.M. By 5 P.M. Wilder was finding his situation precarious, his flanks turned and his rear threatened, so he retired with Lilly's battery to the Viniard farm on the La Fayette road, losing only some of his horses that had been tied in the rear while his men were fighting.

The preliminary affair at Alexander's bridge, where Wilder with only a part of a single brigade and with but four guns of his battery was able to hold off a division with artillery for nearly five hours, was an important milestone in the progress of the war. It confirmed the value in combat of the Spencer repeating rifle with which these mounted infantrymen, through the efforts of their resourceful commander and their own financial co-operation, were equipped.

John T. Wilder was to play an important role in the battle of Chickamauga. His name at times occurs—and should more frequently—among the more spectacular cavalry leaders of the war, perhaps in the second echelon behind the names of Forrest, Stuart, James H. Wilson and Sheridan. He had come out of the Catskill Mountains in New York as a lad, to work in an iron foundry at Columbus, Ohio. His great-grandfather, Seth Wilder, had lost a leg at Bunker Hill; his grandfather had fought at Saratoga and Stony Point; his father, Reuben Wilder, had recruited a company of light horse and fought under General Jacob Brown in the War of 1812. The father still had fire in his heart at the age of sixty-nine; in 1862 he wrote the son in Tennessee, asking permission to serve as an aide during the Stone's River campaign.

Young John left Columbus for Greensburg, Indiana, a town long and still noted for the tree that grew out of its courthouse tower. There he established his own foundry, which employed 200 workmen. It was highly successful, partly because Wilder, who had become an expert in hydraulics, invented a turbine wheel that facilitated his output and allowed him to build up a trade covering Indiana, Kentucky, Virginia, Tennessee, Illinois, Wisconsin. Though a Democrat, he sided wholeheartedly with the Union and when war came, he began to cast cannon in his plant. The next natural step for one of his aggressive temperament was to organize an artillery company, but when it was not accepted into the service with sufficient alacrity he became captain of Company A, 17th Indiana Infantry, a regiment he later commanded as colonel. The 17th was with Reynolds and Rosecrans in West

Virginia, then with Nelson's division at Shiloh; it served in his own brigade at Chickamauga.

As an inventor Wilder attracted the inventive Rosecrans. Before they left Murfreesboro, Wilder exhibited to the army commander his newly devised rail-twister, a method of disabling railroads so effectively that they could not be readily repaired—as was possible when the rails were merely heated in the middle and curved back. Sherman, the greatest of the railroad wreckers, apparently did not take to Wilder's invention when he went to work later in Georgia, suggested by the fact that rails heated in the middle and bent back came to be known as "Sherman's hairpins."

Wilder was a large, intense man, six feet two inches tall, with bright, penetrating eyes and apparently unlimited vitality. John Beatty commented on his "wonderful energy and nerve." At the age of forty-six he could ride and fight as hard as any young trooper in his command; but though he never used tobacco or liquor, he did burn himself out before the end of the conflict and on account of poor health had to retire reluctantly.

On May 18, 1863, Wilder's brigade received their new Spencer repeaters, thus, according to the claim of the 17th Indiana, "making the brigade the best-equipped organization in the service." There can be scant doubt about the assertion. Wilder had inspected the Henry rifle, a gun which, "with a slight twist of the wrist, will throw sixteen bullets in almost that many seconds." But Spencers were available where Henrys were not. They had seven shots instead of sixteen; still the fire power was so extraordinary compared with the muzzle loaders with which the armies were equipped, that at Hoover's Gap, where they were first employed after Rosecrans set out for Tullahoma and Chattanooga, the Confederate General Bushrod Johnson thought when his brigade met Wilder's he was outnumbered five to one.

Quite obviously Stanton was conducting the War Department's procurement branch with the same sort of pinched-up economy that characterized the administration of Secretary of War Dr. William Eustis in the War of 1812. He permitted himself to be handicapped also by a reactionary chief of ordnance, Brigadier General James W. Ripley, who was devoted to the muzzle loader.

But the fault appeared largely Stanton's. When Lincoln, a tinkerer with an inventive trend himself, had tested the Spencer breech-loader (patented by Christopher Spencer of Connecticut in 1860) behind the Treasury and had become so fascinated with it that he invited Stanton to inspect it in a second trial, the Secretary of War was much too busy with other matters to look at the gun which some claim won the war for the North. It came to be known rightly as "Mr. Lincoln's gun."

Although in the spring of 1863 the Spencers were procurable on the market—for Wilder was able to buy them—they were not obtainable yet by War Department issue for soldiers who were fighting in the most deadly of combats. Rosecrans had been clamoring for repeaters for months. Wilder, a direct actionist, decided to purchase them without waiting longer. In order to raise the cash he wrote to his home-town bankers and volunteered to mortgage his plant and other possessions in Greensburg as an earnest for the money. The bankers said they did not need the mortgage, although they did take his personal note which was much the same thing. Then the brigade members said each one would pay for his own gun by deductions from his pay, a sacrifice for a soldier earning no more than tobacco and old sledge money. It was only after their efficacy had been fully established that the War Department decided to pick up the check and refund to each man what he had paid personally. The regiments were extremely happy with the arms, first used at Hoover's Gap but more fully demonstrated at Chickamauga. Said Colonel Smith D. Atkins of the 92nd Illinois: "The Spencer rifles made the sweetest music that was heard during the war for the Union."[3]

But for Walker's Confederates on September 18 there was little harmony in the refrain. General Liddell reported his loss at Alexander's bridge at 105 killed and wounded, which was surely heavy for the nature of the combat. "I can only account for this disproportion from the efficiency of this new weapon," said Liddell.[3]

With Wilder finally out of the way before darkness, Walker crossed his corps over the Chickamauga and advanced into the woods not far from Alexander's bridge.

CHAPTER ELEVEN

Meeting on the "River of Death"

ROSECRANS replied to Bragg's encircling maneuver by extending his left up the La Fayette road toward Chattanooga.

At 4 P.M. on September 18 Thomas began a movement north from McLemore's Cove to thwart Bragg's plan of interposing his army between Rosecrans and Chattanooga.

All night long the road leading northward through Pond Spring and Crawfish Springs was filled with marching columns as Thomas neared and then passed across the rear of Crittenden at Lee and Gordon's mill, to take position on Rosecrans' left. Why had the commanding general designated Thomas to hold the left, rather than Crittenden, whose march would have been shorter? Mainly because he had supreme confidence in Thomas' ability to exercise what amounted almost to an independent or separate command. Thomas would take the left of the army, Rosecrans the right. That much was determined before anyone knew just how the battle would be fought.

All along the route, burning fences at the side of the road provided light to guide Thomas' brigades, and a bit of heat on the cold night. As always, on such a movement over a single roadway in darkness there would be plenty of halts. When they came, the men broke ranks. Some would fall asleep. Others would heap new rails on the fires, warm their chilled hands and joke with Crittenden's soldiers until the bugle once more spoke the notes of "forward." Baird's division was in the lead, followed by Brannan. It was 2 A.M. when the head of Baird's division reached Crawfish Springs, where canteens were filled. Nobody knew it, but this was the last time many of the men would have opportunity to fill their canteens until after the battle. Many others would never fill their canteens again. The woods through which Thomas fought were almost destitute of springs or streams, so dry had been the late summer weather on the south side of the Cumberlands.

It was sun-up on Saturday, September 19, when Thomas reached the Kelly house with Baird's division, and 8 A.M. when Brannan's division marched across Baird's rear and took position as the far left element of Rosecrans' army.

Rosecrans, coming up later from Crawfish Springs, established his headquarters at 1 P.M. at the Glenn house, on the road from Crawfish Springs to Chattanooga. This little log cabin, the home of the Widow Glenn, was a mile and a half to the right of Kelly's and half a mile west of the La Fayette road.

Turchin's brigade of Reynolds' division, which followed Brannan, halted near a tanyard, where the 36th Ohio filled its canteens—the last time for two days—with water impregnated with the peppermint that grew in the pool.

Some were still doubtful about a battle. As the armies closed, the New York *Tribune* correspondent was writing on September 18 that hundreds of Southern soldiers were entering the Federal lines each week and laying down their arms.

"Where the enemy will make its stand is somewhat hard to conjecture," he wrote for the *Tribune's* lead story. "Had he wanted to fight he could have selected no more favorable place than Chattanooga for defense. The evacuation of it only confirms me in the opinion that he wants if possible to avoid a general engagement, by which a part of his army will be saved, and another campaign next spring made necessary."

Here was a reporter who must have been trained in observation and deduction in the school of the pseudo-military Dana! But Rosecrans' marches and countermarches had indeed been confusing to both newspapermen and officers. As a soldier of the 19th Illinois noted: ". . . The reassembling of his three corps by Rosecrans was a tactical proceeding that even the privates could not make heads or tails of."[1]

Far away, men were marching to Rosecrans' assistance. Halleck's frantic appeals were being answered. Pope in distant Minnesota and Schofield in Missouri had sent off soldiers they could scarcely spare. Nearer at hand Hurlburt in Memphis and Sherman in Mississippi put troops on the road. Scattered detachments in Tennessee and Kentucky were ordered to the front. General Parke got out of his sickbed and began to march with his Ninth Corps from Cumberland Gap. Details guarding railroads and bridges along the line to Louisville were reduced to the minimum so that men might be sent to the front. Halleck seemed to recognize that much of the fault of pitting Rosecrans against a reinforced enemy was his, and he was making every effort to overcome it.

Back in Richmond, War Clerk Jones was writing on that day that soon in north Georgia there must be a "fight or a foot race," then, "If we deserve independence I think we shall achieve it." He was observing also that Bragg was becoming unpopular: "But Bragg will fight!"

The armies were about to grapple in the deep woods like two great senseless brutes struggling in the darkness. North and South were waiting. Lincoln walked back and forth to the telegraph office in the War Department. The less robust Davis rested on the couch in his Richmond home and awaited word from Bragg, his favorite.

Rosecrans had directed his staff to telegraph a request to ministers of the North advising them that his army was about to meet the enemy and requesting that they beseech Almighty God to lend His support to the Northern cause. These prayers were beginning to go up in Northern churches. They would rise to their highest volume on Sunday, September 20, while the battle was raging.

The temperature was close to freezing that night along the Chickamauga. The armies lay on the frosty ground. The moon in its first quarter was bright, the sky cloudless. Thomas was marching through the night; here and there Crittenden's men were throwing up log breastworks. All along the Federal lines the fires burned merrily and details were going back and forth bringing in fence rails to keep them blazing. Bragg's soldiers could have no doubt that the Federals were close at hand across the Chickamauga and that the battle likely would begin in the morning.

Trim, determined Kentucky regiments faced each other as the bitterest and most unrelenting of enemies. The great Kentucky statesman and compromiser Henry Clay had declared in one of his last pathetic speeches to the Senate that if war came between the North and South it would be "furious, bloody, implacable, exterminating." Now the Kentuckians were about to make his words come true. Had he looked on, he who had given his untiring labors toward arresting the conflict and preserving the Union, would have seen his grandson fighting in the army of the South, a member of the staff of Lieutenant General Polk.

Some had presentiments. The captain of the Arkansas battery dreamed that the Confederacy would win a brilliant victory. Captain George Y. Williams of the 50th Tennessee, in Bushrod Johnson's division, seemed to know it was his last battle. At Fort Donelson he had won free of Grant's encirclement but had returned because he had promised his men he would never leave them. This night he called an old boyhood friend to his tent, talked of their earlier times in Clarksville, Tennessee, handed over his watch to be given to his mother. On the next day he was the first of his company to fall.

Stewart's Confederate division had come up to the home of old Mrs. Debbie Thedford, the "Mother of Chickamauga," so christened by Buckner's corps, at Thedford's Ford. Her first knowledge that her sons were home with the army was when they and others rushed in and began raiding her potato patch. An officer tried to restrain them.

"Hold on, Mr. Officer!" she exclaimed. "They are my potatoes and my boys. Let 'em take 'em."

During the battle two other sons serving with Longstreet were carried wounded into her house.

Here Bragg had his headquarters much of the time. Bromfield L. Ridley of Stewart's staff sensed the drama of the scene. "Bragg slept sweetly that night . . . for once the forces were nearly equal; Rosecrans on the other hand was restless and perturbed, fearful of his left wing being turned . . ."

That morning Captain Cullen Bradley of the 6th Ohio battery, of Harker's brigade, Wood's division, fired across the Chickamauga at some gray-clad troops in the bushes—one of the many "first shots" of the battle. This brigade lay along the creek bank at Lee and Gordon's Mill. "All night we heard the tread of hurrying feet, and the clatter of galloping hoofs. It was the night before the battle."[2]

The expanse of territory on which the armies were about to meet extends for six miles along the west bank of Chickamauga Creek, in the deeply wooded basin, level in its central stretches, between Pigeon and Lookout mountains, or more technically the Boykin and the Missionary ridges.

The Confederate army had Pigeon Mountain to its rear, the Federal, Lookout. The depth of the combat area was about three miles. It has been well said that on every acre there was desperate fighting.

The Chickamauga, deep, tree-lined, sluggish and wandering, has precipitous rocky banks in most places; the water is often ten feet deep, making it uncrossable for troops except at the bridges and fords, which were fairly numerous. The name of the stream has been given various interpretations, as "stagnant water," from the lower Cherokee tongue, or "good country," from the Chickasaw. But the most fitting tradition and the one that has persisted is that Chickamauga meant "River of Death" in the dialect of the up-country Cherokee. In pioneer days the banks were lined with the villages of the Cherokee who had migrated from the Little Tennessee River. Being joined by recruits from the Shawnee and Muskogee tribes, they harassed the white settlements. Here Chief Dragging Canoe presided, and here Tecumseh in his youth orated and fought with his brother Cheeseekau.

But "The River of Death" came by its title not from the early warfare of the region. It was here that the Cherokee contracted smallpox, which raged through the tribe after the first coming of the white man. Probably it was communicated more readily because the Indians bathed in the river to allay their fever. Because of the havoc played by the disease, often apparently transmitted by the stream, the Chickamauga won the name so appropriate for the sanguinary battle fought along its banks.

Rosecrans had never before seen the Chickamauga country. But Bragg had long been familiar with it. In 1838, as a young lieutenant one year out of West Point, he had been stationed at Camp Missionary Hill while General Winfield Scott was enforcing the migration of the Cherokee out of Georgia, North Carolina and Tennessee to the reservation beyond the Mississippi.

The Confederates fought with the Chickamauga to their backs. A severe defeat would have meant a great deal of jamming at the bridges and fords and perhaps disasters along the line. But Bragg's original intention was to cross the stream below Lee and Gordon's mill, envelop the Federal left, and attack upstream, from the north to the south. He believed that Crittenden's corps at Lee and Gordon's mill was the left element of Rosecrans' army, in which case his plan would have probably proved most advantageous. But Thomas' march across Crittenden's rear on the night of the eighteenth defeated Bragg's intention to attack facing south with his army between Rosecrans and Chattanooga, and compelled him to fight facing west, with his back to the creek.

Much of the area over which the armies fought was in thickets, with a low growth of dogwood, scrub oak, cedar, and pine, matted with underbrush of blackberry briars, honeysuckle, poison oak and trumpet vine. As these two armies had struggled and floundered through tangles of cedar at Stone's River, so they were again to meet this bristling, sticky, irritating obstacle along the Chickamauga. Here and there the underbrush gave way to more cathedral-like forests of great hardwoods: hickory, black gum, maple, white and Spanish oak; while all about were great cedars and shortleaf pine. Occasionally there were clearings—cultivated farms and pasture lands—almost all of them having the small log houses built by the pioneers who had come over the mountains from North Carolina when Tennessee was still a part of that state, and occupied now by the sons and grandsons of the first settlers.

One of the St. Louis correspondents writing about the meeting of the two armies termed it a "soldiers' battle," and such it was, for here, as in few other instances in the war, bands of men fought other bands until one group or both were killed or exhausted, with higher ranking generals having no view of the field and little control over the fighting. It has likewise been properly termed a battle of motion. The armies were shifting positions when they unexpectedly ran headlong into each other and there was little stability to the fighting lines during the two days they were locked in deadly combat.[3]

At Gettysburg, the great comparable battle fought by the armies in the east, the battle lines were clearly defined; at Chickamauga they were fluid. As sandpipers which press closely after each receding wave and then, as the crest stops and turns to surge up the beach once more, scamper nimbly back, giving way not one unnecessary inch, or one second too soon, prepared at any instant to note the wave's high point and turn and follow its recession again—so the two armies surged continuously back and forth at each other through the woods and across the clearings, as watchful as sandpipers to detect when the impact of a wave would be spent, or, like the sea, gathering new strength from a reinforcing wave and plunging forward to the full limit of their strength.

At Gettysburg the units were relatively stable in the positions they assumed at the beginning of the combat. Lee's divisions and brigades fought where they came onto the field. There was virtually no readjustment of the divisions to new places in the battle lines. While Meade shifted some elements to take advantage of his interior lines, even with his army, most of the corps, divisions and brigades held or returned to their original positions. The 12th and 11th Corps remained on the right, Hancock with his 2nd Corps in the center, the 3rd and 5th Corps on the left, and the 6th in reserve.

That was not the case at Chickamauga, where corps were broken apart by the Northern commander, who did not hesitate to issue orders to divisions and brigades directly. Thus in the instance of Crittenden and to a lesser degree McCook he almost deprived the corps commanders of their function, and at times without their knowledge personally assigned units to new positions in the line. The relative position of divisions and brigades in Bragg's army was more stable, but here, too, a major readjustment occurred when the army was divided into wings and assigned to new commanders in the very middle of the battle.

At Gettysburg the armies ended the combat in substantially the same positions where they began it, Meade along Cemetery and Lee along Seminary Ridge. At Chickamauga the fighting was almost continually over new ground and one army ended the battle roughly where the other began it.

Rosecrans was outnumbered. His army aggregated 64,500 of all arms, and 170 pieces of artillery. Bragg had an army of 71,500 of all arms and 200 pieces of artillery. The Confederate superiority in artillery was of scant advantage in a battle fought in heavy timber. Rosecrans' deficiency in cavalry was partly compensated for by the superior arms of many of the Northern mounted men. But never before on any major battlefield of the war had the Confederacy been so favorably situated.

What General Lee could have done with this army is one of the unanswered questions of American history, but it is perhaps well for the cause of the Union that Bragg rather than he commanded here.

CHAPTER TWELVE

Thomas Stumbles into a Battle

So LOW was the visibility in the dense woods that when the commander of the Federal reserve at Rossville, General Granger, sent Colonel Dan McCook up the Chickamauga to help Minty at Reed's bridge, McCook was led into a false impression.

Arriving after Minty had been driven back, he explored around in the gathering darkness. About a mile west and south of Reed's bridge he chanced into McNair's brigade of Bushrod Johnson's division, from which he picked up some prisoners.

Dan McCook bivouacked on the spot, then sent word of his encounter to Thomas, who was marching his corps past Crittenden's to take a position at the Kelly farm. Being ignorant of the fact that the balance of Bushrod Johnson's division and all of Walker's corps were on the west side of the Chickamauga, poised to attack southward according to Bragg's plan to turn the Federal left flank, McCook told Thomas that a single Confederate brigade was isolated west of the creek on the Reed's bridge road. He said he had destroyed the bridge behind it, and believed this brigade could be pocketed and captured.

Thomas had received word from Wilder, as well as from Dan McCook, of the crossing of Walker's corps. Walker had, in fact, pressed ahead toward the Viniard farm on the night of the eighteenth and twice in the darkness had attacked Wilder and Dick's brigade of VanCleve's division, which had come to his support. Bushrod Johnson meantime had followed orders and marched three miles upstream, then bivouacked, leaving Walker's corps the right of the Confederate army on the west side of the Chickamauga.

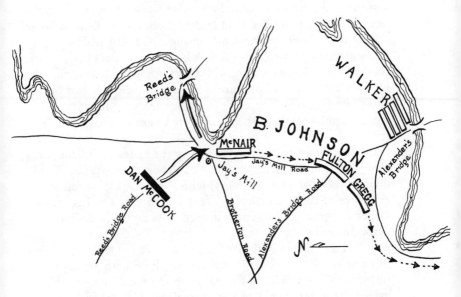

First infantry contact on the battlefield. Dan McCook stumbles into McNair's Confederate brigade, believes it is isolated and sends word to Thomas that it can be captured.

Thomas, always enterprising when the odds seemed favorable, had no intention of passing up the isolated brigade Dan McCook had discovered. Other Federal units were within reach. Richard Johnson and VanCleve were near by, Reynolds' division was coming up, and Palmer was approaching. So with his position well secured, he ordered Brannan, commanding his left division, to put one brigade on the road to Alexander's bridge, where it would receive support from Baird's division on that road, and with his other two brigades to go after the loose Confederate brigade Dan McCook had encountered.

Thomas' order to Brannan was of the first significance because it suddenly put the Federal army, which Bragg presumed to be on the defensive, in the role of the assailant. Instead of Bragg overlapping the Federal left, Rosecrans now overlapped Bragg's right. It was 7:30 A.M. Brannan moved out, Van Derveer's brigade on the left, on both sides of the road leading from the McDonald house (then situated where the Chickamauga National Military Park headquarters now stands) to Reed's bridge; Croxton's brigade was on the right, on the road from Kelly's farm to Jay's sawmill. The mill was close to the Chickamauga and on a side road just off the Reed's bridge road. The roads on which the two brigades moved were roughly parallel for a time, then almost converged at Jay's mill.

In general outline, the initial battle on the Federal left flank was a clash of Brannan's division supported a short time later by Baird's division (both of Thomas' corps) with Forrest's cavalry and Walker's corps of two Confederate infantry divisions. The Federals attacked between the two roads toward Jay's mill. The fighting was desperate and the first results inconclusive. The initial phase might be called the repulse of the Federal attack toward Jay's mill. What this action mainly accomplished was to show both armies that a full-scale battle would be fought along the west bank of Chickamauga Creek and that all of both armies should be hastened to that area.

The second phase was marked by the arrival of the Federal division commanded by Richard Johnson—there was a Johnson in command of a division in each army—and Cheatham's Confederate division. Succeeding phases followed the arrivals of fresh divisions of both armies. An oncoming division of each army seemed to reach the battle zone at about the same time. These newcomers, taking corresponding positions in the relatively fluid battle lines, fought each other until both were spent. Thus the action which began on the north end of the battlefield, nearest to Rossville and Chattanooga, moved southward as the day advanced. By the late evening of the first day the main conflict was being fought between fresh troops of both armies at the far southern end of the field, from Hall's Ford to the Viniard farm, nearest to Lee and Gordon's mill. All day long the troops were marching to the north and the battle was rolling to the south.

From the outset it was clear that in no sense were the lines of the two armies stable. As the columns of troops marched north, the

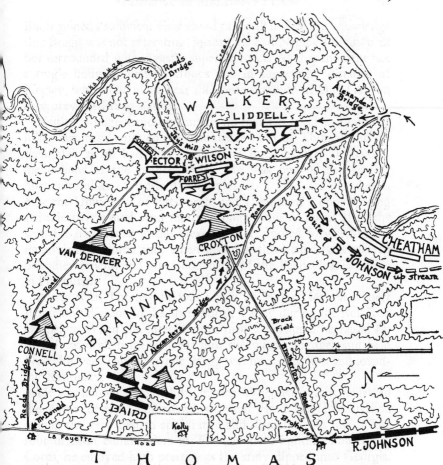

Beginning the battle. Croxton finds that instead of one Confederate brigade, he faces several brigades of Walker's corps. He attacks, supported in turn by Brannan's other two brigades, Van Derveer and Connell, and Baird's division.

Federals turned to the right and the Confederates to the left to face each other, and went into battle in the labyrinths of the virgin forest, where it was usually more difficult to locate friends on the right or left than the enemy supposed to be in front.

As Brannan began his attack, Forrest was forced back and had to call on Walker for infantry help, and thus the battle opened.

Croxton struck the enemy first. His brigade had halted at Kelly's long enough for coffee after its all-night march. The men were a bit refreshed. They faced east toward the Chickamauga with confidence and formed line of battle on the edge of a woods west of Jay's mill. Suddenly the skirmishers sent out by the 10th Indiana came back on the run, pressed closely by Confederate cavalry charging pell-mell over the hill on their heels. "Steady, boys. Wait for the word from our colonel." The enemy horse, reported Private T. B. Kellenberger, reached to within 150 yards of Croxton's line without seeing it. In the letter Kellenberger wrote home his capitalization suggested his sense of the high drama of this initial clash of the main armies.

"Our tremendous volley rang along the whole line. At first all was Smoke, then Dust from the Struggling Steeds. A few riderless Horses were running here and there Save which Nothing was Seen of that Cavalry troop; thus began the battle of Chickamauga."[1]

Croxton's brigade had two Indiana, two Kentucky and one Ohio regiment. The 74th Indiana was on the right, the 10th Indiana in the center and the 4th Kentucky on the left of the first line. When the cavalry screen was driven back, the Northerners were able to feel the enemy line behind it. They learned quickly that instead of confronting an isolated brigade, Croxton was facing two strongly posted Confederate divisions. These comprised Walker's corps, which was to launch the Southern attack up the west side of the Chickamauga in conjunction with Bushrod Johnson, who had already gone ahead up the stream.

An amusing feature was that when Croxton met the Confederate force and learned its proportions, he is alleged to have sent back an oral inquiry to Thomas, asking facetiously which of the four or five enemy brigades in his front was the one he was supposed to capture.

Croxton joined at once into a desperate engagement with Gist's division of Walker's corps, consisting of the brigades of Wilson and Ector, which were assisted by Forrest. Both sides opened in a manner to forecast the deadly fury of this great battle. At the very outset Colonel William B. Carroll of the 10th Indiana was shot fatally in front of his regiment, the first field officer of either army to fall.

Brannan sent prompt help to Croxton from the parallel road. Quickly Van Derveer's brigade came up on his left. Brannan's first brigade, Connell's, which had marched in reserve, hastened to Van Derveer's aid and now the heavy sounds of battle were carried back to Thomas, to whom Croxton reported that he had driven the enemy half a mile but was now encountering obstinate resistance.

Major General William Henry Talbot Walker, whose corps opened the infantry battle for Bragg's army, was still a general of uncertain quality in the third year of the war, though he had served both in Virginia and the western armies. He had done poorly in the class of 1837 at West Point, standing forty-sixth among the fifty graduates, but his record as a young officer was in marked contrast with his lackadaisical cadetship. He was wounded severely three times fighting the Seminoles and again desperately in Mexico, where the surgeons gave him up for dead. He so distinguished himself in the Mexican War that Georgia gave him a sword and the army breveted him major and then lieutenant colonel. Because of his injuries he had to sleep thereafter sitting in a chair. A Federal picket finally would drop him in front of Atlanta more surely than had the Mexicans or Seminoles.

Often retarded by poor health and sick leaves resulting from his wounds, he had advanced only to major in the 10th Infantry when the Confederacy was formed. Though he regretted the break, he resigned his commission in December 1860. After Fort Sumter he was appointed a brigadier general of the Confederacy and took charge of a brigade in Virginia, but resigned that autumn in protest when the Confederate government failed to name him a major general. He sat for a year and a half on the sidelines, then re-entered as a brigadier general. But on the recommendation of General Joseph E. Johnston, who rated him the best division commander in the army, he was made a major general May 23, 1863, assigned to Johnston in Mississippi. When Vicksburg was lost and Bragg required help, Walker was sent to Bragg's army. His "Reserve Corps" was composed of two front-line veteran divisions.

The first, put together during the battle, was commanded by the handsome graduate of Harvard Law School, States' Rights Gist, whose name, pitched for Southern ears, must have raised eyebrows on the Cambridge campus. Gist, a South Carolinian who had come up to brigadier general through the militia, had been an aide to Barnard E. Bee when that lamented general was christening T. J. Jackson "Stonewall" at First Manassas. When Bee was killed, Gist had taken command of Bee's brigade, and he had shown thereafter that his ardor and great effort were as much in his cause as his name. He would survive his corps commander Walker by a few months and fall at the battle of Franklin.[2]

Walker's other division commander, the Mississippi planter, St. John R. Liddell, had dropped out of West Point after sampling the arduous studies for a year. He came up through Hardee's staff to brigade, then division command.

The combat to this point had been carried by Gist's brigades and Forrest's cavalry division led by John Pegram, elder brother of the brilliant young artilleryman William Johnson Pegram of Lee's army.

An episode characteristic of Forrest occurred in this opening combat of marked ferocity. The Southern cavalryman, whom Northern writers delighted to call "the hero of the card table and bowie knife," was supporting Ector. Assailed in front by all he could take care of, Ector worried about his right flank, which Forrest was supposed to be protecting. His brigade was likely to be exposed, since it was on the far right of Walker's corps and Bragg's army. He sent his adjutant, C. B. Kilgore (later Congressman and United States district judge) with the unnecessary warning to Forrest that he should be most attentive to the flank. Kilgore found Forrest deeply engaged in the combat, standing among his guns where he could catch the exhilaration of heavy enemy infantry and artillery fire—unruffled, attentive to everything about him. The colloquy was brief:

"General Forrest, General Ector directed me to say to you he is uneasy about his right flank."

"Tell General Ector that he need not bother about his right flank. I'll take care of it."

Kilgore delivered the reassurance. But it did not satisfy Ector a little later after Wilson's brigade had been worsted on his left. So the brigade commander again sent his adjutant to Forrest to repeat the message that he was uneasy, this time about his left flank. An hour had passed and Forrest had not given way an inch. He was at one of his batteries "blazing away and every man fighting like mad." But when Kilgore delivered his new request Forrest flew into a furious tantrum, and shouted so loud that even the cannon could not drown out his words nor the battle smoke conceal his flashing eyes.

"Tell General Ector that by God I am here, and will take care of his left flank as well as his right."[3]

When Ector was finally pressed back, it was by an attack on his front. Forrest had kept his contract; no enemy assailed Ector on either flank.

Now Walker sent in Liddell's division, which brought timely succor to Ector and Wilson because Thomas, recognizing the gravity of the fighting and the threat to the Federal left, had ordered up Baird to Brannan's support. It was 10:30 A.M. Croxton, whose ammunition was exhausted after a tense hour, was pulled out of the line, and Starkweather's brigade of Baird's division took his place.

Baird at about 11 A.M. began an assault on Ector's and Wilson's brigades and Walker retired them. But Baird could not pursue. He became conscious of an enemy force on his right and directed Brigadier General John H. King, who commanded a brigade of United States Regular Army troops, to change front to the southeast and face this threat in the direction of Alexander's bridge.

King was engaged in this movement when his brigade was hit a sudden and devastating blow by Liddell's division crashing through the woods. Walker was disclosing the soundness of Joseph E. Johnston's judgment and was executing a happy maneuver with Liddell's two brigades, commanded by Govan and Walthall. The first was composed of Arkansas and Louisiana troops and the second of Mississippians. While Govan was directing his men toward King's exposed right flank, Walthall assailed Baird's first brigade, commanded by Scribner.

King's brigade of regulars folded like a jacknife. Battery H of
the 5th U.S. Field Artillery, with its six guns, was captured,
along with the 1st Battalion of the 16th U. S. Infantry, except for
five officers and sixty-two men. Liddell's take of prisoners aggregated nearly five hundred, while King's casualties in killed and
wounded were grievously heavy. What part of King's brigade that
was not captured left the field in confused flight. It overran the left
of Connell's brigade but did not communicate its panic. Connell's
left regiment, the 82nd Indiana, held. Govan's brigade at the same
time broke Scribner's line, took some of his guns and sent his soldiers flying back in disorder.

August Bratnober of the 10th Wisconsin, Scribner's brigade, explained the capture of Scribner's guns by saying the battery was
firing too high. The Wisconsin regiment supporting it was lying in
front of the guns on a slope, with their heels higher than their
heads. Their single volley was close and alleged to be damaging but
the "Rebels were not even slowed." The infantrymen, heads down,
were in no shape to reload and had to retreat. Bratnober's company
had no captain and here lost both of its lieutenants.

Liddell's assault now fell on Connell and on Baird's remaining
brigade, Starkweather's. Starkweather lost five of his guns but
Connell was well prepared for the blow. When Colonel Morton C.
Hunter of the 82nd Indiana saw King's soldiers coming back in dis-
order he told his men to lie down and not to fire until the regulars
had passed over them. Church's 4th Michigan battery, attached to
Connell's brigade, double-shotted each of its six guns and waited.
When Govan in hot pursuit of King reached within fifty yards of
Connell's concealed line the 82nd Indiana fired a volley at the same
time Church unloosed his canister. Church was assisted by Smith's
4th U. S. Battery of the regular army and by the 2nd Minnesota
Infantry of Van Derveer's brigade, which likewise lay down until
King's stampeded brigade had passed, then put in a volley.

The onrushing enemy was checked. When both the Federal infantry and the battery continued rapid-firing, Liddell retired to a
place of security in the woods. Although King's men began to
rally in Connell's rear, neither Brannan nor King was yet in condition to assume the offensive. At this moment the situation looked

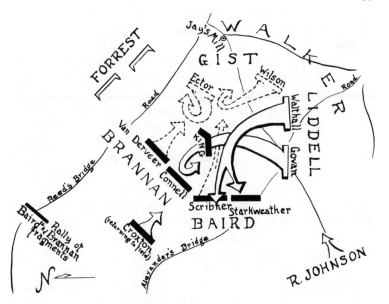

Liddell's repulse of Baird. Brannan is pressing Wilson and Ector when Liddell's division strikes Baird's flank and drives back the Federal line. Baird is saved by the approach of Richard Johnson's division.

unusually bright for Bragg's right, where Walker's two divisions had counterattacked with the greatest vigor and achieved an outstanding success. What they required now was a little help from Bragg's numerous forces.[4]

But Walker and his subordinates would have no opportunity to felicitate one another over the auspicious beginning of the battle. Baird had scarcely been pressed back when succor for his roughly handled regulars appeared. Had the Confederate generals been able to look ahead through the woods and shallow clearings, they could have seen a long blue line overlapping their flanks in both directions and pressing down on them at a moment when they had lost formations and scarcely had opportunity to herd back their prisoners and carry to safety the guns they had captured from Baird.

The newcomers were Richard Johnson's division of McCook's

corps, which Thomas had thrown in on Baird's right, plus Brannan's and Baird's re-formed divisions, now ready to resume the combat.

Walker was driven back relentlessly to some high ground and was unable to retain the fruits of his victory over Baird. Given confidence by its new supports, Connell's brigade of Brannan's division dashed forward. The 31st Ohio recovered the five guns Walthall had captured from Starkweather and which the Confederate had been unable to drag off in his retirement. "Now a Battery is taken, and again retaken," noted Private Kellenberger. "Around these Dead Horses and men are piled in Sickening confusion."

A fresh regiment of Van Derveer's brigade, the 9th Ohio, appeared from the rear, where it had been performing the boring duty of minding Brannan's ammunition train. The regiment had been organized by Cincinnati Germans immediately after Fort Sumter, at a patriotic rally in Turner Hall, and there and within the next few days 1,500 Germans had stepped forward to fight for their adopted country. There were too many for a regiment and numbers had to be sent back home. The 9th had given splendid service under McClellan in West Virginia; then, like several other Ohio regiments, it had been transferred to the western army. Under Thomas at Mill Springs it and the 2nd Minnesota had made a gallant charge that had much to do with giving Thomas a victory.

Always thereafter in the Army of the Cumberland a strong affiliation prevailed between the Minnesotans and the Cincinnati Germans. "Perfect harmony of feeling existed between them, and each was always watchful of the honor of the other." Beautiful handmade flags had been presented to the regiments by the ladies of Louisville, Kentucky, a distinction that went also only to the 10th Indiana and 4th Kentucky, in Croxton's brigade. The 9th Ohio possessed (and what German regiment would not?) a splendid brass band. More than that, it had in Colonel Gustave Kammerling a leader who would go in at the head of his men and with oaths and bluster get the work accomplished in the shortest possible time.

While the 2nd Minnesota was firing at Liddell's retiring line there was a commotion behind it, and bursting through the woods came the Cincinnati Germans, released from their guard duty and seeking their place at the front alongside their Minnesota companions. Kammerling was at their head, riding his horse and turbulently demanding, "Where dem got dam rebels gone?" One of the Minnesotans in Company F, made up of St. Croix raftsmen and lumbermen, showed the direction in which the Confederates had retired, and the 9th Ohio plunged boisterously ahead through the lines of the 2nd Minnesota. Colonel Van Derveer, the brigade commander, was nearby and shouted orders for Kammerling to stop, but such orders went unheeded.

"We could hear them yelling and cheering in both languages long after they had disappeared from sight," said a Minnesota soldier.

They pressed forward a quarter of a mile, from where the fray of a minor battle could be heard. Finally, in response to Van Derveer's peremptory orders, they returned. But what was it they were bringing with them? They were dragging along every gun of the 5th U. S. Artillery; six glistening pieces which they had recaptured from Govan's men.[5]

Walker's retirement of a mile and a half had been as much in response to the sudden attack by Richard Johnson's fresh division as to Brannan's renewed efforts. But now the battle was reaching a new phase. Fresh divisions were crowding up for both armies. Cheatham's division of Polk's corps, the largest division of Bragg's army, consisting of five veteran brigades, was finally at hand to relieve Walker. It was noon. Had Cheatham arrived an hour earlier the entire Federal left wing might very likely have been destroyed. He had crossed at Dalton's ford and had marched quickly as soon as Bragg gave him orders at 11 A.M. His brigades passed through Walker's men and struck Richard Johnson, Baird and Brannan a staggering blow.

CHAPTER THIRTEEN

"Rosey" Follows the Battle by Ear

AT HIS Crawfish Springs headquarters at 9 A.M. Rosecrans heard the heavy firing down Chickamauga Creek as Brannan and Baird became locked in combat with Walker's corps.

Not knowing the proportions of the conflict, he awaited developments until noon, with Assistant Secretary of War Dana remaining close by his side. Finally, when it became clear that a full-scale battle was in progress, the headquarters party moved up the road leading from Crawfish Springs to McFarland's Gap—known as the Dry Valley road—to the Widow Glenn's house.

Dana found that in a reportorial sense this brought him no nearer the battle raging in the deep forest, which, as he said, was "invisible to outsiders." Reports from the generals and sounds of the firing afforded the only means of following its progress.

Dana was happy with conditions at the Widow Glenn's because his wire connection with Washington was soon restored. Rosecrans' signal-corps men had stretched a wire from Chattanooga to Crawfish Springs on September 17. Since the line ran close to the Widow Glenn's, a circuit into the new headquarters was made quickly, and within a hour after his arrival Dana had the telegraph clicking off his optimistic messages to Secretary Stanton in Washington. That day he sent to Stanton eleven dispatches telling what he could see of the battle—which was not much—and forecasting victory unhesitatingly.

Rosecrans was in good spirits. Almost miraculously his army had been reunited and delivered from the great peril into which his enthusiasm and faulty information had plunged it. His men were confident and Thomas was fighting resolutely on his left. His eyes sparkled with such brilliance that one of the reporters described them as black rather than dark blue. He wore a pair of black breeches, a white vest and a plain blue coat. His cheeks were flushed, and he was pictured at this supreme moment as "very handsome."

The Widow Glenn's was from two to three miles southwest from where Thomas' divisions joined the battle with Forrest and Walker. Mrs. Eliza Glenn seems to have been a fairly young widow. She had a child, her second, less than two years old, whom the father, John Glenn, had never seen. He had gone off to war in the Confederate service and never returned. When he left home in 1861 Mrs. Glenn's father, who lived about six miles south, had sent her a slave, John, to work the farm and protect the family. Rosecrans selected the small log house for his headquarters because it occupied a commanding position on an eminence on the Crawfish Springs or Dry Valley road, two fifths of a mile west of the La Fayette road, and overlooking the long sweep of the Glenn and Viniard farms, partly cleared of timber, between the two roads.[1]

After he picked the site, Rosecrans went inside and told the Widow Glenn she would be in great danger during the battle—a truthful prediction because the house was hit by an exploding shell and burned—and that she should seek a place of safety. Later in the day as the battle came nearer, the slave loaded her and her two children into the wagon and drove them off to the home of Hiram Vittetoe, situated behind a spur of Lookout Mountain now known as Horseshoe Ridge. As the battle roared still nearer on the next day, the slave, John, drove her to her father's farm near Pond Spring.

Before her departure Rosecrans got what information he could from her about the surrounding country. He brought out his maps and like Bragg took up a nervous pacing back and forth across the room. While he walked, his engineer with compass and pencil tried to locate the battle on the map, guided only by the Widow Glenn's impressions and the booming of the artillery. "Never was anything so ridiculous as this scene," wrote the New York *Herald* correspondent Shanks, who stood by. He quoted the widow as guessing, when a gun was heard, that it was "nigh out about Reid's [*sic*] bridge somewhar," or "about a mile fornenst John Kelly's house."

Shanks, contemptuous of the high command of the Army of the Cumberland, said that Rosecrans, "fairly quivering with excitement," rubbing his hands as the firing grew more rapid, but not understanding the situation any more than the countrywoman, exclaimed, "Ah! there goes Brannan!" or "That's Negley going in!"

The annoyed Shanks need not have been so mocking, for the sounds were about all Rosecrans had to go on, and he certainly had pitched his army headquarters near enough to the front. Unhappily the battlefield was not in the classic ideal of Gettysburg or Waterloo, with accommodating elevations and clearings so that the commanders might view the fields on which their divisions moved. Subtropical Chickamauga was closer akin to the jungles of World War II warfare in the Pacific than the clean farmlands of Antietam and much of Gettysburg.

Rosecrans' maps were pitifully inadequate. His sketch of the roads and farms of the area has very properly been termed laughable compared with the detailed topographical maps made of this field after the battle had been fought, and the later maps were required only for the rehashes.

During the early part of that afternoon, Rosecrans must have been still confused about Bragg's reinforcements. Otherwise his attitude is inexplicable. When Hood's division had advanced a skirmish line into the woods west of the La Fayette road, Colonel Atkins of the 92nd Illinois, Wilder's brigade, took a prisoner, who proved to be the first captured from Longstreet's corps of the Virginia army. Aware of the intelligence involved in the capture, Atkins escorted him to headquarters at the Widow Glenn's and told Rosecrans he had a prisoner from Longstreet's corps. Rosecrans at once exploded—"flew into a passion," as Atkins put it—and denounced the "little boy" as a liar. Vehemently he declared that Longstreet's corps was not on the field. The prisoner was a country boy of sixteen or seventeen and the result of Rosecrans' high excitement was to frighten him to utter speechlessness. He simply could not say a word.

Atkins must have had a foreboding that the commanding general was a little off beam. The news was too stunning for him to accept it willingly. "In sorrow I turned away and joined my regiment," Atkins said. Later he observed: "Rosecrans found out that Longstreet's corps was there."

Rosecrans got no better information by interviewing a Confederate officer a little later. He invited the prisoner, a Captain Rice of the 1st Texas, Robertson's brigade, to step aside with him. They sat on a fallen tree trunk thirty yards away from the general's staff. Rosecrans whittled. It could not have been a familiar diversion for one of his nervous make-up. He conversed pleasantly and asked the captain where the Confederate lines were.

"General," replied the Texan, "it has cost me a great deal of trouble to find your lines; if you take the same amount of trouble you will find ours."

He could not remember what division or corps he belonged to but acknowledged that he was in Bragg's army. Rosecrans by this time recognized, apparently, the hard fact that Longstreet had arrived and inquired how many men he had with him.

"About forty-five thousand," the captain said without blinking an eyelash.

"Is Longstreet in command?"

"Oh, no, sir! General Bragg is in command."

"Captain," said Rosecrans finally, "you don't seem to know much, for a man whose appearance seems to indicate so much intelligence."

"Well, General," the captain responded, "if you are not satisfied with my information, I will volunteer some. We are going to whip you most tremendously in this fight."[2]

Rosecrans gave up the quest and sent the prisoner to the rear.

Richard Johnson marched his division up the La Fayette road from Lee and Gordon's mill and reached Thomas, who was in the saddle in the Poe field, half a mile south of Kelly's and west of the La Fayette road.

Thomas pushed him into line immediately. Beating his way through the woods to the D. C. Reed house east of the crossing of the Brotherton and Alexander's bridge roads, he fell on Liddell's flank, disorganized his line and pushed him back.

But Richard Johnson was met almost immediately by Cheatham's division coming up from Dalton's ford, deployed with Jackson's brigade on the right, Preston Smith's in the center and Wright's on the left, with Maney and Strahl in reserve. These two divisions, Richard Johnson's well-seasoned Federals and Cheatham's veteran Confederate division that had fought gallantly at Shiloh and Stone's River and in a score of lesser engagements, swayed back and forth all through the early afternoon, locked in a desperate encounter, until both were near exhaustion.

Cheatham had every personal justification to fight for the recovery of Tennessee, for he was a direct descendent of James Robertson, the pioneer settler of the state. A native of Nashville, he had advanced to high command through the Tennessee militia without any formal military education; his service as colonel of Tennessee troops in the Mexican War marked him for distinction and by the time the war came between the states he had reached the rank of major general of Tennessee troops. He was commissioned brigadier general in the Confederate army but was a major general before Shiloh. (His service as corps commander later in the war was marred by long controversy with General John B. Hood, extending into the peace years, for his alleged though by no means proved neglect to cut off the Federal General Schofield at Spring Hill in the Franklin, Tennessee, campaign. He served after the war as Postmaster of Nashville.)

Johnson went into action against Cheatham with the brigades of Brigadier General August Willich on the right and Colonel Philemon P. Baldwin on the left and with the brigade of Colonel Joseph P. Dodge in reserve. All his brigade commanders had come up from being regimental commanders of Indiana troops. Willich, who had been colonel of the 32nd Indiana, an all-German regiment, had been an officer in the German army but had emigrated

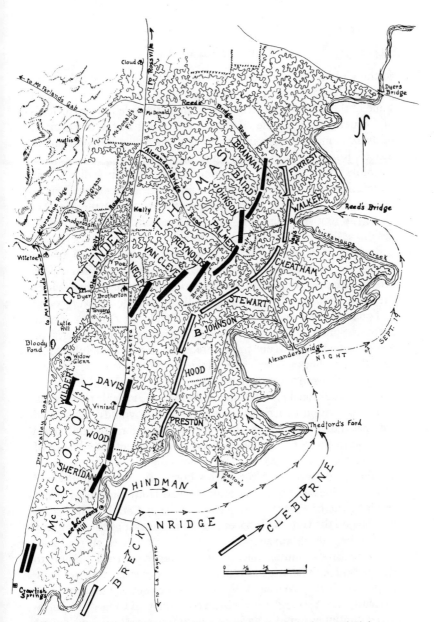

Positions of the two armies on reaching the field. Breckinridge and Cleburne are marching down the Chickamauga to Bragg's right and Hindman is crossing to his left, thus bringing Bragg's entire army to the field before daybreak Sept. 20.

to the United States after the German revolution of 1848. At the time of Chickamauga he still spoke a broken English which caused some of the other regiments of the brigade to smile tolerantly at his oral orders. As a brigade commander he had had the bad luck to be away from his troops just at the moment when Bragg struck at Stone's River, and had been captured.

Colonel Baldwin had taken command of the 6th Indiana after Shiloh. This was the first regiment raised by the state, since, out of respect for the five Hoosier regiments that served in the Mexican War, the first five numerals were set aside and not employed to designate Indiana Civil War regiments.

Brigadier General Richard W. Johnson, a Kentuckian of the West Point class of 1849, was an able soldier plagued by adversity. His division had been on the extreme right at Stone's River, where the main impact of Bragg's attack fell. Johnson lost men, ground and guns. He had been ill at the time of Shiloh but a greater reverse between Shiloh and Stone's River came when with 800 troopers he was detached to intercept the Confederate cavalryman John Morgan, then raiding in Tennessee. Morgan, instead of being bagged, captured him and about half his men.[3]

Heavy additional reinforcements were soon available to Thomas. Palmer's division of Crittenden's corps and Reynolds' division of Thomas' corps entered the line in turn on the right of Richard Johnson to check the attack of Cheatham and meet the advance of Buckner's corps.

Palmer's division of Crittenden's corps had followed Richard Johnson's division up the La Fayette road from Crawfish Springs reaching the battle area from 11 A.M. to 1:30 P.M. Thomas sent it into line on the right of Johnson, in the forest east of the Poe farm. Cruft's brigade in advance struck the Confederates at 1:30 P.M. near the Brock house, south of the Brotherton road leading to Reed's bridge. The brigade sustained three desperate charges from Brigadier General Marcus J. Wright's Tennesseans, but, according to Cruft, "not a straggler was observed going to the rear." The musketry continued rapidly on both sides until 2:30 P.M., and during the lull of an hour that followed, ammunition was sent forward and the cartridge boxes were replenished for the more serious business just ahead. Hazen's brigade of Palmer's division was sent against Preston Smith, Cheatham's center brigade, at 2 P.M. and fought with it desperately for a clump of woods three quarters of a mile east of the La Fayette road and southeast of Brock field. Hazen held possession as the combat subsided. Colonel William Grose's brigade of Palmer's division also met Wright's Tennesseans and a little later the advance of Stewart's Confederate division.

One of Hazen's soldiers battling against Preston Smith and in turn Strahl's brigade of Cheatham's division was Ambrose Bierce, twenty-one years old, a junior officer in the 9th Indiana, who became so attracted to Hazen that after the war he accompanied that officer on a tour of army posts in the Northwest. Thus he gained knowledge of the western pioneer country that became the subject of some of his classic stories and was led to San Francisco, where he wrote many of them. Bierce, born in a log cabin on Horse Cave Creek, Meigs County, Ohio, was the son of a poor farmer who blessed American letters by putting more money into books than plows and thereby kindled the spark that sent his son, who had no formal education, into a distinguished newspaper and literary career. Ambrose was wounded three times. He enlisted as a private and ended the war a major.

Brigadier General William B. Hazen, whose brigade was one of the active fighting units on both days at Chickamauga, was a Vermonter whose family had moved to Portage County near Hiram, Ohio, the home of his boyhood friend James A. Garfield. He was graduated from West Point in 1856, and was wounded severely fighting the Comanche Indians in 1859. The bullet remained embedded in his back. When the war broke he was teaching infantry tactics at West Point. He became colonel of the 41st Ohio and was made a brigade commander before Shiloh. After the war, besides serving in the Northwest, he became chief of the Army Signal Corps.

The division commander, Major General John M. Palmer, was one of the seniors in the army at forty-six, who would serve in later years as Governor of Illinois and United States Senator. He and Confederate General Simon B. Buckner would team up in 1896 to run for president and vice-president as candidates of the "Gold

Democrats" who repudiated the free-silver doctrine of William Jennings Bryan. He had already sampled politics before joining the army as colonel of the 14th Illinois. He had two good military qualities: self-confidence and willingness to fight. When he was serving before Corinth under General John Pope, who commanded Halleck's left wing, Pope sent an orderly to ask if his brigade could hold against the advance of the Confederate generals, Price and Van Dorn.

Palmer's reply was: "Tell General Pope that I can hold my position against the world, the flesh and the devil."

But the attack was spirited and the brigade was forced to give ground. Later when Palmer reported at headquarters there was hearty laughter.

"How is it, Palmer?" Pope inquired.

"Well, General," said Palmer with a twinkle, "I can stand the world, but the devil was too much for me."

Palmer, Kentucky born, had moved to Illinois when fourteen because of an aversion to slavery. He had peddled clocks and worked as handy man to get two years' schooling in Shurtleff College in Upper Alton, had read law, been an ardent Democrat, become a Republican and served as a delegate to the convention that nominated Lincoln. Defeated for Congress in 1859, he fared better in the military service, but in 1864 he requested to be relieved after an argument with Sherman over his refusal to take orders from Schofield, whom he claimed to rank.[4]

Palmer's outstanding army service came at Stone's River, for which he was promoted to major general, and at Chickamauga, where he fought with great resolution on both days of the battle.

Dodge's brigade, which Richard Johnson had held in reserve, went in at 1 P.M. to the relief of Hazen's brigade of Palmer's division, which had been fighting so enthusiastically with Preston Smith's brigade of Cheatham's division that its ammunition was exhausted. Dodge took up the fight with Preston Smith, who was now supported by Strahl from Cheatham's second line.

The 77th Pennsylvania of Dodge's brigade claimed an even more distinguished part at Stone's River than its companion regiment of

Negley's division, the 78th Pennsylvania. "Old Rosey" had tended to confirm its views when before the Chattanooga campaign he had paused in front of the regiment and said to its commander, Colonel Thomas E. Rose:

"Colonel, I see that your regiment is all right. Give my compliments to the boys and tell them that I say it was the banner regiment at Stone River; it never broke its ranks."

Now it was in the midst of an even tougher battle, in even denser woods. Said its Captain George W. Skinner: "The artillery fire for the space of perhaps half an hour was simply terrible. Trees were mown down like grain, and the smoke of battle fell so thick amid the foliage that it was difficult to pierce the gloom with the naked eye for any great distance."

In the 30th Indiana of Dodge's brigade was a red-haired, twenty-year-old captain of Company A, Henry W. Lawton, who would rise to high command in the United States Army, serve as Inspector General, lead a division at Santiago in the Spanish-American War, and command the campaign against Aguinaldo in the Philippine Islands. While at the head of his troops in that campaign he was shot through the heart. His parents had died before he was nine years old and he had lived with an uncle in Fort Wayne, enlisted as a private in 1861 and before the end of the war was commanding a regiment. His courage in action was noteworthy in this war, as in later combats. He was to be an inspiration to a number of officers who knew him in their early army days and later held important posts of command in the First World War.[5]

CHAPTER FOURTEEN

The "Little Giants" Dent Rosecrans' Center

WHEN Thomas marched his corps north from McLemore's Cove during the night of the eighteenth, Reynolds' division of two brigades—Wilder's, the third, being mounted and detached—was in the rear and the head of it did not reach Poe's field until 1:30 P.M. on the nineteenth.

Thomas was awaiting it eagerly. Brigadier General John B. Turchin's brigade was sent to support Palmer, suffering under Cheatham's attack. The brigade commanded by Colonel Edward A. King (not to be confused with John King's brigade of regulars in Baird's division) was dispatched to assist VanCleve, now plugging the Federal center. When Reynolds passed Brotherton's corner en route to Thomas he regained contact with this third brigade, Wilder's, which after roaming the battlefield was ranging from Brotherton's south to the Viniard house.

Brigadier General John B. Turchin was a curiosity in the Northern army, though his brigade of Ohio and Kentucky troops was by common acknowledgment one of the finest. A Russian, born in Don Province, he bore about him the powder smell of Sevastopol and Balaklava. He had attended cadet school in St. Petersburg, had served as a captain and later a colonel on the general staff of the Russian Imperial Guard, and had fought in the Hungarian War of 1848-1849 and the Crimean War before migrating to Illinois, looking for peace but finding a much more deadly conflict. His first

regiment, the 19th Illinois, was reputed the best drilled of the
Army of the Cumberland.

Palmer's hard-pressed brigades were those of Hazen and Cruft
and it was to their assistance that Reynolds directed Turchin. One
of Turchin's regiments was the 36th Ohio, led by the high-spirited
Colonel William G. Jones, of Cincinnati, grandson of Colonel
John Johnston, the noted Ohio Indian agent of pioneer days,
friend of Tecumseh, and one who enjoyed the confidence of the
red men and tried to reconcile the races. Jones was graduated from
West Point in 1860, and had served as Major General Edwin V.
("Old Bull") Summer's aide at Antietam and Fredericksburg. But
he had always wanted to command a regiment from his home state
and the chance came after General Sumner died in early 1863.

On reaching his position at Chickamauga he saw a flurry of
scattering bluecoats. He drew his sword, which one of his men
said "rang like an anvil" against his scabbard, and shouted, "We'll
let them know this is a regiment that can't run." The regiment, recruited in the Marietta, Ohio, region, had tended to merit his assertion by its steady service in the Army of the Potomac in Virginia and at Antietam, where its first colonel had been killed. Then
it had been transferred to Rosecrans' army, with which it was now
beginning its most costly battle.

Despite words as ringing as his scabbard, Colonel Jones had a
clear picture of the desperate nature of the fray he was entering.
He noted in his pocket diary at noon that day: "Off to the left;
merciful Father, have mercy on me and my regiment, and protect
us from injury and death." That afternoon would be the colonel's
last.

While the brigade was awaiting the step-off order, Chaplain
William W. Lyle of the 11th Ohio obtained permission of Colonel
Philander P. Lane to address the regiment. After his words of en-
couragement the men joined him in prayer, their hats off, their
hands clasped around muskets gleaming from care by seasoned soldiers. The 11th also had been in the eastern theater. The colors
that had waved proudly on the Kanawha and at Antietam, were
drooped in the only instance allowable, at the time of supplication.
General Reynolds, who was riding by, saw the ceremony, halted

and joined the men in this reverence; then, when the prayer was finished, he grasped the hand of the chaplain and thanked him. The brigade went at once into the action, its hardest.

Passing over a cornfield and through a strip of woods, Turchin discovered the Confederate line at close range, drove it back, and when threatened again, made a countercharge, the 11th and 36th Ohio regiments in the lead. Colonel Jones fell early and died soon after. For him, the regiment never retreated.

Rob Adney of the 36th Ohio, who had been firing from behind a sourwood tree, thought the assault was spontaneous. "Without orders, as far as I know, the Regiment rose as one man and hurled itself on the rebels in the bush and the bank of white sulpher smoke in a fierce bayonet charge."

Some of Cruft's brigade joined, among them the 90th Ohio. When they had advanced 400 yards, Turchin called out in his Russian accent, "Poys, we go far enough. We know not what is on our right or what is on our left!" That was, indeed, the situation, with the heavy forest all about them, in which waited unseen foes.[1]

Tuchin had just been given temporary relief from Cheatham when formidable new lines of gray-clad soldiers appeared to his right in the woods. Bragg was getting Stewart's division into action.

It was midafternoon and the battle which hitherto had been fought almost completely in the thickets was about to move to the somewhat more open country around the Brotherton, Dyer and Viniard farms, where Bragg began to menace Rosecrans' hold on the La Fayette road, roughly the defensive line of his army.

All through the morning hours, while Forrest, Walker and then Cheatham were battling Thomas, Bragg had been pressing the main elements of his army down the Chickamauga in a persistent, almost blind devotion to his original plan of turning Rosecrans' left and cutting him off from Chattanooga.

Possibly his experience with his subordinates had convinced him that any change of purpose after the beginning of the battle would be misinterpreted or ignored and that the best results would be obtained by following original orders without deviation. But the attack delivered by Thomas on Walker was notice to Bragg that

his purpose was quite well understood and the continued reinforcement of Thomas by heavy Federal columns moving downstream indicated that Rosecrans was massing the greater part of
his army on his left to thwart such a purpose.

Well before noon on the nineteenth Bragg could have seen that
his turning movement against Rosecrans' left had not been wide
enough to put his forces on the Federal flank—that instead of being
able to attack upstream toward Lee and Gordon's mill, from north
to south, he had himself been overlapped and assailed from the
west and was being forced to fight facing in that direction.

Probably at this stage a more resourceful commander, or one in
better control of his subordinates, would have reflected on the developments of the day and taken advantage of what the new situation offered. All through the morning the Confederate army had
been crossing the Chickamauga at the bridges and fords, but
whether on the west or east bank, Bragg was pressing them downstream before putting them into action. Thus Cheatham was
marched three miles across the front of the Federals in order that
Bragg might send him against Rosecrans' left in support of Walker.
D. H. Hill, who at the beginning of the battle was on Bragg's
extreme left, above Lee and Gordon's mill, was required to march
six miles downstream so that one of his divisions might go into action on the extreme right of the Southern army, in further obstinate obedience to the original plan of turning the Federal left.

All the while, as a general of greater mental flexibility might
have sensed, Rosecrans had a gap of varying widths ranging up to
about two miles in the center of his army, between Wood's division at Lee and Gordon's mill and Thomas' concentration at the
Kelly farm. Across this gap columns moving in procession to
Thomas' support might have been taken in flank. Wood at Lee and
Gordon's and those portions of McCook's corps which had not
yet come up from Crawfish Springs could have been severed from
Thomas during the morning of the nineteenth by any sort of de-
termined thrust by Bragg midway between Kelly's and Lee and
Gordon's.

Bragg's opportunities in this area were now about to be exploited belatedly, more fortuitously than by design. He directed

Buckner to send Stewart's division downstream in the wake of Cheatham. When Buckner passed the orders to Stewart, the division commander complied sufficiently to obey them in principle, but believing that the pressure of the enemy could be relieved more by fighting than by marching, and finding favorable ground over which he might move his troops, he turned and delivered an impetuous assault on VanCleve's division which had come into line in time to participate in the repulse of Cheatham.

The result was little short of sensational. It was 2:30 P.M. Stewart's "Little Giant Division," composed of the brigades of Brown, Bate and Clayton, plunged ahead through the woods, driving before it the brigades of Sam Beatty and George F. Dick of VanCleve's division, which contested every step of their retreat with a vigor that made this action one of the most stubbornly fought of the day.

The Confederate Major General Alexander P. Stewart was a man of high attainment, both as educator and soldier. He placed great reliance on personal relationships and frank appeals to his men. John B. Hood, who commended his strict adherence to instructions and the able performance of his troops on a later occasion, noted that before the battle he had gone through his division and talked to the soldiers, telling them it was imperative that they carry everything before them at all hazards, and emphasizing that they should not stop at temporary breastworks. They should charge over every obstacle, get contact with the enemy and rout him from his position. Entrenchments had proved so effective in general use that he felt he should steel the men to supreme courage when they encountered them.

Although opposed to secession at the beginning, he was tenacious and persistent in defense of the Confederacy, and ardent to the very end. In Joseph E. Johnston's last gasping effort against Sherman at Bentonville, North Carolina, it was Stewart, then a lieutenant general, who commanded the remnant of the once glorious Army of Tennessee. Joining it to troops brought up from Savannah by one of his old commanders, Hardee, he served as ably in Hardee's hastily assembled corps in this "Battle of the Generals" as he had at Shiloh, the first great struggle in the West, where his brigade made repeated assaults against the impregnable "Hornet's Nest." There he had his first division command, stepping up in Polk's corps after the wounding of Brigadier General Charles Clark.

Stewart was called by his men "Old Straight," but it seems to have been as much a classroom affection for a mathematician as it was related to his ramrod posture. Born in Rogersville, Tennessee, he was appointed to West Point from that state and stood twelfth in the class of 1842. What time Longstreet was not rooming with Rosecrans at the academy he roomed with his classmate Stewart. The close friendship was disrupted upon graduation when Longstreet went into the infantry and Stewart into the 3rd Artillery, Bragg's regiment. Then Stewart was called back to West Point to teach mathematics, but after he had spent three years in the service he resigned to become professor of mathematics at Cumberland University, in Lebanon, Tennessee. Then he moved on to be a professor at Nashville University, where Brigadier General Bushrod Johnson had been a fellow faculty member. He was at heart an educator, who after the war had opportunity for notable work as Chancellor of the University of Mississippi.

When the states left the Union against the sentiments of such old-time Whigs as Stewart, he stepped back across the sixteen years to the artillery range, tested the guns, erected heavy batteries on the Mississippi at Columbus and Belmont, instructed at the camps and then became a general officer under Leonidas Polk. When Polk was killed after Chickamauga—at Pine Mountain in the Atlanta campaign—Stewart took command of Polk's corps, and in the final phases commanded the Army of Tennessee.

Stewart had crossed the Chickamauga at Thedford's ford during the night of the eighteenth but had been held in Bragg's second line all during the morning of the nineteenth, while Walker and then Cheatham were fighting on his right. It was not until 1:30 P.M. that he was ordered to Cheatham's support. He progressed downstream only a short distance, then turned to the left, a move which took him into line against the Federal center, much softer than Thomas' strongly held left. But the gap in the Federal center that had been so inviting all morning was now being filled by

Rosecrans, who at the Widow Glenn's was taking a firmer grip on the battle, in which control over the fighting line had up to this time been left largely to Thomas.

Stewart formed his division in the heavy woods east of the La Fayette road and went forward in column of brigades, Clayton in front, Brown following and Bate with his "crack brigade" in the rear. VanCleve, approaching with his Federal division, appeared on Stewart's left, which caused Clayton, part of whose troops were not well seasoned, to adjust his line and face this adversary. One of his regiments, the 38th Alabama, had been long in the service but had been kept on garrison duty in Mobile. Some of their company names suggested they had fighting intentions: the Alabama Invincibles, the North River Tigers, the Dixie Rifles. Despite their greenness they attacked with a courage unsurpassed in any of the dogged fighting already witnessed on the field. But they were moving into a veritable inferno.

"Did you ever notice the thickness of rain drops in a tempest?" asked Bromfield L. Ridley, a recorder of this sanguinary affair. "Did you ever see the destruction of hail stones to a growing corn field? Did you ever witness driftwood in a squall?"

That was about what Clayton's men encountered in lead and cannon blasts. Such was the first experience in battle for large numbers of these Alabamans. Though the brigade had only three regiments, they were well recruited. Still, the loss was staggering; 618 killed and wounded, or 200 men per regiment.

At Pensacola at the outbreak of the war, Brigadier General Henry D. Clayton, of Clayton, Alabama, had received the distinction of being made colonel of the 1st Alabama regiment, the initial regiment provided by the Alabama legislature. As the enlistments expired, he had organized at Opelika the 39th Alabama, which at Chickamauga was serving in Hindman's division. After a year with him the men judged him "genial and pleasant," but he appeared firm enough and was called brave and possessed of military skill. As one man said, "He himself was not afraid to go where we were told to follow." He was thirty-six when he fought at Chickamauga. A graduate of Emory and Henry College, and a native of Pulaski County, Georgia, he served after the war as a circuit judge and President of the University of Alabama.[2]

For three quarters of an hour Clayton continued a close-range fight with VanCleve's two brigades, commanded by Brigadier General Samuel Beatty and Colonel George F. Dick. VanCleve's third brigade, commanded by Colonel Sidney M. Barnes, had been left temporarily at Lee and Gordon's mill, and would reach the field later.

Brigadier General Horatio P. VanCleve, a native of Princeton, New Jersey, but a resident of Minnesota when war came, was at fifty-four the eldest of the division commanders of the Army of the Cumberland. His appearance has been described as "patriarchal" because of his long, graying beard, his spectacles, the baldness on the top of his head and the long heavy hair hanging over his ears. Nevertheless he was by no means burned out and was credited by some with having the same energy and zest as the younger officers.

He attended West Point and was graduated in 1831, two years after Lee and Joseph E. Johnston; he served a few years with the 5th Infantry and resigned in 1836. Twenty-five years passed before he again put on the uniform, when at the outbreak of the war he was appointed colonel of the 2nd Minnesota regiment. He commanded it at Mill Springs, where it performed notably. Thereafter he had a brigade in Crittenden's division and took command of the division when Crittenden stepped up to command the corps. Severely wounded at Stone's River, he returned in time for the Tullahoma campaign and resumed command of his division. A plain, unostentatious man, careful but never inspirational, indisposed to promote himself, he had reached his peak as commander of a division.

Sam Beatty's brigade of VanCleve's division had marched at 1 P.M. and on nearing the firing had been ordered to double-quick to the aid of Palmer, then heavily engaged with Cheatham. Corps Commander Crittenden accompanied the brigade and helped form it in two lines on Palmer's right, the 19th Ohio and 79th Indiana in the front line, the 9th and 17th Kentucky in reserve.

Crowding down on Palmer's right flank, which fortunately for him had been given temporary relief by the splendid advance of Turchin's brigade, came Stewart's fresh division. Beatty's men rushed forward 200 yards to meet the gray line in an open field and quickly the battle was joined, the rifles all but touching muzzle to muzzle. "There were no breastworks," said a participant, "no protection of any kind, to shield or screen . . . It was a fight to the death."

Colonel Frederick Knefler of the 79th Indiana saw a Confederate battery come up and unlimber on his left and ordered the regiment to concentrate its fire on the horses and artillerymen. Forty-eight horses were shot down. Then he ordered a charge. His men rushed in amid the struggling, dying horses and captured the four guns, all double-shotted with canister. They were pulled out by the 9th and 17th Kentucky and placed near the La Fayette road. It proved to be the battery of Lieutenant William W. Carnes of Cheatham's division.

Sam Beatty, a Pennsylvanian who had served as 1st Lieutenant with Ohio troops in the Mexican War, and had re-entered the service to be a captain in the 19th Ohio in April 1861, possessed one of the most enviable battle records among the officers of the Army of the Cumberland. Rosecrans had praised him for his conduct at Rich Mountain, as had Brigadier General Jeremiah T. Boyle at Shiloh. At Stone's River, Beatty, by that time a brigadier general, was on the extreme left, the critical post in the turning column that was to envelop Bragg's right. He was the first to get his troops across the river. Then came the shock of Bragg's unexpected counter turning movement. When the brigade was recalled to meet the assault by which Bragg overwhelmed the Federal right, Rosecrans had personally led Sam Beatty's charge to check the Confederate advance.

Now he was engaged in what was undoubtedly his most deadly encounter. VanCleve's other brigade, Dick's, which had been battling Clayton, was alongside Beatty, when the two brigades were attacked savagely by a new wave of Stewart's infantry. It was 3:15 P.M. Stewart had sent Brown's brigade forward to replace Clayton and quickly he was hammering not only at the front of VanCleve at a time when Beatty was becoming exhausted, but threatening also to turn Dick's flank. VanCleve's two brigades were forced back. The Confederates recovered Carnes's guns. In the fury of this fighting the dry woods, parched from the long drought, caught fire, and to the clouds and fumes of powder smoke were added the heavy white billows from the dry leaves and flaming underbrush. Through the smoke Dick's brigade fired a volley and then met Brown's advance with a bold countercharge, which momentarily checked the Confederates.[3]

One of the gray-clad soldiers of Brown's brigade killed in this action was to have a distinction apart from that of all others of either army who fought in the deadly battle. He was to rest permanently on the battlefield from which the bodies of all his fallen comrades and fallen enemies were removed. He was Private John Ingraham of Company G, 26th Tennessee Infantry. When members of the Reed family, who lived near the bridge, were going over the battlefield after the armies had departed, they recognized Ingraham, buried him and marked the spot so that they could find it.

Years later, after the dead of both armies had been returned to their home people or buried in national cemeteries, the Reeds put up a headstone over the grave of the private soldier who stayed behind as the lone watcher over the field. Ingraham's regimental commander, Colonel J. M. Lillard, fell in the same attack.

Fortunately for the Federals at this moment, relief came in the form of three regiments of Colonel Edward A. King's brigade, Reynolds' division, which took position on Dick's right.

General Palmer, on VanCleve's left, who had been listening anxiously to the heavy battle of Stewart's attack on VanCleve which threatened to engulf his own division, rode to his right and was on hand when King's regiments arrived. He encountered Colonel Milton S. Robinson, who had served under him in the Corinth campaign, and who now commanded the 75th Indiana of Edward King's brigade.

This well-filled regiment, which had never been under fire, numbered more than 800. Because of the emergency of the situation, Palmer ordered Robinson, although he belonged to Reynolds' division, to charge into Stewart's advance as it bore down on Van-Cleve. The colonel answered with alacrity, leading his men personally. They stormed ahead with loud shouts that rang through the woods and apparently gave the Confederates the impression that an entire brigade was on them. When the freshly recruited Hoosiers saw the enemy line they rushed at it impetuously. Stewart's men, already disconcerted, were half taken by surprise and fell back rapidly through the woods.

But Palmer was familiar with Stewart's staying power and knew the advantage gained by the courageous attack of a single green regiment would be temporary. He told Robinson the enemy would recover and return, and said he should "keep up appearances as long as he could." Palmer then rode a quarter of a mile back to his own division. When he met Robinson later the colonel told him his regiment had been destroyed. Only fifty remained of the 800! Palmer, the old "pro," advised him there would be more on hand when rations were issued next morning, and such was the case. But no untested regiment could have given a better performance.

Robinson's service at Chickamauga led to a later incident. After the war Palmer went to Anderson, Indiana, campaigning for Horace Greeley, in 1872. He met Robinson, a candidate on the Grant ticket for Congress. Robinson was being assailed for alleged cowardice at Chickamauga. The colonel had brought veterans of the 75th Indiana to the platform to refute the charges, but Palmer supplied the clinching evidence by describing Robinson's gallant attack at the head of his untried troops. Palmer added that he was more impressed with Robinson's military leadership than his politics. Robinson was elected and subsequently served as chief justice of the Indiana appellate court.[4]

But the Confederates were again stirring. Stewart's remaining brigade, Bate's, now came into line on the left of Brown, and despite Edward King's reinforcements VanCleve was overlapped. Suddenly his two brigades broke and he was forced back across the La Fayette road, carrying King with him. VanCleve drew a new line hastily along the Brotherton fields south of the Brotherton house, on the west side of the La Fayette road. The loss of this roadway would be critical if not disastrous to Rosecrans, since it linked his right at Lee and Gordon's with Thomas.

Scarcely was VanCleve in his new position before Bate's gray line, accompanied by Brown and Clayton, burst from the Brotherton woods in an assault which the historian of the 86th Indiana

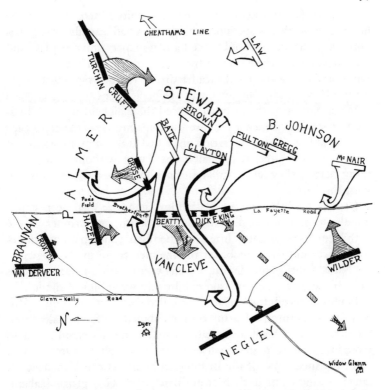

Bragg attacks the Federal center. Stewart's "Little Giant" division breaks VanCleve's line but is forced to retire by the approach of Negley and Thomas' dispatch of Brannan to the point of danger.

could describe only with the word "terrific." Dick's brigade put up a resolute defense. "Without shelter of any kind, in an open field, our men fought with a stubbornness that was never surpassed." Though beaten back once, the Confederates reformed and went forward "with a force that seemed irresistible."

Brigadier General William B. Bate knew something about being and about leading a private soldier. He had served as a private in both the Mexican War and at the beginning of the present struggle. A Gallatin, Tennessee, lawyer, who would twice be elected

Governor of Tennessee and four times United States Senator, he had begun work as a steamboat clerk, then had attended the Lebanon University law school, edited a newspaper, practiced law and gone to the legislature. When the war came he had enlisted in the ranks but he was so natural a leader that he jumped rapidly through the grades of captain and colonel to brigadier general.

When Stewart's division had waded the Chickamauga at Thedford's ford, Bate's men were interested mainly in a chance to capture breakfast. The only ration they had was sorghum stalks cut into six-inch lengths. After half a day's wait without eating anything better, they were still famished and eager to get through with the battle.

Dr. W. J. McMurray of Nashville, Tennessee, had been standing alongside Colonel Thomas Benton Smith, commander of the 20th Tennessee, of Bate's brigade, when Bate rode up on his single-foot sorrel and gave the order for the men to go in.

"Now, Smith, now, Smith, I want you to sail on those fellows like you were a wild cat," he said, briskly scrambling a simile.

Plunging ahead, the brigade had sailed and clawed through Palmer's line, captured the artillery in its immediate front, halted momentarily when VanCleve's blue-coated soldiers seemed about to close in on the rear, and finally had reached the La Fayette road a short distance south of the Brotherton house. When VanCleve arranged his new line in their front, Bate's men, Georgians, Alabamans and Tennesseans, charged abreast Brown and the remnants of Clayton, again pushed him back and cut through his center. They pressed ahead. Clayton's battered brigade reached the tanyard of the Dyer farm on the west side of the Glenn-Kelly road, in the very heart of the Federal position. Bate crossed the La Fayette road farther north. On the advance they captured twelve Federal guns.

Possessed of the Glenn-Kelly road, they could look across the rising land to the ridge overlooking the Dry Valley road, a quarter of a mile distant—Rosecrans' only other link with Chattanooga. Farther to the left was the long sweep to the Widow Glenn's, not three quarters of a mile away. Rosecrans was watching there with some consternation, seeing that the center of his army was all but pierced. King's three regiments, grimy and black with powder stains, were driven back to the Widow Glenn's before the commanding general's eyes.

The assault of Stewart's "Little Giant" division at Chickamauga was similar to the advance of Brigadier General Ambrose R. Wright's brigade of Anderson's division on the second day at Gettysburg, when the Georgians reached the crest of Cemetery Ridge, drove off the Federal infantry, and seized the batteries. It was one of the supreme moments at Gettysburg. But in the end Wright was pressed back by heavy concentrations of reserves, as Stewart's division was now about to be at Chickamauga.

When President Jefferson Davis inspected the battlefield during his visit with Bragg's army a short time later, he passed over the ground Stewart's division had carried in this attack. He came to a dead horse that wore the trappings of a general officer's mount and inquired about whose it was. He was told it was General Bate's sorrel. Then 300 yards farther on he saw a little black mare stretched dead on the ground. When he asked about this he was told it was one of Bate's mounts. Still farther on he saw a "mouse-colored, bobtailed artillery horse," lying on top of some Federal earthworks. This horse, too, he was told had been Bate's. The President manifestly was impressed. Soon after his return to Richmond, Bate received a commission as major general, though at the time of Chickamauga he was the junior brigadier of the army. Half of his brigade had been left between Chickamauga Creek and the Dyer tanyard.

The savior of the Federal center at this juncture was Major General Joseph J. Reynolds, one of the capable officers of Thomas' corps, son of a Lafayette, Indiana, hatter, student at Wabash College in Crawfordsville, Indiana, and tenth in the West Point class of 1843, in which Grant was twenty-first. His friendship with Grant was close and enduring.

Reynolds served with Zachary Taylor in Mexico, then spent nine years on the West Point teaching staff. After a sample of frontier garrison duty he resigned to become professor of mathematics and engineering at Washington University in St. Louis, but just before the war he removed to Lafayette to join one of his brothers in the grocery business. When the war came he was appointed colonel of the 10th Indiana, returned for a time to the grocery business because of his brother's health, then re-entered the army and rose quickly to the command of a division.

Reynolds brought all the available artillery to bear on the gray line and shifted the guns dexterously when the assailants tried to take them in flank. He collected VanCleve's fugitives to provide supports. Fourteen guns belched their canister on the assailants while every Federal musket within range added to the fearful deluge of shot being poured into Stewart's men. Wilder's mounted infantry had been pushed aside by the overwhelming assault but Reynolds, in the critical moment when the Confederates reached the La Fayette road, encountered Colonel Atkins with his 92nd Illinois of Wilder's command. Reynolds told him Edward King's brigade had been broken, then ordered him to dismount his men and try to keep the enemy from pouring through the Federal lines. Atkins had his Illinois regiment dismount and with their authoritative Spencers they drove back that part of the enemy force—"easily," as he described it—advancing in his front. But when the Confederates crowded around his right flank he was compelled to give ground. Atkins thought the condition of the center of the army at that moment was nearly chaotic. He found thousands of Union troops in disorder, "floating off through the woods" toward Chattanooga.[5]

Atkins hunted through the timber with his scouts and patrols and discovered the left flank of the Confederate division that had crashed through the Federal line. Then he hurried with this intelligence to Colonel Wilder, at the Viniard farm. Wilder took his entire brigade back into the action and with his fire power and a series of charges helped Reynolds with his artillery to push Stewart back to the east side of the La Fayette road. In this urgent counterattack the corps commander, Crittenden, was in the front lines doing all he could to rally the center of the army. By this time Federal divisions and brigades had become jumbled. The center was held partly by his own and partly by Thomas' corps.

Crittenden got too far to the east in the timber, and if a company of the 72nd Indiana of Wilder's brigade had not been attentive and beaten back the Confederates from a point of woods near the Viniard farmhouse, the corps commander undoubtedly would have been captured.

No small part in the effective work of Reynolds' artillery in staying the Confederates was performed by Captain Eli Lilly's 18th Indiana battery of Wilder's brigade. A ditch or small ravine created an obstacle to the assailants on the west side of the La Fayette road. Lilly posted two guns in a cornfield to rake this ditch and opened with double and triple charges of canister and grape. Lilly had four other pieces doing terrific havoc as they played on the Confederate advance. Even so tough a fighter as Wilder was sickened by the carnage.

"At this point," he said, "it actually seemed a pity to kill men so. They fell in heaps; and I had it in my heart to order the firing to cease, to end the awful sight."

In such instances the guns were helpful, but they were rare. One of the newspaper correspondents said it was not a battle of generals, nor of artillery, but of musketry. The cannon were gobbled up or lost in the thickets. "Battery after battery went into the woods and never came out."

Fully as important as Reynolds' use of the artillery was the decisive action by Thomas to repulse Stewart. Hearing the swelling volume of the battle on his right, keeping a close watch on all parts of the field, and learning of Stewart's advance across the La Fayette and Glenn-Kelly roads, he decided instantly to strip his left of Brannan's excellent division, which had maintained a fierce élan all through the fighting of the morning, and move it to reinforce the center. The orders, quickly issued, were quickly executed. While Brannan marched from the north, Negley's division of Thomas' corps, which during the morning had been at Crawfish Springs, came into sight across the Dyer and Glenn farms approaching from the south. The converging of these two divisions on Stewart, standing almost isolated well out in advance of the Confederate line, caused the Confederate to reflect, then retire past Brotherton's to the east side of the La Fayette road.[6]

CHAPTER FIFTEEN

Viniard's Farm

IT WAS approaching 4 P.M. and Bragg's poorly organized attack appeared to have been wearing away the Federal army as had his assault on the Federal right at Stone's River, though the greater part of his army at Chickamauga was still unengaged.

As the battle had developed there had been little form or general objective in the movements of either side except to meet the desperate needs immediately at hand. The fighting had been a series of disconnected attacks in the heavy timber and vine-covered thickets, with visibility rendered still more difficult by great clouds of heavy powder smoke. In both armies the combat had been waged mainly by brigades, the largest units that could be seen and directed by the officers under such unfavorable battle conditions.

But it had been, as the St. Louis newspaperman described it, essentially a "soldiers' battle," and in no clash of the eastern or western armies had the determination of the individual soldier to win seemed quite so pronounced. Manifestly the men of both armies, who had been restive during the long lull that preceded this campaign, looked on it as the decisive battle of the West, if not of the war—a battle on which, for the South, the fate of Atlanta and all Georgia depended; while for the Northern soldiers it was the opportunity to cut the Confederacy through the middle and likely end the war before Christmas.

This general pattern of fighting by brigades was now to be continued in two of the most determined Confederate attacks of the first day's battle—that of Major General John B. Hood against the

Federal right and, after that languished, the sanguinary twilight assault by Major General Patrick R. Cleburne against the extreme left of Thomas' position.

The advanced elements of Longstreet's corps had reached Ringgold on the sixteenth without baggage, shelter halves or equipment, and had bivouacked in the open. On the next day they marched west toward Bragg's concentration along the east bank of the Chickamauga. The dryness and ruggedness of the territory struck forcibly the soldiers who were recently in the beautiful rolling farmlands of Virginia, loaded with the heavy harvest of 1863 that was stimulated by war necessity.

"We marched and we marched," said Colonel William C. Oates of the 15th Alabama, "along the dustiest roads I ever saw. We got on the wrong road and marched I don't know where to and camped; got up the next morning and marched back again."

Oates, who had carried the main load of the assault on Little Round Top, set out on the seventeenth with only two days' rations and during the continued marching and countermarching the supplies were exhausted. When the men entered the battle on the nineteenth it was with empty haversacks.

Hood did not reach Ringgold until the afternoon of the eighteenth. There he found Bragg's order awaiting him to take the Reed's bridge road and assume command of the column that had been marching toward the battlefield when the orders were issued, but had now already arrived. These troops comprised three of his own brigades, the Alabamans under Brigadier General E. McIver Law, the Georgia brigade commanded by Brigadier General Henry L. "Rock" Benning and his own old Texas brigade commanded by Brigadier General Jerome B. Robertson. Of his old division, only Brigadier General George T. "Tige" Anderson's brigade was missing.

Hood mounted at Ringgold, one arm in a sling, and about 3 P.M. joined his brigades, which were with Brigadier General Bushrod Johnson's division, waiting on the west side of the Chickamauga for Bragg to order them into action. General Law retained the command of Hood's division, which he had exercised after Hood was wounded at Gettysburg, and Hood took command of the hastily linked corps consisting of the divisions of Law and Bushrod Johnson.

The battle on the Confederate right had lulled. Nearer at hand Stewart and Reynolds were exchanging heavy infantry fire, but Stewart's fierce attack was being pushed back across the La Fayette road and its vigor was all but spent. Hood moved through the woods and brought his men in on Stewart's left so as to attack the Federals in the region of the Viniard farm and drive them back on Rosecrans' headquarters at the Widow Glenn's. He deployed his corps in the woods about 800 yards east of Viniard's.

Hood was devoted to the infantry. He was to be charged later by one of Cleburne's staff officers with either not knowing much or not caring much about artillery and cavalry. However that may be, he did rely mainly on the shock of his infantry, and as a leader of that arm there were few to excel him in either army, at least when he was acting under the orders of such competent superiors as Lee or Longstreet. In the instance of his attack on Viniard's his reliance on the infantry was well justified, for there was scant opportunity for the effective use of artillery in the thickets and underbrush on this or any other part of the field.[1]

The Federal Brigadier General Jefferson C. Davis, commanding a division of McCook's corps, had marched that morning from Crawfish Springs to the Widow Glenn's, where he turned to the east and arranged his lines east of the La Fayette road in front of the Viniard house, forming the Federal right. Later Sheridan followed with his division, excepting the brigade of Brigadier General William H. Lytle, which was left at Lee and Gordon's mill, relieving Wood's division of Crittenden's corps, which all through the morning and until 3:30 P.M. performed the dull assignment of watching the crossing there.

Almost simultaneous with the arrival of Davis came Colonel Sidney M. Barnes's brigade of VanCleve's division, which likewise had been left at Lee and Gordon's but which was able to get away two hours ahead of Wood.

At Stone's River Rosecrans had given Barnes's brigade some personal instructions that had bearing on its attitude at Chickamauga. It had been commanded at Stone's River by a Kentuckian, Colonel

Samuel W. Price, and had behaved well. Rosecrans, coming up to the brigade at a Stone's River ford, asked who commanded.

"I do, sir," Colonel Price answered.

"Will you hold this ford?"

"I will try, sir," said the colonel.

"Will you hold this ford?"

"I will die right here!"

"Will you hold this ford?" This time Rosecrans thundered the question.

"Yes, sir," Price answered.

"That will do," said Rosecrans as he galloped away.

Now the brigade had a critical assignment on the extreme right flank of the battle line. VanCleve left eight pieces of artillery with Barnes and ordered him as he approached the field to go in and act on his own judgment. "I accordingly did go in," the brigade commander reported, taking no chances that Old Rosey might ride up and ask about his orders.

On Davis' arrival at 2 P.M., Heg's brigade, first in the column, took the left, nearest to Crittenden fighting Stewart at Brotherton's. Carlin's brigade took the center, while Barnes fell in on the right. Wilder's brigade was in support just west of the Viniard house. The right of Rosecrans' army consequently was held at this stage by four brigades, Heg's and Carlin's of Davis' division, Barnes's brigade of VanCleve's and Wilder's brigade of Reynolds' division. All corps of the army except Granger's reserve were represented by these four brigades, the first two belonging to McCook's, Barnes to Crittenden's and Wilder to Thomas'. Rosecrans' line was indeed becoming jumbled by the chance manner in which the brigades reached the field. Davis' third brigade was left behind to guard the supply train.

Hood's attack on Rosecrans' right at Chickamauga had the same fierceness as his assault against Sherman's army later in the war at Peach Tree Creek in front of Atlanta. Davis' two brigades were assailed so suddenly and viciously that they were driven back pellmell, almost disorganized. But they rallied from this first deadly affray and came again into the action. The battle swayed back and forth, the compelling shock finally being delivered by Robertson's

Texans. Other elements of Bushrod Johnson's division pressed to the right and formed a juncture with Stewart's division battling VanCleve and Reynolds.

When Hood's blow fell, Carlin's brigade was deployed in the open field east of the La Fayette road, the 81st Indiana on the right, the 101st Ohio in the center, the 38th Illinois reaching into the timber on the left, and the 21st Illinois in reserve. Heg extended the line to the left, or north. An advance on Carlin's left had scarcely been checked by a volley when a large enemy force was seen moving to the left of Heg. Elements of Johnson's division were pressing to their own right, where they formed a juncture with Stewart's division, joined in the battle against VanCleve, and shortly presented an ominous threat to Heg.

Then Carlin was hit in his center by the brigades of Robertson of Law's and Gregg of Bushrod Johnson's division and was overwhelmed and pushed to the west side of the La Fayette road, leaving three guns of the 8th Indiana battery of light artillery and the colors of the 21st Illinois with the enemy. The 21st Illinois had some distinction in the Army of the Cumberland because it had been Grant's first regiment—the so-called "toughs" which the victor of Fort Donelson and Vicksburg had drilled and was alleged to have cowed, though he had appeared before them in his rough civilian clothes.

Carlin's right regiment, the 81st Indiana, being bypassed, took the Confederates who crashed through Carlin's center in flank. The Hoosier riflemen commanded by Captain Nevil B. Boone drove them back. The 8th Indiana battery and the colors of the 21st Illinois were recaptured. Apparently the Confederates had never noticed the colors still clutched in the hands of the dead color sergeant. Barnes's brigade came up in time to give assistance in this recovery of the La Fayette road.

Farther to the left the brigade of Colonel Hans Christian Heg— a handsome, much-admired civilian soldier from Wisconsin, born in the village of Lier, Norway—found itself handled even less gently than had been Carlin.

Brigadier General Jefferson C. Davis, who had risen from the ranks in the regular army and had been with Robert Anderson in

Fort Sumter when Beauregard bombarded it, had apparently not picked up much information on the way up to division commander about what happened to flanks suspended in the air. When he took his position at Viniard's he left half a mile of open country between his own left and the right of King's brigade fighting on the right of VanCleve.

What could be more natural on such a stubbornly fought field than that Hood should send a suitable force into this gap. Benning pressed Heg in front while Gregg and McNair attacked his flank. Heg's brigade took frightful punishment. One of the first Confederate bullets found Heg. A Cincinnati newspaperman saw the brigade lose half its numbers: "flank exposed . . . wide gap between it and troops on left. . . . Bullets tore through the ranks; grape and canister whistled among the brave men . . . [who] stood their ground, not yielding an inch."[2]

Such was the story of Heg's battle. The bullet hit Heg in the bowels and did not kill him instantly. What time he had left he devoted to rallying and protecting his men. Then he rode about a quarter of a mile and collapsed from loss of blood. It was sunset when he died. He was thirty-four years old.

The day before, he had written his wife. "Do not feel uneasy for me. I am well and in good spirits . . . If it is true the Rebels have not gone, Old Rosey will give them one of the biggest whippings they ever had. . . . Goodby, my darling."

Heg was a Viking at heart. Like other adventuresome officers and soldiers in this war, including the Confederate general Cheatham, he had been drawn to California by the gold rush of 1849. By the time he returned, his father had died. He married a Norwegian immigrant girl, Gunild Einong. When he ran for State Prison Commissioner he won, partly because he spoke such fluent English. He resigned to enter the army, and Governor Alexander W. Randall quickly appointed him colonel. An editorial commending him said he was "young, powerful, attractive, honorable, unimpeachably honest" and added that he "had sound sense,"—a quality not too generously dispensed among the officers in this war.

Heg called for 1,000 recruits from among the Danes, Swedes and Norwegians, and they were assembled into the 15th Wisconsin Infantry. One of the striking features of this war was the readiness with which newcomers to America entered the service on both sides. The greater number arriving entered on the Northern side, mainly because the stream of immigration that could not compete against slave labor was directed to the northern cities or northwestern prairie states. Many of the Scandinavians had just reached Wisconsin when they enlisted.

Heg had said in his appeal, "Let us band together and deliver untarnished to posterity the old honorable name of Norsemen." None had ever gone out seeking battles more eagerly than the old Norsemen, and that heritage may have been a factor in sending Heg and his blond-haired band off into a war that had been seething for generations in American politics, and led them ultimately into Rosecrans' right wing at Chickamauga. The complexion of the command could be seen from the fact that in Company F alone there were five Ole Olsens.

Heg's beautifully affectionate letters to Gunild and his children, published by the Norwegian-American Historical Association in 1936, have touched many who have studied this costly battle. When the Chattanooga writer, Robert Sparks Walker, read them he said that "for many days thereafter my heart ached violently in sympathy." He decided then to prepare his interesting series of newspaper articles published in the Chattanooga *Sunday Times* in 1936 under the title "The Pyramids of Chickamauga." The "pyramids," erected of cannonballs by the Chickamauga National Military Park, mark the spots where brigade commanders fell. One seems to encounter them everywhere on the field.

One close observer of this part of the field was impressed by a distinction. On most battlefields the scars on the trees showed the direction of the fighting, but near Viniard's farm the trees were pitted around their entire circumference. The correspondent commented that "there was fighting front to front, fighting on the flanks, enfilading and cross firing." The deadly fighting surged back and forth and all around.

Benning's men rushed a battery, not identified but apparently that of the 8th Indiana, and captured it. But the horses had been killed and they were unable to draw it back. A little later the bluecoats made a spirited charge and recaptured the guns. The Confederate captain who saw them coming jumped behind a tree and observed. He criticized their tactics: they did not pursue his own men while they had a chance. Instead, they "jumped up on the guns and began making speeches to celebrate the recapture."[3]

Benning's brigade, like virtually all others engaged in this battle, was suffering from want of water. Captain Houghton of the 2nd Georgia saw a canteen on what looked like a dead Northerner. He leaned his gun against a tree, crawled the twenty feet, unloosed the canteen strap and pulled it out from under the body, when suddenly the body jumped up, entirely unhurt. "The Yankee was a lot bigger," he said, "but was too scared to do anything but run."

Neither side, according to the captain, knew it was in the proximity of the enemy until the two lines suddenly faced each other at pistol shot. The confused nature of the fighting was indicated by an incident he related. Some Confederate guns had been pushed up to cover ground gained. Their firing reverberated through the woods. Then the Confederate line went ahead again, and found that their fire had swept away one of their own field hospitals. The solid shot had plowed through rows of the wounded waiting for attention. "Among the dead was a young aide. I remember thinking as I looked at him that he was the handsomest man I had ever seen."

Hood's aim had been to locate the right flank of the Federal army and turn it, and sweep away the center and left from in front of Stewart, Cheatham and Walker. But he had been compelled to fight the Federals where he found them, and fight face to face, from the east to the west, instead of from the south facing north. Near Viniard's the Chickamauga bends to the west and flows close to the La Fayette road. The space between creek and road was well covered by Federal forces at Lee and Gordon's mill, on whom Hood would have been compelled to turn his back had he undertaken a flank movement from south to north. The plan of trying to turn the Federal right might have been well enough earlier in the day, when it could have been directed against the forces fighting under Thomas, but it was impractical after the coming in the mid-afternoon of Davis' division. But a frontal attack now appeared as promising as any flank movement.

Very likely Hood would have rolled up and destroyed the Federal right flank had it not been for the timely arrival of Wood's division of Crittenden's corps coming down the Chickamauga from Lee and Gordon's. Wood had two brigades, his third under Wagner still being on garrison duty in Chattanooga. He directed Buell's brigade to a field behind the severely handled brigades of Carlin and Heg to give them support. Buell arrived just in time to become momentarily involved in the near rout of these two brigades. Wood threw Harker's brigade directly against Bushrod Johnson's flank, which had been left exposed when Johnson was pressing Heg across the La Fayette road. This was most effective as Harker got into Johnson's rear. Johnson was compelled to turn, then retire.

Harker's brigade picked up some prisoners from Hood and had not nearly so much difficulty as Rosecrans earlier in the day in establishing that they were Longstreet's men. Zebulon Vance's gift uniforms proved an identifying mark. Harker's men noticed that all of Longstreet's soldiers wore the standard gray Confederate uniform, while the dress of Bragg's army was "go-as-you-please ... with every imaginable variety of garments and head covering." Scarcely any two wore the same kind of clothing. Some said Bragg's uniforms were greasy.

One of Harker's soldiers asked a prisoner, "How does Longstreet like the western Yankees?"

"You'll get enough of Longstreet before tomorrow night." The prisoner was speaking hopefully, but he could not have been more prophetic if he had possessed a crystal ball.

In the fighting between Wood and Bushrod Johnson, Brigadier General John Gregg, commanding a brigade largely of Tennessee troops but including his own early regiment, the 7th Texas, was grievously wounded. Colonel C. A. Sugg of the 50th Tennessee took command of the brigade, which was destined to play an important role in the battle on the following day.

Gregg, an Alabaman, another professor of mathematics, and a lawyer, had moved to Texas and become a member of the Confederate Congress. He resigned after the first battle of Manassas and recruited the 7th Texas. Captured at Fort Donelson, he was imprisoned for nearly seven months in Boston Harbor, and on exchange was given a brigade in Joseph E. Johnston's Mississippi army. He had ridden ahead to reconnoiter but got near the Federal lines in the timber, and a skirmisher dropped him from his horse. His neck wound appeared mortal and while he was lying where he fell he was relieved of his valuable spurs and sword. When Robertson's brigade charged over this part of the woods both he and his horse were recovered. The bullets seemed to have his name on them, for he was killed later in Virginia after he had replaced Robertson as commander of the Texas brigade.

The loss of officers in Gregg's brigade was heavy in this action. When Sugg took the brigade, his two successors as commander of the 50th Tennessee, Lieutenant Colonel Thomas W. Beaumont and Major Christopher W. Robertson, were killed. Lieutenant Colonel James J. Turner, commander of the 30th Tennessee, and Lieutenant Colonel Sam Thompson of the 10th Tennessee, were both severely wounded. Numerous company grade officers fell as well.

Nothing more adequately described the fearful carnage than the story told of an owl that was startled up in front of the 10th Tennessee, an Irish regiment of Gregg's brigade. Some crows saw it in the air, pursued it and soon a battle was raging, while the lines below were firing as rapidly as they could load. An Irishman dropped his gun, gazed upward and exclaimed, "Moses, what a country! The very birds are fighting."[4]

Similarly revealing was the attitude of another private after the colors of the 10th Tennessee had been shot down. Carrying the colors was an almost certain title to six feet of north Georgia soil. When Colonel William Grace ordered a man on the firing line to take the flag, the busy soldier, loading and shooting at high speed, responded enthusiastically, "By the holy St. Patrick, Colonel, there's so much good shooting here I haven't a minute's time to waste fooling with that thing."

Much needless loss of life would have been prevented in both armies in this war if it had not been considered so imperative to carry the colors to the firing line.

Still further help was appearing for the Federals in the form of Sheridan's soldiers. They were reaching the battlefield after the long, wearisome march back and forth over the mountains from Alpine. Instead of being content with the defensive, a role to which Davis had been forced by the onslaughts of Hood, Sheridan sent Bradley's brigade to the east side of the La Fayette road, where a short but exceedingly fierce and bloody conflict was joined. Sheridan was driven back again to the west side.

Two new Confederate divisions were now appearing on the field, but so was darkness. Hindman and Preston came in on Hood's left. Even as they arrived the fighting on the southern end of the battlefield was languishing. Preston sent merely Trigg's brigade to support Hood. Wilder brought his brigade up to the La Fayette road to help prevent another Confederate crossing after Bushrod Johnson had driven Sheridan back from the east side. As the battle lulled, the roadway came to be accepted tacitly as the dividing line between the armies on this part of the battlefield.

The story was told that as Hood's men from the Army of Northern Virginia had gone into action they passed through some Tennessee troops resting behind the lines. "Rise up, Tennesseans, and see the Virginians go in," one of Hood's soldiers shouted.

When Hood suffered a reverse and came trailing back he passed the same body of troops. A man yelled: "Rise up, Tennesseans, and see the Virginians come out."

An anatomical curiosity developed from this battle around Viniard's. Edmund Brewer Tate of the 15th Georgia, Benning's brigade, was one of eight brothers from Elberton, Georgia, in the Confederate armies. As the fighting subsided about sunset he was hit by a Minié ball which entered the left breast directly at the nipple, ranged slightly downward, came out at the back near and to the left of the spinal column, and made sixteen holes as it cut through the blanket rolled across his back.

The path of the bullet would suggest that it passed directly through his heart, but that he was still alive was evidence it did not. When the doctors examined him they discovered to their amazement that his heart was on his right side. They judged it had been knocked over there by the bullet. He survived, and always was looked on as the man whose heart was knocked into the wrong place at Chickamauga. Surely it is more likely the heart had been dislocated since birth, an extremely rare but not unique condition.

The battle in Hood's sector had ended substantially where it began. But Hood's attack had been conducted with the dogged desperation of men who did not know how to lose. Bloody as had been the day's work all along the line, none of the fighting had been more fearsome than here.

The intensity of the firing on this part of the battlefield might be seen from the experience of some loggers after the war. They set up a sawmill about two thirds of the way from the Dry Valley road to Viniard's. The pines the lumbermen felled, loaded as they were with Minié balls, grape and shell fragments, proved more than a match for the teeth of the buzz saws. As late as 1890 there was a standing rule among sawmills of the area not to take logs from the Chickamauga battlefield.[5]

Darkness was falling but the day of carnage was not ended. The bitter fighting on the right of the Federal army was now about to be duplicated on its left.

CHAPTER SIXTEEN

Cleburne's Sunset Assault

ALL THE while the battle was raging that afternoon along the Chickamauga, Cleburne's division of Hill's corps was marching down the stream toward Thedford's ford.

In stubborn adherence to his original plan of turning Rosecrans' left, Bragg had ordered a renewal of the attack against Thomas, which had lulled as the battle rolled southward. While Bragg may have sensed that Thomas had weakened his left to reinforce the center by the shift of Brannan's division, and believed that there still might be opportunity to get between the Federals and Chattanooga, the Confederate commander might well have reflected at this stage on the greater successes he was even then scoring against Rosecrans' weaker center and right, where Stewart had broken VanCleve and Hood was severely handling Davis.

Cleburne was crossing at Thedford's ford at 4:30 P.M., at an hour when Heg and Carlin were suffering and coming close to a general rout under the series of assaults by the divisions of Law and Bushrod Johnson. Behind these two divisions of Hood's corps were the divisions of Hindman and Preston, which Bragg had not yet seen fit to engage. With Cleburne now close at hand, Bragg had enough weight on his left to crush not only Davis' staggering division plus Barnes's brigade and Wood's small division coming up from Lee and Gordon's mill, but also the two brigades Sheridan might bring up in support.

Bragg must have seen this. But one who has been crossed repeatedly is more than normally tenacious with his decisions. So it was with Bragg. With the single exception of Trigg's brigade, Hindman and Preston were not sent into action. Cleburne was ordered to march to the right of the army and report to Lieutenant General Leonidas Polk, who would direct him into line. Cleburne's march of six miles down the Chickamauga already had been delayed by numerous obstacles, detachments of marching troops, and trains of artillery on the road. By the time he reached the ford he was in haste. He did not, as was the custom, give the men a chance to break ranks and find their own way across the stream, but plunged straight ahead in solid column. Colonel Roger Quarles Mills of the 6th Texas, who would serve long in the United States Senate and House, could recall vividly, in later years when he visited the field, this icy bath in a creek fed by mountain springs. The water reached to the armpits. Without halting, the division marched on through the woods, came at length to the Confederate right and pitched in at sundown in wet clothes to battle the divisions of Baird and Richard Johnson.

Sometimes the story of a company tells the story of an army. That of Company B, 33rd Alabama, throws light on the nature and the beginnings of the force Cleburne commanded, which was distinguished above most of the others in the armies of the western front.

When the "Dale County Greys" were organized in May 1861, the Alabama people brought them chickens, eggs, butter, milk, fresh meat and fruits in abundance at Camp Hardaway near Glenville. They had one bass drum and one kettle drum and up to three pipers, and there was thus plenty of martial music. But there were few weapons, particularly guns.

So the blacksmiths got busy and fashioned out of carriage springs knives ranging from fourteen to eighteen inches in length, which the soldiers carried in scabbards. The notion that the South was loaded with firearms at the beginning was a misconception. The "Greys" had to set out armed with carriage springs to look for the Northerners.

They drew uniforms consisting of a round jacket coat reaching down to the hip joint, of the nature of the jackets of World War II, and gray woolen jeans and caps. But the caps were not fancied and were generally tossed aside; the soldiers preferred their civilian hats.

The guns finally issued were ancient unpainted smooth-bore muskets which once had been flint and steel-lock guns, worked over so that they could be fired with percussion caps. A cylinder had been fastened onto the right side of the barrel close to the touchhole so that the powder could be fired by a hammer coming down on the percussion cap placed over the end of the tube. The guns fired buck and ball cartridges—a half-inch ball, in front of which were three buckshot, deadly at close range.

Other equipment included leather cartridge boxes about seven inches square and two-and-a-half inches deep, holding forty rounds, hung over the left shoulder by a two-inch strap and anchored to the belt. The belt had a copper or brass plate with the initials CSA. The men received bayonet and scabbard that fastened to the belt in the rear.

They were never issued blankets. Whereas many in the Southern armies got carpeting from home for blankets, these Alabamans usually took "white bed blankets" with them, made either of natural wool or possibly in instances of cotton. These served until they could capture Federal blankets on the battlefield. Their canteens were small cedar casks fastened with copper hoops. The men liked to exchange these for the well-fashioned, nonleaking Northern metal canteens of prisoners.

The company had their misfortunes. One of the company sergeants was a jeweler and when he got in a supply of watches for repair he deserted to the Federals and took all of them with him.

Their outlook was improved in mid-1862 when they were issued Enfields and discarded the old flintlocks. The regiment elected Sam Adams of Greenville, Alabama, their colonel; he had been a lieutenant in the earlier fighting in Virginia. He married during this campaign and shortly before the battle of Chickamauga his wife visited him at Harrison, Tennessee. One could have foretold that their married life would be brief. When Sam Adams saw the color-bearer of the 33rd faltering after the staff was broken at Chickamauga, he snatched the flag, put himself at the head of the regiment and led it forward. He would survive to be killed in front of Atlanta in the great battle of July 22nd.[1]

All through the afternoon of the nineteenth the 33rd Alabama hurried to the front and about sunset formed in line of battle, a part of Brigadier General Sterling Alexander Martin Wood's brigade of Cleburne's division. The line of battle was formed at sunset and the brigade passed through Walker's corps. Walker's men were lying down but cheered Cleburne's soldiers as they passed. They clambered over a worm rail fence and finally encountered the Federal line.

The 16th Alabama, another typical regiment of Cleburne's command, had gone off from Courtland—the postwar home of Major General Joe Wheeler—in August 1861, armed with flintlocks and the well wishes of all north central Alabama. The departure was accompanied by a great ovation. Nearly every house showed a Confederate flag. One of the members of the brass band, Elijah Stover of Oakville, composed a ballad especially for the departure. The regiment went into Zollicoffer's brigade and fought at Mill Springs, then Shiloh, Stone's River and Chickamauga.

Company E was commanded by W. W. Weatherford, former sheriff of Franklin County, whose peculiar stance caused the men to call him "Parade Rest" Weatherford. One wonders about his relationships. Weatherford was a great name in early Alabama, borne by the stanchest and most admirable of the Muskogee Creek chiefs, the half-breed son of a shrewd and fabulously wealthy Scottish peddler.

Another company was commanded by John H. Bankhead, who had been promoted from lieutenant to captain on the field of "Bloody" Shiloh where he was wounded three times. He would serve long in later years as Senator from Alabama, and one of his sons would be Senator and another Speaker of the House.

Major J. H. McGaughy, commander of the regiment, was killed at Chickamauga. Captain Frederick A. Ashford of Company B took command. His grandfather, Thomas A. Ashford, was fighting alongside Colonel Richard Mentor Johnson at the Battle of the Thames when Johnson killed an Indian chief, alleged in later political campaigns to have been Tecumseh.

This regiment, called the "cream of the fighting material" of northern Alabama, which had left Courtland about 1,000 strong and had fought across the great battlefields of the West, would lose

244 in killed and wounded at Chickamauga and come out of the battle with fifty-one privates, eight noncommissioned and nine commissioned officers.[2]

Cleburne was an inspirational leader who fired his division to extraordinary effort and achievement. No general of the Confederacy ever had a more splendid tribute than that paid to Cleburne by his old commander, General Hardee: "When Cleburne's division defended, no odds broke its lines; where it attacked, no numbers resisted its onslaught, save only once, and there is the grave of Cleburne."

No doubt the title he bore of "the Stonewall Jackson of the West" was a bit strained. Cleburne never had opportunity to display strategical talents like Jackson's in independent command; he did nevertheless show such marked tactical ability that he stood in the very forefront of the natural fighters who came into renown in this war, and none possessed any greater battle ardor than he did behind his rather expressionless face. His countenance has been called "gloomy" and it certainly was not made more attractive by an ugly scar; he had been wounded in the mouth at the battle of Richmond, Kentucky. He was also wounded in the leg at Perryville.

That he was filled with sentiment and charity was indicated by an incident just before his death. The story has persisted (some overly punctilious historians have scrutinized it so closely as to question though not disprove it) that when at Franklin, Tennessee, he saw an Irish lad from Little Rock, Arkansas, marching over the furrows of a frozen cornfield, leaving bloody footprints on the snow because he had no shoes. Cleburne took off his own shoes and gave them to the soldier, and died in his stocking feet.

At times his emotion surged up into fervid outbursts, as when he addressed his brigade before the battle of Tupelo, Mississippi, in what was termed by an auditor "the most stirring patriotic speech he had ever heard." He had told in his most pathetic terms the story of distressed Ireland, crushed down and humbled, and had predicted even more grievous conditions for the South if the Confederacy failed. Then, his head erect, his emotions stirred to all their Celtic depths, he had declared: "If this cause which is so dear to my heart is doomed to fail, I pray heaven may let me fall with it, while my face is turned to the enemy and my arm battling for that which I know to be right."

Cleburne was born ten miles west of Cork, Ireland, of Episcopalian parents, March 17, 1828. When he was four years old, his mother died. His father remarried but his family life appeared to be pleasant and his stepmother sympathetic. He entered Trinity College in Dublin. His chagrin at not being able to pass the examinations for a medical education caused him to enlist at the age of seventeen in the 41st Regiment of British infantry. There he served for three years and rose to be a corporal. In 1849 he bought his discharge and at twenty-one left with a brother and sister for America, where they landed at New Orleans. Another brother and a half-brother followed. One brother served in the Union Army, and the half-brother enlisted in Morgan's cavalry and was killed at the battle of Cloyd's farm in southwestern Virginia.

Pursued by the medical urge, Patrick Cleburne became a pharmacist's clerk in Helena, Arkansas, then part owner of a drugstore, and at length a lawyer who prospered and acquired property. He made it a point not to own slaves. A diligent student of the law and current affairs, a gifted speaker, tall, spare and erect, with a good vein of humor, and a close friend of the Helena Congressman Thomas C. Hindman, Cleburne had become one of the well-known men of the community and of eastern Arkansas before the war. He had gone to Hindman's help in a political street fight in Helena, when a gang attacked and shot his friend, and had been severly injured himself.

His indifference to danger was shown in all his army service, from the time he joined the Yell Rifles of Helena (named after Colonel Archibald Yell who fell at Buena Vista) until he died leading the storming party at Franklin. In May 1861 he was chosen colonel of the 15th Arkansas and soon came under the command of Hardee, a competent superior who quickly detected his fine military talents.

The men of his regiment, his brigade and, after the Kentucky campaign, his division came to call themselves fondly "Old Pat's boys." Trained with the British foot, he was a splendid drillmaster who possessed just enough peculiarities to make him a character to young men who had scarcely ever before been outside their own counties of Arkansas and Tennessee. He never spoke of the "old country" except in terms of affection, and with an accent that disclosed what country he referred to. When he was stirred, the accent turned to heavy brogue. Always the r's would roll along in his striking, "sometimes startling" command of "Fore-ward Mar-r-r-ch!" When telling his officers about the use of firearms he would refer to the rifle "bar-r-rel."

This immigrant Irish corporal rose toward the end to be one of the great men of the Confederacy and none in Bragg's army at Chickamauga commanded greater respect or confidence. Perhaps it was unfortunate that he did not have higher command, for in innate military ability he was nearest to Forrest among all of Bragg's officers.[3]

Thomas had ridden over at 5 P.M. to inspect and consolidate his line on the left, being confident that the enemy would assault in that quarter. He met Baird and Richard Johnson together, showed Johnson where he should place his lines, then followed with instructions to Baird. From Baird's line he went to Palmer and Reynolds farther to the right and drew a line for them in the woods about 500 yards east of the La Fayette road. Brannan was now still farther to the right in reserve at the Dyer farm.

Thomas had barely completed readjusting his line when Cleburne, supported by Cheatham, delivered his furious assault on Johnson and Baird, and, as Thomas mildly conceded, "produced some confusion."

Cleburne attacked with all his fiery impetuosity. His front extended about a mile, with three brigades in line, Lucius Polk on the right at Jay's sawmill, which had been the scene of some of the most stubborn early fighting of the battle; S. A. M. Wood with his four Alabama and two Mississippi regiments in the center, and Deshler on the left. Most of the terrain in their front was wooded but the underbrush became less of an obstacle as the assailants moved away from the creek, and the artillery came into heavy use.

As they were approaching the battle line a soldier of the 18th

Alabama Battalion, of S. A. M Wood's brigade, looked back and noticed that a field officer had a bottle turned up to his lips. He assumed it was whisky; "I further thought he was trying to steady his nerve." The soldier was not surprised when he learned that the officer's horse had fallen and disabled him so severely that he had to go to the rear.

There was no such relief for the men when they neared the firing line. The infantry seemed to open without anyone giving the command, and in three minutes, according to the Alabaman, the battle was "something awful . . . one solid, unbroken wave of awe-inspiring sound. . . . It seemed as if all the fires of earth and hell had been turned loose in one mighty effort to destroy each other. . . . Ever and anon I could hear the Confederate yell of victory and triumph." The din registered so firmly on his brain that for years he found that when he would take a cold all the fury of the cannon and shouting would roar in his head.

Even Cleburne said of the firing, "For half an hour it was the heaviest I ever heard."

On an advance in the darkness laggards had opportunity to slip behind. One difficulty was that they insisted then on firing from the rear and sometimes hit their own men. In that manner Adjutant A. M. Moore of the 33rd Alabama, twenty years old, was killed. He was the son of former Governor Gabriel Moore, and a student at the University of Alabama.

Men in both armies would grow so excited or intense in the action that they sometimes neglected to remove their iron ramrods from the gun barrels before firing. Bent ramrods could be seen sticking here and there in the trees. It was a dangerous mistake, for ramrods were essential.

Long after the war the old veterans liked to talk about this night attack—the deep palpable blackness of the forest glades, the intensity of the firing such as those in neither army ever heard before or after—the sharp notes of a cracking rifle multiplied by the thousands and blended into one shrill continuous shriek—the armies attacking each other guided by sound and powder flashes. For more than an hour the vicious fighting continued in darkness lighted by a pale quarter moon pallid in that gathering mist not infrequent in the early autumn nights in this lower Appalachian country.[4]

Although Thomas was ready with his alignments when the attack came, it took some of the men in the ranks by surprise. Captain C. C. Briant, Company K, 6th Indiana, of Richard Johnson's division, thought the battle of the nineteenth was finished in his sector, as did his men, until suddenly the pickets came scurrying back closely pursued by the Confederates with their "demoniacal yell." They were advancing in heavy, massed columns, at a run. All down the defending line went the order for the companies to fall in.

Then the Federals unloosed a devastating fire. Very quickly a "shower of leaden hail was being belched into their faces" by the Northerners as the gray-coated soldiers advanced. Still they came ahead, "yell after yell," and drew so close there was no longer room for loading. The battle became one of gun butts and bayonets, hand to hand. The lines of both armies would recoil without breaking, then clash again.

Captain Briant, remarking on the "recklessness which characterizes all soldiers after breathing an atmosphere strongly impregnated with powder-smoke," credited the enemy in his front with "loading and firing in a manner that I believe was never surpassed on any battlefield during the rebellion." All the while, his regiment and others along the line were firing at the attackers at point-blank range. Such an action could not last. Finally the Confederates gave way in front of the 6th Indiana, but word came down the line that they had penetrated on both flanks. The 5th Indiana battery had to withdraw with the loss of a gun.

Such was the confusion that a Pennsylvania regiment rushed in as a reserve came over a crest seventy yards in the rear, mistook the Hoosiers for the enemy and opened fire. Lieutenant Colonel Hagerman Tripp rushed back and made them stop. That night he wrote: "Hard fighting all afternoon, continued until 7 o'clock, night. My loss heavy. Camped for the night on battlefield. *O, heavy hour!* Lost 160 men today." He would be critically wounded before the battle's end.

One reason for the retirement of the flanks of the division was that Richard Johnson, seeing Dodge's brigade, which sustained the first impact of Cleburne's attack, give way, ordered his other two brigades, Willich's and Baldwin's, to retire abreast it. Willich was able to execute the movement, but Baldwin, now being under heavy close-range attack, was unable to conform and instead decided to charge forward rather than go back.

Colonel Philemon P. Baldwin, who formerly led the 6th Indiana and now commanded the brigade, was on the right of the brigade line when the enemy came on impetuously. He, too, had "breathed atmosphere strongly impregnated with powder smoke." The high point of the assault was the moment he regarded as timely for a countercharge. Though they were in the open on a cultivated farm known as Winfrey field, he leaped his horse to the front of his men and, seizing the flag as the color sergeant was falling, shouted, "Follow me!" He could scarcely do more than get the words out of his mouth. The lines were only a few yards apart. Rider and horse were shot down instantly.

"The regiment very sensibly did not obey an order that should never have been given," said the captain who recorded the story of Baldwin's death. The captain said he should merely have ordered, "Stand fast and give 'em hell!"

About a quarter of a mile from where Baldwin fell, the Confederate Brigadier General Preston Smith dropped in front of his men at almost the same instant. Johnson had succeeded in pushing back Deshler, and Preston Smith was bringing his brigade of Cheatham's division up in support. In the darkness Smith could not be sure of the Federal position and stumbled into it without warning while he was picking his way in advance of the brigade. He was killed by balls from the first enemy volley.

Because of the confusion about where the lines were, Deshler's Confederate brigade was also caught in its own fire and casualties resulted.

Much of the time the Confederate artillery in the darkness fired too high to cause heavy damage except for the havoc it wrought in the timber.

"Tree-tops, limbs and twigs were clipped off over our heads

and fell all around us," said the historian of the 38th Indiana. "It was a display of fireworks that one does not like to see more than once in a lifetime." The 15th Ohio came to have new admiration for their German brigade commander Willich that night, as he stood out in front of the regiment amid Cleburne's tremendous fire of bursting shells and bullets.[5]

Night rather than a success for either side ended this sanguinary fighting between forces that could do little more than grope for each other and slug in the darkness. Old Pat's boys settled down to sleep on the ground where they were, their only meal dry crackers. Thomas' line had been pushed back about a mile in some places but it was unbroken.

CHAPTER SEVENTEEN

Driving Thirst in the
Deep Shadows

WATER was the main problem in the Federal army that night, and to a smaller extent a problem among the Confederates.

The sudden concentration of 120,000 or more men largely into twelve square miles of territory having only a few wells and two or three weak springs, intensified by the tremendous number of parched, wounded soldiers scattered over the field, made the supply of water a supreme emergency. The accounts of both armies abound with stories of aching, maddening thirst.

The 39th Indiana mounted infantry of Willich's brigade collected all the canteens it could lay hands on and brought up from Crawfish Springs 1,000 canteens full of spring water. These were delivered before midnight to suffering Federal soldiers. The supply was pitifully small in relation to the demands, but the distance was three miles to the Federal right and eight or nine from Thomas' position, and no large casks for hauling water were on hand.

The spring at Dyer's farmhouse, now all but dry, could not have been bold even in the days of the battle, judging by the contour of the land. There were two springs in the neighborhood of Viniard's, apparently neither yielding a good flow. East of Hiram Vittetoe's house was another weak spring.

About the only source of water on the right of the Federal lines was a pond, long since dried up, in the rear of the Widow Glenn's and east of the Dry Valley road. This was called "the Sink" by inhabitants of the area but during and after the battle became known as "Bloody Pond." The name resulted not because of any heavy near-by fighting but because many thirsting wounded soldiers dragged themselves to die on its banks on the night of the nineteenth and all through the next day.

So much blood was shed when they tried to drink that the water became stained close by the shores. The pond was foul, having no inlet or outlet, and could not have been either sanitary or inviting before the battle, but as one of the survivors remarked when he looked on the stagnant little pool some years afterward, "We could drink anything in the form of water those days."

An officer wrote: "How we suffered that night no one knows. Water could not be found; the rebels had possession of the Chickamauga, and we had to do without. Few of us had blankets and the night was very cold. All looked with anxiety for the coming of the dawn; for although we had given the enemy a rough handling, he had certainly used us very hard."

Captain Lemark Duvall of the 90th Ohio, Palmer's division, said he had not experienced a more uncomfortable night since his enlistment. After a few minutes of sleep he awoke "almost frozen." Perhaps the severe cold was felt so keenly because it was the first of the season. His detachment got up and moved a quarter of a mile to where they saw a small fire. To reach it they elbowed their way "through a crowd of Md's," which stood not for doctors, but mule drivers. Around the fire they were able to sleep.

Lieutenant Colonel Archibald Blakeley of the 78th Pennsylvania, Negley's division, was stirred by the events. "I shall never forget that night, the meditation the conditions produced," he said. "We were in the solitude of a wilderness, and in absolute darkness, a thousand miles away from our Northern homes where loved ones thought of us and prayed for us."[1]

George Morgan Kirkpatrick, of Evansville, Indiana, one of six brothers in the 42nd Indiana, Negley's division, who went off to fight with War of 1812 flintlocks, had a mild disaster just before the battle. He took off his blouse and shirt to wash himself in a brook and hung them on a branch, but somebody stole them. He went through the battle with a dirty shirt he had salvaged and no coat. That night when the cold wave swept the territory he got the "shivers." He cut a hole in a blanket, stuck his head through it and used it as a coat.

"There was vermin in our clothing," he said, "and now as before, our socks, when we had any, were not on speaking terms with us. We did not take them off until they were rotten, and only removed our shoes once a week."

The unseasonable coldness could be seen from the fact that youthful Captain W. P. Herron of Wilder's brigade—"I never saw a man fight so hard"—wounded severely in the battle on the Federal right, bled during the night and had to be chopped loose from the ground in the morning. His side wound had stuck to the frosty ground. It was freed carefully by comrades. But the bullet that hit his head so blinded him that he had to stay in a darkened room for five years. He survived to be a prosperous banker of Crawfordsville, Indiana, and serve on the Chickamauga National Military Park Commission.

During the night some of the Federal losses of the last combat were moderated. Cleburne's vicious assault had overlapped Richard Johnson's right brigade, Dodge's, and two of his regiments, the 77th Pennsylvania and the 79th Illinois, were taken in the rear. Substantially all of the Pennsylvanians and a good part of the Illinois regiment were made prisoners, along with brigade commander Dodge. But it proved impossible for the Confederates to hold them in the forest gloom and amid the battle confusion. The larger part, including Dodge, disappeared into the shadows and stealthily made their way back into the Federal lines.

The only comparable Confederate reverse during the night fighting—and that was spoken of as "slight"—was the capture of part of Preston Smith's brigade of Cheatham's division when it became disorganized for a time after its commander fell.

In the Federal army conversation turned to the poor performance of King's brigade of regulars when Baird's division came under attack early in the day. Generals Wood and Harker, who had come up through the regular army, dwelt on it and Wood thereafter was more sympathetic toward volunteers.

"The battle is not over yet," he said that night. "No doubt we will have to fight again tomorrow. If I were given my choice between regulars and volunteers, I would choose volunteer troops. They will 'stick'; you can fight them as long as you please. I say this from my experience with them at Stone River and in the battle today. The regulars are too sharp. They know when they are whipped but the volunteers don't; they will fight as long as they can pull a trigger."[2]

Orders were issued against fires all along the Confederate lines. They were not always complied with, but most of the battlefield was in utter darkness. Thin beams of the moon at the first quarter, often obscured by clouds and mist, penetrated the heavy foliage here and there. As one of the Confederates described it: "Dead and wounded all around us, friend and foe writhing in pain; litter bearers working to exhaustion . . . cries for water from the wounded rending the air, and yet a threatened night battle." The water situation was much better in the Southern than the Northern army because Chickamauga Creek could be reached, though for some it meant a walk of up to two miles through the dark night; and for the wounded lying in the woods it might as well have been a rivulet on the moon.

As after all battles, wretches stole through the woods looking for loot. One old soldier brought in a story that he had been out between the lines and had seen a "human vampire" hovering over a soldier who had a valuable watch, waiting for him to die. He did give the wounded man a drink. When the soldier died, the vulture relieved him of his watch and disappeared in the darkness.

Up the Chickamauga on the Confederate left, where Hood, Preston and Hindman held the line, few slept because the battle raged intermittently through the night—mostly exchanges of picket firing but swelling in volume at times with the booming of cannon. Here too sounded the cries of the wounded. Lewellyn A. Shaver of the 1st Battalion, Hilliard's "Alabama Legion," now of Gracie's brigade, said the night was so cold, the clothing so thin and the supply of blankets so inadequate that, with no fires allowed, very few in the legion slept at all.

Another distraction, partly to the ears but mainly psychological, was the ringing of the Federal axes. For soldiers about to fight again the next morning this sound beat on the eardrums and jangled the nerves. As at Gettysburg where Brigadier General John B. Gordon could not sleep amid the noise from Meade's men fortifying Culp's and Cemetery hills in his front, knowing the formidable line that would be reared above him by morning, so at Chicakamauga the Confederate soldiers turned and twisted while the battle-wearied Federals crashed down trees and fashioned abatis, certain that the lines which had been difficult enough when defended only by artillery and rifles would be forbidding barricades by daylight.

This agonizing labor continued during most of the night, at times along a line of five miles but mainly in front of Thomas. All through the night sounded the rumble of Federal wagons and artillery trains as Rosecrans shifted his forces and prepared to receive the assaults he knew were inevitable. He had long since abandoned all idea of the offensive. His aim was to maintain his army unbroken in the face of the merciless hammering.

The Texas Colonel Roger Quarles Mills, trying to sleep amid the commotion in the pine woods and finding it impossible, said he remembered no night of the war so distressing. One reason was that a wounded Federal officer between the lines in front of his regiment groaned so pitiably the men could not sleep either, but kept coming to him with requests that they be allowed to do something for "the Yank." He knew it would provoke firing from the Federals close by if there was stirring between the lines. Finally he had to yield and told his men to "do as you please but it's dangerous."

A few of the Texans took off their shoes, got a blanket and stealthily made their way through the deep darkness toward the groans. They brought the enemy officer back in their blanket, found he had bled profusely and was well-nigh frost-bitten from the cold. Again they forgot orders and built a fire behind an old house to make their enemy comfortable. Mills said it was the only fire on that part of the battlefield. Then as morning approached they went back to their places and prepared for the bitter fighting everyone knew would follow.[3]

Dr. Edwin L. Drake, who at one stage of Cleburne's intense battle found that he was one of nine men crowded behind a single average pine tree, said that some of Cleburne's wet men, indifferent to orders, built small brush fires to dry by. The Federal artillery would have none of it. As quickly as the flames disclosed the position the guns opened and skirmishers came creeping through the woods. They had to be repelled, and a night battle of some proportions resulted.

That was the story elsewhere on the field. Some of the 18th Tennessee who wanted to smoke invited bullets every time they lighted a match.

Possibly it was a harbinger of the events of the next day, but several noted the depression that ran along the Federal lines that night. Edwin K. Martin told how the 79th Pennsylvania of Baird's division sensed "something terrible and oppressive about the dark forest—something which one could feel but not describe." Later any number of them remarked on it. He thought the physical exhaustion of the men might have had some bearing. The lack of food and the empty canteens played a part, but there was a grim presentiment that was not lightened by the bursts of night fighting.

"Put the combatants in a woods so dense that the foliage obscures the Heavens, so black that you cannot distinguish friend from foe, then open the throats of ten thousand rifles and you have it," Martin explained.

While the 79th Pennsylvania was forging ahead earlier in this sporadic night battle an exploding shell killed the color sergeant, but before the flag touched the earth others of the color guard seized it and took it on. The incident was taken by the sculptor for the memorial to the regiment.[4]

Lieutenant Colonel James M. Ray of the 60th North Carolina, in Stovall's brigade, Breckinridge's division, told how the men, when they reached the battlefield that night, sensed the atmosphere charged with battle and quickly altered their attitude. "Curses were changed to prayers, cards in the pockets were replaced with Testaments and a quiet determination took the place of jests and ribaldry," he said.

They had marched that night "hour upon hour" coming down the Chickamauga from below Lee and Gordon's mill. They crossed at Alexander's bridge and it was near dawn before the division had cleared the creek and settled down for a short sleep. Then almost at once came the long roll—"a sound that like the rattlesnake's warning notes, never failed to put all hearers on the alert."

At daybreak the regiment was formed and ready. The soldiers noticed that the commanding officers of troops on their right and left were making speeches and called on their commander for some remarks. Ray stepped out in front of them.

"I hardly think it just the time for a speech," he said. "Later it may be necessary. We know full well what is before us. I am no more anxious for the conflict than the rest of you, but I mean to do my full duty and have confidence that you will do the same."

The men must have listened, for theirs was one of the stellar performances on the field that day.

After the hard fighting on the Confederate left, Hood, following the custom he had always practiced with General Lee in the Virginia army, rode to army headquarters to give Bragg an account of his corps' fighting and progress.

To his amazement, he encountered such thick gloom around the headquarters that he could have cut it with a dull bayonet. This was his first opportunity to meet the outstanding officers of the main western army of the Confederacy, some of whom he had known in old army days. Being a Kentuckian, he had been acquainted with Breckinridge, though he was about ten years his junior. They talked and Hood asserted that the army would put the Federals to flight on the next day.

Breckinridge had been sitting at the foot of a tree but when Hood made the prediction he leaped to his feet with delight. "My dear Hood," he exclaimed, "I am delighted to hear you say so. You give me renewed hope. God grant it may be so."

Hood appeared to be the only one present with an optimistic view of the next day's battle. The depression apparently led to his prompt departure when he had received orders from Bragg to attack after the troops on his right had gone into action. That was to be the battle plan, a succession of attacks from right to left, and as those procedures usually worked out it might mean that Hood's men would not be stepping off until afternoon or, as was the case with Ewell's corps on the extreme left at Gettysburg, until the approach of darkness.

Hood's men were poorly equipped for campaigning because they did not have their trains, not a single wagon or ambulance in fact. They had no reserve ammunition, merely the forty rounds each man carried in his cartridge box. As Hood said, except for this they were destitute of almost everything but pride and spirit. He had no camp equipment either and camped that night with Buckner.[5]

CHAPTER EIGHTEEN

Rosecrans Talks, McCook Sings

AFTER most of the fighting had died down, Rosecrans, according to his practice, called a council of war to meet at the Widow Glenn's at 11 P.M. The council concluded that if Bragg did not retreat—and there appeared to be some hope he would—the battle would be continued along the same lines on the next morning, Sunday the twentieth.

Garfield had a map of the battlefield on which, for the convenience of the council, he marked the position of the different divisions. There does not appear to have been any accurate summation of losses, though the corps commanders made estimates and they were clearly heavy. On the favorable side, as Rosecrans canvassed the situation, were the points that he now had a fairly continuous battle line, much shorter than when, at the beginning of the engagement, the army was scattered from Crawfish Springs to Kelly field; that he retained his grip on the La Fayette road; and that, having been on the defensive, he had not been dislodged, and might well claim victory as long as he held the field.

The little log house was packed with officers and a few observers, among them Dana, whose newspaper instincts did not sense the full drama of the event, for he chronicled it but briefly. The attentive John McDonald was somewhere around headquarters, eager but unable to break away to tell Bragg what he knew of the opinions reflected by the Yankee generals. McDonald, resident of the area of the battlefield where the fighting had begun, had been encountered by Wilder, who saw at once that he was well acquainted with the Chickamauga country and a good man to have available, and carried him off to army headquarters. Rosecrans made him a guide and later took him to Chattanooga and held him prisoner for ten weeks. He and his wife Priscilla had lived near the crossing of the La Fayette and Reed's bridge roads for seventeen years.

Rosecrans also picked up Robert Dyer for guide and information purposes. Dyer and his wife Carrie and family lived half a mile west of the crossing of the Brotherton and La Fayette roads. Of their five children, two sons, Spill and John, were in the Confederate army fighting at Chickamauga. The father had better luck than John McDonald and was able to escape before the end of the battle.

The Federal commander, who delighted in these round-robin night discussions, passed the ball around and asked everyone's views about the results of the battle that day and what should be done on the morrow. Ten or twelve officers participated. These included not only the three corps commanders, Thomas, Crittenden and McCook, but also Garfield, Horace Porter, Rosecrans' chief of ordnance and later the staff officer and close confidant and biographer of Grant, along with Dana and unidentified others. Thomas was exhausted, having marched all the previous night and fought a most difficult and uncertain battle all that day. Dana represented him as falling asleep every minute or so but awaking and sitting upright and attentive whenever the commanding general shot a question in his direction. He would put in his advice, invariably that "I would strengthen the left," then go back to sleep in his chair before Rosecrans could speak his rejoinder: "Where are we going to take it from?"[1]

Thomas' chaplain, Thomas B. Van Horne, who wrote with General Thomas' blessing and with his corps papers for a guide, gave a different view of the general's recommendations. Thomas proposed that the right and center of the Federal army should be pulled back from the region of the La Fayette road to the spurs of Missionary Ridge overlooking the Dry Valley road. With keen soldierly instinct he seemed to sense the weakness of the army's right, even though he had not inspected it.

After the assaults of Hood and Bushrod Johnson, the right had been recessed. It ran that evening from a point on the La Fayette road half a mile south of Brotherton's, thence across the fields to the Widow Glenn's, and on to the Dry Valley road. The right wing consequently faced southeast. Under Thomas' suggestion, the right would face south. Apparently assured at this stage that he could hold the La Fayette road and prevent Bragg from interposing his army between Rosecrans and Chattanooga, Thomas would have the right of the army cover securely the Dry Valley road running through McFarland's Gap.

Van Horne's view—and it may be taken as a reflection of Thomas'—was that this readjustment of the line would double the defensive strength of the army's right. Thomas would still have covered the area east of the La Fayette road from McDonald's to Kelly's and the right would have turned back to the strong defensive spur on which the Snodgrass house was situated.

Rosecrans was more satisfied than Thomas with the position into which the chance arrivals of the different units had thrown the army; and after everyone had offered suggestions he issued his orders that if Bragg did not retreat, the army would fight the next morning on substantially the same line it occupied on the nineteenth. Thomas was to draw his line back a bit and make it more compact, but he still would face mainly east, half a mile on the east side of the La Fayette road. His line would run from the McDonald house on the left and, moving south, would encompass the Kelly farm and bend back and cross the La Fayette road in the vicinity of Poe's, where there was a cathedral-like forest of great trees relatively free of underbrush. Thomas had already ordered that his line be strengthened with abatis and now while the generals meditated, his men, mindful of the desperate encounter that faced them, labored with axes—in marked contrast to the manner in which the night had been spent idly between the two days at Shiloh.

Rosecrans ordered McCook to close his two divisions on Thomas. His third division, Richard Johnson's, was still detached and serving on the left under Thomas' personal orders. Similarly Crittenden had one division, Palmer's, detached and forming a part of Thomas' line. Crittenden's other two divisions, those of

Wood and VanCleve, were to be held in reserve in the center at the junction of Thomas and McCook.

Rosecrans took the precaution of having the orders written and then read to the assembled generals. That done, the time had arrived when by custom it was the period for relaxation and social exchanges at headquarters. Hot coffee was brought in and while it was being sipped the blithe commander of the 20th Corps, Major General Alexander McD. McCook, lately the instructor in infantry tactics at West Point, entertained the high-ranking crowd by singing a plaintive love ballad that had been making the rounds for the last fifteen years, entitled "The Hebrew Maiden's Lament." [2]The song, of German origin, told the story of a Jewish girl torn between the faith of her fathers and love for a Gentile youth, and of how, out of family loyalty, she abandoned her loved one.

The English words by C. Beaunom Burkhardt were set to P. Lindpainter's mournful melody:

> In that sombre chamber yonder,
> Father's taper still burns bright;
> Bending to his breast his aged,
> Care-worn face he prays tonight.
>
> Open wide before the righteous
> Lies the Talmud which he reads,
> And his child e'en is forgotten,
> 'Fore his God, and Israel's deeds.
>
> List'ning then a few short moments,
> I may by this lattice stand,
> And may watch yon little window
> Of our neighbor's nigh at hand.
>
> Oh! in yonder friendly chamber,
> Whence the light now peepeth forth,
> Lives of Christian youths the fairest,
> Lives my life, my all on earth . . .

Dearest youth whose care worn image,
Graven in my heart will be,
Ah thou seest not the bitter,
Bitter tears I shed for thee . . .

Donn Piatt, who referred to him as "the genial, full-stomached McCook," said "he owed his elevation to favoritism, the McCook and Stanton families having been at an early day almost one in their daily intercourse and affiliations." Both were from the Steubenville area.

The observant fellow-Ohioan John Beatty not only called him a "chucklehead," and one affecting the "rough and ready style," whatever that may have meant in 1863, but likened him to Wood as given to swearing "like pirates."

Beatty happened to be with Negley during the Tullahoma campaign when McCook, whose corps was near by, called. Beatty's diary entry after the meeting read: "He looks, if possible, more like a blockhead than ever, and it is astonishing to me that he should be permitted to retain command of a corps for a single hour."

Everyone in all the corps knew him quite well because of his habit of riding out with his wife and staff. On such trips, as in headquarters, he had the bearing and front to give the casual observer the impression that he was an outstanding military leader.

The McCook family as a whole did such notable work for the Federal cause that they came to be known as "the Fighting McCooks." Alexander's father and eight sons and his uncle and five sons were in the army. Some of them gave highly distinguished service, some their lives, to their cause. Alexander, the only West Point graduate among them, no doubt would have fared better in other commands or on another field, but he scarcely possessed the quick resourcefulness or sturdiness required for corps command in this battle of tense drama and rapid change, a battle fought under such blind conditions that a high degree of military intuition had to be brought into play. Buell and Rosecrans had pushed McCook along to command three splendid divisions, but either might well have described him, as Napoleon did Berthier with less cause, as "a gosling I have made an eagle." The advancement has been used with some justification in contending that while Rosecrans knew strategy he did not understand people.

Even if on no other basis than that McCook was a bad-luck man, Rosecrans might have reflected seriously on giving the corps to another general. McCook's service at Perryville and Stone's River had been anything but satisfactory. It is impossible to make a case, as some have undertaken to do, that Rosecrans trailed along with McCook in order to remain in good standing with Stanton. Having done everything else possible to belittle and snub the Secretary of War openly, almost from the moment he took command of the army, Rosecrans would scarcely have hesitated about throwing McCook back on him because of any obsequiousness.

McCook shaved his face, which was uncommon. He had the misfortune to be engaged in this time-wasting pursuit when Cleburne and McCown hit his corps and rolled it up at Stone's River. Being caught off guard, he did not have much chance to put up a resolute defense, but was saved by Thomas' strength in holding the center. Thomas wore a full beard and it might be cited as a case where shaving almost lost a battle. But the reasons for McCook's failure were deeper than his whiskers, or lack of them. At Perryville, where Bragg was supposed to have been defeated, McCook suffered the humiliation of seeing not only many of his men captured, but also some of his staff officers, his servants and his personal carriage and baggage carried off by the retreating foe.

He has been referred to as "dashing"—but at Chickamauga it was in the wrong direction—and as a "hail-fellow-well-met who did not take war too seriously," but it was more from lack of depth than willful indifference.

McCook was thirty-two years old at Chickamauga, a West Point graduate in 1852, thirtieth in his class, and a captain in the regular army when the war came. He went in as colonel of the 1st Ohio and was commended for the handling of the regiment at the first Manassas. Promotions came rapidly and by the time of Bragg's Kentucky campaign he was a major general commanding a corps of Buell's army. Acting beyond his orders he brought on the battle of Perryville, for which Buell censured him, but when

Rosecrans took over the command from Buell he was continued in command of a corps.

Early in the war McCook was the object of complaint as being a "slave-catcher," because when fugitive slaves came to his command in Tennessee he listed them and held them for their owners, should they appear. According to the Ohio newspaperman Whitelaw Reid, his political views before the war were "Southern and Democratic." McCook's trouble, in Reid's opinion, was that his familiarity with tactics from teaching the subject at West Point was mistaken for military genius, and: "High promotions naturally ensued long before he had any opportunity to grow . . . up to them, and . . . repeated disappointments in his performance led to a revulsion which went, perhaps, as far to the other extreme."[3]

Although there was much talk and some festivity about headquarters that night, the high command maintained a surprising isolation from those who had been on the actual firing line. That is a fair assumption from the treatment accorded Palmer. His division had been in the heavy fighting virtually all day and Palmer himself had not slept for forty-eight hours. When the battle died down he got some supper and then went to look for a superior officer to get orders for the next day. After some groping he located the army headquarters at the Widow Glenn's but the door was closed against him. He was informed that he could see neither Rosecrans nor his corps commander Crittenden. The rebuff would have seemed incredible except that Palmer reported it himself, though he did not specify the hour when he reached the Widow Glenn's. More likely it was while Rosecrans was holding forth with his council of war than while McCook was supplying entertainment for tired generals and assistant secretaries. He rode back to his division and went to sleep. Next morning he had the satisfaction of talking with a general not too occupied to receive his reports and give him orders—Thomas.

When the council at the Widow Glenn's broke up and the generals went back to their commands, Dana and Horace Porter slept on the floor and the wires to Washington were silenced.[4]

CHAPTER NINETEEN

Rosecrans Delivers a Costly Rebuke

THOMAS left the Widow Glenn's after midnight but did not get back to his corps until 2 A.M. There he was confronted with a report from Baird, who held the army's left. Baird said his division would not stretch all the way to the Reed's bridge road near which stood the McDonald house, and still be strong enough to hold in the middle.

Thomas consequently sent a message to Rosecrans asking that Negley's division, of his own corps, the last division to arrive from Crawfish Springs, and virtually unengaged during the first day of the battle, be sent to the left of the army to fall in behind Baird and thus give reassurance that this part of the lines, on which the safety of the army was so dependent, would not be crushed or turned.

Rosecrans replied that Negley's division would be sent immediately. The movement of this division and its consequent replacement in the line by Wood's division would come to have a decisive bearing on the battle of the twentieth, but its progress toward the left was slow indeed for such an officer as Thomas, who as he catnapped that night seems to have had his subconscious mind on a watch for the arrival of Negley. Dawn came, then 7 A.M., but not Negley.

Thomas meantime had found a protruding root of a tree near the Snodgrass house in rear of his lines and using this knot he laid his hat and sword close by, pulled his coat over him and slept. The old man George Washington Snodgrass told the story of it, but not without dispute. One of the soldiers, E. P. Burlingame, insisted that Thomas had his bivouac not at the Snodgrass place but about 500 yards west and a bit north of Poe's. This would not have been too far from Snodgrass', but they clearly were not talking about the hump of the same big oak tree.

The tree old man Snodgrass referred to—probably the authentic one—was close beside a tree into which a horseshoe had been driven long before the battle. The tree had grown around the shoe and embedded part of it, leaving an iron loop to which a horse might be hitched. The outside edge of the curve of the horseshoe was still visible in the 1890's but the inside of the shoe had become fully embedded. Here Thomas tied his horse that night. Nobody has ever tried to advance the interests of any other tree for the distinction.

Near by was a tree with the root that arched itself three or four inches above the ground, which Snodgrass long pointed to as Thomas' pillow. This was fairly close to the little Snodgrass log house and was not Burlingame's tree at all. Possibly the root grew uncomfortable and Thomas tried a second tree.[1]

Sunday morning came, cold on the hills, foggy in the bottoms. Officers at headquarters looked through the haze and smoke at the early sun, rising blood red. Garfield pointed to it and said, "It is ominous. It will indeed be a day of blood."

Rosecrans has been blamed severely for not retiring during the night into Chattanooga. This criticism is, of course, based on the conclusions of history and not on the information of the moment, which was the only thing available to Rosecrans that night of September 19. Retreat into Chattanooga was out of the question. Withdrawal in such a heavily-wooded country would have been difficult enough in daylight; impossible—if such a word enters into the purview of capable generalship—at night. Certainly Rosecrans could not have pulled back any kind of an organized force through McFarland's Gap in the darkness. The army would have disintegrated into a disorganized mass. No doubt the gap and the pass of Rossville might have been held until he could have reformed in Chattanooga, but he would have conceded defeat on the nineteenth, which would not have been justified by what had actually occurred on that day. Surely his best plan was to remain on the field and be content with the defensive. Bragg might batter the Confederate army to pieces against his lines. If unable to dislodge him, it would be Bragg who would be compelled to withdraw. If the soldiers in the gloomy woods did have forbidding presentiments, they were not shared by Rosecrans at headquarters.

By shutting his eyes to what seemed unpleasant incidentals, such as the appearance of some of Longstreet's men on the battlefield, Rosecrans might well consider the events of the day salutary and the prospects of the morrow brilliant. He had thwarted decisively Bragg's effort to turn his left and had imposed staggering losses on the enemy corps and divisions which had assaulted Thomas in turn rather than in mass. He had been able to fill in his center and unite his wings while the battle was being waged, always a difficult procedure. His own army had been severely punished but he had in Negley and Sheridan divisions that had been only lightly involved, while his reserve corps under Granger at Rossville, and Lytle's brigade on his right, had not been in action.

At the end of the first day Bragg did hold all the ground over which the battle had been fought but he could claim no more than that and it was far short of impressive. The men in both armies had fought with supreme courage but had fought indecisively. Further bloody combat would be necessary to determine a victor.

Something of Rosecrans' confidence was reflected at 6 A.M. on the twentieth as he rode along the lines. When he arrived in front of the 6th Ohio of Grose's brigade, Palmer's division, he appeared washed out from lack of sleep, but his words were enthusiastic: "Fight today as well as you did yesterday and we shall whip them!"

"I did not like the way he looked," said one of the Ohioans, "but of course felt cheered, and did not allow myself to think of any such thing as defeat."[2]

Through the morning frost and haze, Rosecrans passed along his entire army, followed by his staff and the omnipresent Dana. Instead of merely inspecting, he tore things up considerably everywhere he went. Negley had not yet moved, and the commanding general directed him to go to Thomas at once. Then he told

McCook to move his line farther back and close in to the left in order to compensate for the departure of Negley. Similar instructions to close on the left were issued to Crittenden. Almost since the first gun had been fired, the army had been drifting toward the left and now considerable nudging was added to the process.

Then Rosecrans went to see the left himself. The frequent criticism that he did not exercise close enough control over his formations is not borne out by a review of his actions. His tendency was to interfere too impetuously with the placement of smaller units and to leave little for his corps commanders, with the exception of Thomas. On reaching Thomas' position Rosecrans was told the enemy still appeared to be moving toward the Federal left. Rosecrans answered, "You must move up, too, as fast as they do." Thomas then told him how his own corps and the two divisions he had on loan were posted.

Thomas, with the enthusiasm of a born fighter and with what seemed almost the guileless exuberance of youth, lost his reticence when he talked with the commanding general about the battle of the nineteenth.

"Whenever I touched their flanks they broke, General, they broke," he said excitedly.

Then when he saw that the Cincinnati newspaperman Shanks was within hearing, he flushed, as was not uncommon with him when caught off guard, and drew back into his shell of reserve.[3]

If Negley should arrive, Thomas would have under his command three fifths of the Federal army present on the field, excepting Granger's reserve corps at Rossville. He would have his own four divisions of Baird, Negley, Brannan and Reynolds, plus Richard Johnson of McCook's corps and Palmer of Crittenden's corps. This would leave to McCook the divisions of Jefferson C. Davis and Sheridan, and to Crittenden the divisions of Wood and VanCleve.

After reviewing the left, Rosecrans shared Thomas' belief that the Confederate attack would again fall on that flank. He went back to prod Negley, who was exhibiting unaccountable reluctance to get under way. When the commander reached the center he saw to his amazement that Negley had not yet moved, nor had McCook brought over his troops or consolidated his line in order to compensate for Negley's departure. In short, nothing had happened.

Bragg, long inured to such contempt of his orders, might be tolerant of it, but not Rosecrans. None could let loose a greater torrent of high anger and vituperation. The day was advancing and Bragg long since had been expected to strike. His guns might sound at any instant. Apparently giving up hope for the moment that McCook would be able to extract Negley, and anxious to have that general en route to Thomas, Rosecrans told Crittenden to put Wood's division into the line to fill the place Negley occupied. Then he rode off to the right, found McCook, told him his line was still too thin and strung out, showed him where to correct it, and again went back to his center—only to find that his division commanders were moving with the deliberation of pachyderms and that Wood was not yet in line, nor Negley in motion. Negley's excuse was that Wood had not come to take his place.

The commanding general himself started off John Beatty's brigade of Negley's division toward the left, and its arrival proved most fortuitous. Negley then got under way but went on a route that took him not to Thomas but out of the Army of the Cumberland. A little later Ambrose Bierce of Hazen's brigade saw Negley going off on a tangent that would lead him into a quiet sector, and offered to show the way toward the fighting. Bierce, a penetrating observer and writer as well as a self-educated topographical engineer, noticed that Negley's mind seemed to be wandering and that at this moment it was "back in Chattanooga behind the breastworks."[4]

When Rosecrans found Wood, on whom he appeared to place the principal blame for the slow departure of Negley, he upbraided him severely in the presence of his staff. It proved the most costly reprimand Rosecrans ever delivered. Wood did not repeat the language in his official account, but none had a more caustic tongue than Rosecrans when he became excited and in this instance he was agitated into a fury.

"What is the meaning of this, sir?" he shouted to Wood, according to one version of his remarks. "You have disobeyed my specific orders. By your damnable negligence you are endangering the safety of the entire army, and, by God, I will not tolerate it. Move your division at once, as I have instructed, or the consequences will not be pleasant for yourself."

Whether the admonition was in precisely these words is immaterial, but succeeding events warrant an assumption that they could not have been less severe. Wood merely saluted and ordered his men to march. He still had the three brigades he had taken into the battle on the previous afternoon on the army's right. The commanding general had assigned Barnes's brigade of VanCleve's division to act under his orders. His division, depleted by the detachment of Wagner to garrison Chattanooga, was thus brought back to full strength.

He had passed the night behind the lines on the eastern slope of Missionary Ridge but now stepped forward and occupied an interval of about a quarter of a mile in the line in a fringe of woods behind the house and cultivated fields of the Brotherton farm. Barnes was on the left, in contact with the right of Brannan's division; Harker in the center, and Buell on the right.

His instructions were to be prepared to repel any enemy advance but not to initiate an engagement. When he threw out skirmishers across the Brotherton farm to the east he stirred up a hornet's nest showing that the enemy was in force in the woods immediately in his front. Colonel Frederick A. Bartleson took part of his 100th Illinois too near the enemy and was dropped from his horse severely wounded.

On Wood's right was Davis' division and beyond that Sheridan's. Rosecrans continued to shift his brigades about during the morning but the most important event that occurred in the early hours, as far as the fortunes of the day were concerned, was his merciless rebuke to Wood for failure or at least lack of promptness in obeying his orders. Wood could not have been very dilatory. On him fell the wrath Rosecrans had been nursing all morning against Negley and McCook.[5]

to the United States after the German revolution of 1848. At the time of Chickamauga he still spoke a broken English which caused some of the other regiments of the brigade to smile, good-naturedly at his oral orders. As a brigade commander he had had the bad luck to be away from his troops just at the moment when Bragg struck at Stone's River, and had been captured.

Colonel Gleason had taken command of the 9th Indiana after Shiloh. This was the last regiment raised by the state, since, out of respect for the five Hoosier regiments that served in the Mexican War, the first five numerals were set aside and not employed in designating Indiana Civil War regiments.

Brigadier General Richard W. Johnson, a Kentuckian of the West Point class of 1849, was an able soldier plagued by adversity. His division had been on the extreme right at Stone's River, where the main impact of Bragg's attack fell. Johnson lost men, ground and guns. He had been since the spring of Shiloh but a greater reverse between Shiloh and Stone's River came when with scarcely any he was detached to intercept the Confederate cavalryman John Morgan, then raiding in Tennessee. Morgan, instead of being bagged, captured him and about half his men.

Heavy additional reinforcements were soon available to Thomas. Palmer's division of Crittenden's corps and Reynolds' division of Thomas' corps entered the line in turn on the right of Richard Johnson to check the attack of Cheatham and meet the advance of Buckner's corps.

Palmer's division of Crittenden's corps had followed Richard Johnson's division up the La Fayette road from Crawfish Springs, reaching the battle area from 10 A.M. to 11:30 P.M. Thomas sent it into line on the right of R. Johnson, in the forest east of the Poe farm. Craft's brigade in advance struck the Confederates at 11:30 A.M., near the Brock house, south of the Brotherton road leading to Reed's bridge. The brigade sustained three desperate charges from brigadier General Marcus J. Wright's Tennesseans, but according to Craft, "not a straggler was observed going to the rear." The men fought confidently on both sides until 12:30 P.M., and during the lull of an hour that followed, ammunition was sent forward and the cartridge boxes were replenished for the more serious business

PART **III**

LONGSTREET:
Whirlwind in the
Forest

CHAPTER TWENTY

Old Peter Reaches the Battlefield

Events of the highest significance were occurring in Bragg's army. Longstreet reached headquarters at 11 p.m. on the nineteenth. Handsome in his new gray uniform, the tall, robust, bellicose lieutenant general, already established in history as an eminent tactician, left the cars at Catoosa about 2 p.m. This small platform and woodshed where the locomotives got fuel was the nearest rail approach to the Chickamauga battlefield. It is no longer in existence.

Accompanying Longstreet were the inseparable Lieutenant Colonel G. Moxley Sorrel, his chief of staff, one of the reasons for Longstreet's sure handling of his corps, and Lieutenant Colonel P. T. Manning, his chief of ordnance. Most of his staff officers and aides were on later trains, as were the horses.

For two hours Longstreet and the two colonels had to walk back and forth along the Catoosa platform, listening to the far-off roar that told them the battle of Chickamauga was being fought. The absence of any staff officer or guides from Bragg to meet them informed them also that the commanding general of the Army of Tennessee was either indifferent to their coming or lacked the graces and amenities customarily associated with high military command that would suggest recognition of the arrival of so distinguished an officer as the second in command of the Army of Northern Virginia.

Some of Longstreet's familiars were missing. E. Porter Alexander, his main reliance with the guns, was working his way across South Carolina and up from Augusta. Lafayette McLaws, whose division had crushed Sickles in the Peach Orchard salient at Gettysburg and brought Meade's army close to disaster, was back in

Atlanta. His place at the head of Longstreet's first division had been taken by the always reliable South Carolinian, Joseph B. Kershaw. Kershaw's troops, along with those of the Mississippi Brigadier General Benjamin G. Humphreys, successor to the lamented Barksdale who fell at Gettysburg, had preceded Longstreet by a short time and were marching toward the battlefield.

With the force already present under Hood which had fought on Bragg's left on the nineteenth, these acquisitions would mean that Bragg was being reinforced by five brigades of the Army of Northern Virginia. They were those of Law, Robertson, Benning, Kershaw and Humphreys. The remaining brigades of Hood's and McLaws' divisions would not come in time for the engagement.

The horses arrived at 4 P.M. Since there was no unloading platform for animals, Longstreet jumped his mount from the car, as did the two others. As speedily as the saddles could be put on the backs of the horses the party was riding toward the sound of the guns. Someone at Catoosa told them to "follow the main road," on which was moving the wreckage of a great battle—ambulances carrying the wounded, wagons lumbering along in both directions, ammunition carts, stragglers and fugitives. While it was easy to distinguish the main road in the late afternoon, twilight was soon on them, then darkness. The route became difficult and they confused. Longstreet thought when he wrote of it that the woodlands along the side of the road were "quite open, so that we could see and be seen," but Sorrel said they "wandered by various roads and across small streams through the growing darkness of the Georgia forest." In any event, they were suddenly hauled up by the challenge of a sentry who apparently did not drop his R's, for the Confederate party was at once suspicious.

"Who comes there?" rang the challenge.

"Friends," was the prompt answer.

The sentry was no more reassured than Longstreet. As they parleyed in the darkness, either the general or one of his party asked the guard what his outfit was. He answered in numerals to designate his brigade and division, which alerted Longstreet further because the Southern custom was to name brigades and divisions after their commanders whereas the North more frequently used numbers. The fact was, as Sorrel reported it, they were in the "very center" of a strong enemy picket. Where or who it was cannot be determined, but since Longstreet referred to the sounds of the battle on his right as he rode toward the field, he had probably brushed into one of Minty's or Dan McCook's patrols bivouacked far down on one of the roads from Rossville east of the Chickamauga, in the rear of Bragg's army.

Longstreet also noticed some obstructions on the road ahead which put him as much on guard as did the sentry's answer. The moon, though at the quarter, was bright and the sky at the time cloudless. To make a run for it would be to invite a bullet in the back. Longstreet turned to the two colonels and said in unperturbed voice, loudly so the guard might hear, "Let us ride down a little and find a better crossing."

They rode into the cover of some large trees, untouched by the bullets of the surprised guard, who according to Sorrel fired hastily. Once in the shade, they were able to turn back in safety and ride at a gallop to regain the main road from which they had strayed. Receiving better information from a civilian, they at length reached Bragg's headquarters.

The commanding general was asleep in an ambulance but Longstreet did not hesitate to arouse him. The two talked for an hour, none others being present. Said Sorrel, "An hour was quite enough to settle the plan and details, since nothing could be simpler than the operations proposed for Rosecrans' destruction." Then the lieutenant general and his staff officers pulled up some leaves and made beds under the great oak and hickory trees and slept in the open until dawn.

At their conference Bragg advised Longstreet that he was dividing his army into two wings. Lieutenant General Polk would command the right wing, composed of the divisions of Breckinridge and Cleburne, in Hill's corps; Cheatham's division; the two divisions of Walker's corps, Liddell's and Gist's. Forrest on the right was directly under Bragg. The left wing under Longstreet would consist of the divisions of Law and Kershaw, comprising Hood's corps; Stewart, Bushrod Johnson, Hindman and Preston. Stewart's and Preston's divisions formed Buckner's corps.

Wheeler's cavalry was still on the army's left flank where it had little more part in the battle than to neutralize the Federal cavalry under Brigadier General Robert B. Mitchell.

None could expect much understanding or companionship between the irascible, dyspeptic Bragg and the blunt, domineering, never-wrong Longstreet and they were not forthcoming. The hour-long conference was their only contact until late in the battle and thereafter relations grew continually less pleasant.

As Sorrel expressed it, "the order of the day was simple in the extreme." The army already was in position. When the battle was joined the attack would be taken up from right to left until the entire army would be advancing against the enemy.

Before Longstreet's arrival, Bragg had given instructions to this effect to Polk, who had visited army headquarters at 9 P.M. Polk was not pleased with the division of the army into two wings because it was in effect a rebuff to D. H. Hill, newly appointed a lieutenant general especially for this campaign. He would have a subordinate role in the battle to that of the other lieutenant generals, Longstreet and Polk.

Polk's idea was that instead of two wings, the army should have right, center and left divisions, each under a lieutenant general. How firmly he advanced this suggestion to Bragg is not clear, but it was discussed sufficiently to bring out the fact that Bragg still nursed his anger against Hill for the failure to bag Negley in McLemore's Cove; that he thought Hill was insubordinate and, quite obviously, that he wanted to insulate himself from his fellow North Carolinian during the battle and deal with him only through Polk. In view of the fact that relations between Bragg and Polk had been strained over a considerable period, Bragg's desire to deal solely with Polk showed that his dislike of Hill already had become keen, though their association had been brief.

Bragg's orders for Polk to attack with his wing at daylight were delivered orally. The plan was a renewal of that of the nineteenth. Bragg's aim still was to turn the Federal left, cut Rosecrans off from Chattanooga and drive him back into McLemore's Cove, where fate would be kind to him if he were not captured.

After Bragg gave his orders, Polk requested what was normal

in a general beginning an attack—more troops. He said the fighting
of the nineteenth showed that Rosecrans was massing his army
toward the Confederate right, while Granger's corps in Rossville
would be on his flank when he, with Bragg's right wing, undertook
to envelop the Federal left. Bragg was not so sure Rosecrans had
concentrated in that direction heavily, but believed him still in
force near Lee and Gordon's mill. He thought Polk had ample
troops.

En route to his headquarters at Alexander's bridge—the place
where he told Bragg he could be reached, Polk met Breckinridge,
who had just crossed Alexander's bridge with his division of men
fatigued from their difficult march over the crowded roadway
leading down the Chickamauga. Time was allowed them to sleep
awhile in a field, but Polk directed the division commander, who
according to Bragg's plan would launch the attack against the
Federal left, to have his men in attack formation by dawn. Then
from his headquarters Polk issued orders to Hill, who commanded
Breckinridge and Cleburne, to make the daylight attack. He ordered Cheatham to follow on Hill's left and directed Walker to
hold his corps in reserve. These orders, in writing, were given to
couriers for immediate delivery.

Everything appeared to be in proper order, but Bragg had been
guilty of one bad slip-up. He had not yet notified Hill that Polk
had been placed in command of the right wing, and Hill consequently was not advised that he was supposed to be acting under
Polk's orders.

Longstreet, up early, rode at once to the left wing of the army
to take over his new command. The divisions placed under his
direction had never before acted in concert, nor was he acquainted
with the quality of the troops or the combat ability of most of the
officers. The first of his stipulations to General Lee, that he have
opportunity to win the confidence of the men before leading them
in action, obviously could not be complied with because the battle
had been joined and would have to be fought through to a conclusion. He was of course intimate with five of the left-wing
brigades and it was to his subordinate Hood that he rode first to
begin his preparations for the day.

Hood already was arranging his columns for attack when he saw "Old Peter" Longstreet approaching, riding through the woods. Always interested in the attitude of the individual soldier and reluctant to expend men except for grand results, Longstreet's first inquiry was respecting the spirit of the troops, how they had entered into the fighting on the afternoon before and how the enemy had met their assaults. Hood told him he had never seen better feeling among officers and men, said they had pressed the enemy back fully a mile on the afternoon of the nineteenth and would do even better before sunset on the twentieth. Longstreet replied with confidence. As Hood later related it:

"This distinguished general instantly responded with that confidence which had so often contributed to his extraordinary success, that we would *of course* whip and drive them from the field."

Remembering the dismal, down-at-the-mouth attitude he had encountered at Bragg's headquarters on the night before, Hood told Longstreet how delighted he was to hear such sentiments, and added that Longstreet was the first general he had come up with since his arrival who was talking in terms of victory.

After he had reviewed with Hood the matter of posting the troops, Longstreet went to see his old West Point roommate, the tall, cultivated, urbane professor of mathematics, Alexander P. Stewart. Stewart saw him riding unescorted even by a staff officer. Work had been assigned to every one of his staff in the preparations being made to take the left wing into action.

Stewart was one of the most entertaining conversationalists in the army. (In later years, as a member of the Chickamauga National Military Park Commission, he would master perhaps more than any other individual of either side the details of this complicated battle.) As he and Longstreet talked briefly of old times the conversation could not have missed touching on Longstreet's other roommate, the near-genius Rosecrans who commanded the great army awaiting them on the other side of the La Fayette road.

That night the Federal army received minor, the Confederate major reinforcements. Lytle's brigade of Sheridan's division, which had accompanied the baggage of McCook's corps all the way from Alpine and which on the first day of the battle had remained at

Lee and Gordon's mill, moved up to the Widow Glenn's. Every unit of Rosecrans' three corps was now on the field, except one brigade of Wood's division.

On the Confederate side, Breckinridge's fresh division had crossed Chickamauga Creek, had passed across Cleburne's rear and had taken position on Bragg's extreme right. Kelly's and Gracie's brigades had reached Preston's division. Gist's division, which included the units that had pressured the engineer into service at the point of a pistol at Rome, Georgia, had been augmented to fill out Walker's corps. The arrival of Longstreet's remaining units completed Bragg's army, the largest that had been assembled by the Confederacy in the western theater of the war.

The order of the two armies as they lined up to battle each other on the morning of Sunday, September 20, was as follows:

FEDERAL	CONFEDERATE
Baird	Breckinridge
Richard Johnson	Cleburne
Palmer	Cheatham (Recessed)
Reynolds	Walker (Recessed)
Brannan	Stewart
Wood	Bushrod Johnson
VanCleve (Recessed)	Hood
Negley (Recessed)	Kershaw
Davis	Hindman
Sheridan	Preston

Granger with the Federal reserve corps was still at Rossville. VanCleve was behind Brannan. On the Confederate side, Cheatham was in support of Breckinridge and Walker was in support of Cleburne.

CHAPTER TWENTY-ONE

Paralysis on Bragg's Right

MAINLY because chance had thrown the first troops arriving from the Army of Northern Virginia to Bragg's left, where Longstreet would naturally have the command, the conduct of the army's right wing fell to Leonidas Polk, whose controversies with Bragg already had rocked the Army of Tennessee and called into play President Davis' full conciliatory powers.

Polk stood apart in the Southern army because in many respects he was still more prelate than soldier. While he seemed to enjoy the trappings of high command, and was reputed to have the most elegant staff between the Rapidan and the Mississippi, he was less versed in battle tactics than some of his subordinates—notably Cleburne and Cheatham, who understood how to get the maximum from their troops and were admired more for their military insight than for any dominant personality such as Polk might claim. Nor was Polk's attitude toward Bragg as much cheery support as irksome submission.

Polk's family connections were distinguished. His grandfather Thomas Polk had served as a brigadier general under General Nathaniel Greene, had helped draft the Mecklenburg resolutions for independence, and was a founder of both the University of North Carolina, the first of the state universities, and of the town of Charlotte. His father William Polk likewise was a soldier of the Revolution who became a large landowner in North Carolina and Tennessee. Leonidas was a fairly close kinsman of President James K. Polk, who was a great-nephew of Brigadier General Thomas Polk.

Leonidas, born in Raleigh in 1806, was in the class of 1827 at

West Point, in the period of Lee, Jefferson Davis, Joseph E. Johnston and Magruder, but he resigned as a brevet second lieutenant five months after he was graduated and commissioned and began theological studies for a ministerial career. His abrupt transition from the military to the church resulted from the inspirational leadership of a chaplain who appeared at West Point during his fourth year, Dr. Charles P. McIlvaine, later Episcopal Bishop of Ohio, who aroused the cadet corps spiritually "as by a thunderbolt."

Polk progressed in the church and was Bishop of the Southwest stationed in New Orleans when the war came. His close friend President Davis gave him a commission in the Confederate army. He had the distinction, rare if ever duplicated in the line, of jumping, after thirty-four years in civilian life, from brevet second lieutenant to major general.

When he shed the cloth and took up the sword he was rebuked by his fellow bishop William Meade, who said he already had a commission in a different kind of army. Polk's attitude to the war could be seen from his reply:

"I shall only prove the more faithful to it [the church] by doing all that lies in me to bring this unhallowed and unnatural war to a speedy and happy close. We of the Confederate States are the last bulwarks of civil and religious liberty; we fight for our hearthstones and our altars; above all, we fight for a race that has been by Divine Providence entrusted to our most sacred keeping."[1]

As a minister Polk had never attained the eloquence of the chaplain who moved him to lead the "praying squad" at West Point. He was rated a dry speaker but he possessed a magnificent military presence, which for many seemed a substitute for sound generalship. His influence was so strong in the army and behind the lines, and Bragg's so weak, that the bishop-general appeared to take some advantage of his commanding officer. If he did not treat Bragg with actual contempt, he did withhold a measure of enthusiasm and confidence that would be likely to inspire the most diligent and unquestioning execution of his chief's orders. If he had not been a widely popular bishop who enjoyed the President's close friendship, he might have been looked on as a marplot.

Even though he may not have been the instigator of the cabal against Bragg after the retreat from Stone's River, his prestige gave elevation to it and his own disquiet became so pronounced that he wrote President Davis about the dissatisfaction in the army and suggested the appointment of another commander.

The final break came after Chickamauga. When Lieutenant Colonel David Urquhart of Bragg's staff saw an order from Bragg placing Polk under arrest, he went to Bragg's tent to dissuade him from issuing it. Bragg held up the paper pending overnight reflection. But as one might expect, the general's strict sense of duty triumphed. Next morning he summoned Urquhart, thanked him for his intercession, said he appreciated that execution of the order would arouse feeling against him, but "he felt that the urgent exactions of discipline made General Polk's arrest absolutely requisite." So Polk was put under arrest, President Davis had to intercede on his behalf, and Bragg's popularity again took a plunge.

Though Joseph E. Johnston's inspection trip to the Army of Tennessee after Stone's River had tended to alleviate temporarily the strain between Bragg and his generals, Urquhart made it clear that the situation had worsened again before Chickamauga. Bragg was not entirely at fault. The bishop had been supreme as a prelate and did not appear to enjoy or understand fully a subordinate role except on his own terms. He had disclosed earlier in the war that he was not above studying a situation and deliberately disobeying orders if he considered his own judgment better. In the Perryville campaign, when Bragg at Lexington learned that Buell was advancing from Louisville, he ordered Polk (sending two copies in writing) to advance from Bardstown and strike Buell in the flank and rear while Bragg with Kirby Smith hit him in front. Polk had been under orders to retire to Bryantsville. Polk scrutinized Bragg's orders, laid them before a council of war and decided to disobey them and follow the original plan. He did notify Bragg so that he would not attack Buell with Kirby Smith's troops unaided. Whether for good or bad, it was disobedience.

Large, erect, striking—"the first glance revealed him as a man to be obeyed"—Polk had many commendable qualities. He had disclosed his fearlessness on the field, where he would die. At Perryville he had mistakenly ridden into an Indiana regiment. He had bluffed it out and issued commands in the dull light until he could regain his own lines. His dark eyes sparked fire and his thin mouth was compressed grimly with resolute purpose. Though he had the consolation of a deep faith, he was inclined to be pessimistic. Mrs. Chesnut referred to him as "a splendid fellow" but became a bit confused in refuting the charge that he slept when he should have been attacking, saying "he has too good a conscience to sleep so soundly." Ordinarily a good conscience would seem to invite sleep. What she was apparently trying to say was that the bishop should not be criticized.[2]

Bragg, rarely resourceful in dealing with personal situations, clearly erred in giving Polk command of the right wing at Chickamauga, whatever may have been his rank. There were other recourses. He might have made Polk second in command of the army, as Halleck had done with Grant when he wanted to get shut of him in the Corinth campaign. This would have relegated Polk to a minor role.

Another and not uncommon method of dealing with such a situation would have been for Bragg to pitch his headquarters on the right near those of Polk, perhaps in the vicinity of Jay's sawmill, where he could personally supervise the beginning of the attack. He could have kept either Polk or Hill, or both, in his presence until the battle was well under way. Then he could have moved down the line as the attack passed from right to left, until he again reached the center. Bragg did go to the right later, but after much time had been lost.

As it was, Polk received the most important assignment of the day, of launching the attack on which the actions of all the other units on the field would be keyed.

Whatever the past, here at Chickamauga he was face to face with his greatest opportunity of the war where by skillful command of the right wing he might hope to drive the Federal army and cut it off from Chattanooga, even destroy it and revive the hopes of the Confederacy desponding after the failure at Gettysburg and the loss of Vicksburg and Chattanooga. His troops were ample and one division was altogether fresh. What was called for was promptness and good tactical management.

At about 5:30 P.M. on the nineteenth, Polk, who was behind the line on the right, told his engineer officer Captain W. J. Morris to set up a corps, or, as it later developed, a right-wing headquarters, behind his center. His ambulance, he said, was at Alexander's bridge and there Morris found it. It was east of the Chickamauga, distant a trot of three or four minutes from where Polk was directing the battle. Morris guided it into the woods and located Polk's bivouac fifty yards from the bridge and east of the road. Bragg's headquarters were about a mile away at the Thedford house.

Polk's staff slept on both sides of the roadway that crossed Alexander's bridge. Polk took the precaution to station sentries at the bridge, told them to build fires, apparently considering himself far enough in the rear not to be visible to the enemy, and ordered that they give directions to anyone seeking him, and to keep a sharp watch for General Hill, Cheatham or Walker. Walker did come that night, and a Lieutenant Reid of Hill's staff, and it was not until 2 A.M. that the sentinels were withdrawn.

Polk had talked with Breckinridge while they had supper that night, but there is doubt that he ever mentioned the attack. Cheatham and Walker received their copies of the attack orders, but the one courier who carried the orders to Hill could not find him. This is understandable, considering the dark woods, winding roads and general nature of the field, but it had a most unfortunate bearing on the development of the battle. On behalf of Polk it may be said that he had expected to see Hill that night and go over the plans personally. He had asked Hill to come to his headquarters and had entrusted this message to two members of Hill's staff, who had delivered it before midnight.

Less impressive is the defense of Polk based on the supposition that Bragg also would deliver the attack orders directly to Hill. But Polk did have a right to expect that Bragg would give notice to Hill that he had been placed under Polk's orders and should look to that general for instructions about the battle for the twentieth. Hill learned indirectly during the night that he had been put under

Polk, but he did not get Polk's attack orders and claimed to know nothing whatever about them.[3]

Hill had been with Cleburne during the night attack of the nineteenth. After the fighting ceased, he rode at 11 P.M. to find Bragg, who was supposed to be at Thedford's ford, five miles from where Hill was on the extreme right of the army. Two of Hill's staff members, Captains Coleman and Reid accompanied him. En route some soldiers told him that Breckinridge's division of his corps had reached the field. Hill sent Captain Reid to escort the Kentuckian's division to the right of Cleburne. Reid found that Polk had allowed Breckinridge's men a rest period but at 2 A.M. the division marched, with Reid as guide, to Cleburne's right. Hill said it did not get into position until after sunrise, in which case it could not have delivered a "day dawn" attack.

Meantime Hill and his aide Coleman reached Thedford's after midnight, found that Bragg was absent, and searched for him vainly. Hill did receive a message from his own chief of staff, saying Polk had sent notice that Hill's corps had been placed under him as wing commander. Polk also requested that Hill come to Alexander's bridge but according to Hill did not utter a peep about any kind of a daylight attack order. When Hill wrote of this in later years, he asserted that Polk had not even mentioned the attack to Breckinridge, with whom he had spent most of the evening. Hill when he wrote had before him a statement from Breckinridge to that effect. It does seem that the good bishop had in mind some other topic of conversation to which he gave preference and did not get around to talking about next morning's business.

Hill said he did not see the attack order until nineteen years afterwards in a letter from General Polk's son and staff member, Captain W. M. Polk, to the Southern Historical Society.

Another mishap was that when Hill reached Alexander's bridge at 3 A.M. the sentry who was supposed to be on hand to conduct him to General Polk had been withdrawn. Hill left an aide there with directions to hunt up Polk and tell him that Hill could be found on his battle line. It was daylight when Hill returned there after a sleepless night spent searching for his superiors to learn what their orders were for the day.[4]

Captain Polk's version—and he wrote a lengthy explanation of all that happened that night—was that Hill passed almost through Polk's camp at about 4 A.M. without reporting himself at headquarters, and continued ahead to his section of the line. An hour later Polk learned that his courier had not reached Hill with the orders, so he sent fresh orders in duplicate directly to the two division commanders of Hill's corps—Breckinridge and Cleburne. These orders explained that the wing commander had been unsuccessful in an effort to find Hill and therefore ordered the division commanders to "move and attack the enemy as soon as you are in position." The orders explained that Cheatham on their left had been directed to attack simultaneously. By the time these orders were delivered the day was advancing and Bragg was beginning to grow restive because he did not hear the sound of the guns.

Probably the fact that the battle was being fought in the thickets was the main reason for the series of misunderstandings that delayed the attack by the Confederate right wing, but there were others. One was that Polk had sent a single copy of his order to Hill and thereafter had neglected the matter until he learned at about daybreak that the order had not been delivered. Issuing the order for Hill to attack at daybreak was Polk's main duty that night and it was not performed well. Only ordinary precaution would have suggested that duplicate copies be sent by separate messengers. In view of the high importance of the attack, the uncertainties of the field and the devious routes that could lead to confusion in the woods, he might well have had a good part of his staff combing the countryside for Hill to make certain that Bragg's plan would not miscarry. Thus the original fault appears very clearly to have been Polk's.

Hill a little later, and with more deliberation, contributed to the delay. Bragg was not well served during the early part of the morning by either subordinate.

Polk's orders sent directly to Breckinridge and Cleburne early on the twentieth, after Hill could not be found, were carried by Captain J. Frank Wheeless, who gave an account of his mission, the high point of which was Hill's cavalier reaction to them.

Wheeless reached Cheatham first, left his copy, then found Cleburne, Breckinridge and Hill together at a campfire in rear of Cleburne's command. When he said he had orders from Polk, Hill reached for them, but the captain explained, "These orders are for Generals Breckinridge and Cleburne." He told Hill that Polk had sent orders to him during the night but when he could not be located the wing commander was sending these attack orders directly to the division commanders.

One of the generals—Wheeless did not specify which—handed the orders to Hill after reading them and said the men could not attack until rations had been distributed. Hill agreed to this. Instead of moving out at once in response to Bragg's desires, Hill saw reasons for delay. No doubt being cast in a subordinate role, he wanted to assert to the limit what authority he retained. He had proved in the eastern army that though a tenacious fighter when engaged, he could be as headstrong with his superiors as he was combative with his enemies.

Captain Wheeless inquired if Hill had any message for the wing commander and Hill then said that Polk had promised to have a courier at Alexander's bridge but none was there when he arrived. Here he was conceding his own lack of enterprise, or manifesting a desire to complain, for if he had shouted or looked around a bit near the bridge he undoubtedly could have obtained directions how to find Polk's bivouac near by. A pistol shot or some vigorous oaths would have brought half a dozen aides scurrying to the bridge. Captain Wheeless told Hill he knew Polk had couriers at the bridge until a late hour but he could not be certain when they were withdrawn. He waited ten minutes until Hill could write a note to Polk, all the while observing how unready the divisions were for an attack. On his return he met Polk and delivered the note. Polk read it and handed it back to the captain, who, after he had read it, said:

"General, you notice General Hill says it will be an hour or so before he is ready to attack. I am confident that it will be more than two hours before he is ready to attack."

Wheeless did not give the time of these different transactions but it must have been close to 7 A.M. when he returned from Hill and met Polk. The wing commander said he was riding to the lines, gave directions about the establishment of headquarters near where they had been on the nineteenth, west of the Chickamauga near Alexander's bridge, and after fifteen minutes left for the battle line. He had scarcely departed when Bragg rode up and asked for him. Captain Wheeless told Bragg that Polk had gone to learn the cause of the delay and would return to headquarters but that Bragg could find him quicker by riding to the lines himself.

"General," the captain volunteered, "in case you should not find General Polk, I will tell you what has been done this morning."

Then he related to the commanding general everything he knew about Polk's original orders to Hill, the later substitute orders to the division commanders, about the incidents connected with the delivery of those orders and the content of Hill's note to Polk. Again he said he felt Hill would be unable to attack within two hours but he put in the remark that he should have attacked at daylight. This caused Bragg to ask how Hill could be expected to attack even before he had received the orders.

The captain was ready with an answer: "General, you will remember, when General Polk sent me to you yesterday evening, you instructed me to say that you would send a staff officer for him and the other generals, as you wished to have a conference with them. My last remark was made under the impression that General Hill was, of course, present at that conference and understood that he was to make the attack at daylight, and that General Polk had renewed the orders himself so that there could not possibly be any mistake."

Captain Wheeless did not report any clarifying remark from Bragg as to why he had not summoned Hill and given him the attack orders direct, but it is apparent that he preferred to deal with Hill through Polk. Wheeless then addressed Bragg further: "General, General Cleburne reported to General Hill this morning, while I was there, that the enemy was felling trees on his front all night."

"Well, sir," Bragg replied, "is this not another important reason why the attack should be made at once?"

"Yes, sir," the captain responded, "it does certainly seem so to me; but it did not seem to impress General Hill that way."

What Hill said in his note, in addition to notice that his attack would be delayed "an hour or more" because the men were getting their rations, was that because the Northerners had been felling trees all night they were "consequently now occupying a position too strong to be taken by assault." He wanted to know what should be done when the Federal fortifications were reached.

Polk when he received Hill's note wrote to Bragg about it and gave 7 A.M. as the hour of receiving it. "Day dawn" was already well passed and the attack was still two hours or more away. According to Hill's timing it was 7:25 A.M. when he heard from Polk and then wrote the note.[5]

It is necessary to go back and review briefly some of the earlier developments of the day.

Bragg's morning up to that time had been one of frustration.

When daylight began to creep across the field on Sunday morning, September 20, men in both armies were stimulated by the arrival of one of the crisp, clear, early-autumn mornings so familiar to residents of the lower Appalachians.

Those on some sections of the field noticed a mist or fog, which must have been spotty, for it was inconsistent with reports of frost on the hills where many Federal soldiers camped. The mist was on the Confederate side, rising from the Chickamauga. Part of it was the smoke of the battle of the nineteenth.

Sam R. Watkins of "Co. Aytch," 1st Tennessee, noticed that "the sun rose over the eastern hills clear and beautiful" and thought "the day itself seemed to have a Sabbath-day look about it." Captain Lemark Duvall on the Federal line said "it was a beautiful day indeed," with everything quiet, not a shot being heard. But the silence itself was ominous as the two great armies began to stir and the clank of mess pans and cups was heard in the Federal companies when steaming hot coffee was poured.

Bragg was mounted at dawn. Surrounded by his staff, he waited near the Thedford house for the sound of the guns that would tell him of Polk's attack on the right. But as on the morning at McLemore's Cove, when he paced impatiently up and down listening for the noise of Hindman's firing, the silence informed him that his orders, so easy of execution, were again being ignored. Sunrise was at 5:47 A.M. on the twentieth. Already the enemy was being allowed to complete by daylight the fortifications on which they had labored with less sureness in darkness.

As Sam Watkins gazed out across the battlefield and its trees and undergrowth "that ever since the creation had never been disturbed by the ax of civilized man," he said, "It looked wild, weird, uncivilized." The thought that ran through Lemark Duvall's mind was that "something dreadful was in preparation."

While Bragg waited in the saddle the sun began climbing up the sky. His impatience rose with it. Finally he sent Major Pollock B. Lee of his staff to learn what was causing Polk's delay and to urge him to speed the assault.

Lee returned and told Bragg he had found Polk "at a farm house three miles from the line of his troops, about one hour after sunrise, sitting on a gallery reading a newspaper and waiting, as he (the Genl.) said for his breakfast." The quotation is Bragg's, who added that "it was 9 o'clock before I got him in position and about 10 before the attack was made."

There appears no good reason why Major Lee would have invented such a story, though denials were forthcoming. None of them seems to mention any other place where the bishop-general got his breakfast. It might be argued that if he were continually present on the field, as his supporters insisted, he might be more accountable for the failure to obey the attack orders, than if he were away getting breakfast.

Major Lee's report came to be told with embellishments. One version was that he found Polk, who loved military ostentation, surrounded by his superbly garbed staff, seated at a hearty breakfast. When queried about the attack he said he had ordered Hill to make it, then added:

"Do tell General Bragg that my heart is overflowing with anxiety for the attack—overflowing with anxiety, sir."

When Bragg heard Major Lee so quote the Bishop he uttered what was termed "a terrible exclamation," which included references to his generals with especial compliments to Polk and Hill. Then he turned again to his staff officer.

"Major Lee," he was quoted as saying, "ride along the line and order *every captain* to take his men instantly into action."

The order probably was not delivered in exactly those words but no doubt Bragg felt like going over the heads of his generals and directing his line officers to make the attack. Instead of that, he did rearrange his plans on account of the delay. Instead of having the divisions and corps attack in sequence after the battle should be joined on the right, if that came to pass, he directed what was more reasonable, that a general assault on Rosecrans be made all along the line.

When he heard that Polk was reading the newspaper Bragg decided to go to the lines personally, and he set out with part of his staff. Sometime between 7 and 8 A.M. he finally caught up with Polk. The wing commander made a full explanation of the delay. It did not impress Bragg, who had been thwarted again as at McLemore's Cove, in a conscientious effort to get an attack launched at daybreak. That was not a difficult task in this war even for troops that had marched through the night like Breckinridge's, to get into position. Hancock was able to get his Northern troops into formation by dawn at Spotsylvania after marching them through the night across the rear of Grant's army. Slocum's men marched back from Meade's left in the night and attacked the Confederates on the slopes of Culp's Hill at 3:45 A.M. All that was required at Chickamauga was zest and determination on the part of the wing and corps commanders, or of either. Certainly neither Cleburne nor Breckinridge could be blamed for the failure. Bragg later referred to Cleburne as "one of the best and truest officers of our cause."[6]

Major Dick Person of Cleburne's staff had had a disturbed night and then an encounter with the commanding general which disclosed how truly agitated Bragg was over Polk's failure to carry out his instructions.

Major Person had been aroused mainly by the ominous night labor of the Federal army on its fortifications. When he tried to sleep he happened to be near a Northern soldier with a bullet through his groin. Repeatedly the major got up and went out between the lines to see if he could help the suffering soldier.

"I think that when daybreak came," he said, "I was feeling as bad as I ever felt in my life." He was afraid his nervousness would reveal itself to others, so he walked back some distance behind the lines to an open space in the woods and here he began to pace back and forth, thinking "If I could get some circulation started the boys wouldn't see how badly broken up I was."

Just then Bragg suddenly appeared. Having met Person in North Carolina before the war, Bragg recognized him, then "with some feeling" asked him, "Major, can you tell me why you are not engaged here?"

"No, sir, I cannot," the staff officer answered. When he told of it later he said he volunteered nothing else because he distrusted his voice.

But Bragg went on: "My instructions were to assault at daybreak. Where is General Cleburne?"

Major Person saw Cleburne with his staff through the woods and pointed to him. "There he is, sir." Bragg said no more but rode to Cleburne.

It was now eight o'clock. Hill was with Cleburne. When Bragg rode up and asked why he had not attacked, Hill told the commanding general he was then hearing about the attack order for the first time. He quoted Bragg as saying angrily,

"I found Polk after sunrise sitting down reading a newspaper at Alexander's bridge, two miles from the line of battle, where he ought to have been fighting."

Either Hill or Bragg was in error in this statement, for it was Major Lee, Bragg's assistant Adjutant General, who reported Polk to be so engaged.[7]

Bragg could readily perceive that the troops were unprepared for the assault and that time would be required to align them and send them against the enemy.

Meanwhile Walker and Cheatham had been ready in the rear of Hill to give support as quickly as the assault should be launched. On the left, Old Peter Longstreet had been in the saddle since dawn, riding down his lines, his ear tuned for the signal that would send his divisions forward. But time wore on. Here and there along the lines could be heard the desultory firing of pickets. Otherwise the clear, mellow autumn day was unjarred by battle outbursts.

From the explanation given of Polk's actions by his son and aide and by other defenders, the impression is gained that he was up most of the night issuing orders and was in the saddle riding the lines early. But the other side of the story is Hill's statement which claimed he was unprepared because uninformed.

By passing on to Bragg Hill's excuse for not attacking, Polk was scarcely serving as a corps commander, but more as a courier. The thing called for was to make Hill attack without delay, and in that Polk was altogether wanting. Hill said Polk consented to the delay. His lack of vigor would seem to warrant any disciplinary action Bragg might elect to take against him. Bragg called for a written explanation after the battle and when he found it unsatisfactory—it placed the blame on Hill—he suspended Polk from his command. "The case is flagrant and is but a repetition of the past," he told President Davis, and added ". . . I suffer self-reproach for not having acted earlier."

At 9:45 A.M. Hill was finally ready and Breckinridge advanced his division to the attack, the brigade of Adams on the right, Stovall in the center and the Kentuckians, the "Orphan Brigade," under Helm on the left.

Major General John C. Breckinridge, lately Vice President with President James Buchanan, at the age of thirty-six, and the youngest Vice President in American history, possessed such a warm, strong and resolute personality that he made one of the capable generals of the Southern armies, though he had no military education and scant army background before the war.

One of the tests of military competence is quite obviously the response a leader can get from his soldiers. There was no occasion when he was serving under Bragg, or when commanding his own army in the Shenandoah Valley, or leading a division under Lee at Cold Harbor, on which Breckinridge did not have the most ardent response and warm affection of his men. Under his command the youths of the Virginia Military Institute cadet corps came out and fought with the gallantry of veterans at the Battle of New Market, and lost 8 killed and 46 wounded of the 225 engaged.

"Surely there were never nobler leaders than Breckinridge and Cleburne," said D. H. Hill, their corps commander, of their work at Chickamauga. Breckinridge was a graduate of Centre College at Danville, Kentucky. He studied law at Princeton and Transylvania College in Lexington, but when he tried practicing in Iowa he yearned so for the Bluegrass that he returned happily to the more crowded Kentucky bar and gained eminence in it. He served as major in the 3rd Kentucky regiment in the Mexican War.

By the time he went to Congress—his grandfather James had been an outstanding Senator from Kentucky—in 1851, at the age of thirty, he was recognized as an able orator, and five years later, as of sufficient ability to strengthen the ticket headed by the aging Buchanan, the "Buck and Breck" Democratic ticket elected in 1856. In 1860, after he had been elected to the Senate, he was the unsuccessful candidate for President on the ticket of the Southern Democratic faction. He opposed secession but when the break came sided with the South. The Senate expelled him when he cast his fortunes with the Confederacy.[8]

Polk's Futile Brigade Assaults

HILL finally had his divisions formed by 9:30 A.M. and under way at 9:45 A.M., and at ten o'clock Breckinridge's attack was sounding the full length of the Confederate line.

Far off to the north the church bells of Chattanooga could be heard between the blasts, calling the distressed citizens to divine worship. As Breckinridge went into action two of his brigades, Stovall's and Adams', reached beyond the Federal left, although Baird's division had been given help on its left by Dodge's brigade of Richard Johnson's division. Forrest's cavalry watched Breckinridge's right.

But John Beatty's brigade of Negley's division, which Rosecrans at Thomas' request had dispatched personally at top speed from the Union center, was arriving as Hill's corps began its belated attack, and Thomas used it to extend his left near Kelly's. Then he advanced it a quarter of a mile to the ridge at the McDonald house and faced it north to meet Hill's turning effort.

Stovall and Adams consequently confronted Beatty on ground free of fortifications, which the Federals had not prepared for their defense during the night or the four hours of daylight they had received as a bonus. Helm, on Breckinridge's left, advanced more directly against the formidable field works consisting of piled-up logs, brush loppings and bristling abatis. The spade and pickax, which were becoming favorite military weapons of Robert E. Lee at this stage of the war, had not been brought into use by the Federals at Chickamauga, partly no doubt because the closeness of the trees and their interlocking root systems would have made trench digging in the darkness difficult, and partly because Rosecrans did not have opportunity to advance his trains, in which most of his entrenching tools were stored.

Adams commanded a splendid brigade composed of five Louisiana regiments, one additional Louisiana sharpshooter battalion, a Louisiana battery and one Alabama regiment. The Alabamans, organized at Mobile, appreciated martial music so much that the regiment's first colonel, Alexander McKinstry, set up a fancy pay scale for musicians probably not topped in the Confederate army. The band leader received sixty dollars a month and each of the eleven other members of the band received forty dollars a month. An over-all payment of a hundred dollars a month was added, altogether a neat sum for musicians in the days before Confederate money was on the skids. The music may have contributed something because the regiment had helped Forrest on some of his successful exploits.

Daniel W. Adams was an intrepid brigadier general who had lost an eye at Shiloh and had been wounded again at Stone's River. His brother, William Wirt Adams, was a brigadier general of Mississippi cavalry who served under Forrest in the Vicksburg campaign and in the later stages of the war. The Adams brothers, both Kentucky-born, had trouble with the press. Daniel before the war had fought a duel with an editor who criticized his father, and killed him. After the war William had a street altercation in Jackson, Mississippi, with an editor who killed him.[1]

On this far left of the Federal line, where there were no fortifications, Breckinridge pressed the enemy hard and seemed on the verge of an easy victory. Then he met the resolute John Beatty who had been posted personally by Thomas and who contested every step stubbornly as he was pushed back. The presence of the rest of Negley's division that was wandering toward the rear would have been of inestimable help at this critical moment. Negley's disappearance, in fact, accounted for Beatty's main difficulty. When he was stationed facing north near the McDonald house, a gap remained between his right and Baird's left. This quarter of a mile should have been filled by Negley's other two brigades, Stanley's and Sirwell's. They did not come. When Breckin-

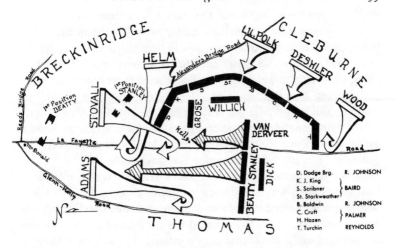

Breckinridge assails the Federal left. He attempts to envelop Thomas' flank and capture the La Fayette road. Helm's attack is shown passing the left of Thomas' fortified line, where it receives heavy enfilade fire.

ridge's division advanced, Adams' brigade found this opening and pressed through it, struck the 42nd Indiana, Beatty's right regiment, and rolled it up on the 88th Indiana, which was compelled to change front from the north to the south to meet the enemy in its rear.

Colonel George Humphrey, the Scotsman who commanded the 88th Indiana, had been born in Ayrshire, in the house where Robert Burns was born, and his grandfather had been one of the bard's confidants and companions. The Colonel had organized the regiment in Fort Wayne at the time Bragg and Kirby Smith had invaded Kentucky and threatened to go farther north; it had left at once for Louisville and, though green and untested, had been pushed with Rousseau into the thickest of the fight at Perryville. Now, seasoned and steady, it was preventing the disintegration of Rosecrans' left wing at Chickamauga. Behind this protection the 42nd rallied.

Beatty's brigade, famous at Chickamauga, left its mark in military terminology for quite another reason than its steadiness. When shelter tents were issued and the men found they were so small they could not stand up in them, they promptly termed them "dog tents" and hung placards on them. These signs read, "Pups for sale," or "Terriers" or "Sons of Bitches within." Rosecrans passed along the line at inspection. The men got on their hands and knees and greeted him with calls of "Bow wow! Bow wow!" All the general could do was laugh and promise he would try to procure better living quarters for the troops, who had been accustomed to squad tents. But the small shelter tents had been named. Always thereafter the army knew them as "pup tents."[2]

Beatty was putting up a creditable resistance when unexpected help came. This was in the form of Stanley's brigade of Negley's division, which freed itself from Negley and followed Beatty, who had encountered it when he had gone back during a lull, looking for help. For a brief period an intense battle raged between Stanley and the Confederates. Adams, relentless in his pressure, advancing boldly, was shot down severely wounded at the head of his troops, and captured by Stanley when the Confederates fell back. Meantime Beatty was sending his aide in search of Negley. According to Beatty's information, Negley had ordered Stanley back to Chattanooga just before Beatty intercepted him. Negley could be found nowhere. Beatty thought that if Stanley had come an hour earlier, the Federals would have fared better on their far left flank.

Breckinridge was accompanied on his advance by a six-gun battery of the Washington Artillery, a company of the old and famous New Orleans organization that did not go with the other Washington Artillery batteries to Lee's army in Virginia. There the Washington Artillery distinguished itself in numerous campaigns and fired the opening guns for the Pickett-Pettigrew-Trimble assault on Cemetery Ridge at Gettysburg.

While the battle was at its height between Beatty and Adams, the Confederates received a one-man reinforcement, worth almost the coming of a fresh brigade, which accounted in large measure for their ability to wrest the La Fayette road from the Federals and hold it for a time.

J. A. Chalaron, an officer of the 5th Company of the Washington

Artillery, on Breckinridge's right, witnessed the repulse of the Confederates when Thomas first threw in Beatty and then supported him with Stanley. Breckinridge's men were reforming behind the guns when a newcomer appeared among them. Said Chalaron: "In the midst of the indecision of the moment, among the first who arrived at our guns I noticed a splendidly-mounted, magnificent looking man, commanding in stature and appearance, in full Confederate-gray uniform, who seemed to be a general officer. I heard him say to them: 'Rally here, Louisianans, or I'll have to bring up my bobtail cavalry to show you how to fight!' "

Such a remark immediately identified the handsome officer to Chalaron. It was Nathan Forrest, coming in from his cavalry outpost when he saw the uncertain situation on Bragg's right flank.

"I recognized in his face," the artilleryman continued, "the lineaments I had often heard described as peculiar to Forrest. He looked like some knight-errant dropping into our midst from out some battle picture of romance—some Richard Coeur de Lion —some Black Douglas. That knightly apparition ever since has been ineffaceably fixed in my recollection."

In the presence of such force and determination, it is little wonder that Adams' Louisianans rallied. Though Adams had been wounded and captured, his men soon returned and with renewed spirit pressed their attack on Stanley so vigorously that he was driven back. Left unsupported, and assailed in flank a little later by Breckinridge's other brigade—Helm's, Beatty's two Indiana regiments, the 42nd and 88th, retreated to the left and rear.[3]

In a narration of their attacks on Thomas, Breckinridge's three brigades must be dealt with separately, but they advanced against Thomas' line in concert and attacked simultaneously. Thus, while Stovall and Adams were making good headway and then encountering stubborn resistance from John Beatty and Stanley, Helm's "Orphan Brigade" appeared in front of the breastworks farther to the Confederate left, where it met a withering infantry fire and heavy discharges of canister. The check of Helm was as much responsible for arresting the farther advance of Stovall and Adams as was the Federal infantry and artillery fire in their front. The two light brigades could not be sent off on an isolated march

238 CHICKAMAUGA

toward Thomas' rear so long as the Confederate line on their left was unable to advance.

Helm's fight was in many respects as heart-rending as any in all the sanguinary battle along the Chickamauga. One of President Lincoln's several brothers-in-law in the Confederate service, Helm was thirty-two, dashing, and among Bragg's most competent and promising brigade leaders.

The "Orphan Brigade," sometimes called the "Blood of Boone," named partly after Daniel and partly after their Tennessee rendezvous, Camp Boone, was composed of the 2nd, 4th, 6th and 9th Confederate Kentucky regiments, the 41st Alabama and Captain Robert Cobb's Kentucky battery. The 2nd Kentucky under Colonel Roger W. Hanson had the misfortune at Fort Donelson of having been captured in its entirety. It had been forced back into the works while Forrest was riding through with his cavalry to safety. When Bragg invaded Kentucky, the 2nd Kentucky and parts of two Kentucky brigades were combined to form a brigade under Hanson, a veteran of the Mexican War. Identified officially as the 1st Kentucky brigade, it was more familiarly known by the "Orphan" designation.

Hanson was killed at Stone's River, where the Kentucky "Orphans" performed well, and Helm, a West Point graduate, who had come up in the Confederate service in the Baton Rouge area, was transferred to Bragg's army to succeed Hanson.

However high Lincoln's admiration for Helm may have been, it probably was not so excessive as implied by the remark attributed to him that Helm would be worth more to the Union cause than the whole state of Kentucky. In view of Lincoln's early attitude that if Kentucky seceded the jig would be up for the Union, he could scarcely have thought Helm weighed so heavily.

Helm's battle was sanguinary and well fought. As he advanced he threw out the 4th Kentucky as skirmishers and moved with the 2nd and 9th Kentucky and the 41st Alabama, holding the 6th Kentucky in reserve. His attack fell on Baird's salient in the Federal line, one of the many "bloody angles" of the war, where it turned back to the left near a small stream that rose on the Kelly farm. Helm's left regiments faced the breastworks of logs while his right regiment, the 6th Kentucky, and the 4th Kentucky skirmishers, pressed ahead in conjunction with Adams against the flank of John Beatty's brigade. Beatty was in the field to Helm's right, without cover, his flank exposed. Beatty, with Stanley's assistance, was now battling two of Helm's regiments and Breckinridge's other two brigades. He was fairly chewed up and cut through the middle. Helm had his post on the right of his brigade, at the point of his action with Beatty.

John Beatty was helped by a section of Bridges' Illinois battery, which was supported by the 15th Kentucky Federal regiment. Helm's fight therefore pitted Kentuckian against Kentuckian. Helm's 4th Confederate Kentucky under Colonel Joseph P. Nuckols struggled hand to hand with the 15th Federal Kentucky under Colonel Marion C. Taylor. Helm drove the Federal Kentuckians back, felled Captain Lyman Bridges, commanding the Illinois guns, killed all his artillerymen and horses, and took the guns, then turned them about and got in some shots at Beatty's retiring men.

Here Benjamin Hardin Helm, of Bardstown, who seemed to typify the old, aristocratic culture of the Bluegrass, son and grandson of distinguished Kentucky statesmen, President Lincoln's favorite brother-in-law, was shot down by a Kentucky bullet through his right side. Even a hurried glance showed that the wound was mortal. He was carried back by his aides, Lieutenant John B. Pirtle, and Lieutenant William Wallace Herr, who after the war married Mrs. Lincoln's half-sister. He died behind the lines that night.

This part of Helm's brigade had been caught in an enfilade fire from King's brigade of regulars in the fortifications, who were free to concentrate on the "Orphan Brigade" because Polk had not yet sent in Cleburne's division to assail Baird's front.

Few if any events of the war caused President Lincoln greater anguish than the death of Helm. David Davis was with him just after he received the news and it appeared almost to prostrate him and overshadow every other detail of the battle.

"I never saw Mr. Lincoln more moved than when he heard of the death of his young brother-in-law," Davis said. "I called to see him about 4 o'clock on the 22nd of September; I found him in the greatest grief. 'Davis,' he said, 'I feel as David of old when he was told of the death of Absolom.' I saw how grief stricken he was so I closed the door and left him."

Mrs. Lincoln was on a shopping trip to New York. The President sent her a telegram telling her of the tragedy in her family and the tragedy of the battle for the Union cause.

Helm had gone to Springfield, Illinois, in 1857, on law business, and his sister-in-law, Mary Todd Lincoln, had decreed that he should be welcomed both as a Kentuckian and a brother. "And also as the grandson of the 'Kitchen Knife Whetted on a Brick,' " put in Lincoln, with reference to his grandfather Ben Hardin, the Kentucky pioneer lad of the 1780's who had served two considerable stretches in Congress and different posts in the state legislature and government. Helm's father, John La Rue Helm, governor of Kentucky in the 1850's, supported the Union cause in a state where so many families were torn asunder, and became governor again for a short period after the war. His mother was Lucinda Barbour Hardin, daughter of the pioneer and longtime Congressman.

Lincoln was charmed with his young brother-in-law during the Springfield visit, talked points of law with him, told stories about Helm's neighboring Hardin county. His wife was Mary Todd Lincoln's "Little Sister." When Lincoln was in Lexington years before he had lifted her into his arms; now, grown to beautiful young womanhood, she had married the handsome young graduate from West Point and lawyer from Harvard, who had entered the Military Academy when he was sixteen and was graduated when twenty. A good student, he stood ninth in a class of forty-two. But a year later he resigned from the army, sampled Harvard, and read law in the office of his eminent father at Bardstown, then hung out his own shingle, first in Elizabethtown and then in Louisville.

Close as he was to Lincoln in family and affection, he voted against him for the Presidency. That did not seem to dampen the warmth of the President's reception when Helm came to see him in the White House after the firing on Fort Sumter when war was in the air. This mid-April visit, made at the President's invitation, was followed by another on April 27, as Helm was preparing to return to Kentucky.

"Ben, here is something for you," Lincoln said at their parting. "Think it over by yourself and let me know what you will do."

When Helm broke the seal he found a commission as major in the Federal army. Lincoln appears to have misjudged his young friend's temperament slightly, for the commission was in the paymaster's department instead of in the line where a high-spirited Kentuckian would want to be. Another offer came from Lincoln: that Helm would be assigned to the frontier if he chose, so that he would not have to fight against the South. Mrs. Lincoln was pressing, too, for she wanted "Little Sister" to live with her in the White House. Emilie Todd had married Helm in 1856 when he was serving in the Kentucky legislature. She was as loyal and sympathetic to his political views as her sister Mary was to Lincoln's.

Helm appears to have done considerable shopping around before determining his course. Undoubtedly it was more to gain ideas and test sentiments than to seek any personal preferment, which could have come most readily through his brother-in-law Lincoln, cast so unexpectedly into the Presidency. While Helm was in Washington he called on Colonel Robert E. Lee, on the very day Lee shed the United States uniform. They touched on war and politics. Lee told his young caller that he could not fight against his own people and speculated that Helm's brother-in-law Lincoln would find the situation growing too chaotic for his control. The remark suggests that Lee, like most others, did not at that time sense Lincoln's innate strength.

Helm went back to Kentucky and talked with Simon Buckner, the bellwether of the Southern sympathizers there, then on to Montgomery, Alabama, for a talk with Jefferson Davis. He did not at first accept Davis' advice to go home and work to bring Kentucky into the Southern federation. Obviously torn in his sentiments, he followed the will-o-the-wisp of neutrality awhile, then recruited the 1st Kentucky Cavalry and put on gray. Most of the Todds were going with the South, ignoring sister Mary's family connections. Alexander H. Todd, twenty-three, was killed while serving under Helm at Baton Rouge, a loss which caused Mrs. Lincoln to drop to her knees and cry out in anguish, "Oh, little Aleck, why had you to die?"[4]

When Helm fell, Colonel Joseph H. Lewis of the 6th Kentucky took command of the Orphan Brigade. The loss as Kentuckian fought Kentuckian had been frightful. Of the 1,400 who had gone into action with the brigade, 471 were lying on the field, among them the colonels of the 4th, 2nd and 9th Kentucky regiments.

The 41st Alabama of Helm's brigade—the only regiment not from Kentucky—lost 189 men in these futile, determined assaults.

Helm's death and the terrible loss of life in his brigade tended to slow the Confederate flank attack. But as it faltered, Cleburne launched his assault against Baird's right and the division of Richard Johnson. Meantime the vicious manner in which Breckinridge conducted his attacks caused Thomas to call again on Rosecrans for more men, and Rosecrans to begin the further dispatch of troops from his center and right.

Thomas' first desire was for the return of Brannan's division, which he had sent on the afternoon of the nineteenth to safeguard the center when it seemed likely to crumble from Stewart's attack. At the council of war in the Widow Glenn's house Rosecrans had agreed that Brannan's division should be left as a mobile reserve in the Federal center. Now, when Thomas needed it badly, he learned that it had already been placed in line in the Poe woods, between Reynolds and Wood. The brigades of Connell and Croxton were in the front line and Van Derveer was in reserve.

Van Derveer's brigade was quickly snatched from its place behind the center and at 10:30 A.M., half an hour after Breckinridge's assault had been launched, it was marching double quick to the north and the Federal left flank. It reached the La Fayette road near the juncture with the Reed's bridge road east of McDonald's, at the critical moment when Stovall and Adams were advancing from the north to the south down the La Fayette road. Their piercing yells gave concern that they were about to crush the Federal flank. Van Derveer met them with the 2nd Minnesota and 87th Indiana deployed in his first line. The 9th Ohio—which under Colonel Kemmerling on the day before had recaptured the guns of the 5th U. S. Artillery—and the 35th Ohio were in the second line. The onsweep of Stovall and Adams was checked and the flank of the army that had been threatened with disaster was momentarily relieved.

The 60th North Carolina of Stovall's brigade claimed that when it confronted the 2nd Minnesota at noon, it made the farthest advance "in this famous charge" of Breckinridge's division. This has given rise to the contention at times that North Carolina made the farthest advance at Chickamauga, as it did at Gettysburg. But other Confederate troops later in the day made a farther penetration of the Federal position, of course.[5]

One reason for the failure of Helm's attack was that Polk and Hill had not yet sent in Cleburne on Breckinridge's left, and his effort was largely unsupported. Finally Cleburne moved forward. His front was so extended that his brigades became separated in the woods and they too carried on a series of isolated attacks which Baird and Richard Johnson behind their barriers were able to repulse in detail.

The brigade of Lucius Polk was on the right and was supposed to use Breckinridge's division as a guide. But the delay and the underbrush separated it and it parted also from Wood's brigade on its left. Polk was alone when he advanced against the Federal barricade where it was held by the brigades of Scribner and Starkweather.

Lucius Polk, his companion of the old Yell Rifles days, and Cleburne represented a combination of the aristocratic Southern planter with the Irish newcomer, brought together into a common cause by their martial ardor and love of freedom. Lucius was perhaps a better tactician then his more distinguished uncle, the bishop-general. His charge at this point with the first of Cleburne's brigades was audacious. Captain William Cairnes of his staff rode alongside him and watched the assault on Thomas' outer breastworks.

"I never witnessed a more enthusiastic charge, and it carried everything before it," he said. The first Federal line—he said it appeared to be a heavy skirmish line, for Baird's division must have been stretched thin—was pressed back behind a more formidable log barricade. Cairnes added: "Such was the impetuosity of the attack that our men rushed up to and over these works, driving the troops there, in utter confusion, back on the main line."

Lucius Polk turned to him. "Go back and tell the old general [Leonidas Polk] that we have passed two lines of breastworks; that we have got them on the jump, and I am sure of carrying the main line."

Cairnes rode at his best speed to the lieutenant general, who was in a little glade near Breckinridge's left. Breckinridge and Cheatham were with him. When Polk heard of his nephew's success he turned to the others. "Push your commands forward, gentlemen," he said, "and assault them vigorously all along the whole line."

To the young captain, Cleburne's advance was much more impressive than it was believed to be elsewhere along the Confederate front. He said they picked up small arms and equipment scattered all about. Sorrel, watching and waiting with Longstreet, thought that Wing Commander Polk "does not appear to have achieved a decided success."[6]

Lucius Polk was, in fact, arrested and hurled back when he reached the main Federal line. For the next two hours, Wing Commander Leonidas Polk continued his hammering against Thomas' line. It was more a series of blows in succession than a steady pressure, and everywhere it failed. Sometime after 11 A.M. heavy firing began to be heard down the Confederate left, which caused curiosity among Cheatham's soldiers awaiting the order to attack.

Polk rode along the line in front of the 1st Tennessee. Some of the men called to him and asked, "Say, General, what command is that . . . engaged now?"

"That is Longstreet's corps," Polk replied. Then it was the bishop as much as the general who added: "He is driving them this way, and we will drive them that way, and crush them between the upper and nether millstones."

It must have been at the time Captain Cairnes reported, because Cheatham was still near by. Polk said to him, "General, move your division and attack at once." Cheatham gave the attack order, which was: "Forward, boys, and give them hell!" Polk reinforced the order but the attentive soldiers noticed he skirted the profanity. "Do as General Cheatham says, boys," he told them.

Cleburne again attacked ahead of Cheatham down the Alexander's bridge road and overlapped Baird's Federals on their right. This assault brought S. A. M. Wood's and Deshler's brigades of Cleburne's division into conflict with Palmer and the left of Reynolds. Along this line the log works proved of inestimable value to Thomas' men. All that could be seen by S. A. M. Wood and Deshler as they advanced was the sheet of flame issuing from the barricade. Rarely were Cleburne's soldiers able to get an enemy target in their sights. Firing into the logs and loppings, they exhausted their ammunition in a futile battle, the advantage being entirely on the Northern side.

Deshler's men had been firing so rapidly that their ammunition was running low, which prompted Colonel Mills of the 6th Texas to inform the brigade commander by courier. Within a few minutes Mills saw Deshler approaching from the right of the line, obviously coming to determine for himself the condition of the cartridge boxes, a mission on which he had declined to send one of his staff. As he approached the Texas regiment he was hit in the chest by a bursting shell, which literally tore his heart from his bosom. Thirty years after the battle Colonel-Senator Mills visited the pine forest east of Kelly field and pointed to the spot where Deshler fell.

Deshler, the son of Pennsylvanians who had moved to Alabama, was in the West Point class of 1854. He had cast his lot with the South and had been critically wounded during the Cheat Mountain campaign. He had served in the Seven Days battles around Richmond before being promoted brigadier general and transferred to Cleburne's division.[7]

It required less than an hour to demonstrate to Cleburne conclusively that the log works defended by artillery and heavy infantry supports could not be carried by frontal assault.

One peculiarity the surgeons noticed from this in-the-woods fighting was the unusually large number of men wounded in the left arm. As the soldiers shot from behind the small trees, they kept their head back on the right but crooked their left arm to hold the gun while shooting. In later years the old soldiers returning to the field for reunions were noticed to be almost as scarred as the trees. One of Cleburne's captains, identified in the press only as "Frazer" displayed scars of wounds on either side of his neck. He did not know what had happened until he tried to give an order and found blood gushing forth more readily than words. He had been shot through the windpipe. When the surgeons came by looking for those who might be salvaged for other battles, one said of Frazer, "No use taking him. He's good as dead already." "Old Frazer" was attending reunions heartily at least twenty-seven years after the battle.

Undoubtedly the main mistake in the morning assault was that Bishop Polk did not hurl his entire wing *en masse* against the enemy. Instead, he conducted what amounted to a series of isolated brigade actions. It is true that on the greater part of the battlefield brigades remained the largest unit that could be kept in view by a commanding officer, but the assault nevertheless showed lack of the careful preparation that might have given greater concert and avoided piecemeal defeat.

Bragg was still resolute in his determination to drive back the Federal left under Thomas, and while Breckinridge and Cleburne were failing to make any important impression, he and Polk sent in Walker and Cheatham. Walker's corps was pulled around to Bragg's far right. There it came under the command of Hill, who instead of following Bragg's idea of launching it against Thomas' flank, facing it south and attacking down the La Fayette road, seemed apprehensive of a Federal counterattack. He used it to relieve Breckinridge and Cleburne after their attacks were spent. Liddell's division which had helped to open the battle on the morning of the nineteenth went into line relieving Lucius Polk and Stovall, while Gist's division passed through the ranks of the "Orphan Brigade," still shaken by the loss of Helm. Leading Gist's advance was Colquitt's fresh brigade of Georgia and South Carolina troops. They were the first to reach the Federal line. Colquitt had advanced in a manner that would seem impulsive, without throwing forward skirmishers, but this was due to his belief that there were Breckinridge men still in front of him. As he passed

Baird's flank he encountered a severe flank fire from Baird's breast-works.

Colonel Peyton H. Colquitt (brother of Brigadier General Alfred Holt Colquitt, later the capable Governor of Georgia and United States Senator) commanded Gist's brigade when Gist took command of the division. He advanced through a dense section of the woods where it was difficult to maintain contact with commands on either flank. The men had little more than their rifles and ammunition boxes. All of their baggage had been left behind at Rome, and Colquitt had felt himself fortunate, considering the railroad congestion, to reach the battlefield at all.

Now he was out in front of the main Confederate line, in an advance on which, in World War I terms, he had overrun his objective. The enemy seemed all about him. He maintained a stubborn, deadly fight. While he was going forward to reconnoiter his position, he was shot down. Another pyramid stands close to that marking where Helm had fallen. His casualties were frightful. One of his regiments, the 24th South Carolina, lost 169 out of less than 400 engaged. Numerous other officers of his small brigade fell. His remnants were driven back to a line held by Gist's other brigades.

Liddell's own brigade under Govan, attacking farther to the Confederate right, achieved fair success. Govan scattered the already severely handled John Beatty but had to retire when Thomas, always alert to the condition of his flank, threw the brigades of Van Derveer and Grose against him.

In Govan's brigade the 2nd Arkansas was inspired by an intrepid young officer, Major Elbridge Gerry Brasher, who won compliments for his coolness, though at the age of twenty-two he was undoubtedly one of the younger field officers in the Confederate service. He fell badly wounded in the front of this charge. He had the compensation of being able to recuperate at the beautiful plantation home of Judge Stocks near Greensboro, Georgia, under the care of his brother. The Brashers liked the names of distinguished statesmen—his brother was Dr. Thomas Jefferson Brasher, an army surgeon. The doctor handled him so well that he was able to return to his regiment in six weeks.[8]

Thomas estimated that the first attacks of the brigades of Lucius Polk and Walthall, which fell on Richard Johnson, Palmer and Reynolds, lasted two hours. The Confederates, in Thomas' words, made "assault after assault with fresh troops" until exhausted.

Palmer's division was placed where it could see the country ahead, an area almost clear of undergrowth. Had Polk attacked at day break as Bragg ordered, Palmer conceded that "the battle would not have lasted an hour" and that the Federals would have "gone to Chattanooga on the run." Now they were prepared. The enemy came ahead on the double quick. The fire from the defenses "seemed to sweep the field to our front." According to Palmer the charge had such momentum that the gray-clad soldiers reached within thirty yards of the log breastworks before they fell. "These assaults were repeated with an impetuosity that threatened to overwhelm us."

Captain Lemark Duvall of the 90th Ohio, in Palmer's division, said that during this fighting it was useless to give orders because they could not be heard. "The rebs charged in three distinct lines but each time they charged they were driven back with fearfully decimated ranks."

Irrespective of the question whether Polk was reading his newspaper when he should have been launching his attack, his generalship on Bragg's right was deficient and ill prepared him for his later criticism of Bragg. Inquiry and analysis of what Stonewall Jackson probably would have done in the circumstances have been made in almost every instance where an important Confederate officer failed to rise to his opportunities in this war. The situation on Bragg's right at Chickamauga has not been overlooked in such comparisons. It has been well pointed out that when Breckinridge's division was assailing Thomas' flank it was 400 yards beyond the Federal line of breastworks, poised for a turning thrust to the Federal rear.

Breckinridge's two brigades that made this encircling movement —Helm's being engaged in a frontal assault—numbered 2,200 rifles and one battery. He won the La Fayette road, crossed it, wheeled to the left, was in position and was actually beginning to sweep down the road with one of his brigades on either side, against Thomas' flank. It was an instant for which more capable generalship might have been on the alert. Surely Jackson would have driven hard and fast.

Polk had immediately at hand three divisions, Gist's and Liddell's of Walker's corps and Cheatham's large division acting directly under his own orders. These were in addition to the divisions of Breckinridge and Cleburne, already engaged. Had Polk's attack been more carefully planned and its possibilities prepared for, these reserve divisions, instead of being employed in frontal attacks on Thomas' log works or, as in the case of Cheatham, allowed to remain idle, might have been sent in promptly behind Breckinridge. Such masses might readily have rolled up Thomas' flank.

Bragg's plan, though stubbornly adhered to in the face of better opportunities for victory elsewhere along the line, had the merit that if successful it would yield the grandest results. By rolling up the Federal left he would almost certainly cut Rosecrans off from Chattanooga. By defeating his center or right, he would tend to drive Rosecrans back on Chattanooga. No victory was to be scorned in a battle being fought to the death by both sides, but the opportunity for the more splendid triumph rested with Polk's wing.

"It was a capital moment," said the Confederate Lieutenant Colonel Archer Anderson of the invitation presented to support Breckinridge and drive behind Thomas' log works. The comparison of Polk's opportunity with Jackson's flank attack at Chancellorsville is pertinent except for the nature of the opposing generalship. Whereas Jackson faced the Federal corps commander Oliver O. Howard, a courageous but by no means gifted fighter, and the erratic Hooker in command of the Army of the Potomac, Polk was battling in Thomas one of the ablest generals of the war. Thomas would not have hesitated to shift troops from his log works if the Confederates failed to assail them simultaneously in force, and he would have fought along a new line, facing north, if the emergency required it. Rosecrans, too, understood Thomas' needs and would have been a much stronger reliance than the baffled Hooker.

Still, from a Confederate standpoint, a wider encircling movement of the entire wing, attacking *en masse* behind Breckinridge, would have offered more promise than a series of costly assaults against the hastily constructed but formidable log works that protected Thomas' front.[9]

Breckinridge's brigades, severely handled in battling John Beatty and Stanley and finally Van Derveer, settled down for more routine fighting. As the battle moved down the Confederate line toward Bragg's center and left, the hostile forces on the north end of the battlefield exchanged long range fire for the balance of the morning.

CHAPTER TWENTY-THREE

Wood Leaves a Gap

DIVISION commander Thomas J. Wood of Rosecrans' army was energetic and capable, but his greatest glory in the war was to come near its close when he commanded with high competence the largest corps and the center of Thomas' army at Nashville, in what was perhaps the outstanding Union triumph.

John Beatty said Wood "knew how to blow his own horn" but that does not appear to have been an offensive characteristic, for others did not notice it. Everything about his military career was distinguished except ten momentous minutes at Chickamauga. About those ten minutes his superiors, the home public and historians have divided sharply.

A Kentuckian from Munfordville, he was fifth in his class at West Point, where Grant was his first roommate. His good grades gave him a commission in the engineer corps. He sacrificed his leave to get to Zachary Taylor in time to be an important factor in the Battle of Palo Alto, where he employed ox teams to haul up the guns. In quite another manner he distinguished himself at Buena Vista, where with skill and daring he conducted a reconnaissance behind the Mexican lines. Then he took to the dragoons and rose in the cavalry arm to the rank of lieutenant colonel. He was on the Utah campaign with Albert Sidney Johnston.

On leave in Egypt when news of secession reached him, he returned immediately and performed a notable service in Indianapolis in the next half year mustering 40,000 Hoosiers into the Federal Army. Of all the divisions at Stone's River, his in the Federal center was the one that held its ground unmoved through

251

the entire battle. Thomas, who commanded the center, could not have had other than high confidence in him. It endured throughout the war and was persuasive testimony to Wood's ability.

(Later Wood would have opportunity to justify that confidence. His men were first in the Confederate works on Missionary Ridge. As he had declined to leave the field when wounded at Stone's River, so he did when wounded severely at Lovejoy's Station in the Atlanta campaign. He wrapped his shattered leg in a robe and stayed with his command, an act which won from Sherman the remark that his example of courage was worth 20,000 men. As appeared to be the pattern with the more capable Federal generals named military administrators in the South after the war—examples being Thomas and Winfield Scott Hancock—he instituted a humane rule. In after years he was a member of the Board of Visitors at West Point.)

The spirit of his division could be seen from the attitude of an Irish member. When the women of Haskell, in La Porte County, Indiana, presented a flag to a Hoosier regiment, General Wagner received it from the chaplain, saying, "Tell the young ladies of Haskell that when the war is over their then sanctified gift shall be returned to them, unless torn to shreds by the enemy's bullets."

"An' thin we'll take 'em back the pole!" exclaimed a private from Erin, speaking out impulsively from the ranks. A laugh went along the line because of the breach of discipline, but the general must have appreciated the sentiment because he gave the soldier a pass to town the next day.[1]

Wood reached his fortieth birthday five days after the battle of Chickamauga. Regarded as "second to none in experience and cultured intellect," an officer of sensitivity whose service had been nothing short of distinguished since the first battle of the Mexican War, he had been deeply hurt and mortified by Rosecrans' merciless, crude censure in front of his staff and troops earlier in the day for his alleged slowness in relieving Negley. It was not to be expected that he would look lightly on any further orders.

At 10:30 A.M. the position in the Federal center was substantially unchanged since Wood went into line except that Barnes's brigade which had been lent to him from VanCleve had been returned, then dispatched at 9 A.M. to the aid of Thomas. Wood's two brigades, Harker's and Buell's, were undisturbed in their positions by the removal of Barnes, except to fill what he had covered. Wood's line ran through a fringe of trees parallel to and in front of the Glenn-Kelly road where it passed in rear of the Brotherton house and farm, roughly a quarter of a mile west of the La Fayette road.

Wood's left touched Brannan's right gently, for Brannan's line was somewhat in advance of Wood's and ran through a forest of great trees, fairly clean of underbrush but so heavy as to obscure any view of the troops from one who might pass in their rear along the Glenn-Kelly road. Brannan's left was *en echelon* behind Reynolds, whose line was on the east side of the La Fayette road. Edward King's brigade of Reynolds' division was bent back to face south down the La Fayette road and make a fair contact with Croxton's brigade of Brannan's division, which faced east. Van-Cleve's division was in reserve behind the juncture of Wood and Brannan, occupying the Dyer farm west of the Glenn-Kelly road.

Such was the situation when Captain Sanford C. Kellogg, of Thomas' staff, who had come up through the New York militia, had been a sergeant in the 37th New York and had won his captaincy and appointment to Thomas' staff just before the Tullahoma campaign, passed along the Glenn-Kelly road with one of Thomas' requests to Rosecrans for reinforcements. Two other aides had just reached headquarters from Thomas in rapid succession, and in response to their urgency Rosecrans had ordered Sheridan to send two brigades and VanCleve to go with two brigades to Thomas' support. Rosecrans was following his remark made early in the battle that Thomas must hold the road to Rossville "if he has to be reinforced by the entire army."

Captain Kellogg knew little of the battlefield, though after a long cavalry career he would study it intimately as the official mapmaker of the Chickamauga National Military Park. Perhaps he was not attentive to what the forest might conceal. As he passed in rear from Reynolds to Wood, he thought Reynolds' flank was in the air, not being able to discern his communication with Brannan, nor to see anything whatever of Brannan's division through the numerous trees and heavy foliage between the Glenn-Kelly and La

Fayette roads. Reaching headquarters, he reported to Rosecrans that as he passed he had noticed "Brannan was out of line and Reynolds' flank exposed." This wording of Kellogg's report was given by Lieutenant Colonel Gates P. Thruston, of McCook's staff, and in substantially the same language by Rosecrans in his report. Possibly it was more disconcerting, for the alarm conveyed to Rosecrans was that there was a wide gap in his line, with no troops between Wood and Reynolds.[2]

The situation at army headquarters at the time was one of tense activity. Rosecrans had returned to the Widow Glenn's after his ride along the lines. Couriers were coming minute by minute. Rosecrans was shifting units, mostly to answer the appeals of Thomas. Garfield was putting his orders into lucid writing. Headquarters at midmorning felt that the battle was progressing satisfactorily. No ambiguities had crept into the orders. Of Garfield it has been said, "His clear, unmistakable English had not a doubtful phrase or a misplaced comma."

As the picture of headquarters was presented at 10:30 A.M., another aide from General Thomas galloped up with information to Rosecrans that there was "a chasm in the center" of his army, between Reynolds and Wood. The commanding general's fault has not been deemed by some so much in the order he issued as in his choice of a staff member to write it. This error has been attributed to his excitement at the moment. Garfield "was deeply engaged in another matter," although what was more urgent than writing an order to save the army's center is not known. Rosecrans turned to Major Frank S. Bond and told him to write an order immediately. The order, so fateful to an army and to any number of its soldiers and officers and to many military careers, can be appreciated only by reading it:

> "Headquarters Department of Cumberland,
> "September 20th—10:45 A.M.
> "Brigadier-General Wood, Commanding Division:
> "The general commanding directs that you close up on Reynolds as fast as possible, and support him. Respectfully, etc.
> "FRANK S. BOND, Major and Aide-de-Camp."

Major Bond was Rosecrans' confidential aide who had charge of all the army's ciphers and was as near being the general's amanuensis as anyone at headquarters. Garfield's biographer, John Clark Ridpath, gives assurance that "had Garfield been consulted that order would never have been written" and bolsters it with the impressive argument that Garfield knew the exact position of every division on the field and would have known there was no gap between Wood and Reynolds. That is undoubtedly true; he was constantly relocating units on his map. But when coincidence enters to control a situation, it often comes not in a single event but in a chain of circumstances. One of the links here was that Garfield was not available when the order was written. It happened to be the most consequential order issued during the battle, and it was the only order issued that he did not write.

Rosecrans' lack of attentiveness to detail at this moment—he does not appear to have read the order after Bond worded it—suggests that he was feeling the strain of the battle. Taken with his outburst against Wood that morning and his capriciousness on the preceding day, it gives evidence of the approach of an instability dangerous for the leader of a great army in the presence of resourceful enemies. For weeks as the campaign against Chattanooga developed he had leaned on the stanch character and clear intellect of Thomas, but Thomas now had his hands full and Rosecrans was left to his own resources at headquarters.

What has been described as Rosecrans' "apparent lapses, neglect, and want of promptness" was due unquestionably to mental strain and physical exhaustion. The anxiety during the days when the army was divided and vulnerable had been a severe trial for him. Certainly on the second day at Chickamauga he was not the general of Rich Mountain, Iuka, Corinth or Stone's River.[3]

The question of what Wood should have done when he received the order was long discussed in the Army. One of the sane views was that of Palmer, who thought the fault was that the order should have been sent through Crittenden, the corps commander, instead of direct to Wood the division commander. Palmer's contention was that when orders were sent through a corps commander that general by virtue of his rank could modify them as circumstances dictated and could supervise their execution. It is true that the corps commander would have wider latitude. Rosecrans maintained in his own defense that division commander Wood should have used his discretion, that he should have perceived the consequences of strict obedience and have assumed that the order had been issued without a full knowledge of the situation. But Rosecrans failed to remember that only an hour or so earlier he had stormed at Wood with such words as: "You have disobeyed my specific orders . . . and, by God, I will not tolerate it!" It is difficult to blame a general for prompt and explicit obedience of peremptory orders on the battlefield. As Palmer summed it up: "Wood was merely unfortunate; he had attempted to obey an order dictated by ignorance of the situation."

Turchin analyzed the question at length and reached a conclusion different from Palmer's, one more sympathetic toward Rosecrans. He felt that on its face the order was not capable of execution and should therefore have provoked inquiry. If Brannan's division had not been between Wood's and Reynolds' the order would make sense. Wood could simply move his division to the left on the same line—nudge over, in effect—which would be closing on Reynolds and supporting him. So, also, if he had been in the rear of Reynolds the order would have been intelligible. He would simply move his division up behind Reynolds at a supporting distance. But with conditions as they were, Turchin held, the order contradicted itself: "The first part of it meant for General Wood to move his division to the left *in the line* and join Reynolds, and the second part meant to move it *out of the line* and place it in the rear of Reynolds. According to the phraseology accepted in military language the order had no sense; one part of it was contradicting the other part. Why then not to ascertain the meaning of it from the person who wrote the order before moving?"

Turchin went on to say that Wood was aware of the presence of the enemy in his front. About that there could be no question because of the reconnaissance he had already conducted. It would have required only a few minutes to ascertain the meaning of the order.

Such was the issue presented. Turchin's clincher was: "The idea

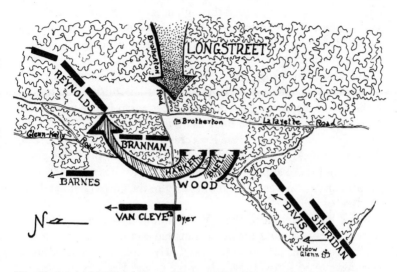

Wood's fatal withdrawal. In response to Rosecrans' order to "close up on Reynolds . . . and support him," he moves across the rear of Brannan and leaves a gap in the Federal line at moment of Longstreet's advance.

of implicitly obeying orders by such officers as commanders of divisions, without reasoning about them is absurd. . . ." But had Turchin just been blasted by Rosecrans for not stepping lively and been warned of the unpleasant consequences of disobedience?

Thomas' confidant and biographer, Chaplain Thomas B. Van Horne, tended to absolve Wood of blame, saying, "The fact that this order was not sent through General Crittenden, the corps commander, emphasized the requirement to make the movement as fast as possible."

Those very words often overlooked in the order are "as fast as possible." How much time for inquiry does such a phrase allow?

The newspaper correspondent Whitelaw Reid, who wrote admiringly of Rosecrans but still retained some objectivity, found no merit whatever in Wood's position. He said that "even if literal execution of the order had been possible, obedience to it approached criminality." He pointed out the well-settled principle that a subordinate has the privilege of disobeying an order that is sure to be disastrous, or is clearly issued through misapprehension of the facts. Wood knew that execution of the order would be dangerous, but he could not know Rosecrans' plans or what replacements he might intend to send.[4]

But how about the general who impetuously issues—through other than his routine staff channels—an order churning up his line of battle on the mere hearsay that there is a gap in it, without any personal inspection of the field? The first fault was Kellogg's but the major fault was of course Rosecrans'. He could have ridden to Wood as quickly as he could send a staff officer. But if he could not go, and there appears to be no reason why he could not, then his proper course was to assign the duty to the corps commander—Crittenden.

Some have contended that Wood should have gone at once to Rosecrans, but should not Rosecrans have gone to Wood before issuing the order? Rosecrans was fairly close by. The Widow Glenn's looked across the fields to the Glenn Kelly road where it crossed the Dyer road. A gallop of four or five minutes would have taken him to Wood's position. Rosecrans had been in close contact with his battle line that morning, but here was an instance where he was not, and it was the critical moment of the battle.

Wood's comment that he was glad he had the order in writing, often cited to show he was at fault, seems to have little bearing on the central question, which turns on the matter of the spirit in which peremptory orders sent to the battle line should be obeyed. In this war of frequent disaster and much complaint, it was often well for a subordinate to have his orders in writing.

McCook was present when an orderly from Rosecrans handed Wood the order at 10:55 A.M. That tended to relieve Wood of some of the responsibility, though McCook was not his commander. McCook felt that Wood would be required to take his division out of the line; before he rode away he said he would close the gap thus created. Wood then sent orders to his brigade commanders to begin the movement at double quick and they responded at once. There can be little doubt that Wood acted in good faith.

"The order was not only mandatory, but peremptorily mandatory," he later explained. "It directed me to close upon General Reynolds, a movement of one body from the rear to another body in front of it. But it gave me the reason for the movement—viz., to support the body of troops in front—the most important reason that can exist on the field of battle.

"With this order in my hand, with Brannan on my left, with no knowledge of Reynolds' position, but with a peremptory order to close up on him and support him, it was physically impossible to obey it in any other way than I did—viz., by withdrawing from the line, passing to the left, finding Reynolds' position, closing up on him, and supporting him."[5]

When Wood had his command in motion and marching across the rear of Brannan to the support of Reynolds, he rode ahead to ask Reynolds where his troops should be posted. Unable to find Reynolds, he met Thomas, told him of the order he had received from Rosecrans, and asked where he should place his command to support Reynolds. Thomas advised him that Reynolds did not require support but Baird could use it and that he should go to Baird on the extreme left of the line. Wood then showed Thomas his order—having only related its contents previously—and asked if the corps commander would assume responsibility for altering it. Thomas at once said he would.

Thomas supplied a staff officer to guide Wood to Baird. Wood sent Barnes's brigade ahead—it already being on the way to Thomas —and rode to get his own two brigades that had moved out of line and were in column marching toward the rear of Reynolds.

They had not been out of line ten minutes but in that brief period the entire aspect of the battle had changed.

CHAPTER TWENTY-FOUR

Piercing the Federal Center

LONGSTREET had waited impatiently through the morning, all the while making good use of the time by aligning his divisions. Instead of attacking on a wide front as Polk's wing had done on both days—Cleburne's single division had a front a mile wide—Longstreet massed his troops in a grand column of assault, much superior in weight and depth to his attacking force on the third day at Gettysburg, or to anything Polk or Bragg had undertaken thus far at Chickamauga.

When Longstreet had attacked at Gettysburg with the divisions of Pickett, Pettigrew and Trimble consisting of nine brigades, four of them already had been shattered and grievously weakened during the first day of the battle. At Chickamauga he formed on a front of half a mile eight brigades, all relatively fresh and some not yet tried in action. His Chickamauga column was superior and it had the protection of the forest, whereas the Gettysburg advance was across open ground.

Turchin, the Russian-born brigadier general who had engaged in warfare on two continents and was one of the best students of method in the Northern army, observed that "Longstreet's experience in these matters was much larger than Polk's or Hill's," and it led him to use columns of attack in place of Cleburne's and Breckinridge's single lines.

Longstreet's main column had a front of two brigades of Bushrod Johnson's division. McNair was on the right with his one North Carolina and four Arkansas regiments and Captain James F. Culpeper's South Carolina battery. Bushrod Johnson's old brigade, commanded by Colonel John S. Fulton, was on the left, all Tennesseans except the Georgia artillery battery under Lieutenant William S. Everett. Gregg's strong brigade of one Texas and six Tennessee regiments made a second line except for the Texans, who were brought up on Fulton's left. Gregg's brigade included Bledsoe's efficient Missouri battery, commanded by Lieutenant R. L. Wood.

Behind Bushrod Johnson, Longstreet stationed Hood's old division commanded by Law, consisting of Law's brigade under Colonel James L. Sheffield (who had led the 48th Alabama up Little Round Top at Gettysburg), Robertson's Texas brigade (formerly Hood's) and Benning's "Rock Brigade" of Georgians. Filling out the column in rear of Law was Kershaw's demidivision, a part of the troops McLaws had led at Gettysburg, consisting of Kershaw's and Humphreys' brigades. Humphreys' was Barksdale's old brigade that had crushed the Peach Orchard salient at Gettysburg.

This column of assault aggregated about 11,000 men and was under the immediate command of Hood. On Hood's right was Stewart's "Little Giant" division, which had reached the Dyer farm on the preceding afternoon, while on his left was Hindman's fresh division of three brigades, supported by Preston's division of three, which held the Confederate left and had not yet been engaged. Thus Longstreet's entire assault party aggregated about 23,000 men.

Though Stewart was under Longstreet's command, he had received attack orders directly from Bragg after that general had become exasperated by Polk's delay and had sent broadside instructions to every captain—or was alleged to have done so, though it would seem the orders reached the generals ahead of the company commanders—to begin the action. Stewart had scored a brilliant achievement in penetrating deep into the Federal center on the afternoon before and was anxious to repeat his performance. He moved forward and encountered Brannan's Federals at the La Fayette road. The battle was hot but inconclusive.

At the time Stewart attacked, Longstreet had not yet been advised that Bragg had cast aside his first plan and put the battle under the control of the division commanders and the captains, to attack at will and at once. When he received that intelligence he rushed off a restraining order to Hood, fearful that he would advance before the brigades of Kershaw and Humphreys were in position in the rear of Law's three brigades. Now Old Peter was free of any curbs imposed by Bragg's plan, and could fight his own battle. Finally the grand column of assault was ready. All of the preparatory work had been done in the deep woods screened from the Federal pickets. The column straddled the Brotherton road, down which the attack would be made.[1]

Irrespective of what would be said about his politics in after years, Longstreet was systematic as a general. On reaching his command he not only inspected his troops, most of whom he had never seen, but also studied as fully as he could the character of the battlefield. The Brotherton farm of 700 acres, partly cleared, offered an objective directly in his front. Because of the timber, he could not reconnoiter effectively, so before he went to sleep on the night of the nineteenth he inquired about residents of the neighborhood who were in the Confederate army. He hit on Tom Brotherton as the man he wanted to see. Tom was found and taken to Old Peter. Jim Brotherton, his brother, told of it afterward:

"We was raised right here and knew every pig trail through these woods. Saturday night as soon as he got here the gineral sent for Tom. Tom he sez to me: 'It's a sorry lad that won't fight for his own home, Jim. Remember that tomorrow.' Then he left me and he was with the gineral all that night and the next day."

With Tom Brotherton filling in the details, Longstreet's movement conformed to the conditions of woods and trails. A newspaper correspondent later wondered about credit for the attack: "How much of it belongs to Longstreet the general and how much to Tom Brotherton the private?" Longstreet was at least needed. As he was guided by Tom Brotherton, so one of the Dyer boys who had been reared on the farm adjoining Brotherton's guided Preston's division.

One of Bragg's scouts was Maurice Thompson, nineteen years old, Indiana-born but Georgia-reared, who flitted about the north Georgia hills and red lands he knew so well, and from which he had already begun to write nature and bird stories that were to become one source of his fame. Perhaps his greatest achievement was that he and his brother Will, another Confederate soldier, reversed the carpetbag procedure after the war, went North to work on a railroad, and married the two daughters of the railroad president. Maurice, who became one of the most gifted of Hoosier poets, always cherished memories of his Confederate soldier days:

> ". . . I am a Southerner;
> I love the South; I dared for her
> To fight from Lookout to the sea,
> With her proud banner over me."

He became a lawyer at Crawfordsville, Indiana, and a prolific writer whose best-known work, *Alice of Old Vincennes*, was published after his death. He also led in establishing archery as an American sport and wrote much about it, while Will Thompson was five times national archery champion.

Maurice Thompson gave us the poem quoted on the title page. Even while he was Bragg's scout he had time for literature. His close friend and fellow townsman, Meredith Nicholson, said that while Thompson was a Confederate soldier he always had a book with him—likely a book of De Quincey's essays or Carlyle's. It would appear that Longstreet learned more about the lay of the battlefield than Bragg, possibly because Tom Brotherton was not bothered with De Quincey.

Jim Brotherton, "long-legged, short-bodied, spry as a cat and quick of tongue," whom the newspaperman regarded a fair type of Confederate mountain soldier, fought "the best he knowed how" while his brother scouted for Longstreet.

Years later when Longstreet visited the battlefield one of his first acts was to go to the Brotherton house looking for his old scout, but Tom was dead.[2]

When finally organized, Longstreet's front was about 300 yards east of the La Fayette road and roughly half a mile in front of the position held up to that time by Wood's Federal division. Longstreet had only forty-two guns on his left wing. The paucity of artillery was due to the fact that neither Bushrod Johnson's division nor Hood's corps had their artillery with them when they reached the field. Alexander was missed by Longstreet. However, Old Peter did not waste much time in search for a substitute chief of artillery because his survey of the field showed it to be mainly a heavy woodland poorly adapted to the use of artillery. Another difficulty for Longstreet was that some of the men were without rations. Their wagons had been lost in the woods. Some wagons came up in darkness and some after daylight and while the left wing was waiting for Polk to get into action a breakfast of what was available was cooked along the lines.

Longstreet surveyed his preparations: "The hour of battle was at hand."

Now Bushrod Johnson, at Longstreet's order transmitted by Hood, began one of the most spectacular advances of the Confederate war. Sweeping through the woods and covering quickly the 300 yards east of the La Fayette road, he encountered a heavy line of Federal skirmishers scattered along that roadway and hidden behind the fence of the Brotherton farm. Davis had set up a battery in the cleared field south of Brotherton's which opened on the advancing graycoats and did considerable damage to the front of the column. But the Federal fire, while galling, was coming from Davis' troops diagonally situated to the left or from Brannan's diagonally to the right, and the column soon noticed that it was advancing without heavy resistance in its immediate front. Bursts of grape came from the Federal guns, though canister was used to a much greater extent in the eastern armies. Minié balls whistled more from the flanks than front.

As Fulton's brigade emerged from the woods and encountered this fire, Lieutenant Colonel Watt W. Floyd of the 17th Tennessee called out, "Boys, do you see that battery?"

Then men answered with a hurrah and "We do."

"That's ours," commanded the colonel.

At that instant Bushrod Johnson rode up and talked briefly with Colonel Fulton, the brigade commander, who then turned and shouted, "Attention, old brigade!" The soldiers knew he meant Johnson's "old brigade," and snapped to attention. Fulton's next order was "Forward, double-quick!"

"We started on the run," said Elijah Wiseman of the 17th Tennessee, "raised the 'rebel yell,' and in a few minutes those guns were ours."

Johnson's division gained impetus as it advanced. At the Brotherton house it split, McNair's brigade passing to the north of the house, moving on both sides of the road leading west to the Dyer farm. Fulton's brigade passed south of Brotherton's, plunging across the fields which Jim and Tom Brotherton had rotated in corn and hay as long as they could remember. Inside the Brotherton house one of Johnson's squads picked up the wounded Colonel F. A. Bartleson of the 100th Illinois, who had ventured out in front of Wood's line—without orders, according to Wood. He had been wounded and taken into the house by his soldiers on the skirmish line.

At no place on the battlefield was there heavier concentration of fire than at Brotherton's, where the battle already had surged back and forth on the nineteenth when Stewart made his penetration of the Federal line, and where it now struck like a tornado as Bushrod Johnson came out of the woods. Yet all through the fray the four Brotherton cows munched the grass contentedly, unconsciously evading bullets that fell thick and the high explosives and storms of grape. What was more remarkable, they also avoided the foragers of the Northern army, who a little later in the war would leave nothing on four legs behind them as they passed through Georgia under Sherman.

Adaline Brotherton, one of the heroines of the Chickamauga story, returned to the farm at milking time each day to milk the four cows and give the milk to the wounded of both armies being cared for in the little log Brotherton house. George and Mary Brotherton, father and mother of the seven Brotherton children, had remained in the house during the battle of the nineteenth, but left late Saturday afternoon to camp with those children who were not fighting in the Confederate army, and with their neighbors. These included their daughter and son-in-law, Sarah and Larkin H. Poe, who lived a short distance up the La Fayette road, between the Brothertons and the Kellys.

How the fighting went around the Brotherton house might be

judged from the fact that when the family returned after the battle they found nine dead Federal soldiers in their front yard. All of the wounded had been taken to improvised hospitals.[3]

Bushrod Johnson's brigades passed the Brotherton house without halting and reached on a run the strip of woods behind the cleared fields. Here, in front of the Glenn-Kelly road, up until 11 A.M., ten minutes before Longstreet's step-off, Wood's division of Crittenden's corps had maintained its battle line. On the left of the advancing troops could be seen Davis' division rushing across the fields toward this position, and, scarcely more distant, Sheridan's two brigades moving north.

On Bushrod Johnson's right and close at hand was the last of Wood's two brigades, Buell's, already in column on the Glenn-Kelly road and beginning its march on the mistaken mission to "close up on and support" Reynolds.

Enemy troops were on both sides of Johnson but nothing was in front. Buell's brigade was ready prey—a "sitting duck." Its flank and rear were exposed and, being in no manner deployed for action, it could offer scant resistance. Davis was hit as he rushed to stem the gray flow through the fatal gap.

Everett's battery of Fulton's brigade was set up in the field south of the Brotherton house to cover the advance to the front and left. While each gun was firing six rounds, Hindman entered the attack on the left, and Hood's brigades in rear of Johnson began to incline toward the right to find a place in the line. Brannan from his position in the Federal woods threw such a heavy fire into McNair that the brigade faltered and some of the men began to retreat, but Johnson was able to rally them. The heavy column burst over the empty log breastworks that had marked Wood's old line and swept forward, as Johnson described it, with "great force and rapidity."

When Wood's division had been pulled out of its position at the double-quick to "close up on and support" Reynolds, the right of the 17th Ohio of Brannan's division was left exposed. As Bushrod Johnson's men moved up the Dyer road past the Brotherton house they took Brannan's position in flank and savagely attacked the Ohio regiment in front, flank and rear. The regiment gave way in confusion, the men scattering over the fields of the Dyer farm.

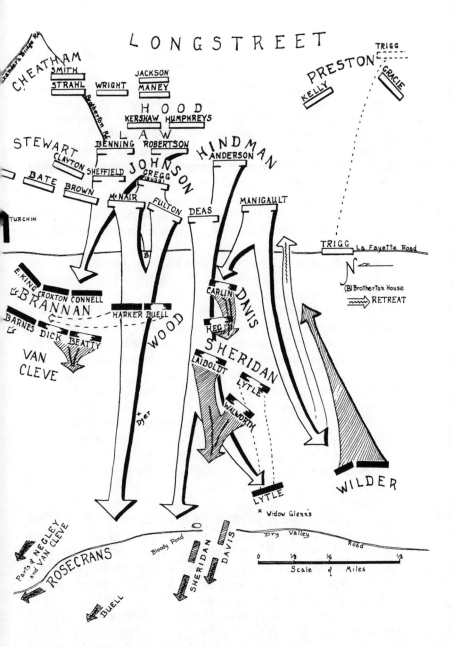

Longstreet's massed attack on Federal right. Bushrod Johnson's division moves through gap left by Wood and cleaves through the Federal right center. Hindman's division routs divisions of Davis and Sheridan and Rosecrans' right wing is driven from field.

Only Company B managed to hold a formation. It moved compactly 300 yards to the rear, halted, gave three cheers and sounded what the men termed the rally cry of the regiment, something that had not been needed at Mill Springs or Stone's River, where its brigade had been the victorious assailant instead of the retiring assailed. About 200 men assembled to the call and what was left of the regiment made an impetuous but futile charge against the advancing gray line, a heavy mass that outnumbered them ten to one. This charge alone cost the Ohioans 100 casualties. The remaining 100 retired for a second stand before they passed off the field. By this time the regiment had shrunk to fifty-two.[4]

Bushrod Johnson tore like a whirlwind through the Federal line at the quarter-of-a-mile gap left so invitingly for him by the shift of Wood. The division came out of the trees and faced the open fields of the Dyer farm. Here his right brigade, McNair's, was halted momentarily by heavy flank fire, until Colonel Cyrus A. Sugg of the 50th Tennessee, who commanded Gregg's brigade after Gregg had been wounded on the nineteenth, brought up his regiments which had formed the second line as the division advanced. Fulton inclined his brigade to the left and McNair to the right to make room for Sugg. The division resumed its rapid advance, bursting from the timber, crossing the Glenn-Kelly road, and driving ahead onto the cultivated ground of the Dyer farm.

Federal batteries were booming forth on the long incline toward the Snodgrass farm to Johnson's front and right, posted there earlier by Thomas for a protection mainly of his left from a turning movement by Polk's divisions. Across this incline streamed back the blue-coated soldiers of Buell's brigade and parts of Davis', Sheridan's and VanCleve's divisions. VanCleve's, who had been exposed by the withdrawal of Wood and the retirement of Brannan, largely disintegrated in the rout, but another molesting Federal battery was holding its ground at the corner of a peach orchard southwest of the Dyer farmhouse.

Bushrod Johnson was entranced with the picture as he emerged from the woods. "The scene now presented was unspeakably grand," he said. "The resolute and impetuous charge, the rush of our heavy columns sweeping out from the shadow of the gloom of the forest into the open fields flooded with sunlight, the glitter of arms, the onward dash of artillery and mounted men, the retreat of the foe, the shout of hosts of our army, the dust, the smoke, the noise of fire-arms—of whistling balls and grape-shot and of bursting shell—made up a battle scene of unsurpassed grandeur."

Still, Johnson knew it was no time to halt and contemplate the magnificent pageant of high triumph and supreme tragedy that comes at the moment when a great army is suddenly put to rout on a battlefield. As his three brigades began their movement across the Dyer farm, Hood rode alongside and gave him the last order the corps commander issued on the battlefield: "Go ahead, and keep ahead of everything." Only a few minutes more of command were left to Hood.

Johnson did exactly as ordered. The center of the Federal army had been pierced. He ascribed the victory up to this point to the depth of the attack column and "the force and power with which it was thrown upon the enemy's line." The assault as he surveyed it had broken completely Rosecrans' center and "cast the shattered fragments to the right and left."

Johnson advanced Everett's battery again to play against the retreating masses of Federal soldiers. Half a mile to the left he could see Hindman's division, which had advanced abreast him and was now shattering Sheridan, moving past the Viniard farm and up the slopes toward the Widow Glenn's. Johnson, the point of the wedge which Longstreet was driving into the Union position, splitting and widening the gap with each new hammer blow, had now reached the Dyer farmhouse, shaded by great willow oaks. Fulton's brigade passed on either side of the house.

The battery that had been firing from the peach orchard west of Dyer's lay just ahead. Johnson's center brigade, Sugg's, inclined slightly to the right in order to take this battery in flank, and easily picked up the nine guns. The adjutant of the 50th Tennessee, Fletcher Beaumont—the customary order of the names of the great Elizabethan playwrights had been reversed here to no loss of dramatic effect—required the Northern drivers to limber and haul off the pieces with their own horses; so quickly had the capture been made that neither could the men escape nor the animals be driven to Northern safety. The novel feature was that the four three-inch rifles involved in this capture belonged to the 1st Missouri Federal battery, commanded by Lieutenant Gustavus Schueler, of Laiboldt's brigade, Sheridan's division. They passed into the hands of the 1st Missouri Confederate battery (Bledsoe's), commanded by Lieutenant R. L. Wood.[5]

Meanwhile McNair's brigade, which won in this action the title of "the Star Brigade at Chickamauga," advanced on Johnson's right, moving toward the Federal guns that had been sending in an oblique fire from the rolling land rising toward Snodgrass Hill. McNair was hit in the advance and Colonel Robert W. Harper of the 1st Arkansas was wounded mortally. The command fell to Colonel David Coleman of the 39th North Carolina. Although origin of the term "Tarheels" has been attributed in North Carolina folklore to Hoke's division of Lee's army, it was employed with the 39th North Carolina many months before Hoke ever became a major general and had a division. A Montgomery newspaper correspondent writing of Chickamauga used the term as one currently applied to Coleman's men, "perhaps from their tenacity of purpose as well as their having been enlisted in the piny woods of the old North State."

The formidable collection of Federal guns consisted of two batteries, which Coleman's men rushed and took. Eight of the pieces were sent at once to the Confederate rear and two others were removed later, but Bragg, in recognition of the capture, ordered that three of them should be assigned to Coleman's command. As the Montgomery correspondent described this high point of the advance, the batteries were strongly supported by Federal infantry, but "McNair's brigade charged so rapidly, loading and firing as they went, that the Yankees were surprised and routed. The assault was ferocious, and the victory complete."

Coleman was in front of his brigade in the rush and was the first to put his hand on a captured cannon. The correspondent reaffirmed that the Federal artillerists put up a much stronger battle than the support. The infantrymen appeared to have been caught in the contagion as the army collapsed about them. But the artillery, devoted to their precious guns, fired and loaded as long as they could, then flung grapeshot and shells with their hands into the faces of the Confederates as they rushed amid the pieces. The second battery was about 100 yards distant. When the two had been captured the "Tarheels," who led the movement, let out a shout and raised the flag of the 39th North Carolina—an all-mountaineer regiment—over the guns. Losses on both sides were heavy, those of McNair's brigade aggregating 40 per cent.[6]

One of the regiments distinguished in the fighting was the 1st Arkansas Rifles whose Colonel Robert W. Harper, mortally wounded at the beginning, was succeeded by Lieutenant Colonel Daniel H. Reynolds. He led it so ably during the battle that his commission as colonel was dated from September 20, 1863. Destined to command McNair's brigade, known in the later stages of the war as Reynolds' brigade, he was a Northerner like his division commander, Bushrod Johnson, and his fellow lieutenant colonel, R. Bogardus Snowden, commander of the 25th Tennessee of Fulton's brigade. Reynolds had come up from captain of the Chicot Rangers of Little Rock, Arkansas, and he gave brilliant service to the Confederacy until he lost his leg in the closing days at Bentonville. He was born near Centerburg, Ohio, and attended Ohio Wesleyan University, at Delaware, Ohio, in Rosecrans' home county. A fellow student was another Ohioan, now the Confederate Brigadier General Otho French Strahl, who across the fields on Bragg's right was commanding ably a brigade of Cheatham's division. Reynolds and Strahl had studied law and had been admitted to the bar together at Somerville, Tennessee, and both were practicing in the South when war came.

Colonel Coleman, who commanded the brigade for the balance of the battle, was from Buncombe County, North Carolina. At Camp Patton in Asheville he had organized "Coleman's battalion," out of which the regiment had grown. As Lieutenant Theodore F. Davidson of the 39th North Carolina described his advance, the brigade was well out in front of the Confederate line when Coleman decided he must silence the guns on the elevation ahead. To make sure of the capture, he told his men to shoot down the horses instead of the enemy soldiers. After the Federal infantry support broke, the defiant gunners fought hand-to-hand until killed or wounded. This was the place and the time which, as discussed among the Carolinians, came to be called the "Famous Break of the Federal Center" and, though it was not known to be so at the time, was the decisive moment of the battle.[7]

After Johnson had passed the Dyer house and the main batteries that had been impeding his advance had been captured, he noticed the narrow strip of woods on the western edge of the Dyer farmlands and beyond this strip an elevated ridge, cleared of timber, running north and south, parallel with his own battle line. He judged the elevation to be 600 yards from where the nine Federal guns had been captured in the peach orchard west of the Dyer house. This was an overestimate, for the ridge is little more than a quarter of a mile from the house. It was one of the most important elevations on the entire battlefield, for it overlooked the Dry Valley road, the link between Rosecrans' right wing and Chattanooga.

Sugg's brigade had halted, apparently in something of the same exultation as the Hoosier regiment when it had recaptured a battery and turned to speechmaking on the afternoon before. While the Confederates did not engage in oratory, time was being wasted in getting the Federal cannon to the rear. Bushrod Johnson prodded the men and got them on the move again. They reached the ridge at about the time Fulton's brigade was climbing it on their left.

Johnson had now penetrated a mile into the heart of the Federal position. From his elevation he could look down the sharp western face of the ridge to the Vittetoe house on his front and right. Beyond this a scant 100 yards was the Dry Valley road leading from Crawfish Springs through McFarland's Gap to Rossville and Chattanooga. South of the Vittetoe house was a large cornfield in a cove between the ridge just reached by the Confederates and the first ascents of Missionary Ridge. North of where Johnson stood, Missionary Ridge shot eastward a spur, the eastern end of which was Snodgrass Hill, where elements of the Federal army were assembling. The back part of the spur has been known since some of the early literature about the battle as Horseshoe Ridge, a designation that does not seem to occur in contemporary accounts. Johnson could see along the Dry Valley road the telegraph wires which linked Rosecrans' headquarters with Chattanooga. As he looked northwest his eye caught a moving train of Federal wagons jamming the Dry Valley road, while around the Vittetoe house nearer at hand was a Federal battery set up to give protection to the train as it withdrew.

Johnson's men overran the ridge quickly. The Federals already had scattered from their breastwork of fence rails here and had also abandoned what proved a neat prize for the Confederate soldiers—a large heap of knapsacks dropped apparently far in the rear of the Federal line where they would be presumed safe.[8]

As soon as he had viewed the territory ahead from his place of vantage on the ridge, the Confederate general looked to his flanks and rear and discovered that he was standing alone. It was not quite noon. In less than fifty minutes Bushrod Johnson's three brigades had split the Federal army and threatened the road along which a large part of it was retiring. While the assault had been prepared by Longstreet, whose management and alignment of the troops had been an essential factor, the drive and resolution had been provided by this Ohioan in gray, who now judged that his main need was artillery and infantry support to maintain his position overlooking the Dry Valley road. He sent his aide-de-camp, Captain W. T. Blakemore who had been with him in Fort Donelson, back to Longstreet to report his position and request more troops and guns.

Johnson needed support because his advance had been costly. Sugg's ranks were sadly thinned as the men reached the ridge. Company A of the 30th Tennessee, from Robertson County, went into the battle with twenty-two men. Nine were killed and nine left wounded on the field during the plunge through the Union army. When arms were stacked that night on Snodgrass Hill, it had to be done carefully to make them stand, because there were only four muskets.

An instance of natural leadership asserting itself occurred in the 10th Tennessee of this brigade—"The Bloody Tinth," a regiment which lost half its numbers.

Clarence Malone was attending the University of Mississippi when war came. He wrote home that he was joining the "Uni-

versity Greys," which became Company A in the celebrated 11th
Mississippi of Lee's army. But his grandfather persuaded him to
return home and join the "Columbus Riflemen," and take his servant, Matt, along. Since he was only a private he was not au-
thorized to have a servant, but he made an arrangement with the
captain that Matt should go along and attend to the needs of both
of them. After much campaigning elsewhere, Malone found himself in the "Tinth," originally an Irish regiment recruited in Nashville.

On this bold Sunday morning advance at Chickamauga, the captain was hit. Malone was kneeling by his side to see the extent of
the injury when another shell severed the captain's head from his
body, cutting it off clean at the shoulders. Seeing no one else to
lead the men, Malone jumped up, waved his sword and shouted,
"Follow me!" He was made a captain after the battle. It was a
rather empty honor. Only six men remained in the company for
him to command.

Bloody as was the battle and costly the sacrifices, evidence was
presented in later years to show that Tennessee did not lose here
all its sturdy fighting stock. Forty-seven years after the battle
James B. Kirk of Company A, 44th Tennessee, Fulton's brigade,
who was wounded in the advance at Chickamauga, had at the age
of eighty-two a progeny of fifty-three children, grandchildren
and great-grandchildren, without a death having occurred in the
family. His brother, who also served in the Confederate army for
four years, had a progeny of sixty-four, with but a single death.

One of the novelties of the 41st Tennessee, Sugg's brigade, was
that Company E, formed in Petersburg, Tennessee, had three sets
of twins, which probably was a pair or two more than any other
company in the Confederate army could boast about. One set had
caused General Gregg difficulty. Edwin R. and Walter S. Beardon
were identical twins. Though too young for mustaches, they were
lieutenants. During a heat wave at Port Hudson, Louisiana, Walter
was serving as officer of the day. Ed was going about his business
when General Gregg suddenly pounced on him and put him under
arrest for not having his coat buttoned and sword belt fastened.
Such disarray was no pattern to be set by an officer of the day. Ed

reported under arrest, but just then the general happened to notice the true officer of the day, Walter, pass in faultless military attire. The general laughed, and Ed laughed with him.

Ed led Company E of the 41st Tennessee at Chickamauga, where a bullet broke his ankle bone. Walter suffered a similar severe leg injury in the Atlanta campaign. When they returned to Petersburg in May 1865, one walked with a crutch, the other a stick.

The company's other twins were Captain John F. and James Fly, and the Reverend Messrs. Sam O. and J. Allen Woods.[9]

After sending Captain Blakemore to Longstreet, Bushrod Johnson took a defensive position along the ridge with Sugg on the right, his flank turned back so that he faced mainly north, in the direction of the Snodgrass-Horseshoe Ridge spur. The part of his brigade facing north had a cover of trees and the position was strong. Fulton's brigade faced west, about 100 yards to the left of Sugg. McNair's brigade, when it returned to Johnson after capturing the two batteries, was still farther to the right, held in reserve.

As quickly as Johnson could throw out skirmishers and consolidate his line he brought up Everett's Georgia artillery battery to open fire on the Federal train moving up the Dry Valley road toward McFarland's Gap. The consternation among the teams and drivers could be witnessed from Johnson's remote position. Wagons were overturned. Some were dashed into trees, others left the road and tried to make their way up the steep, rugged hill. The Confederate pickets opened a rifle fire to aid in the confusion. Lieutenant Everett detached a single gun and sent it to a knoll in the cornfield south of Vittetoe's, where it could fire more directly up the road, which runs through a gorge southwest of Horseshoe Ridge. There the Confederate fire caused the greatest panic.

The Federal battery close to Vittetoe's fired a few rounds and retired, one of its rifled guns having been dismounted. Johnson's skirmishers advanced and captured the wagons, heavily loaded with ammunition, the caissons and four pieces of artillery, along with a number of prisoners.

Bushrod R. Johnson, who had effected this breakthrough—brilliantly executed even though it depended on the fortuitous

removal of Wood's division and on catching other Federal elements in motion—had been drawn south from Ohio as a teacher,
and it would seem he was one of inspirational qualities. Lieutenant
Colonel Snowden of the 25th Tennessee had been a student of his
at both Georgetown, Kentucky, and Nashville, Tennessee.

Johnson was born in Belmont County, Ohio, opposite Wheeling,
then in Virginia. The name Bushrod, which occurs in George
Washington's family, suggests Virginia connections. Probably it
was place of residence rather than heredity that took Johnson into
the Confederate army. He was twenty-third in his West Point
class; ahead of him, standing eighth, was William T. Sherman, and
the twelfth was George H. Thomas. He resigned after seeing
action under Zachary Taylor in Mexico and became professor of
chemistry, mathematics, engineering and philosophy and for four
years superintendent of the Western Military Institute at Georgetown, Kentucky. Then he went to the University of Nashville to
teach civil engineering.

When war came his situation was similar to that of his classmate
Sherman, who was superintendent of Louisiana State Military
Academy, but the two made different decisions. Johnson had been
a colonel in the Kentucky militia and retained the same rank in
the Tennessee militia when he moved to Nashville. Under the Con-
federacy he became a colonel of engineers. Wounded severely at
Shiloh, where he led one of Cheatham's brigades, he accompanied
Bragg on the Kentucky campaign, and commanded a brigade in
Cleburne's division at Stone's River.[10]

Johnson's story, which has distressful aspects, should be completed. After Chickamauga he went with Longstreet to the seige
of Knoxville and into Lee's army, where his division was an important factor at Bermuda Hundred, the Petersburg crater and
until he surrendered with Lee at Appomattox. Returning to teaching, he became Chancellor of the University of Nashville, but the
school had no funds or income and was compelled to close. Education was not very remunerative in the South during the lean Reconstruction years.

Johnson put his family and most treasured possessions in a wagon
and with two mules drove to Macoupin County, Illinois, to become

a farmer. As one might expect, his principal cargo was his books. For his last six years he struggled rather ineffectually to make a living from the land, part of his effort going into the sale of locust posts to neighboring farmers. His farm was near Miles Station, northeast of Brighton. The station is now scarcely a town but then was the seat of Colonel Jonathan Rice Miles, a Union army veteran. He and Johnson became close friends, and another friend was Brevet Brigadier General John I. Rinaker of Carlinville, old colonel of the 122nd Illinois. While the former Confederate was not successful financially, he became an inspiration to the neighborhood through his books and scholarship.

From the folklore of the neighborhood it would appear that General Johnson was admired for his intellectual brilliance and pitied for the manner in which he would allow others, sometimes his farm help, to impose on him. Competent as soldier and teacher, he had no capability in farming or business. But he lent books to boys in the neighborhood and, more than that, discussed their contents with the lads when the books were returned. Some born in the section can recall the appreciation voiced by their fathers for the opportunity the old general gave them in the back country of the 1870s, which retained many aspects of the pioneer society of Abraham Lincoln. The level of country schoolteaching was not very high by modern standards.

Johnson, his health broken by the war, never recovered his full vigor and died in 1880 at the age of sixty-two. His grave is in the little country cemetery of an earlier generation, once the yard of a Methodist church, now churchless, unfenced and unsupported by public funds. But the graves are still cared for, and the plot is mowed by near-by farmer Frank M. Stubblefield, whose grandfather used to recall how the Confederate general, an expatriate almost from both North and South, came to the southern Illinois country behind a pair of mules.

A slim white shaft of soft stone rises above Johnson's grave, bearing only the inscription

Gen. Bushrod R. Johnson
Died Sept. 12, 1880
Age. 62 yrs. 5 days.

The base of the column, which stands about eight feet high, is of coarse concrete, in which is molded the name JOHNSON. Just above the base, in the soft stone of the shaft, are faint traces of what was once an additional inscription. R. D. Fletcher of Thayer, Illinois, who was on business in Miles Station in 1907, noted down this inscription, a verse which one of Johnson's friends had cut in the stone:

> "A valiant leader, true-hearted and sincere;
> An honored soldier who held his honor dear;
> A cultured scholar with mind both deep and broad;
> An honest man, the noblest work of God."

Shortly after this writer's visit at the cemetery in the spring of 1960, a severe storm blew down the white shaft, but Frank Stubblefield took on the responsibility of setting it again in place. Eventually the remaining inscription of Johnson's name and age will be worn from the face. Though he conducted one of the spectacular assaults of the Civil War and was a leading factor in winning one of the great battles, he has received little attention in the story of the Confederacy. The main difference between his attack on the Union center at Chickamauga and of Pickett's at Gettysburg is that his was successful. The rate of casualties appears to have been about the same.[11]

CHAPTER TWENTY-FIVE

Poe's Field to Snodgrass Hill

HOOD had been fighting for some time, though it could not have been as late as 2:30 P.M., the time he gave, when the Federals rushed out of a woods and took the Texas brigade under Robertson in flank and rear, throwing it into confusion. Being about 300 yards behind the brigade, Hood galloped forward and helped realign the men to face the foe appearing from an unexpected quarter. Kershaw came up, Hindman was advancing on the left, and the Confederates, emitting a shout that ran along the entire front, charged into the woods, carried the defenses and, in Hood's words, "thus achieved another glorious victory to our arms."

When Hood described this action he did not fix his position on the field, but he was clearly relating what happened when Harker's brigade of Wood's division, moving ahead of Buell's brigade, turned back and viciously assailed Law's flank, and forced him to retreat until he was relieved by the arrival of Kershaw. The fight occurred near the Glenn-Kelly road, where it was little more than a corduroy trail through the woods, in the northern end of the cleared fields of the Dyer farm.

Hood was not able to enjoy his triumph long. A Minié ball hit him in his upper right leg and knocked him from his horse. He considered it a coincidence that though he was then commanding a corps, he should be caught as he fell by some of his old Texas brigade troops. He was riding a handsome mare that day—a "valuable mare," as he referred to her. His roan, "Jeff Davis," had been wounded the day before. Because "Jeff Davis" had been laid up with a bad leg at the time Hood was wounded at Gettysburg, his soldiers—and nearly all soldiers look for good-luck and bad-luck omens—got the idea that he was safe only when he was riding his favorite roan, "Jeff Davis."

Hood was carried back to the division field hospital, where his leg was amputated by the New Orleans surgeon, Dr. T. G. Richardson, the medical officer of the Army of Tennessee, who later served as president of the American Medical Association. The general was sent a little later to Atlanta, where he recuperated for a month before going on to Richmond. He could not mount again until mid-January 1864. The war was tearing him apart—an arm badly damaged at Gettysburg and a leg lost at Chickamauga.

As soon as the fighting subsided, Longstreet sent a telegram to Richmond recommending that Hood be made a lieutenant general. Bragg also so recommended. When the appointment was made early in the following year, the commission was dated September 20, 1863.

Hood at this time was at the height of his fame, which dimmed as he was thrust into greater responsibilities. He was feted almost as the hero of Lee's army; the performance of his brigade and later his division was so outstanding that they were greeted with a popular ovation when they passed through Richmond. He had now proved his competence as a combat leader in the western theater. But after the newspaper stories about him and his wild Texans, those who met him were likely to express surprise at his gentle mien.

A Wilmington, N. C., newspaperman who saw him a month or so later, when he was visiting General W. H. C. Whiting while en route from Atlanta to Richmond, said his personal appearance, like that of "many other men of signal bravery," was the very opposite "of the conventional idea of a fire-eater." The scribe added:

"Somewhat bleached by illness rendering his delicate features more delicate, with soft hair of light brown and beard nearly golden, he looks like a mild, sensitive and amiable man. . . ."

The fame of his old Texas brigade never dimmed. John H. Reagan, who served under four governments—the Republic of Texas, state of Texas, the Confederacy and the United States—who was Postmaster General and Secretary of the Treasury in the

Confederate cabinet, and both before and after the war a member of the United States Congress in both Senate and House, gave late in his distinguished career an indication of the public admiration of this body of troops:

"I would rather have been able to say that I had been a worthy member of Hood's Texas brigade than to have enjoyed all the honors which have been conferred upon me. I doubt if there has ever been a brigade or other military organization in the history of this war that equalled it in heroic valor and self-sacrificing conduct of its members and the brilliancy of its services."

Back in Camden, South Carolina, Mrs. Mary Boykin Chesnut, who could condense battles into a pithy sentence or two, wrote that Hood had been ordered to hold a bridge but had "already driven the enemy several miles beyond it when the slow generals were still asleep." She summed it up: "Hood has won a victory, though he has only one leg to stand on."[1]

One of Benning's captains, J. H. Martin of Hawkinsville, Georgia, told of Hood's battle. When less than twenty feet from a Federal battery, while he was trying to capture its flag, Captain Martin was shot through his jaw, the bullet crushing the bones so that the effects of the injury were always with him. Every officer and man of his company was killed, wounded, or at least hit by a ball. Benning had three horses killed under him "and the last I heard of him before I was taken off the field he was rushing the enemy, riding bareback an artillery horse without taking time to take the harness off." When someone suggested to the general that he remove the harness, he said there was no time then to saddle horses. The enemy was on the run and his brigade must keep after them. Bragg would have benefited from some of Benning's zest.

The captain's narrative tended to relieve Benning of the mild censure by Longstreet, who encountered him and thought he was excited. Benning told Longstreet, according to the lieutenant general's account, that Hood had been killed, his own brigade had been "torn to pieces, and I haven't a man left." Longstreet asked if he didn't think he could find one man, and the question seemed to quiet his apprehensions. When Longstreet met Benning he was riding the artillery horse, using a piece of rope for his riding whip.

Probably he was not so agitated as Longstreet thought, for he did not communicate any doubts to his men.

A Georgia soldier, Robert H. Murray, writing home to Calhoun County, told how the Yankees were swept from their position, and he attributed the victory to Confederate hunger. "I don't know how we did it but we did. We were anxious to fight, and the boys knew that if we whipped the Yanks we would get food. We got it. The enemy ran from our assault and we chased them. When the ammunition gave out, we threw rocks down on them. We didn't mistreat the prisoners but we took food when we found it on them for we were always hungry."

Notable in Hood's attack was Colonel William C. Oates of the 15th Alabama, lately one of the toughest Confederate fighters at Gettysburg. Had he been allowed to wait five minutes there until his water details returned with the regiment's canteens, being filled at a near-by well, he very likely would have reached the summit of Little Round Top ahead of Colonel Strong Vincent's Federal brigade, which beat him by minutes, then resisted his furious assaults for hours.

Here at Chickamauga his own Alabamans were in Hood's front line with Robertson's Texas brigade. The balance of Law's brigade, commanded by Colonel James L. Sheffield, and Benning's brigade made up the second line.

It will be recalled that Stewart, on the right of Longstreet's column of assault, had attacked earlier, on signal from Bragg, and engaged in a spirited battle with Brannan's division. S. A. M. Wood's brigade of Cleburne's division co-operated with Stewart. The assailants crossed the La Fayette road and battled Brannan in the woods, but that excellent officer and his stanch division, thoroughly imbued with the spirit of their corps commander Thomas, had driven the Confederates back to their protecting woods east of the roadway.

When Longstreet advanced at 11:10 A.M., Stewart already had been repulsed and did not move abreast Longstreet's column, though he did maintain a strong fire that protected the column's right flank. As Bushrod Johnson pressed ahead in the lead, Hood inclined his corps to the right to fill in much of the space across

Stewart's front. This took him directly against Brannan at the time when Johnson was striking and scattering the Ohio regiment on Brannan's right.

Oates's men charged through the portion of the woods frequently referred to in this account as "cathedral-like," because the trees were great first-growth hardwoods, with few saplings and virtually no undergrowth. The grounds appeared to have been grazed by cattle or sheep, and were so clean as to be inviting for outdoor religious services or picnicking. One of the striking artist's conceptions of the fighting at Chickamauga shows the charge of the 15th Alabama through these woods.

As Sheffield advanced on the first day with the brigade that had won such fame in Lee's Pennsylvania campaign, he was injured when thrown from his horse. The command passed through Colonel William F. Perry of the 44th Alabama, whose regiment became detached, to Colonel Oates, who led the brigade against the Federal line securely fastened in the woods. Oates' men had finally been well fed. The rations wagons had been so far behind that they had not had an officially issued morsel all day on the nineteenth, but when the wagons arrived at 1 A.M. on the twentieth they were awakened—or awoke from instinct or the roll of the wagon wheels —and "ate most ravenously" in the darkness.

While his men waited during the morning Oates had been unimpressed by Polk's battle against Thomas, feeling that it was begun late and not pushed with much vigor, and saying later that this part of the battle was "wavering and fluctuating." Finally, when advancing and finding a place in the line on the right of Bushrod Johnson, the Alabama brigade passed through a portion of Stewart's line, which had been firing at a range of about 200 yards, and struck the barricade of tree trunks. Brannan, taken in flank and front, retired his units abruptly, giving up some as prisoners.

One factor that apparently helped Oates, unpleasant though it was to both sides, was the heavy dust on the La Fayette road resulting from the season of unusual dryness and the heavy use of the roadway. Weeds and bushes were coated with dust along the roadside. When the Confederates crossed the road they raised a "tremendous dust," and the first thing Oates could see after it settled was the Federal line of log emplacements in his immediate front and a scattering of Northern soldiers running toward the rear. If he had not been able to see through the dust, neither had the Union defenders. They knew only that a heavy body of troops was coming on, firing as they advanced. Bushrod Johnson was moving at the same time against their right and rear and it was a choice between retreat and being surrounded.

After winning the log breastworks in his front, Oates saw that the Confederate line had become ragged. He had no connection with the other regiments of his brigade. But to his left he saw a fight in progress—apparently in front of the Dyer fields where the Texas brigade was being attacked by Harker, though Oates claimed the Confederates were Deas' brigade of Hindman's division. Two fieldpieces were playing on the Confederate line. He moved toward this combat at a run and came up behind one of the retreating Confederate regiments. Knocked down by a piece of shell that hit his left hip, he was quickly up again with little more damage than a rent in his uniform, and caught up with his men who were advancing and firing. Soon the Federals here also were retiring.

In the ordeal of this fighting through the smoke and dust there was manifestly a great deal of confusion and uncertainty about where the lines of either army were. More properly, there were no lines, only moving units. Oates must have passed at some stage across the rear of Bushrod Johnson, for he adhered to the claim that he supported Hindman instead of Johnson or Hood. He did meet Colonel Samuel K. McSpadden of the 19th Alabama, Deas' brigade, who warned him that the Federals were approaching in his rear. Oates completed his story:

"I stepped out of the smoke and saw four regiments coming up in splendid style, each carrying the Confederate battle flag. They were Patton Anderson's brigade (Hindman's division). As soon as I discovered they were Confederates I ordered a charge." Hindman's division was sweeping ahead and Oates joined forces with it to assail the right wing of Rosecrans' army.[2]

Before entering into the details of Hindman's attack on the Federal right, it is necessary to go back and review briefly how the brigades in Rosecrans' center were responding to the assaults of Bushrod Johnson and Hood.

When Longstreet, with Johnson at the front of his column, struck the Federal line, the timing could not have been more exact had he been able to regulate the movements of both armies. As at Gettysburg, where it would seem his assault on the second day was delayed fortuitously until just after Sickles had marched the 3rd Corps of Meade's army to a position half a mile in front of the lines and with it formed a salient almost impossible to defend at the Peach Orchard—so his attack in column at Chickamauga was delivered at the exact instant Rosecrans had most of his right wing in motion marching to Thomas across the Confederate front, and when his army had by a train of coincidences been made vulnerable by a gap a quarter of a mile wide in its center.

Longstreet was sufficiently modest in attributing the breakthrough to chance instead of his own superb generalship. "As we approached a second line," he said, "Johnson's division happened to strike it while in the act of changing position of some of the troops, charged upon and carried it, capturing some artillery. Hood's and Hindman's troops pressed in close connection."

The Federal Captain Lemark Duvall could observe the attack from Palmer's line. He could see the dense white smoke columns rising to the south. An "unearthly yell" burst from the woods, "which we knew too well came from the throats of the rebs." A few minutes passed, then blue-coated soldiers could be seen rushing from the woods "in considerable disorder." He saw reinforcements going in—this may have been Davis marching north or Harker turning back to confront Hood—but they too were overwhelmed. "No human power could have withstood the avalanche of men which were hurled in such demoniac fury against our right on that memorable Sunday."

Though the breastworks seemed formidable to the attackers, a correspondent for the Richmond *Sentinel* who went over the field a few days after the battle described the Federal defense line as "mean, consisting of old logs, badly thrown together." He said he saw one park of thirty-three pieces of captured artillery and 19,000 muskets in good order.

What happened to the Federal side was that Johnson and Hood thoroughly shattered the Union forces in the Poe and Dyer woods. Harker's brigade had led Wood's division as it pulled out of line and was en route to Reynolds when Johnson came through. It was far enough advanced to be clear of the calamity. But Buell was hit while he was in column behind Harker. He was overthrown, his organizations were broken up, his artillery was captured, and his men were scattered over the Dyer fields.

Buell had left skirmishers in his rear when he marched. He had moved only 500 paces before the blow fell. His skirmishers were killed, scattered or captured. Then the brigade and everything about it seemed to disintegrate as the enemy came through the opening "in great force." All gave way together.

Buell said, "My little brigade seemed as if swept from the field." About the first thing that happened was that his artillery was rendered immobile. Thirty-five horses were shot down. Then the battery was captured. Buell with part of his troops kept up the fight from every hill crest for three quarters of a mile, and at one point he had the spunk to turn and try to advance a little with his remnants, mainly survivors of the 58th Indiana. But it quickly appeared that he would be surrounded.[3]

Sam Beatty's brigade of VanCleve's division in like manner was hit while it was in column, beginning the march in response to Rosecrans' order for VanCleve to go to Thomas. Brannan, though in front of VanCleve, was able to maintain a better organization in some of his units, but he was dislodged and sent across the fields toward the Snodgrass spur of Missionary Ridge. Connell's brigade on Brannan's right suffered the greatest confusion and disorder, pursued closely by Hood.

As the Union soldiers streamed back across the fields, groups rallied here and there; individual regiments turned and began small, resolute attempts to check the oncoming gray tide. The 82nd Indiana under Colonel Morton C. Hunter, of Bloomington, fought a series of spirited holding engagements. The 82nd was a part of Connell's brigade of Brannan's division. It had lost heavily in the battle at the breastworks when the Confederates first struck, and although its fight there had been stubborn, it had to retire or be gobbled up. Hunter ordered the men to wheel about every fifty yards and fire on the pursuing enemy. This was continued for half a mile or more, by which time the regiment had reached the Snodgrass elevation. Fugitives from the battle line were moving across the fields by the hundreds, many from Rosecrans' right wing which had now come under attack by Hindman. Some of them Hunter stopped and put into formation on the left of the 82nd.

Disgusted with running and wheeling and firing, Hunter looked about his Snodgrass Hill elevation and said, "I will not retreat another inch." That, in the opinion of his good regiment, was the beginning of the Snodgrass Hill rally so fateful to the future of the Federal army. In any event, the 82nd Indiana was the first organized body of troops to take a position on that hill. Colonel Gustave Kammerling, whose Cincinnati Germans had recaptured the regular-army battery lost by John King's brigade on the first day of the battle, brought his 9th Ohio of Van Derveer's brigade, Brannan's division, to the right of the 82nd Indiana a little later and a line began to be formed by Brannan's units. Buell showed up with part of the 58th Indiana, all that remained serviceable of his brigade.

Harker's brigade of Wood's division, which had turned back to fight Hood and had been worsted when Kershaw came up on its flank, and Stanley's brigade of Negley's division arrived at the east face of the hill. A rallying point was provided for units still disposed to carry on the battle. The diligent Brannan was on hand to give directions and put what was left of his buffeted division into position for more fighting. He had been battling desperately on both days but he knew a fresh enemy attack would soon be raging about him.

Negley was not with Stanley's brigade. Negley was engaged in his last campaign. The trust his superior Rosecrans and some of the other generals had imposed in him was being lost on the field of Chickamauga, though he always insisted his fault was not having been in the West Point coterie. One of his detractors asserted also that he had won his commission of major general at Stone's River not through his own merits but because of the splendid work of one of his brigade commanders, Colonel John F. Miller, who, disgusted with Negley, assumed direction of the attack and pressed it with such vigor that he captured and held a key position without orders.[4]

CHAPTER TWENTY-SIX

Rout of Davis and Sheridan

HINDMAN's division was in assault formation 600 to 800 yards east of the La Fayette road when at 11:10 A.M. Longstreet issued the attack order. Moving sharply through the woods the division came abreast Bushrod Johnson, then encountered Federal skirmishers.

Deas' Alabama brigade was on Hindman's right, Manigault's brigade of Alabama and South Carolina troops on his left, and Patton Anderson's Mississippi brigade was in reserve. They crossed the La Fayette road and hit the two brigades of Davis' Federal division, Carlin's and Heg's, the latter now under the command of Colonel John A. Martin of the 8th Kansas. Davis' third brigade, Post's, was on the far right with the cavalry.

Davis' men had built a line of crude barricades running through the fields south of the Brotherton house, consisting partly of trees felled during the night and early morning and partly of stones gathered from the fields. Davis' line had been altered once or twice and the fortifications lacked the strength of Thomas' more carefully constructed works.

As Hindman advanced Manigault's flank was in the air. Preston's division had not yet come into action on Hindman's left and Manigault consequently was the left of Longstreet's column of assault. Hindman's division front covered a quarter of a mile, as did Bushrod Johnson's, which meant that Longstreet was assaulting on a half-mile front with four divisions—Johnson, Law, Kershaw and Hindman.

By sheer shock Hindman quickly overpowered Davis, overran his fortifications and hurled him back in headlong flight. Rosecrans' indifference to his right wing was bearing a harvest of thorns and thistles, of blood and disaster. The moment chanced to be the one when Sheridan, in response to Rosecrans' orders to go to the assistance of Thomas, was marching two of his brigades directly across the rear of Davis. These were the brigades of Laiboldt and Bradley, the latter now commanded by Colonel Nathan H. Walworth of the 42nd Illinois after Bradley had been wounded on the nineteenth.

When Davis' division lost its organization and tumbled back, a mass of fugitives pressed closely by Deas and Patton Anderson, it broke through the ranks of Sheridan's division, spread its own panic to Sheridan's troops and threw the column and almost the entire right wing of the army into disorder. As quickly as the wind shifts battle smoke, Rosecrans' right became more like a mass of hunted fugitives than the veteran brigades that had fought stanchly on many fields. Laiboldt did not have time to fire a shot.

As Colonel Smith Atkins of the 92nd Illinois described it: "McCook's corps was wiped off from the field without any attempt at real resistance," floating "like flecks of foam upon a river." The artillerymen cut the traces and dashed away toward Chattanooga. "The rout of McCook's corps was complete."

Of Hindman's brigades, only Manigault was brought to a pause. The attacking force approached the elevation at the Widow Glenn's, an apparently irresistible wave pushing the driftwood and wreckage ahead of it. Then Manigault's exposed flank was struck suddenly by Wilder with his Spencer repeaters, aided by the 39th Indiana, another mounted regiment armed with repeaters. This was the regiment that had carried a thousand canteens of water the night before. The fire from Wilder was devastating and could not be withstood, and Manigault was driven back three quarters of a mile from the Widow Glenn's to beyond the La Fayette road. And while this action was developing, Hindman's other two brigades ran against the only serious resistance offered by Sheridan's division, which came from Lytle.

Sheridan in his own account of the catastrophe told of Davis' troops plunging back in a disorganized mass. McCook happened to be with Laiboldt and ordered him to charge the oncoming Confederates. Laiboldt had time to deploy and pass through Davis' confused ranks, but the Confederates surged on him without being checked, and his brigade broke and rushed to the rear. Before McCook was borne away in the disaster, he ordered Sheridan to bring his other two brigades, those of Bradley and Lytle, into action. Scarcely had they been aligned, according to the division commander, when "the same horde of Confederates that had overwhelmed Davis poured in upon them a deadly fire and shivered the two brigades to pieces."[1]

Although it is true that McCook was caught at a disadvantage because both Davis and Sheridan were engaged in or about to begin movements to the left when they were hit by Hindman, there was not much glory to be passed around among high-ranking officers in the right wing. Sheridan's division was the freshest in the army. It had been merely scratched on the afternoon before. Its strength was about 4,000. Taken with Davis' two brigades, numbering about 3,000, McCook had available a force which exceeded that of Hindman, whose three brigades aggregated about 6,000. Wilder's brigade, which fought the most resolute battle of the forces on Rosecrans' right wing, also was available to McCook. No prompt and vigorous action by the high command, from Rosecrans through McCook to the division commanders Sheridan and Davis, appears to have been forthcoming, once Longstreet's assault had developed its full impetus. The resistance was disorganized, feeble and irresolute, and was left largely to brigade commanders. Lytle and Wilder were notable for continuing the action on their own initiative.

There was no good reason why McCook should have been caught with no kind of effective defense whatever against Hindman. Early in the morning Colonel Smith Atkins with his scouts of the 92nd Illinois had detected Longstreet's preparations, had seen the formation of the heavy assault column, and had witnessed the beginning of the march against McCook's corps. Said Atkins: "I repeatedly sent him information on the approach of that heavy column of the enemy, but he testily declared there was no truth in it, and refused to send a skirmish line of his own, that he might easily have done, and found out for himself."

Sheridan did manage to rally his troops about 300 yards beyond the Dry Valley road and to make a counterattack on the Widow

Glenn's ridge from which he had been ousted, but the success was brief.

Wilder himself in later years made cogent observations about leadership in the battle. Speaking in 1890 at a reunion of Confederate veterans, who invited remarks from one of their old enemies, he said:

"All this talk about generalship displayed on either side is sheer nonsense. There was no generalship in it. It was a soldiers' fight purely, wherein the only question involved was the question of endurance. The two armies came together like two wild beasts, and each fought as long as it could stand up in a knock-down-and-drag-out encounter. If there had been any high order of generalship displayed the disasters to both armies might have been less."[2]

Wilder spoke in generalities. There were specific instances of generals to whom his remarks were not applicable, among them Lytle.

Lytle was one of the most beloved brigade commanders of the Union army, not only because his clear lyric poetry won for him widespread admiration but also because of the gentle affection with which he led his men. Most brigades and regiments returned what they received. His troops seemed to respond more to his moderation than many in other commands did to severity and aloofness.

Almost every schoolboy of an earlier era knew his "Antony and Cleopatra," which the Ohio historian Emilius O. Randall called "a stroke of genius and true inspiration." The first stanza ran:

> "I am dying, Egypt, dying,
> Ebbs the crimson life-tide fast,
> And the dark Plutonian shadows
> Gather on the evening blast;
> Let thine arm, Oh Queen, enfold me,
> Hush thy sobs and bow thine ear,
> Listen to the great heart secrets,
> Thou, and thou alone, must hear."

The poem had been published in the Cincinnati *Enquirer* in 1857 and had been reprinted and read so widely before the war that, after Rosecrans and Thomas, Lytle was perhaps the best-known officer in the Army of the Cumberland. Among his other poems, which were collected into a small volume published in 1894, were "Popocatepetl," which recalls that he had been a soldier in the Mexican War; "Macdonald's Drummer," another oft-recited piece; "Jaqueline," "The Volunteers," "Sweet May Moon" and "Farewell."

Lytle's brigade had not been engaged on the nineteenth but had reached the battlefield after dark, exhausted from seventeen days of constant marching with the corps baggage. He took a position near the Widow Glenn's. When he looked over the terrain he was much pleased with it. He made his headquarters on a wooded knoll on the east side of the Dry Valley road and north of the Glenn house, on what has since been called Lytle Hill. During the morning of the twentieth he stationed his regiments to cover the approaches to the Widow Glenn's. The 21st Michigan was immediately around the small log house. The cultivated field to the south and east was strewn with bodies from the fight on the nineteenth and already the big oak trees were girdled and splintered by bullets and shell fragments.

The Michigan regiment went to work promptly to make the knoll defensible. Rosecrans and his staff were in the saddle on a companion knoll to the north, so the Michigan men took over the house, knocked the chinking from between the logs, and tore down the barn, corncrib and stables to use the lumber for fortifications. Company B of this regiment was armed with Colt's revolvers. Sheridan, who was giving personal attention to his line, sent this company under Lieutenant A. E. Barr to the front on the right as skirmishers and then directed Lieutenant C. E. Belknap with six men of Company H to a position on their right. These six men were turned back to face south. They were the extreme right flank of Rosecrans' army, except for the cavalry in and beyond Crawfish Springs, and with Company B they made a pitifully weak flank guard during a great battle, even with their Colts. Still, every available contingent was going to Thomas, along whose lines what was presumed to be the main battle was raging.

While thus engaged, Lytle was suddenly ordered by Sheridan to put his men on the road and double-quick to the north to the aid of Thomas, following Sheridan's other brigades already moving across the rear of Davis' division.

Lytle merely had time to begin the movement. Just then the Confederates broke through the center and assailed the right of Rosecrans' army and Lytle could see the masses of gray-coated soldiers rushing up the gentle slopes of the elevation on which the Glenn house stood. Hindman's division did not seem to have been slowed as it crashed through Davis' barricades. With the enemy coming on, Lytle ordered his brigade out of the column into which it had just been thrown for its march to Thomas, and into battle line.

Overlapped on both flanks by Hindman's advancing brigades, standing on Rosecrans' far right flank, from which Sheridan's other two brigades and Davis' division were departing, Lytle could see at a glance that his situation was hopeless. But he had no thought of retreat.

Turning to one of his staff officers, he said that if they had to die they "would die in their tracks, with their harness on." Again, he remarked as he pulled on his gloves—and the words suggested something of the knight-errantry still abiding in warfare at that period—that "if I must die, I will die as a gentleman."

When Lytle surveyed the field in front of him he conceived that the only defensive for his little brigade would be in boldness. A spirited offensive might arrest the enemy until someone could re-form the lines in his rear or do something to save the right wing of the army. In addition, it would help Laiboldt, whose brigade was crumbling. Lytle was in front of the 88th Illinois, which faced south to meet Hindman's flank attack from that direction. To the regiment he said, "All right, men, we can die but once. This is the time and place. Let us charge." Then, because cold desperation can use the warmth of a little hope, he said words which Captain E. B. Parsons, Company K, 24th Wisconsin, overheard: "Boys, if we whip them today, we will eat our Christmas dinner at home."

When Lytle called for an advance his men responded. "Into this tornado of war the brigade rushed," said the recorder for the 21st Michigan. The enemy at first seemed to be repulsed, but then came swarming up again, mainly on the left, north of the Glenn house, where a hand-to-hand conflict developed. Both sides used bayonets, gun butts and stones. What was surprising was that the meager flank guard of seven men on the right held until it could retire step by step to the Glenn house. It fought resolutely and miraculously, with the loss of only one man who was killed instantly.[3]

Lytle, born in the family mansion on Lawrence Street in Cincinnati, was an author-lawyer who had wanted to go to West Point and follow his forebears in the military service, but yielded instead to the artistry in his nature gained from his writer mother, Elizabeth Haines. His great-grandfather had been a captain in the French and Indian War and the Revolution; his grandfather fought Indians in the Northwest Territory and served as a major general of Ohio militia in the War of 1812; and his father General Robert Lytle was a congressman, friend of Andrew Jackson and an Ohio militia officer.

William followed his father as a student in Cincinnati College and was graduated when sixteen. He read and practiced law, served in the legislature, went to Mexico as a captain, became known as a splendid orator, and ran for lieutenant governor, and all the while poetry controlled him.

When war began between the states he was appointed colonel of the 10th Ohio, a Cincinnati Irish regiment, and was wounded while leading it at Carnifex Ferry in West Virginia. Again wounded at Perryville, he was given up for dead and left on the field; but was captured and paroled. Upon his recovery he was made a brigadier general and given command of the 1st Brigade of Sheridan's division, previously led by General Joshua W. Sill, who was killed at Stone's River.

Shortly before the battle Lytle's old 10th Ohio, then serving as headquarters guard for Rosecrans, presented to their fondly remembered colonel a gold Maltese cross set with diamonds and emeralds, apparently for no other reason than that they liked him. Before the battle others had been pressing him—a well-known Ohio Democrat—to become a candidate for governor of Ohio, but he declined.

Lytle's face seemed to glow in combat. His aide, Captain Pirtle, termed it "an indescribable expression caused by what is called battle fire." It was "a spirit of enthusiasm brought on by the tremendous excitements of the conflict which irradiates every feature." His eyes sparkled and his nostrils seemed to quiver. "I can almost see him now," said the captain in later reflections.

He wore his overcoat, which suggests that the day was still chill at noon. His breeches were dark blue. The overcoat, buttoned at the neck, was plain. The only sign of rank was the gold cord around the crown of his hat. Nothing would have made him a target unless it was his beautifully caparisoned horse.

Lytle had scarcely begun his counterattack when a bullet found him. He told one of his staff officers that he had been wounded in the spine and was afraid he would have to retire, but he stayed on his mount and remained in front of his men. Meantime the Glenn house hill was inundated by the gray tide and Lytle's men were pressed back to the hill on the north. There, still in front of his brigade, he was hit by three bullets almost at the same second and was dropped from his horse.

Closest to him was his staff officer, Captain Howard Green, who quickly dismounted and caught the general as he fell. The wounded hero must have been suffering great pain from bullets in his spine and body but he did not utter a murmur, and merely smiled gratefully at the captain who eased him to the ground. Others rushed up—officers and orderlies—and tried to carry him back out of the inferno raging around them. Two of the orderlies were shot dead as they undertook to raise him.

Lytle retained consciousness but did not speak. As the group continued around him despite the casualties and heavy firing the general emphatically motioned with his hands for them to leave and save themselves. They laid him under a big tree on the knoll where his brigade was making its last stand. He unfastened his sword and handed it to an orderly and again motioned them to the rear. There under the tree he died.

Colonel William B. McCreery of the 21st Michigan remained near his body. Some of McCreery's men were still fighting on the right of the Widow Glenn's. But while he watched, the colonel was critically wounded. By this time the knoll was stripped of defenders and he was left on the field for dead.

Probably the wound that caused Lytle's immediate death came from the bullet that struck him in the face, but his first wound very likely would have proved mortal in time.[4]

Lytle had delivered a stirring address after the presentation of the Maltese cross. In the group that heard him was Sergeant Richard Realf, a poet who had been with John Brown in Kansas. He was so stirred that he wrote a sonnet, couched in the lofty phrases of the day. Later he gave a copy to General Lytle. The general must have liked it for he had it in his pocket at Chickamauga and one of the bullets that hit him passed through the manuscript. The last lines read:

"Lead on, that we may follow, for I think
The future hath not whereupon we should shrink,
Held by the steadfast shining of your brow."

Colonel William C. Oates, whose 15th Alabama had wandered far from Law's division, saw what he described as a "richly caparisoned horse" near where the Federals had broken. He rushed over, hoping to make a prize of the animal. But the horse had been shot through the joint of a foreleg and was unserviceable. Within a few steps was the body of General Lytle, who was identified to him by prisoners.

Oates found the body "lying in the hot sun," a phrase rather inconsistent with the testimony of the aide that the general was wearing his overcoat in battle, unless the mountain weather was proving tricky. Oates took the body by the arms and dragged it into the shade, then went on with his regiment.

The Southern officers would not leave Lytle's body unattended. After Oates had passed on, Captain Douglas West of Deas' brigade took up the watch. He secured the general's pistol, spurs, sword belt, scabbard and memorandum book. The major had been fond of "Antony and Cleopatra" and with a sense of obligation kept guard. Other Confederate officers came—Major William M. Owen, who had known Lytle before the war now requested that the body be guarded carefully, and finally General William Preston, who commanded the division on the Confederate left.

"What have you there?" Preston asked.

"General Lytle of Cincinnati," the officer answered.

"Ah!" exclaimed Preston, "the son of my old friend Bob Lytle. I am sorry it is so."

Someone had carried the news to the Confederate surgeon E. W. Thomasson, who had trudged through Mexico with Lytle. He identified the body, had it taken to his own tent, then cut off a lock of hair to be sent to the general's sister. Along with the lock he sent Lytle's pocketbook and a copy of another poem, entitled "Company K," which Lytle had in his pocket when he died. None knew the author but there was speculation that it might have been Sergeant Realf and of course some thought it was by Lytle, though the copy was printed and not in his hand.

Not even the commander of either army could have had more tender care than that given the Ohio poet. The night he died the Confederate officers sat around their fires and recited the lines of "Antony and Cleopatra," which many knew. Lytle fought for the North but his genius was not sectional. Thomasson dressed the face wound with green leaves and covered the face with a silken net. He arranged for funeral services and burial of the body at Crawfish Springs. A little later, when Rosecrans was being besieged in Chattanooga, both armies made arrangements so the body of the poet-general might be taken home. Under a truce, Lieutenant Colonel William M. Ward and ten soldiers of the 10th Ohio passed through the Confederate lines and marched to Crawfish Springs. There they disinterred the body, then carried it back to Chattanooga, and thence to Louisville. There it was placed aboard the mailboat *Nightingale* and taken to Cincinnati. Upon its arrival on October 21, the city observed mourning. The funeral was the largest held in Cincinnati to that time.

"Company K," the other poem found in General Lytle's pocket when he was killed, was touching both to the army and the home public. The first stanza read:

> "There's a cap in the closet;
> Old, tattered and blue;
> Of very slight value,
> It may be, to you;
> But a crown, jewel-studded,
> Could not buy it today
> With its letters of honor,
> Brave Company K."

The report that Lytle wrote another stanza for "Antony and Cleopatra" as he was dying is clearly without foundation. For one thing, he did not have time.[5]

The other notable defense against Hindman was Wilder's. Back at the Widow Glenn's, he received through Captain A. S. Burt of Rosecrans' staff an order to cover the retreat of the right wing of the Federal army. From his elevation he could survey the battlefield with its masses of fugitives and recognize the critical nature of the moment. His brigade was southwest of the Glenn house and faced south toward Crawfish Springs. Bringing it up to the ridge on which the house stood, he was just in time to pour his fire into Manigault's brigade, then to follow with a charge by the 17th Indiana and 123rd Illinois.

Manigault gave way. The Federal regiments captured 220 prisoners and pressed Manigault for the better part of a mile, until he was relieved when Longstreet sent in fresh troops. Longstreet, seeing the repulse of the left of his assault column, ordered up Trigg's brigade and then the balance of Preston's division, which held the left of Bragg's army. Old Peter was watching the attack closely and striking with all he had. With Preston in action, his left wing and Bragg's army were at last fully employed.

The Indiana and Illinois regiments returned to Wilder in time for him to use them in assailing Hindman's two other brigades which had passed around his left, crushed Lytle and reached the Dry Valley road west of a point between the Glenn house and the eminence where Lytle had made his last stand. Wilder now attacked Hindman around the "Bloody Pond" and claimed to have driven some of his men through the pond and others around it. The action was sharp but short. The Widow Glenn's house was in flames during this fighting. It had been hit by an exploding shell.

Hindman now had Manigault, who had re-formed and returned with his brigade in fairly good shape, and he prepared to resume his advance in an effort to intercept some of McCook's flying soldiers on the Dry Valley road moving toward McFarland's Gap, when he received a request from Bushrod Johnson for help on Hindman's right. Hindman extended his line to connect with

Johnson and forgot the matter of the pursuit. Wilder remained within striking distance, ready for more fighting.

That Hindman had achieved a splendid triumph was apparent from the fruits of victory about him. On his advance he had captured seventeen pieces of artillery. Ten of them had been abandoned in a gorge west of the Dry Valley road. He had 1,100 prisoners, among them three colonels. The ground about him was strewn with small arms, and 1,400 were gathered by his soldiers. They collected an abundance of other equipment, and 165,000 rounds of ammunition, 40 horses and mules, an ambulance, five caissons and five stands of colors.[6]

At no point in the battle was there more brilliant fighting than by Deas' brigade in this assault. Deas, a wealthy cotton broker, had equipped his original regiment, the 22nd Alabama, at his own expense at the beginning of the war. He rose from command of the regiment at Shiloh to serve as brigadier general until the end of the war. He, like some others, reversed the carpetbag process and moved to New York City after the war, where he again acquired wealth as a member of the stock exchange. At Chickamauga his brigade not only was the main factor in breaking Davis' division, but also fought the battle against the unfortunate Lytle, and, in co-operation with Patton Anderson, drove Sheridan from the field.

"Little Phil" was rarely at his best when the odds were even. He and Davis were actually more disorganized than hurt. Lytle's brigade had done the heavy fighting but four others might have been rallied somewhere in the rear. Wilder had shown it was not necessary to leave the battlefield. There was no pursuit. Whatever may have been Sheridan's merits as a commander at a later period, he failed to disclose either tenacity or resource while in charge of the right division at Chickamauga.

It has been well pointed out by other critics of Chickamauga that if Sheridan and Davis had rallied and reorganized their commands within a mile of the field, where they were safe from pursuit, they could have reappeared during the battle to the discomfiture of Longstreet, whose exposed left flank could have been struck when two hours later he was assailing Thomas on Snodgrass

Hill. Thus a tragic defeat might have been turned into a triumph. As it was, Sheridan went all the way to Rossville before turning back toward the battlefield after the fighting had ended. Sheridan has often been lauded for halting at Rossville instead of proceeding, as McCook had done, into Chattanooga, but the question was why he ever got to Rossville at all.

The 22nd Alabama of Deas' brigade, organized at Montgomery, lost 5 color-bearers and 205 killed and wounded of the 371 who began the advance, or 55 percent of its strength.

The nature of the men Deas commanded may be seen from the story told by Captain H. W. Henry, Company K, 22nd Alabama, about the eighteen-year-old lad who came through the woods on the night of the nineteenth, looking for Company I. He wore butternut homespun but had a "clear, healthy complexion and bright, steadfast look." When he said he wanted to volunteer he was mustered in on the spot, though he had never been drilled an hour in his life. The lieutenant in command of "Eye" company asked if he could shoot, and he answered that he could knock the nose off a squirrel in the top of the highest tree. He seemed unconcerned when told the company would fight on the morrow.

Next day the regiment was in what Captain Henry said was the hottest fire he had ever seen. The men were lying down and edging forward when he saw the recruit standing in the open, loading deliberately, picking out his man as though he were on a squirrel hunt and, when the target did not seem to suit him, bringing down his gun and surveying the enemy until he could get a better sight.

Captain Henry, expecting him to fall at any minute, shouted, "Lie down, you fool! You will be riddled with bullets. Get behind a rock or a tree and shoot." But the lad, not accustomed to obeying orders, paid not the slightest heed to the captain, who lost touch with him as the battle rolled around them.

That night Captain Henry went to Company "Eye," asked the lieutenant about the recruit and was surprised to learn that he continued to enjoy good health. When the captain found him he asked why he did not lie down when told to.

"It warn't any use," the youngster replied indifferently. "I was just as safe as you was behind a tree, for a man don't get killed until his time comes, nohow."

Other volunteers appeared here and there among the Confederates. J. B. Hall, seventeen years old, came up to join his brothers in Company K, 24th Alabama, a Mobile regiment in Manigault's brigade. He fought as an independent volunteer, insisting on keeping at a distance in front of the line. There he was dropped, mortally wounded. The Spencer repeaters were not weapons to be scorned in this close-range fighting.[7]

Another who fell wounded during Wilder's flank attack on Manigault was a private soldier, upward of sixty years old, named Challon, brother of a Catholic priest in Mobile. The old-timer had been in Kansas when the war broke and had made his way on foot to Louisiana, where he enlisted in a Louisiana regiment in hope that he might eventually join troops from Mobile. This opportunity came during the Corinth campaign. Soon he was a favorite in Company A of the 24th Alabama. So pleasant was his personality that General Manigault often called him to his campfire merely to enjoy his conversation.

Private Challon's thigh was broken when the flank fire hit the brigade and he was left behind when it retreated. He waved on those who stopped to help him, telling them to save their time and "go whip the Yankees." But shortly the woods caught fire, as they had on this section of the battlefield the afternoon before. After the brigade rallied, a group of officers went out to bring back old Challon and others endangered by the flames. Challon already had been burned but had battled the fire and crawled from it, dragging his broken leg. He survived both burns and bullet. Some of the soldiers called on him in the hospital, where he greeted them cheerily.

"No matter if the old man dies," he exulted, "we whipped the rascals."

One of Deas' regiments was the 39th Alabama, the oldest regiment in the Confederate service because it was the reorganized 1st Alabama, the initial regiment mustered in by the Jefferson Davis government. It originally was commanded by Henry D. Clayton, who at Chickamauga was leading a brigade of A. P. Stewart's division. One of its difficulties had been with walnuts. Tom Beacham of Opelika had to pick up about ten bushels before he could pitch his tent on the assigned ground. Then the next morning he got a gift of walnuts sent from Alabama by his wife. He claimed the nuts from home were superior to the Tennessee walnuts, at least for eating. The regiment plowed through Davis and Sheridan and won what its Colonel Whitfield Clark called a "complete victory." For the army as a whole he had a different thought. Had the high command taken advantage of the broken condition of the enemy and pursued, "a different page of history might have been written."

Lieutenant A. B. Renfro of the 22nd Alabama had obtained leave of absence to visit his home in Jacksonville, Alabama, roughly eighty miles from the battlefield. When he heard a battle was about to be fought he hastened to his regiment and, due to the urgency, his father, the hotelkeeper of the town, drove him back in a buggy. They arrived during the night of the nineteenth. The lieutenant searched the field and finally found his command. He led it in the first assault, took the colors from the fallen bearer, and was shot dead as he approached the enemy's second position. The father had waited behind the lines. The last the men saw of them, the father was carrying the boy's body off the battlefield in the buggy in which they had come, going back to Jacksonville to bury him.

W. H. Cunningham of the 19th Alabama, in a letter to his brother John Cunningham in Evergreen, Alabama, written immediately after the battle, told of Hindman's advance. "It might appear like vanity in me to say that never did men more fully perform their whole duty. The day's work was one continual charge of the bayonet—that terrible weapon which invariably wins when properly manned and used in the right cause."[8]

In the days after the war any old soldier who had been in Hindman's advance at Chickamauga could well take great pride in it. The stories told at the reunions were abundant. One was that a captain in Patton Anderson's brigade, John N. Sloan of Pontotoc, Mississippi, made an extraordinary find when he returned to the battlefield thirty-two years after the celebrated attack. He finally found the place where he had been shot down and had lain among the dead and wounded. He turned to some of the other old vets who were going over the field with him and said he hoped he could find his teeth and jawbone.

"Captain, here are your teeth," someone called to him a bit later. Sure enough, another veteran had picked up three teeth, which Sloan identified—as nearly as one could after thirty-two years—as his.

While Davis, Sheridan, VanCleve and part of Negley's force were being pushed off the field, Longstreet was moving forward with his staff to keep in close touch with the advance of his divisions. He established his new headquarters at the Dyer house in what had been the center of the Federal position when he began his attack. The great oaks, today more than 200 years old, towered above the little log house in Longstreet's day. Across the open fields masses of Federal soldiers had gathered on Snodgrass Hill. Along the Kelly-field line Thomas' fortifications were still intact. While Longstreet's divisions were realigning themselves to face north instead of west, preparing for a fresh assault on Thomas, Longstreet and his staff at 2:30 P.M. had a mess of sweet potatoes for lunch, served under the trees of the Dyer yard.

He had not heard from Bragg since launching his attack, but while he was eating, a messenger brought word that the commanding general wanted to see him. He rode to the rear and announced his success, making an estimate from the reports he had received that he had captured sixty guns. He asked for reinforcements in order to hold his position, follow the routed Federals down the Dry Valley road, seize McFarland's Gap and cut off Thomas' retreat.

Bragg was anything but fired by the prospect of a great victory. It was 3 P.M. and the battle was about to enter its last phase, but Bragg was not the controlling factor in it. As Longstreet judged the commanding general's attitude, Bragg thought the battle had been lost, not won.

In answer to Longstreet's request, Bragg gave the peculiar and disappointing answer that none of the troops except those with Longstreet "had any fight in them." He did have Cheatham's division, which had not been severely engaged that day. Gist's division had been only partially employed. These troops might have been placed under Longstreet's vigorous leadership and used to good purpose.

Bragg made another strange decision—to go to the right of his line at this moment of triumph on his left. Could he have felt that his chance of defeating Rosecrans rested still with the right wing of his army that had "no fight left in it?" To Longstreet he said, "General, if anything happens, communicate with me at Reed's bridge." Reed's bridge was far away at the other end of the line. The most feasible plan at this stage of the fighting was to mass troops under Longstreet and further turn the Federal right, and close McFarland's Gap in the rear of Thomas, but Bragg did not seem to understand it.

Longstreet returned to his troops soon after 3 P.M. Four hours had passed since he had launched his assault. Wilder had been the most delaying factor he had encountered on the Federal right wing. Probably Wilder's attacks on Hindman had given Thomas the needed margin of time to draw a new defense line running from Kelly field to Snodgrass Hill. Longstreet faced this new line. Some of the hardest fighting of Chickamauga was still ahead.[9]

PART IV

THOMAS:

Rock of Chickamauga

CHAPTER TWENTY-SEVEN

The Panic Overwhelms Rosecrans

PROBABLY in no other engagement of the war except at the First Manassas was there such a headlong, tumultuous flight of panic-stricken soldiers as on Rosecrans' right at Chickamauga. None other involved the actual flight of the commanding general from the field.

Rosecrans had been in the saddle in rear of Davis' division when Longstreet's men had surged across the La Fayette road, brushed Davis aside and rolled back Laiboldt. A number of the accounts by participants or others dealing with this phase of the battle speak of Rosecrans being "caught" or "carried away" in the whirlwind of defeat raging back toward Chattanooga, swept up and blown along by the "driving mass of teamsters, stragglers and fugitives." The fact is that Rosecrans, accompanied by Garfield, Bond and others of his staff, rode along voluntarily with the horde. They passed up the Dry Valley road before Bushrod Johnson had his troops or artillery in place in the region of Vittetoe, or Hindman had reached the Bloody Pond.

McDonald, the impressed scout who lived on the battlefield, was standing beside Rosecrans when the gray tied surged through the hole in his line and the wave came across the Brotherton, Dyer and Glenn farms to inundate his right wing. The general first made his best efforts to rally the men who rushed past him. Then he turned to his staff and others, including McDonald, and said: "If you care to live any longer, get away from here." That was the signal for departure from the battlefield.

Panic such as that which overcame the right wing could cast no permanent reflection on the Army of the Cumberland. Even in the most veteran and stalwart of armies, a commander can take few precautions against panic. Panic was as old as combat. It occurred in the Punic Wars quite as suddenly as in the War between the States. As has been said, "Demoralization is an element impossible to foresee, difficult to arrest."

Lieutenant Colonel William D. Ward, commanding the 37th Indiana, Sirwell's brigade, described the rout: "Many of the officers of all ranks showed by their wild commands and still wilder actions that they had completely lost their heads and were as badly demoralized as the private soldiers. Many of these had thrown away their arms, evidently thinking only of saving themselves by flight." At a defile blocked by some cannon a badly agitated colonel shouted excitedly to his men, "Get out of here at once! The Rebel cavalry are right on you." It caused the artillerymen and teamsters to jump from their horses, abandon their guns and run on foot.

Nobody has exactly prescribed what a general is to do when his army suddenly decides to leave the field—whether to stay and be killed or captured as a captain stays on the bridge of his ship, or go with the army in hope of reorganizing it to return and fight another day. It would appear that when Rosecrans' force panicked he followed the normal course of going along with it. The attitude of the men might be seen from the statement of one of them: "Things looked desperate, and I began to think of Libby." The capture of a commanding general in battle is the token of supreme defeat. Flight is preferable.

Lincoln was tolerant toward homesick young men who took unsanctioned furloughs, or those charged with cowardice in battle, some of whom he pardoned. To him they were "leg cases"; their hearts were in the right place but their legs were not. Experience might make good soldiers of them where a firing squad or prison term would not. But at Chickamauga "leg cases" were not confined to recruits as they were at Bull Run. Except in the minor instance of John King's brigade, they did not occur under Thomas. They may be ascribed mainly to the fact that in this battle Rosecrans' right wing was not well handled.[1]

The main dereliction was that neither Rosecrans nor McCook

appears to have had in mind how to defend himself at every instance from a massed attack, should it come. The guards were
down when parts of their forces were in motion. The withdrawals
in the presence of the enemy were not made carefully, by stages.
Instead, brigades went into column and marched off, leaving scant
protection, if any, between them and a massed enemy close at
hand. Certainly if the account of Colonel Atkins is correct, blame
would attach to McCook for not putting out adequate skirmishers
or heeding the warnings of the mounted infantry that an attack
was impending.

Rosecrans, McCook, Crittenden, Sheridan and Davis all made
their most determined efforts to rally the troops but none was able
to accomplish much. Still, it was by no means inevitable that they
should have permitted themselves to be "swept" through McFarland's Gap and thence in to Rossville and Chattanooga. Wilder
managed to continue resistance. He kept his mounted infantry
enterprising and in no manner did it become affected by the break-
up of the army about it. The Union force had been cut in two by
the advance of Bushrod Johnson and Hood, to be sure, but the
slice was not so clean but that McCook's staff member, Major
Gates P. Thruston, managed to make his way with a detail of
troops directly across the rear of the army to Thomas. He did not
follow the long, indirect route through Rossville which Garfield
and others employed, but rode across the fields.

Thruston had been sent by McCook to bring up the 39th Indiana
from Crawfish Springs at a time when Sheridan was ordered before
the Confederate breakthrough to reinforce Thomas. This mounted
regiment was to fill in some of the gaps on the army's right, left by
the withdrawal of Sheridan. It has been noted that it arrived in
time to assist Wilder in his attack on Manigault.

Thruston, who had a small escort, took charge of the 200 prisoners captured from Manigault. Since Longstreet's forces were about
to overrun the region of the Widow Glenn's, he conducted the
prisoners north—in the direction of Thomas—at a double-quick.
They passed within 300 yards of the advancing Confederates and
Thruston thought that the gray uniforms of the prisoners, which
predominated in his party as it moved across the front of the Con-

federate line, saved them from being shattered by Confederate fire.
They pushed the prisoners "at the point of the sword and carbine"
and finally caught up with Sheridan and Davis retiring up the Dry
Valley road. The two generals had remnants of their five brigades
with them.

Thruston reported that "General Phil was furious." He compared him with "the great Washington on several occasions" as
"*swearing* mad," but there the comparison ended. Thruston
thought there was ample reason for the profanity because Lytle
and "the truest and bravest" had fallen in a battle where they did
not have a chance. "He [Sheridan] had lost faith," a phrase which
the major did not explain. Faith in Rosecrans? Or in himself?
Thruston could hear the roar of battle to the north and offered to
go to Thomas and learn how he was faring. His account is signifi-
cant because it shows what sometimes has not been recognized, that
contact with Thomas was possible after Davis and Sheridan had
been swept from the field. Thruston left at a gallop and rode
toward the sound of battle. His escort was a detachment of Company I of the 2nd Kentucky cavalry, the headquarters troop of
McCook's corps.

"As we neared the firing," said Thruston, "we came suddenly
upon a line of gray much too close to be agreeable. Fortunately it
was intent on other game in its front, and we escaped with only a
few whizzing compliments. We were too far to the right. We had
struck the wrong side, and were behind the Confederates. Circling
to the left we were soon among the soldiers in blue in rear of the
Union lines."

Soon he found Thomas and reported to that sturdy soldier the
break of the army's right wing. Thomas told him to go back and
bring the troops of Davis and Sheridan up to reinforce his right,
which at that moment was a thin line with which to confront the
attack expected from Longstreet. Thruston and his escort rode
back and arrived at the place on the Dry Valley road where they
had left Davis and Sheridan. "Strange to say, no Confederate
cavalry or infantry appeared, and there seemed still no pursuit."

But Davis and Sheridan were gone. Thruston rode after them
down the Dry Valley road and caught their divisions in McFar-

land's Gap. The road there was jammed with fleeing soldiers. He worked ahead, moving toward the front of the column, all the while entreating the regimental and company officers to stop and return to the field. All he could get from them was "See Jeff" or "See Phil." One old-timer shouted from the ranks: "We'll talk to you, my son, when we get to the Ohio River!"

It took Thruston half an hour to reach the head of the column. There he found Sheridan, Davis and (of all people!) Negley, many of whose soldiers were back on Snodgrass Hill with Thomas. Negley, too, had been "caught" in the rout and "carried away" by it. They were then, according to Thruston, halfway between the battlefield and Rossville.

Thruston told them the situation: Thomas was still fighting and needed reinforcements on his right. Davis at once ordered his troops to about-face and march to the battlefront. By that time the panic had subsided sufficiently for them to obey. Thruston in his account of it took pains to explain a bit for "Little Phil":

"Sheridan was still without faith. He may have thought there was danger at Rossville, or that his troops had not regained their fighting spirit. He insisted on going to Rossville. Darkness would catch him before he could reach the field from that direction. Negley was vacillating: he finally went to Rossville."[2]

When Davis turned back, Lieutenant Colonel William M. Ward with his "glorious old Tenth Ohio" which had been Lytle's regiment, decided to turn back also, though it was a part of Sheridan's division, serving as part of Rosecrans' General Headquarters detachment. Night was coming on when Davis and Ward reached the battlefield again.

Rosecrans was ahead of Davis, Sheridan and McCook. Major Frank S. Bond's version was that when the commanding general's party reached the fork of the road where one road led back to Thomas and the other into Chattanooga the party halted "to breathe their horses." The flight must have been rapid if the horses were winded. There Rosecrans told Garfield to go on to Chattanooga and take charge, forward ammunition and prepare for the defense should Thomas be forced back. Rosecrans intended at that stage to return to the battlefield and join Thomas.

But Garfield began to ask questions and show hesitancy. He did not seem to want to undertake "the great responsibility." So Rosecrans said to him:

"Very well, I will go to Chattanooga myself. You go to Thomas. He . . . will undoubtedly hold his position until nightfall. Tell him then to put out a double line of skirmishers, and after dark withdraw his troops to Rossville Gap; and you report to me at Chattanooga as to the condition of affairs with Thomas."

Garfield thereupon departed on his ride, celebrated by his biographers in later years, to convey directions to Thomas, while Rosecrans went by the other road into Chattanooga. That was the story told by Bond.

Rosecrans gave his own account of the conversation and parting with Garfield. He too placed it at the point on the Dry Valley road where the Rossville road led back to Thomas. Rosecrans said to Garfield:

"By the sound of battle we hold our ground under Thomas. Sheridan has orders to halt on the first good position for holding the enemy from advancing this way on the Dry Valley road yonder, and form with his own and Davis' division and any fragments of VanCleve's who may come that way." (Here he told Garfield the measures necessary to bring the commissary train into Chattanooga and the defense that should be set up in that town.) "And lastly, General Thomas must be communicated with to know his situation, and to inform him of the dispositions which are thus to be made."

Garfield, according to Rosecrans' account, said there were so many orders he thought it better that the commanding general give them, and that he should be sent to Thomas. Garfield urged further that a new line of defense should be selected in advance, if it be necessary for Thomas and the rest of the army to retire, and that the selection should be made by the commanding general instead of a substitute. The commanding general should be on hand to assign the returning units to their positions.

This seemed to impress Rosecrans. The colloquy continued:

ROSECRANS: "They are indispensable precautions in the present condition of things, and one of us must give them, while the other must go to General Thomas, and ascertain how the battle goes there."

GARFIELD: "I can go to General Thomas and report the situation to you much better than I can give those orders."

ROSECRANS: "Well, go, and tell General Thomas my precautions to hold the Dry Valley road, and secure our commissary stores and artillery, and report the situation to me, and to use his discretion as to continuing the fight on the ground we occupy at the close of the afternoon, or retiring to a position in the rear near Rossville."

The conversation is of interest because of Garfield's later complaints against Rosecrans, among them that he fled the field during the battle. The great mistake of Rosecrans' career was in not going back to Thomas instead of sending Garfield. Then he could not have been charged with abandoning the army on the battlefield. And it was quite clear that he went to Chattanooga on Garfield's urging.[3]

One other factor may have contributed to take Rosecrans to Chattanooga. At Rossville he asked some of the milling troops, who were "striving in hot haste to be among the first to reach Chattanooga," about the situation of the army. Apparently they did not recognize Rosecrans and Garfield for they gave the fantastic report that Rosecrans and Thomas were killed, McCook and Crittenden captured and the entire army routed. Of a small group Rosecrans inquired what command they belonged to and was told they were Negley's and that he was at Rossville rallying stragglers. Since Negley had been directed to reinforce Thomas, Rosecrans assumed that Thomas had been defeated and would soon be falling back in confusion. That, at least, was Cist's explanation of why Rosecrans went back to prepare for a defense.

By this time the firing had died down. Rosecrans and Garfield dismounted, put their ears to the ground. They were unable to hear artillery, only a rattle of small arms. The commanding general concluded that Thomas had fared no better than McCook.

Cist regarded it as unfortunate that the plan of sending Garfield to Thomas was carried out and thought the roles should have been exchanged: "Rosecrans should at once have gone to the front, and by his presence there aided, as he did at Stone's River, more than any other thing to retrieve the fortunes of the day, and pluck victory from disaster." If Rosecrans had been at the front, Cist thought he probably would not have ordered the retirement of Thomas to Rossville that night. "That was the turning point, and his hour had arrived." But he was not there to meet it.

Rosecrans was considerably more broken up than these accounts indicate. Captain Alfred Lacey Hough of Negley's division rode into Chattanooga that night to find Rosecrans' headquarters, where he saw the general weeping in despair, undertaking to gain spiritual comfort from his priest.

Hough did not obtain any orders from the commanding general. All he got was advice from some unnamed lesser generals to have Negley "close on the center," wherever that may have been in the scattered condition of the army.

Physically exhausted, broken in spirit, emotionally jarred and confused, Rosecrans had to be helped from his horse when he reached the house where department headquarters had been set up. He still thought from his contact with the party of Negley's men that the rout embraced the entire army. He sat with his head in his hands, as beaten and shattered as his right wing.[4]

Dana, who had stayed with Horace Porter on the night of the nineteenth after the council of war, had been with Rosecrans riding the lines in the morning. At noon, since it was warm and, as he explained it, he had slept but little during the last two nights, he decided to take a nap on the grass. Obviously he was off in his timing, because the battle had begun to rage on this part of the field shortly after 11 A.M. and was largely over by noon. Dana must have been operating on erratic time that morning, for he placed the opening of Polk's attack on Thomas as "half past eight or nine," when it was an hour or more later.

He was awakened by "the most infernal noise I ever heard." As he wrote about it, "Never in any battle had I witnessed such a discharge of cannon and musketry." His experience in battle had of course been limited but there was no doubt about the blasts of Longstreet's assault being devastating to eardrums and morale. Dana sat up on his grassy couch. The first thing he saw was Rosecrans crossing himself.

"Hello!" said Dana to himself, as he later recorded his thoughts. "If the general is crossing himself, we are in a desperate situation."

Dana mounted at once. As he looked toward the source of the noise in his front he saw the Federal lines "break and melt away like leaves before the wind." The newspaperman might have found a better figure than having blown leaves "melt" but his description of what he saw was graphic:

"Then the headquarters around me disappeared. The graybacks came through with a rush, and soon the musket balls and cannon shot began to reach the place where we stood. The whole right of the army had apparently been routed."

Dana soon became separated from Rosecrans. He did not explain how it happened, but his remark that "my orderly stuck to me like a veteran" would imply perhaps that others in the group about him pulled out for Chattanooga before he did. He and the orderly retired a short distance to a woods, where he met two of Rosecrans' staff, Captains Horace Porter and James P. Drouillard, trying to stay the routed men.

"They would halt a few of them," said Dana, "get them into some sort of line, and make a beginning of order among them, and then there would come a few rounds of cannon shot through the tree tops over their heads and the men would break and run."

He saw one man charge at Porter with a bayonet but the soldier desisted when the captain refused to give way. Dana's next experience was to "stumble" into an organized body of troops, Wilder's brigade of mounted infantry. There was something naïve, well-nigh incredible in Dana's later statement that Wilder asked him for orders. He wrote it at least twice and no doubt sincerely believed it, but it is clear from Wilder's substantiated account that Dana was in a state of high agitation at the time and gave orders impetuously. It is probable that in later years when he recorded the events of Chickamauga his memory was tricky. Though he was to become a boldly assertive New York newspaperman he was at that moment a very badly frightened Assistant Secretary of War.

Wilder, after his fight around "Bloody Pond," had sent a staff officer, who found Sheridan three quarters of a mile in the rear and asked him to rally his men and come to Wilder's assistance, in which case the mounted infantry would lead the counterattack. Sheridan sent back word that he could not rally his men. He advised Wilder "to get out of there." Wilder noted that Sheridan was falling back through the woods in disorder, though he was not pursued.

Wilder had dismounted his brigade and put it into a hollow square and had decided to attack and try to cut his way through Hindman and Bushrod Johnson, who separated him from Thomas. He had ordered the advance and already moved 100 yards when, as he told the story, a hatless, redheaded man rode up rapidly from the north and excitedly asked Wilder what body of troops he had. Wilder, who was in front, halted his men and gave him the full load of the designation, saying it was the "1st Brigade, 4th Division, of the 14th Corps, Wilder's Brigade of mounted infantry on foot."

The newcomer then announced that he was Charles A. Dana, Assistant Secretary of War. Wilder said he knew him, said he was going to attack and asked if he knew where Rosecrans was and how the battle fared elsewhere. Again the emotionally upset man announced that he was Charles A. Dana, Assistant Secretary of War. He told of having been with Rosecrans, said the enemy had "run over them," that Rosecrans was either killed or captured, the army badly routed and things in general were in a distressful condition—"as bad if not worse than at Bull Run." He told Wilder that his one brigade was the only part of the army left intact. Then he directed Wilder to take him at once to Chattanooga so he might send a telegram to Washington describing the situation.

Wilder was more concerned at the moment with saving a cause and a nation than telling Washington how they had been lost. He told Dana that the Assistant Secretary had been going in the wrong direction from Chattanooga and would quickly have been inside of Bragg's lines if he had not encountered the brigade. Wilder said also that the firing heard to the north had not changed position for the last hour. Though Wilder did not point it out when he later reviewed the conversation, it was quite obvious from the heavy battle still being fought that his brigade was not the only one in the Federal army which had preserved its formation.

"With a scared look," said Wilder, "[Dana] insisted that it was the enemy pursuing, and killing Thomas' men."

For the third time Dana gave his full name and asserted that he was Assistant Secretary of War. Wilder was directed more positively "to move my command, escorting him to Chattanooga that he might communicate with Washington at once." Naturally Wilder, a common-sense man as well as a hard fighter, did not obey. Instead, he told Dana he had scouts who knew the country toward Chattanooga and they could guide Dana as quickly as Wilder could get up his lead horses and his men mounted. Dana agreed to accept the scouts as an escort. But he issued more orders, which were for Wilder to fall back to Chattanooga as quickly as possible, to put his command on Lookout Mountain, "hold it at all hazards," and send his wagons to the north side of the Tennessee River.

The issuance of such orders by a civilian Assistant Secretary of War on the battlefield was preposterous, but it was naturally disconcerting to the leader of this intrepid brigade. While Wilder had been one of the most active factors in the battle, he, like many other Federal brigade commands, was only a colonel. Stanton had been as niggardly with promotions as with mules. Wilder's rank was scarcely sufficient to let him defy contemptuously the man who was supposed to have a more intimate approach to the Secretary of War than anyone else present with the army.

"I hardly knew what to do," said Wilder. The orders had enough weight to cause him to desist in his intention to cut through Longstreet and join Thomas. Longstreet's brigades by that time had changed front to face north for their attack on Snodgrass Hill and its back spur, Horseshoe Ridge. One of the unanswered questions about the battle is what would have happened if Wilder with his six regiments, including the 39th Indiana of Willich's brigade, all armed with the Spencer repeaters, and Eli Lilly's efficient battery, had been allowed to attack Hindman in the rear. He had already demonstrated his ability to drive one of Hindman's brigades by a frontal attack earlier in the day.

Colonel Smith Atkins had been on the skirmish line with his 92nd Illinois and had rejoined Wilder, who told him of his intention to charge through Longstreet's corps. Then Dana had come up. According to Atkins' account, "Dana ordered Wilder not to make the charge, declaring the battle was lost, and ordering Wilder to Chattanooga by the Dry Valley road." Atkins was more blunt in saying Wilder defied the order than was the brigade commander himself. Wilder at length reached Rossville, but it was not until the next day. And it was not until after he had done highly important service in bringing in the hospitals from Crawfish Springs and saving part of the artillery McCook's corps had abandoned on the field.[5]

When McCook's corps gave way, the hospitals at Crawfish Springs, which were in the army's rear when the battle was begun, were severed from both Thomas on the field and from Rossville and Chattanooga. Wilder provided a shield for them as they retired toward Chattanooga. As Atkins put it, Wilder "lingered long on the field" after receiving Dana's positive orders to leave it. His was the one command on the Federal right that was never driven away. Finally he drew back slowly to McFarland's Gap and went to work clearing it of abandoned caissons, limbers, wagons, ambulances and other vehicles.

While he was thus engaged, at 4:30 P.M., Major Gates P. Thruston and his small escort, about the only splinter of McCook's corps left on the field, reached Wilder with orders from Thomas, who on Snodgrass Hill was continually worried about his right. He ordered Wilder to establish a line running from the Vittetoe house across the hills to the base of Lookout Mountain and thereby prevent the Confederate cavalry from circling around and taking Thomas in the rear. Wilder responded to this order immediately, established the line and remained in that position all night. It was not until daylight on the next day that he received intelligence from a sergeant sent by Thomas that the left wing of the army had retired to Rossville and that he could fall back.

Wilder had at least one compensation. When he had a chance to talk with Thomas for a few minutes on the twenty-first, the day after the battle, the old warrior told him that the check he had administered to Longstreet had been just enough to allow Thomas to rally broken elements of the army and set up a defense on the right of his corps on Snodgrass Hill.

Probably the only other instance where a high civilian figure gave orders to an American commander on the battlefield was when Secretary of State James Monroe reorganized the front line of Stansbury's brigade at the Battle of Bladensburg in the War of 1812. Monroe won censure from the Secretary of War as a "busy and blundering tactician," but the conditions were vastly different. Monroe had served under Washington in the Revolution and had military judgment, whereas the American commander at Bladensburg, General William Henry Winder, had demonstrated he did not. Dana on the other hand had behind him a newspaper and Brook Farm career, while Wilder had shown command capabilities as strong as those of any other brigade officer on the field. What damage if any was done by Dana's upsetting orders cannot be known, for none can tell what Wilder's brigade with its sensational repeating rifles might have done by plowing into Longstreet's rear when he was heavily engaged with Thomas in front.

Monroe had been in the first line in Washington's attack on Trenton; Dana had instigated the battle of a different complexion at Bull Run. Still, as President Madison remarked on the field of Bladensburg—in Madison-like language—the civilian authorities should "leave to the military functionaries the discharge of their own duties on their own responsibility." That rule would have been better for the inexperienced Dana to follow at Chickamauga, as it was also for the experienced Monroe at Bladensburg.

In one of his later comments Wilder expressed the opinion that his charge would have been successful. "I would have struck them in flank and rear with five lines of Spencer rifles in the hands of the steadiest body of men I ever saw." He called Dana's orders that prevented the attempt "peremptory."

Dana's version was that he told Wilder he had no authority to give orders but "if I were in your situation I would go to the left, where Thomas is." That is what Wilder was planning to do when checked by Dana's arrival. Dana's ride into Chattanooga was uneventful except that he encountered everywhere evidences of the

disaster; heaped-up baggage wagons, caissons, guns. In Chattanooga he rejoined Rosecrans. "In the helter-skelter of the rear, he
had escaped by the Rossville road."[6]

One of the least consequential features of the flight seems to
have been what happened to the commander of the 21st Corps,
General Crittenden. He followed Rosecrans into Chattanooga, but
it scarcely reflected discredit because he had already become a
corps commander without troops.

Palmer's division had been taken from him and lent to Thomas
in the opening stage of the battle. Then Wood had been pulled
out of line and sent to Thomas just before the Confederate break-
through. Finally VanCleve had been dispatched to Thomas. With
the exception of Barnes's brigade, VanCleve had been caught in
the rush from the battlefield. Apart from a few fragments, his division had been carried back to Rossville. Barnes had been lent to
Wood early on the twentieth, then had marched to the extreme
left of Thomas to help Baird.

Since he had no command on the field whatever, it is understandable that Crittenden should follow the commanding general,
from whom any orders controlling his personal activities would
come. He was not in any practical manner in command of anything when the crisis of the battle arrived. As far as influencing
the outcome is concerned, he might as well have been back in
Kentucky. Even when he was on the field, Rosecrans had been
issuing orders to his division commanders over Crittenden's head,
to the fatal consequences of the army.

CHAPTER TWENTY-EIGHT

Snodgrass Hill

THOMAS "is not brilliant," wrote Bragg to his good friend Sherman before the war, "but he is a solid man."

That firmness—mental and spiritual quite as much as physical—was now about to undergo its most severe test as Longstreet, not without stubborn qualities himself, prepared his victorious brigades to push Thomas off Snodgrass Hill and encircle the right flank of the Union army.

Already at this stage of the war, before the Chattanooga and Atlanta campaigns and his great Nashville triumph, discerning soldiers and civilians on both sides were detecting that Thomas possessed military attributes of the highest order. From the beginning he had been prudent, cautious without being dilatory, adept in his strategy and well prepared and resourceful in his combats, and, what was of greater importance, invariably successful.

Had he possessed a modicum of McClellan's brisk egotism he would no doubt have advanced more rapidly in the early stages of the war, when blatant self-confidence was winning awards of shoulder straps and stars. But modesty and self-effacement and apparently an uncontrollable sense of timidity when attention was focused in his direction, revealed by a tendency to blush, retarded him as much as did official curiosity about how a Virginian and slaveowner would conduct himself in combat against his home people.

Stanton snubbed him. The Secretary of War did not even mention his name in orders issued after he had won the battle of Mill Springs, the first Federal victory in the west. Nor was he recommended for promotion. Lincoln earlier had seemed to doubt him, and had referred to him as "the Virginian," not the most flattering classification at the time. He had neither political friends in Washington nor burning personal ambition to push him along.

He might have done better also had he gone to the trouble, as many other generals did, to meet Lincoln before he went west. Though he came to be rated by many competent authorities the most capable Northern general developed by the war, he and his commander in chief Lincoln never saw each other.

To a man of Rosecrans' mental agility and impulsiveness Thomas must have seemed mentally ponderous, because old Pap "usually reflects twice before he speaks once," and then his language was "carefully measured." But at times, when questioned, his remarks were likely to be concise and conclusive, as when, after there had been much talk of retirement at Stone's River, his opinion was sought and he said with simple conviction: "This army can't retreat." He more than any other factor kept it on the field, and it was Bragg instead of Rosecrans who retreated. The staff-member Bickham commented that he was composed but not intellectually heavy. The simplicity of his manner and dress, the absence of show or vanity, caused this observer to say that "you might easily mistake him for a substantial western farmer."

Inconsistent though it might seem, there is ground for wonder if a faint touch of display, or yearning for attention, did not lurk beneath the inordinate shrinking. When he was made a brigadier general he continued to wear his colonel's eagle for months. When made a major general, again months passed before he put on the second star. Such reluctance would tend to draw more notice to him than a simple conformity to the regulations. Fellow officers found his attitude wholesome and never covetous or ambitious. If there was an inner groping for attention, it was never revealed by unseemliness. Of this Turchin said, "If he had an ambition, it was honorable and legitimate; and he never stooped to cross another man's path for the sake of profiting himself."

Piatt said his ambition "came solely from his consciousness of capacity." Thomas' own attitude was that it was much better to deserve a position and not get it than to get it without deserving it.

Turchin thought he possessed the intuitive qualities that attend talented generalship: "foreseeing the moves of the enemy and preparing means to defeat them." At Chickamauga he was never caught unaware, and he usually anticipated Bragg's next move.

It was only characteristic that when Garfield asked Thomas to what he attributed his success, the corps commander answered quickly, "To my men." Then he added a more precise explanation: "I made my army and my army made my success."

For some, Thomas' greatness was of an illusive quality. It was clearly there, but his naturalness and lack of any form of ostentation caused wonder if he himself were aware of it. Donn Piatt speaks of his reserve force and added: "There are two types of eminent men we are frequently called upon to study. In one we are amazed at the man having achieved what was claimed for him; in the other we are astonished that he did not accomplish more. In this last class George Henry Thomas stands conspicuous."

Again Piatt commented, after observing Thomas at the Buell court of inquiry, that he "made one feel his presence before he uttered a word."

The reserve quality seems to have been akin to that possessed by George Washington. Rosecrans caught it in West Point days: "Years ago, at the Military Academy," he said, "I noticed there were points of strong resemblance between his character and that of Washington. I was in the habit of calling him General Washington."

Thomas was a huge man—"massive" is the term at times applied to him—and although six feet in height he appeared shorter because of his huge shoulders and girth. While in the 1850s he weighed only 175 pounds, he took on many pounds during the years of conflict, until just after the war, at the age of fifty-two, he weighed 246 and was going higher. Probably his sudden death from heart failure when he was fifty-four was due as much to overweight as to the emotional upset that followed his reading of a letter claiming credit to General Schofield for the victory at Nashville—an unfair letter to which he was preparing a reply.

The soldier-scribe Bickham said his "full rounded, powerful form . . . gradually expands upon you, as a mountain which you approach." More than in his bulk, there was firmness in his countenance, especially the square jaw, heavy overhanging brow and steady blue eyes, which were dominating through the bushy eyebrows, heavy, light brown hair and sandy beard. Bickham noted his "ruddy, weather-stippled complexion" and the "glow of cheerfulness on his countenance," and thought the first indicated robust health while the second "irresistibly" inspired confidence. He was erect and "had a walk which was at once military and easy."

Horace Porter of Rosecrans' staff called Thomas' appearance "leonine" and said "he had a great deal more fun in him than is generally supposed." But the example Porter offered would scarcely persuade one that the husky corps commander possessed a delicate sense of humor. A jackass emitted some unrestrained brays and a startled soldier asked, "Did you hear him purr?" The inquiry amused Thomas so much that he would call it up from his memory time and again, and laugh uproariously about it. One laugh would seem enough. Porter said that when entertainers came to camp and recited or sang comic songs, the general would beat time and, when something struck him as especially funny, would "roll from side to side and nearly choke in merriment."

His wit could descend to a pun, and a poor one: "Gentlemen, we will defer bragging until we capture Bragg."

Very likely it was the Welsh temperament that made Thomas fond of music. His laugh had a clear, musical ring. He could be found where there was good singing. The 73rd Illinois, one of the Methodist regiments, held religious services each night and Thomas enjoyed the hymns. There is a plaintive note in his remark that the hymns carried him back to his boyhood and the good people he had known in his Virginia home. Home and family were closed sternly against him now that he had followed the Union cause. Never would his two sisters in Virginia speak to or of him again, but the words suggest that he must have thought of them wistfully at times.[1]

Thomas diligently guarded his personal life from public scrutiny, which accounts for the fact that there are fewer intimate glimpses of him than of other leading generals. Although his chaplain Van Horne had access to his military papers when he wrote the history of the Army of the Cumberland and later the life of his old commander, he did not see Thomas' personal papers, which the general declined to open to biographers. His widow withheld them after him.

"All that I did for my government are matters of history," said Thomas, "but my private life is my own, and I will not have it hawked about in print for the amusement of the curious."

Was it shyness? Or a healthy reticence and dignity? Or a matter of individual expression?—of being different? Or was there an underlying hurt caused by the bad things said about him in the South when he, a Virginian, turned away from his state, and by the reception in the North, lacking in warmth, when he determined to remain with the Union? Surely it was more a wound than shyness.

As has been pointed out by one of his subordinates, while he was retiring he was not austere, and while never familiar in manner with soldiers, he was always accessible to them and his dealings were kindly and sympathetic.

Usually, but not always, Thomas got prompt response from his men, who came to him freely, even with requests for furloughs. Though these were matters that should have been handled in the companies or regiments, he gave them attention. While he was at Murfreesboro a man asked for a pass, needed for a variety of reasons, the clincher being: "I ain't seen my old woman, General, for four months."

"And I have not seen mine for two years," said Thomas. "If a general can submit to such privation, surely a private can."

"Don't know about that, General," said the soldier. "You see, me and my wife ain't made that way."

No doubt Thomas did a great deal of soul searching, as did many others, before determining which side to support when the war came, but he took what was clearly the harder course, which would not accord with the charge that he was governed by what seemed personal advantage. The correspondence available does not throw conclusive light on how his decision was formed as war approached. Very likely he would have won independent command earlier in the Southern army. The astute Confederate General Dabney H. Maury bemoaned his loss to the South.

Of the Northern generals he said: "They had none like the Virginian Thomas." He summed up Thomas' power: "There was in his demeanor, in the massive proportions of his person, in his clear blue eye, in the kindliness of his countenance and his manly voice, all that impresses men with that personal magnetism so potent in the crisis of battle."

Nor is there cause for belief that he went with the North merely because of the urgency of his Troy, New York, wife. Mrs. Thomas stated that he never said one word about the question to her and she let him work out the momentous decision without intruding advice. It surely was more than ordinarily difficult for Major Thomas of the 2nd Cavalry, because the other field officers in the regiment, Colonel Albert Sidney Johnston, Lieutenant Colonel Robert E. Lee and the senior major, W. J. Hardee, resigned and offered a strong example of going with their native states.

But Thomas took the oath of allegiance to the Union twice on the same day and severed himself from his family, his dearly beloved sisters and his Southern friends. Though it led to considerable bitterness among some Southern officers, they in time, after the war passed, came to recognize his military competence and greatness.

Other participants or students of the war held him high. Moxley Sorrel, Horace Greeley and General Joe Hooker rated Thomas at the top of the Union generals. Henry Cist, who had opportunity to observe him closely, called him "the grandest figure of the War of the Rebellion."

Thomas passed through the Civil War without a physical wound. The only time he was wounded in his army career was when as a major of cavalry in 1860, in the western mountains, he was hit by an Indian arrow. It passed through his chin and pinned it to his breast. Though the injury was exceedingly painful he drew the shaft, tossed it aside and continued after the party of Indians.

Thomas fully understood the psychological aspects of warfare. He thought emotions could be subdued by seasoning and careful training to a point where the men could control them in battle. He believed military success came more from practice than intuition or sudden inspiration. Donn Piatt observed that rarely did he dwell on the actions of his fellow officers and almost never did he criticize them. But he did comment softly one night about Mc-Clellan, saying that he was gravely mistaken, during the nine months when he was organizing and training the army in front of Washington, not to skirmish daily with the enemy. McClellan's method, said Thomas, was like that of the woman "who consented to have her daughter learn to swim, but warned her not to go near the water."

Thomas that same night was irked that Rosecrans had not allowed him to do some demonstrating against the enemy. The commanding general thought the army could not spare the mounts and artillery animals.

"It is a great error in the government," said Thomas, "not to supply us with enough horses to enable us to feel daily the enemy at our front. It is the best training to give our men, while it gives us information and the enemy a healthy regard for us."

Heavily outnumbered in the cavalry arm, Rosecrans and Thomas were restrained from engaging in the type of warfare Thomas favored. Very likely Thomas was present at a dinner given at Rosecrans' headquarters before the Tullahoma campaign, to a visiting congressman, who told the party of a conversation he had with President Lincoln just before coming west. Lincoln was quoted as saying:

"I cannot understand this difference between rebel and Union soldiers. We are all of the same people, and our men ought to march as far and fast, and fight precisely the same as the rebels. They make impudent raids to the rear of our armies, why can we not teach them that two can play at that game? I think the fault is in our generals. As soon as we commission one, he sits down and yells for more men. He won't move, and he will yell."

Rosecrans yelled for horses, not more men, and he did need them. But Thomas on an earlier occasion had expressed a different view on this perplexing question of why the Southerners seemed to win the battles. He was telling, with the enthusiasm that at times made his cheeks glow and his eyes burn intensely, about how his men were being taught to be soldiers "in the only school of practical instruction . . . in the field." His thought was that familiarity with the roar of artillery showed that there was more bark than bite in the guns—that for every man killed, his weight in lead was wasted.

Standing against artillery was a matter of morale, and morale was achieved by seasoning. Said Thomas: "Put a plank six inches wide and twelve feet long five feet from the ground, and a thousand men will walk it in safety. Lift that plank five hundred feet from the ground, and one man in a thousand will walk it in safety. It is a question of nerve we have to solve and not dexterity."

Thomas thought the South entered the war better equipped in this respect than the North.

"At the South, men were more accustomed to violence and, therefore, more familiar with death. What we have to do is to make veterans. The great error in McClellan's organization was in his avoidance of fighting. . . . His one congratulatory report was 'All quiet on the Potomac.' The result was a loss of morale. Our troops came to have a mysterious fear of the enemy."[2]

By this time everyone around was giving rapt attention to Thomas' words. It must have disconcerted him, for he broke off the conversation suddenly. He did find fault with brother generals, but not in the sense that Lincoln did, because they clamored for more men. Thomas' view was that it was not a matter of more men, but of properly trained men. And proper training meant familiarity with the enemy, with gunfire, explosions, death—everything that went to make up the world of violence.

Certainly there were staying qualities in Thomas' make-up that were infused into his men that Sunday afternoon on Snodgrass Hill.

It has been noted that at the time of Longstreet's break-through Colonel Morton C. Hunter of the 82nd Indiana, Connell's brigade, had halted on the Snodgrass elevation and declared he would not retreat another inch, and that soon he had Colonel Kammerling with the 9th Ohio Germans, Van Derveer's brigade, by his side. Both of these regiments belonged to Brannan's division. Soon they saw Brannan coming with the survivors of his other regiments and scatterings from elsewhere. These drew the line farther to the right, facing south, reaching toward Horseshoe Ridge, west of Snodgrass Hill. By 1 p.m., when the Confederates appeared to be massing for a continuation of their assault, Brannan had about 2,000 men along the ridge.

Many soldiers unwilling to leave the field came to the ever-increasing concentration on the Snodgrass elevation and augmented the force there under Brannan. It is a mistake to say that Thomas selected Snodgrass Hill as a rallying point for forces that would protect his right. Chance, first prompted by the resolution of Colonel Hunter of the 82nd Indiana, had more to do with it than the corps commander. But chance was putting these scattered elements in the exact place where Thomas had recommended—at the night council at the Widow Glenn's—that the right flank of the army should rest. Now, with a large segment of the army gone, he would have to fight a battle that might have been fought better along the same lines if they had been selected and prepared, and if the fleeing divisions had remained on the field.

Dick's brigade, buffeted and parted by Breckinridge on the far left, was not involved with VanCleve's less fortunate soldiers. It made its way in two parties to Snodgrass Hill, where it reported to Brannan. Already it had seen heavy service on the left flank, where in its front, during the attack by Breckinridge, the Confederate Brigadier General Daniel W. Adams had been wounded and captured. The brigade was rallied in two sections and both continued the fight.

Thus after the diverse elements had drifted back and gravitated naturally to the strong defensive spur of the mountain, on which the Snodgrass house stood, the line that was hurriedly thrown together largely by Brannan consisted, first, of parts of his own division on the right, bearing south along the Horseshoe Ridge.

John Milton Brannan, one of the great names of the battle, was forty-four years old, a native of the District of Columbia, resident of Indiana, and graduate of West Point in the class of 1841. He had come up through the artillery and would become chief of artillery of the Army of the Cumberland after his services in this battle. Part of his early training had been with the historic 1st United States Artillery, where he served as adjutant when its role of officers contained the names of T. J. Jackson, A. P. Hill, McDowell, Hooker and Magruder. Here on Snodgrass Hill he had opportunity, almost for the first time in the battle, to make good use of the artillery, which could sweep the southern and eastern approaches.

The spur of Missionary Ridge, on which the most desperate fighting of the entire battle along the Chickamauga was now about to rage from 1 P.M. until darkness, has at times been called Horseshoe Ridge, perhaps to preserve the tradition that there should be one on every battlefield. It is in no manner shaped like a horseshoe, nor is it possible while the trees are in foliage—as they were on September 20—to gain a very clear conception of the outlines of the elevation, which would more closely resemble an octopus with shortened tentacles, or an irregularly shaped starfish, than a horseshoe. It is high ground with a number of ridges or "hogbacks" extending from the center toward the south and east, and consequently with a number of ravines, most of them relatively shallow, running up toward the center of the hump. Lieutenant Colonel Archer Anderson called these ridges "bastionlike spurs," and so they proved to be. To the rear or west the elevation drops to the Dry Valley road near Vittetoe's, a good half mile from the Snodgrass house near the eastern slope. Northeast of the Snodgrass house one of the ridges—the only one cleared of timber—trails off and descends to the more gently rolling Snodgrass farmlands.

On this cleared ridge, where the brigades of Harker and later Hazen joined Stoughton, some of the early and late desperate actions of the Snodgrass Hill battle were fought. Here Kershaw unloosed the initial bolt of Longstreet's assault on Thomas' new position, and here the Alabama brigade led by the New York City-bred Archibald Gracie delivered its bloody attack as the battle neared its close.

West of the bare eastern face of Snodgrass Hill, the elevation is heavily wooded, and the frequent ravines offered protection for the Confederate assailants.

Stoughton found a place in the line on the left of Brannan, between him and Wood. Wood placed Harker's brigade on the east slope on Snodgrass Hill. Interspersed between and beyond Bran-

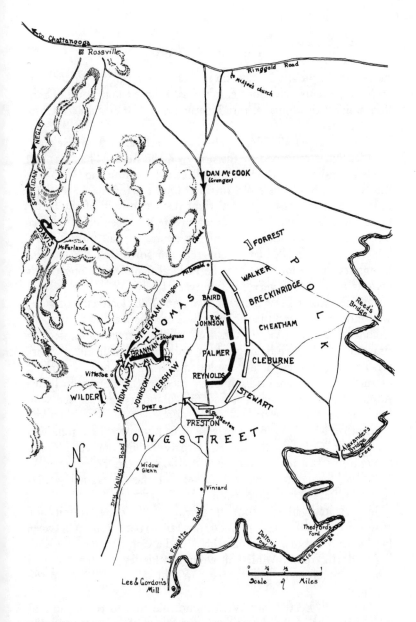

Thomas' battle lines 1 to 3 P.M., Sept. 20. Polk remains inactive in front of Federal left. Longstreet assails Brannan, whose right on Snodgrass Hill is saved by timely arrival of Steedman.

nan on the right and Harker on the left of the ridge were lone intrepid regiments of various commands, almost a confusion of random units: 82nd Indiana, 17th Kentucky, 58th Indiana, 13th Ohio,
44th Indiana.

Thomas came to Snodgrass Hill in the early afternoon. He commanded what remained of the army on the field. What was still
the left consisted of Baird, Palmer, Richard Johnson and Reynolds,
mostly occupying their old fortified lines east of the La Fayette
road, still facing east. Thomas' right flank consisted of the forces
concentrated on and west of Snodgrass Hill, a position of unusual
strength. The weakness was in the center, a half-mile interval
which was never adequately covered, but fortunately Bragg and
Longstreet were interested in the Federal flanks and Longstreet's
assaults never drove very hard between them.

Colonel Moses B. Walker of the 31st Ohio, Connell's brigade,
was under arrest, and the regiment was commanded by Lieutenant
Colonel Frederick W. Lister. But Walker attached himself to
Brannan's staff when he might have enjoyed confinement to quarters behind the lines. A shell exploded near by and he was relieved
of further worry about disciplinary measures. It permanently injured his spine and shoulder and his volunteer staff service won
him a brevet for gallantry.

Another who fought as a private after his troops had gone was
Lieutenant Colonel Charles H. Grosvenor of the 18th Ohio,
Stoughton's brigade of Negley's division. Later, after terms in
Congress, he would serve as chairman of the Chickamauga Na-
tional Military Park commission.

John Beatty gathered some fragments of his scattered units and
moved from the left flank to Snodgrass Hill to take position between
Harker and Brannan. En route he passed a Confederate lad bleeding to death from a Minié-ball wound in his leg. Beatty dropped
him a handkerchief as he rushed past and shouted, "Bind up the
leg tight."

On the hill Beatty met Wood, who told him to round up and
take command of the mixed bodies of men having no leaders. He
tried, though many of them drifted on toward the rear, refusing to

recognize or obey a strange general. But most of the Federals who rallied on the hill were eager to fight and erase the humiliation of McCook's defeat.

The ex-Russian Turchin noticed the independent spirit of the American volunteer soldier, who liked to fight on his own, and saw how it now came into play: "This spontaneous rally on Horseshoe Ridge was an opportunity for just such independent spirits to join the crowd and to fight in their own way and not under subordination and strict orders. And they fought splendidly."[3]

The Snodgrass house, built of logs and clay, stood on the north slope of Snodgrass Hill. Farther down the hill to the north was a clump of dead trees. There Thomas took his position that afternoon and directed the battle, about 400 yards from the firing line. Wood was with him a great deal and there Garfield joined him in the late afternoon. Thomas had plenty of generals around him but could have stood more soldiers. Brigade commanders fought much like privates, among them Sirwell, Stoughton and John Beatty, all of Negley's division. Colonel William Lewis Stoughton had taken command of Stanley's brigade after Stanley was wounded.

As the 2nd Minnesota of Van Derveer's brigade was being conducted across the fields to Snodgrass Hill by an aide, Thomas rode out to meet the regiment and, astride his horse, watched it fondly as it moved up the slope. There was a fatherly softness in his eyes when the regiment that had served him so well in his first triumph at Mill Springs passed in good order, after the notable fighting it had already done under Van Derveer on both days of this battle. Thomas complimented the Northwesterners on their appearance. They were scarcely in line when the left of Kershaw's gray assaulting columns, famed after the Peach Orchard and Wheat Field at Gettysburg, began to ascend the slope. "Ranks followed ranks in close order, moving briskly and bravely against us." But the Minnesotans aimed carefully and the enemy seemed to melt before them. This process of attack and repulse was repeated again and again until the Minnesotans could scarcely see the ground in front of them because it was so covered with dead and wounded.

Thomas could not have been other than gratified by the presence of Van Derveer with his regiments now reassembled. This had been Thomas' old brigade, commanded and trained by him before Mill Springs, and still showing his own solidness.

In its general aspects the battle of Snodgrass Hill, the most determined and sanguinary fight of all this grisly meeting of the two armies along the Chickamauga, and comparable in its hot fury to Gettysburg, Peach Tree Creek and Spotsylvania, consisted of a series of hammerlike blows by Longstreet against a citadel obstinately defended and constantly being strengthened by the erection of barricades as the afternoon wore on. Both sides seemed to recognize that all the fury of fighting of the two days had been only a prelude to the final test on Snodgrass Hill. As Lieutenant Colonel Archer Anderson expressed it: "The Federals fought with the desperation of men standing in their last stronghold, the Confederates with eager yearning for that complete and crowning victory which they now saw suspended like a dazzling prize on the very crest of the fated hill."

The battle of Snodgrass Hill had three distinct phases: Kershaw's attack on Harker and Stoughton; Bushrod Johnson's attack with his own and Hindman's division; and, finally, the all-out assault by the aroused Longstreet who seemed determined to carry the heights if the last round of ammunition and the last gray-clad soldier had to be expended in the process. Longstreet was no man to waste troops, and the prize he envisioned from victory here was stupendous. Longstreet had his mind fixed on a triumphant march to the Ohio and now it seemed to be passing from the realm of fancy.

Even before his lunch of sweet potatoes—which he considered a delicacy because they were not obtainable in Virginia—Longstreet began his assault by sending Kershaw ahead. It appeared at that stage that the Federal right was in such disorder that a single Confederate division might push the refugees off Snodgrass Hill and complete the process of rolling up the flank. Before Harker had rallied on Snodgrass Hill, Kershaw, in a continuation of his first advance, had pushed the Northerner's brigade off of a knoll to the south. This knoll, because of his stubborn defense there, still bears the name of Harker's Hill.

Then Kershaw moved against the Snodgrass lines, with Humphreys' brigade on the right and Kershaw's own brigade on the left.

Stewart's division, badly mangled from its fight on the nineteenth and the flank fire suffered from Brannan just before Longstreet's break-through, did not enter into this assault on Snodgrass Hill, though it was near by, nor did any of Law's division take part except Colonel Oates with his ubiquitous 15th Alabama. This regiment returned from helping Hindman in his attack on Davis and Sheridan in time to go with Kershaw against the last Federal position near the Snodgrass house. Oates said his men had ended their attack "panting like dogs, tired out in the chase."

Oates was crossing the fields over which he had passed earlier in the day when he spied Bryant Skipper, a lad from his Company G, about fifteen years old, lagging behind and crying. The colonel cheered him, told him he had not been hurt yet and might even live through the battle, and said it wasn't time to be frightened.

"Afraid, hell!" wailed the boy. "That ain't it. I am so damned tired I can't keep up with my company." The boy did survive the battle and the war, had ten fine children and served as sheriff of Henry County, Alabama.

As the 15th Alabama traversed the Dyer field where Kershaw had fought Harker earlier, Colonel Oates identified one of the bodies left on the field as that of Lieutenant Colonel Elbert Bland, commander of the 7th South Carolina, which he had led at Chickamauga and during the equally deadly fighting against the Federals De Trobriand and Caldwell in the Wheat Field at Gettysburg. Glory had come on one field, death on another. He had been a surgeon in the Mexican War, then a line officer after Fort Sumter. Oates could not help recalling the beginning of their acquaintance on Bull Run in the winter of 1861, when the army was stirred by the duel fought by Bland and Major Seibles, both of whom "belonged to the regular kid-gloved aristocracy of the Palmetto State." They had quarreled over a game of chess and in the exchange of fire each took a bullet. Since neither was killed, they became warmer friends after the tradition of the code, and apparently good chess companions again.

Oates found a hole between the 7th and 3rd South Carolina regiments and moved into it, and fought along with Kershaw the balance of the day. Kershaw began a series of attacks against the eastern slope of Snodgrass Hill that were repulsed again and again and did not cease until darkness.

Back and forth the battle surged. Here and there the gray tide reached the crest of the hill and seemed about to overrun it, only to be thrown back by a renewed effort from the defenders. Kershaw was finally driven to the base of the hill where he awaited some supporting effort on the part of the Confederate divisions on his left.

Thomas was everywhere giving commands. To Harker, who had brought up his brigade in good order after its tussles earlier with Kershaw's men, he said, "This hill must be held and I trust you to do it."

"We will hold it or die here," Harker promised him.

The brigade was conspicuous from that time for its battling and holding and did much to retrieve the glory of Wood's division after its disastrous withdrawal from the line.

Though "Little Charlie" Harker was having a big day at Chickamauga, he was one of Wood's capable officers who would not share in the glories of the Battle of Nashville. He stormed Missionary Ridge a little later, and he burned his seat by enthusiastically jumping astride a hot Confederate cannon just after it had been captured on the ridge. But he was killed in the great assault on Kennesaw Mountain, north of Atlanta.

Cheers went up many times for Colonel Emerson Opdycke of the 125th Ohio, Harker's brigade, who sat coolly on his horse amid the hailstorm of bullets. Thomas had ridden to him also and said, "This point must be held." Opdycke answered in words like Harker's: "We will hold this ground or go to Heaven from it."

When the first enemy attack reached his front he ordered his men to fix bayonets and shouted, "Men, I will lead you. Follow me!"

The 125th plunged forward, followed by all of Harker's brigade. The Confederate attack was broken and forced back.

But there were other attacks. After one of them had been beaten off, Harker rode up and complimented the Ohioans. As the fury of the battle increased, most of the mounted officers had the good sense to send back their horses and command on foot. The men of the 125th Ohio noticed that at length Opdycke was the only officer along the lines who retained his mount. His voice could be heard above the battle din. Several bullets hit his horse and one went through his blouse and stained his uniform with blood, but horse and man stayed up.

As the afternoon wore on, the 41st Ohio in which Opdycke had once served, came up in support of the 125th Ohio. Some of the men recognized the colonel who had been their captain in earlier days and gave him a great cheer as he passed them, still mounted, his hat in his hand. Because of its gallant fight that afternoon Rosecrans complimented the 125th Ohio and Wood gave it the name it carried into history, the "Tiger Regiment." You will see a tiger on its monument erected where it stood on Snodgrass Hill.

Opdycke, of Newark, Ohio, had entered the army as a private in 1861 and would leave it a brevet major general. Few earned higher praise than he did from Thomas after the battles of Franklin and Nashville. But mainly he is remembered as the leader of "Opdycke's Tigers" at Chickamauga.[4]

Longstreet was directing the battle much after the fashion he had learned from General Lee—making careful preparations and entrusting the details of the assaults to his subordinates. Never having acted before in concert, they became confused at times about who was in command on the firing line. Thus, while Hindman, who ranked Bushrod Johnson, now considered that he commanded the left flank for the balance of the afternoon, Longstreet gave Bushrod Johnson the *de facto* command there. Still later, Hindman was hit in the neck by a shell fragment, and Johnson took charge by Longstreet's order of the two left-wing divisions.

The Federal General Turchin, as has been pointed out, was a competent critic as well as a capable soldier. Perhaps of all the heroic and omnipresent brigades of the Federal army, his vied with Van Derveer's and Wilder's among those outstanding. While he was observing the Snodgrass Hill battle as the commander of the right brigade of Reynolds' division, turned back to face south after Reynolds learned that his flank had been passed and the enemy was in his rear, Turchin of all the Federal brigade officers seemed to keep about the closest check on the progress of the battle. He thought that Bushrod Johnson was "one of the best, if not the best" of Bragg's generals. Johnson more than any other division commander had brought the Confederate army to the verge of a great triumph. Now, with McNair's wandering brigade reunited with his other brigades under Fulton and Sugg, and having command of Hindman's three brigades as well, he prepared to renew the advance he had halted on the ridge in front of Vittetoe's at noon, and assail the right flank of the troops on Snodgrass Hill.

Johnson passed over the wreckage of the battle as he moved against the southwest and west face of the elevation—the so-called Horseshoe Ridge. His force was formidable. From left to right it consisted of the brigades of Deas, Manigault, Fulton, Sugg and Patton Anderson, with McNair in reserve behind Fulton. Deas on the far left was advancing almost from west to east, moving from the Vittetoe cornfields against the west face of Horseshoe Ridge. The other brigades of the two divisions were attacking from south to north. The line menacingly overlapped Brannan's right flank. Accompanied by an ample artillery, Johnson seemed destined to pass Brannan, reach his rear and give him the alternatives of surrender or destruction.

This was quite obviously the critical moment for Thomas. If Johnson crushed Brannan's right he might easily cut the road to McFarland's Gap and all but surround the Federal army. Given any sort of support by Polk's wing, which Bragg was permitting to remain idle while Longstreet was at the supreme moment of the battle on the Confederate left, the entire Union army might be captured.

But before Bushrod Johnson could reach and turn the Federal position and add fresh glories to his and Hindman's troops which had performed already the stellar roles of the battle, one of those fortuitous developments that arise at times to turn the entire course of great events interposed now to rescue Thomas and the Union army from destruction. Back at Rossville and on the road south, Gordon Granger and "Old Steady" Steedman with Rose-crans' reserve corps had been listening to the roar of Thomas' fierce fight when Breckinridge crossed to the west side of the La Fayette road. They had detected that the sounds were moving westward, which would indicate that the Federals were being pressed back. Without more delay they had decided to do something about it.[5]

CHAPTER TWENTY-NINE

March of Granger and Steedman

A COMMON misconception about Chickamauga is that Granger marched to the relief of Thomas without orders, or in violation of orders directing him to hold the Rossville gap. Why anyone should persist in wanting him to hold the gap while the army was being destroyed in front of him is an unexplained phase of this version. But he is supposed to have risked court martial and heroically marched to the sound of the cannon and saved the army.

Rosecrans was not the kind of a general who would fight and lose a battle with orders for one of his corps to stand by idly disengaged. Granger had ample orders. Thomas was in touch with him from time to time on the nineteenth, reporting the progress of the battle. This precaution he took to make sure that Granger remained close enough to give help. That night he asked Granger if the reserve corps were in supporting distance and received a reassuring reply from Steedman, who reported his position at McAfee's church. At 8 P.M. Rosecrans sent an order to Granger through chief of staff Garfield saying, "You must help us in the fight tomorrow by supporting Thomas." No time was specified for the march—a corps commander is ordinarily allowed some discretion in such matters—but the instructions were explicit. Thus Granger's march was made not without orders, or contrary to orders, but in response to orders.

Again, on the morning of the twentieth, Thomas advised Granger of his plans, said he intended to extend his left down the Chickamauga, and once more asked if Steedman remained in supporting distance of his left. Thomas, who left nothing more to chance than circumstances compelled, was making doubly sure that he could rely on Steedman. Steedman's partisans after the war gave him the full credit for marching to Thomas and insisted that he did so without orders from Granger and even over Granger's protest. There seems little doubt that "Old Steady" was the more aggressive spirit in the march, but neither is there reason to believe other than that he and Granger concurred in the necessity for the movement. Granger, who maintained headquarters on the nineteenth in Rossville, moved at 9 A.M. on the twentieth to Mc-Afee's church, three miles from Rossville and a mile and a half east of the La Fayette road. Thus he and Steedman were together when just before eleven o'clock, after studying the sounds from the battlefield, five miles away, they reached the decision to march at once. Steedman moved at eleven, and the head of his division reached Thomas at 1 P.M. The complete division was on the field by 1:30 P.M. The battle had not reached Snodgrass Hill when he marched but it was at the crisis there when he arrived.

When Steedman had his division under way, Captain William C. Russell, Granger's Assistant Adjutant General, sent this dispatch to Colonel George E. Flynt, Thomas' chief of staff:

"Col. Flynt:
"General Granger is moving Steedman with two brigades to General Thomas' assistance.
W. C. RUSSELL,
Captain and Assistant Adjutant-general."[1]

This is ample confirmation that the march was being made by Granger's orders. Granger was not only unpopular with the men but had difficulty with his superiors. He later suffered such strained relations with both Grant and Sherman that he was sent to a quiet sector on the Gulf Coast. The lack of warmth in his character probably accounted for the tendency of the army to give the more magnetic "Old Steady" credit for the march that saved Thomas from destruction. The veterans even changed his name at the reunions from "Old Steady" to "Old Chickamauga." They sent him to the Ohio senate and helped make him chief of police of Toledo. A glory almost as great as that he gained at

Chickamauga came when he commanded a provisional unit of Thomas' army in the defeat of Hood at Nashville.

"Steady," who rose from a destitute orphan boy to be an outstanding Ohio editor and, after the war, publisher of the *Northern Ohio Democrat* in Toledo, appears to have had only one fear. He left what amounted to a provision in his will as a safeguard against it. It was that when his newspaper published his obituary, care should be taken to spell his name Steedman, instead of the way the reporters so often got it—"Steadman."

Zestful and anxious among Steedman's soldiers were members of the 115th Illinois, the Methodist preachers' regiment that had aroused Granger's wrath by foraging over the countryside when it reached Rossville, and whose roving members he had threatened to have horse-whipped. The 115th had camped with Whitaker's brigade on the night of the nineteenth near the McAfee church. They had coffee and hardtack on the morning of the twentieth, and then, when the guns began to roar four to five miles away, speculated on the role they might play in the battle. Isaac H. C. Royse talked with Lieutenant Colonel William Kinman, veteran of the Black Hawk and Mexican wars, who had a premonition that this bright pleasant Sunday would be his last.

"Oh, no, Colonel," said Royse: "you will go through it all right, and live to fight many other battles." But the colonel persisted in his foreboding. A few hours later he led a charge up Horseshoe Ridge.

The 115th Illinois carried old-fashioned .69-caliber Remingtons, whereas Steedman's other regiments had later-model Enfields or Springfields. Steedman had two brigades, Whitaker's and Mitchell's, made up of Illinois and Ohio troops, except for a single Indiana regiment, the 84th, in Whitaker's brigade. Some of Whitaker's regiments had never been involved in a major battle. Two of the Illinois regiments, the 96th and 115th, had been under arms for more than a year and were well drilled but had fought nothing but skirmishes. Whitaker's other permanently assigned regiments were the 40th Ohio and 84th Indiana, but two regiments, the 22nd Michigan and the 89th Ohio, had been temporarily attached to his brigade before the battle. This gave Whitaker a strong brigade of six regiments.

Steedman's division, concentrated around McAfee's church, held under arms, ready to march at a moment's notice, listened to the roar of the distant guns. The soldiers detected as quickly as the officers that the sound was moving to the west. Everyone in the ranks seemed to sense that Thomas needed help, though they could not foresee that the army's right would give way and that Rosecrans would leave the field. Then just before eleven o'clock they knew somebody had made a decision, for Steedman's division was brought to attention and put on the roadway, Whitaker's brigade in the lead, followed by Mitchell's. Dan McCook's brigade was left near the McAfee church for a time to perform the duty that had belonged to the corps of guarding the Rossville gap. With good judgment many of Steedman's soldiers filled their canteens at a spring near the church. The water was precious on Horseshoe Ridge that afternoon.

Had Steedman been less resolute he could have found many reasons for delaying his march toward Thomas. Most apparent was the annoyance by Forrest's cavalry, which had to be pushed aside and left menacingly in his rear. A good many generals would have found Forrest a reason why they could not reach Thomas that afternoon. As the column neared the La Fayette road, Forrest opened on it with three batteries firing simultaneously. He forced Whitaker to go from column into line of battle, facing east near the Hein house. Whitaker sent a wave of skirmishers against Forrest, who gave way slowly, only to return to the harassment when the pressure on him was relaxed.

At twelve o'clock Whitaker's brigade passed the Cloud house on the La Fayette road half a mile north of McDonald's. Forrest's cavalry was galloping back and forth on its left sending volleys into the flank of the column, which was moving at "even more than a double-quick." Here Whitaker recaptured a Federal hospital which had been in Forrest's possession several hours.

At Cloud's the Confederate artillery again opened on the column. Whitaker's men could see the flash of a gun in time to warn them that a shell was coming. The roadway had a shoulder on the eastern side, high enough to give protection while the men were lying down in the roadway. The column marched with eyes to the

left. When the men saw a flash they would drop quickly to the
ground without orders and watch the shell go screeching over-
head or explode harmlessly. Then they would rise and resume the
march. The procedure did not suit their Major Poteet, who repri-
manded them and remained erect during the firing. Then a shell
almost hit him. Thereafter he did not admonish them for ducking
and dodging.

When the column was in the region of the Cloud house it passed
a part of Negley's division leaving the battlefield. Negley's men
held to their direction toward Rossville although Steedman's column was directly between them and the Confederates. The two
commands had different aims.[2]

From Cloud's the distance was a mile and a half to the Snodgrass
house. There, in order to be free of Forrest's annoyance, the column left the La Fayette road and passed down a hill until it came
to a shallow valley about 600 yards west of the road. Down this depression it moved until it reached the cleared fields of the Mullis
and Snodgrass farms.

While Steedman was marching, Thomas was on the northeast
face of Snodgrass Hill behind Harker's brigade, where he could
look across open fields and over the woods to the La Fayette road
toward Rossville. The dust rose in a heavy billow above the trees.
The New York *Herald* correspondent Shanks watched closely. He
said Thomas was deeply concerned over this march of troops
toward his left rear: "It cast a cloud over his spirits which was
plainly visible to one who observed him, as I confess I did that day,
with ever increasing admiration."

Thomas' anxiety was well founded. If the distant column were
fresh enemy troops, he was doomed; if friends, he might still save
his wing from disaster. From the communications that had gone
back and forth he had a right to expect Granger, but time after
time during the battle, as in the instances of Negley, VanCleve and
Sheridan, he had counted on reinforcements that never came.
Scarcely an hour earlier a column of Longstreet's men was mistaken for the approach of Sheridan.

Thomas turned to the group of officers about him. "Take my

glass, some one of you whose horse is steady," he said. "Tell me what you see."

One of them took the glasses and all waited. Somebody even had the farfetched idea that it might be Burnside coming down to Rosecrans' relief from Knoxville. The officer could distinguish nothing except a moving mass of men. But he affirmed that they were infantry. That seemed to satisfy Thomas. If cavalry, it would undoubtedly be Forrest; if infantry, Granger probably would be approaching from Rossville and McAfee's church. Just then Captain Gilbert M. Johnson of the 2nd Indiana Cavalry, serving as inspector general on Negley's staff, rode up and reported for duty "of any character." He had been separated from Negley's division—or the division from him.

"Captain Johnson," said Thomas, "ride over there and report to me who and what that force is."

Johnson was off at a gallop. Thomas' group watched him as he rode across the fields and into a clump of willows. They heard the rattle of firearms in his vicinity as he came under the fire of Southern patrols, then saw him emerge from the trees, put spurs to his horse and dash into the woods again toward the rising dust cloud. They waited eagerly and finally saw him come out of the woods, riding back in their direction, but through their glasses they could see that behind him was another rider carrying aloft the red, white and blue flag with a white crescent, the battle flag of Gordon Granger's reserve corps. A wave of excitement and exultation passed through the group surrounding Thomas. Help was at hand!

The newspaperman breathlessly described the scene: "We had wished for night, and it was Blücher who had come to us. At a quarter past one, Steedman first, and Gordon Granger afterwards, had wrung the hand of the statue Thomas, who had gone through the terrible scenes of the last two days' battle to be melted and moved at this hour. As Granger came up, I felt that from the face of the heavens a great cloud had passed, and that the sun was shining once more upon us."

The clasp of Steedman's hand seemed to impart to Thomas fresh strength. Someone saw his eyes light with "a strange, bewitching smile" while his mouth retained its "mysterious fixed solidity that revealed the inflexible determination of a soul that knew not how to yield." But his voice came with its normal, measured, practical words. Still, for Thomas they were emotion-laden.

"General Steedman," he said, "I have always been glad to see you, but never so glad as now. How many muskets have you got?"

"I have seventy-five hundred muskets, General."

"It is a good force," he said meditatively, "and needed very badly."

Steedman brought with him something else that delighted Thomas almost as much as the 7,500 soldiers. This was 95,000 extra rounds of ammunition. The supply has been likened to "water in the Sahara." The cartridge boxes on Snodgrass Hill were almost empty. One of the army's main ammunition trains had been involved in McCook's disaster and the shortage was growing acute all along Thomas' line.

When Steedman was approaching across the Mullis farm, Thomas had intended to put his division into line on the left of Wood and thus employ it to fill the half-mile gap between his right wing on Snodgrass Hill and his left wing behind the barricades east of the La Fayette road. That indeed was his first order. But even as Steedman began to obey it the emergency on Brannan's right, created by Bushrod Johnson's attack with his own and Hindman's divisions, imperiously demanded that the two fresh brigades be sent on the run to the heavily wooded Horseshoe Ridge area now already being occupied by the Confederates. Granger, who arrived later, remained with Thomas. Steedman led the two brigades, Whitaker's and Mitchell's, consisting of ten well-filled infantry regiments and two batteries, into action.[3]

CHAPTER THIRTY

Horseshoe Ridge

THE arrival of Steedman was one of the dramatic moments of the battle. The bluecoats charged up the hill, Mitchell on the right, Whitaker on the left, and advanced through the undergrowth, trees and rocks to the crest, where they could see the enemy already in line. As they neared the summit they noticed that because of the thin rocky soil, the trees there were retarded and the undergrowth scant, and the hostile lines were in full view of each other. The Federals had the advantage of having their bayonets fixed, and the steel gleamed threateningly as they approached. They could hear the rustle and hum of Confederate detachments coming up the other side of the hill.

Whitaker's brigade moved in two lines, the first having the 96th Illinois on the right and the 115th Illinois in the center. The 22nd Michigan on the left touched Brannan's right. In the second line were the 40th Ohio, 84th Indiana and 89th Ohio.

Steedman gave a signal and the men ran forward with a shout which they said equaled the rebel yell at its best. The battle quickly became desperate. The 115th Illinois, like many another regiment in its first heavy battle, began to break. Forceful Jesse H. Moore, the pastor-colonel loved by his soldiers he would not have whipped at Granger's orders, was back and forth along the disturbed line rallying the men. Lieutenant Colonel Kinman was killed as he had predicted. Other officers helped to stay the break.

At the moment of the panic Steedman caught up the regiment's flag and dashed forward. He was the personification of force and purpose: "a great, hearty man, broad-breasted, broad-shouldered,

a face written all over with sturdy sense and stout courage." He
was compared in one of the contemporary accounts with "stout
old Morgan of the Revolution." When he took the flag from the
color-bearer and looked along the line, he roared with a voice
heard above the din of battle, "Go back, boys, go back; but the
flag can't go with you!"

That was enough. The men cheered him, turned around and
followed him toward the enemy. His horse was shot down and his
hand severely injured by the fall, but he continued to lead on foot.
While thus dismounted he saw others beginning to give way. He
ordered the retreating men to halt. When they would not respond
he grabbed up stones from the ground and began pelting them,
driving them back into line. Long he held the colors in his own
hands, showing that he did not fear the most dangerous assignment
on the battle line.

What happened was that the suddenness and initial ferocity of
Steedman's attack startled the Confederates. They retreated eighty
to a hundred yards, then rallied and drove Whitaker's first line
back on his second. This was the critical moment for Steedman,
and his personal exertions as much as any other factor prevented
the repulse of his division, the loss of Horseshoe Ridge and perhaps
the rout or capture of the army. His raw soldiers gained steadiness
and eventually were fighting like veterans. Hindman's men were
driven back again and Steedman occupied the crest of the ridge,
at the cost of 1,000 casualties. He prolonged Brannan's line the
better part of half a mile to the right, then turned the flank back to
face west. The line now ran from the east end of Snodgrass Hill
to the west face of Horseshoe Ridge.

His men had a rest, which they used for a quick meal of hardtack
and tasty raw fat pork, described as "very sweet!" But the respite
was brief.

Edwin K. Martin of the 79th Pennsylvania caught a picture of
Thomas as the battle of Snodgrass Hill raged around him and the
bullets cut the leaves from the trees over his head. Not a muscle on
his face moved. He issued orders in polite, conversational tone.
"There is no figure in military history more sublime than that of
General Thomas in the midst of this line of fire that nearly en-

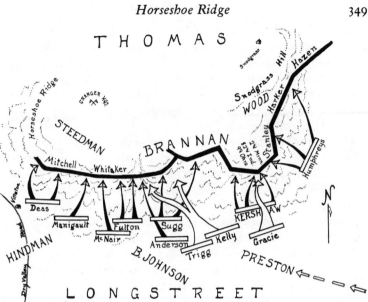

Longstreet's sustained attack on Thomas on Snodgrass Hill. Preston's three Confederate brigades—Trigg, Kelly and Gracie—are shown passing through Kershaw and Bushrod Johnson for their final desperate assault on Brannan.

circles the Horseshoe Ridge . . . wrenching victory from the jaws of defeat . . . making amends for the sins of a whole campaign."

Admiral Perry sloshing across the bloody deck of the *Lawrence* on Lake Erie; Andrew Jackson on the veranda of the Macarté plantation house at New Orleans; Colonel William Travis drawing the line with his sword at the Alamo; Washington riding "aflame" at Princeton, were indeed epic scenes, but no more lifting or exalted than this view of Thomas at the supreme moment of his stand at Chickamauga.

There were shortcomings and misdeeds for which Thomas was now making payment: "For Halleck's misconceptions and blunders at Washington; for Rosecrans' excessive confidence that in the face of his foes scattered his army over sixty miles when it should have occupied six; for the failure of Burnside to co-operate from Knoxville; or of Grant from Vicksburg."[1]

Bushrod Johnson's second advance against Steedman and Brannan was determined and deadly. Although his initial battle on the ridge had lasted only half an hour, the action now developed into a series of attacks that continued through the balance of the afternoon. The defenders of the hill watched as the long line of two divisions came steadily forward. Steedman opened with his artillery and did fearful execution.

During the lull that preceded this enemy advance, he had got his two batteries into position on Horseshoe Ridge. The Confederates, far from being routed, opened an incessant rifle fire on the Federal line and Steedman had his guns reply. Mounted on a fresh horse, he rode along the artillery. An efficient lieutenant named Closskey was leaning against a caisson watching the effect of his fire. Steedman told him to double-shot his guns.

"Been doing it for ten rounds, General," said Closskey.

Steedman looked down the slope and saw the enemy forming. "Then treble-shot them," he ordered.

"Never heard of it before," declared Closskey. But he turned to his gunners. "Treble-shot 'em, boys," he ordered.

The heavy charges tore away the rifling from the guns, and tore equally well into the ranks of the Confederates.

But the gray lines continued, surged up the hill, fought from behind trees and stones, and fought in the open.

The two lines came so close together that a soldier of the 121st Ohio in Mitchell's brigade reached out and snatched the colors of the 22nd Alabama of Deas' brigade and took them off as a prize. This Ohio regiment, which had been worsted during Bragg's invasion of Kentucky, went into action crying, "Wipe out Perryville!" Its youthful Colonel Henry B. Banning won from Granger the praise that, to him, "as much as to any other man, is owing the remarkable obstinacy with which two brigades . . . for more than seven hours held the key of the position on the battlefield." Granger said the regiment saved the army from destruction. Governor David Tod of Ohio, in acknowledging the receipt of the Alabama colors, thanked the regiment for "glorious achievements on that desperate field."

Another flag incident occurred when a South Carolina color-bearer planted his banner on the hill.

"A captain's commission to the man who gets that flag!" shouted a Union brigade commander. Almost a whole Ohio regiment dashed after it. The color-bearer fell backward as he dropped dead from a bullet. In a dying effort he cast the flag over his shoulders into the arms of his companions, who retired it when the attack was repulsed.

Jim Brotherton, the Confederate, still fighting where he caught glimpses of his own house, went from tree to tree. He had a blanket rolled over the knapsack strapped to his back, a hump that would stick out, like the left arms of some of the less experienced in-the-woods fighters. After the battle Jim counted thirty-seven enemy bullets and two buckshot caught in his blanket roll and knapsack. He probably did not exaggerate the number. Robert Y. Hiett, color-bearer of the 2nd Alabama Bn., had eighty-three bullets pass through his battle flag. By the time he had planted the colors on Snodgrass Hill at the end of the battle he had been wounded three times and his flagstaff had been shot away.[2]

Farther to Johnson's right, Patton Anderson's Mississippi brigade of Hindman's division met mainly the 21st Ohio, which demonstrated that a regiment with efficient small arms could stand off two or three times their numbers.

Seven companies of the 21st were armed with Colt's revolving rifles. The other three companies had good Enfields, but all five chambers of the Colts could be loaded as quickly as the one-shot Enfields. Ordinarily after a volley had been fired by a defending line the attackers had breathing time in which to rush forward while the defenders were reloading. Longstreet's troops who came up in front of the 21st Ohio were amazed to find that they had no period of safety after sustaining a volley. A second and then other volleys caught them almost at once.

The Ohio regiment was commanded by Lieutenant Colonel Dwella M. Stoughton and was a part of Sirwell's brigade, Negley's division. It numbered 535 men but made up in weapons what it lacked in numbers. As a member of the regiment said, "One man was like five in shooting power." Five separate charges against the regiment's front were repulsed. The cost to the assailants was staggering; to the defenders, heavy. Lieutenant Colonel Stoughton was mortally wounded, but the line held.

"The scene at this time was horrible," said a regimental account. Artillery had set fire to the brush and leaves. Ammunition was running low. Search was made through the cartridge boxes of the dead. The field hospitals in the rear were combed through and the cartridge boxes of the wounded were sent to the firing line. By economizing and making every shot count as much as they could, the Ohioans held on. The 535 men of the regiment expended 43,550 rounds of Colt's ammunition, in addition to some Enfield cartridges, which, it was discovered during the fray, could be employed in the Colts.

What Colonel Hunter of the 82nd Indiana remembered was that from about 1 P.M. through the rest of the day the Confederates made a series of furious attacks, "charge after charge." Each repulse seemed to add to their fury. "The very earth trembled with musketry." He could hear no artillery above the rattle of the small arms, though artillery was employed heavily on both sides. The ground in their front seemed "mowed smooth" by bullets, but "we stayed as if frozen to the hill."

When Johnson's attack was finally repulsed, it was repulsed decisively. The Confederate leader called the retreat down the hill "precipitate." He had to use every effort to prevent some of the troops from breaking into a rout. But he opened again with his batteries and shelled the heights, though the artillery had to work amid a shower of Federal bullets. By late afternoon Hindman's three brigades—Deas, Manigault and Patton Anderson—which during the day had delivered one of the best performances of the war, were played out and had to be relieved from further offensive action. Johnson settled down to artillery and infantry fire. Some of the Southerners thought that if he had had one more brigade, he could have flanked Thomas and carried the ridge.[3]

Longstreet had now attacked Snodgrass Hill and Horseshoe Ridge with three divisions—Kershaw's, Hindman's and Bushrod Johnson's. He still had a fresh division, Preston's, the largest of his left wing, which he had husbanded all through the two days of battle, except for the minor employment of Trigg's brigade on the late afternoon of the nineteenth. There is ground for wonder, along with the inquiring Turchin, why he did not employ this splendid force to test the situation in the woods between Thomas' two wings—the half-mile gap guarded by no more than Willich's brigade, which was rather used up after the first day's battle and Polk's attack on the morning of the twentieth. Turchin—with the advantage of hindsight, to be sure—suggested that by bringing up Preston and adding Stewart's division, which had been idle since it had been repulsed at midmorning by Brannan in Poe's woods, Longstreet might have hurled an overwhelming force against Thomas' weak center and cut his army in two.

About the only explanation of Longstreet's failure to exploit the opportunities existing between Snodgrass Hill and Reynolds is that he was unaware of them. The interval covered only by Willich was so heavily wooded that Longstreet could not have had the vaguest knowledge about how strongly it was defended. He did know the Federals were in force on Snodgrass Hill. His attitude, much like that of Lee at Gettysburg, was that "the enemy is there and I am going to strike him." Undoubtedly it was the more attractive plan to find the right flank of the enemy on Horseshoe Ridge, turn it, cut off the retreat to McFarland's Gap, and drive the Federals back on Polk's wing, which might contain them even if it had not been able to dislodge them. Willich appeared threatened at one time by an enemy force, probably Law's division, and was subjected to heavy artillery fire, but he held his ground.

At 3:30 P.M. Longstreet ordered Preston to go through Kershaw's ranks and hurl his division against the southern slope of Snodgrass Hill. The hour for an all-out effort had come. The division made a beautiful appearance as it passed across the La Fayette road and the Dyer farm, Gracie with his four Alabama battalions, one Alabama regiment, and one Tennessee regiment on the right and Kelly with his mixed brigade of four regiments—the 65th Georgia, 5th Kentucky, 58th North Carolina and 63rd Virginia—on the left. Trigg was held in reserve by Buckner, who supervised the advance.

Kershaw and the scattering from Law's division were opening

a place for Preston, and Colonel Oates of the 15th Alabama scrutinized the fresh troops.

"As we moved out," he said, "we passed Gracie's brigade going in, in echelon of battalions, as handsomely as a command ever moved to such perilous work. It never had been in battle and its ranks were full."

William Preston, the distinguished Congressman and diplomat of Lexington, Kentucky, whose home had been the scene of brilliant festivities for Bragg and Kirby Smith on the Kentucky invasion, was courtly, dignified, finished at Harvard, and a fitting representative of the Bluegrass aristocracy that had sided with the South. His father had been one of Anthony Wayne's officers who stayed in the West after the "Blacksnake" finished Blue Jacket's warriors at Fallen Timbers. An old-time Henry Clay Whig, Preston had become a Democrat when the Whig Party dissolved, had served as Minister to Spain under Buchanan, then had come home to lead in the movement to take Kentucky out of the Union.

He had been a lieutenant colonel in the Mexican War and none could question his high ability after his service on the staff of Albert Sidney Johnston, his brother-in-law, and his able conduct in nearly all the western battles. Longstreet, who met him for the first time at Chickamauga, referred to him as "the genial, gallant, lovable William Preston." Jefferson Davis a little later took advantage of his diplomatic talents to send him as ambassador to Maximilian in Mexico, but he was never able to reach his post.

Preston's, the last of Longstreet's attacks, was the bloodiest and most vicious of all.

By the time he reached the Federal lines on the ridge, they were consolidated, protected by works of trees and stones, and given great strength by well-posted artillery. Nothing could provide a more inspiring yet more heart-rending picture than the advance of Gracie's brigade, moving forward as on parade, without firing a shot until it came to a narrow shelf or terrace in front of the Federal line. Apace with it marched Kelly. On they came until they were less than forty paces from the sheltered Federals. There, the one side protected, the other standing in the open, the two lines blazed away at each other, volley on volley. The remarkable feature of this action was that Gracie and Kelly maintained it for more than an hour.

The eyes of the Southern army were fastened on Colonel John H. Kelly, little more than a lad, who commanded the soldiers of one of Preston's brigades. Two months later, at the age of twenty-three, he would become the youngest brigadier general in the Confederate service. He was an orphan boy from Carrollton, Alabama, who gained an appointment to West Point. He resigned his cadet-ship when his state seceded and became a second lieutenant of Alabama artillery. Quickly he proved that he was an enterprising youth who, like boyish Brigadier General Dodson Ramseur of Lee's army, understood war and got the devoted response of his men. In command of a battalion at Shiloh, he led a regiment at Stone's River and a brigade at Chicakamauga. He enjoyed but briefly the star on his shoulder, for he fell in a skirmish at Franklin, Tennessee, on September 2, 1864.

Nothing in this battle, marked with gallantry so frequent that it became commonplace, surpassed the courage of these two brigades as they watched their ranks thin minute by minute and still doggedly refused to yield an inch of ground. The observant Turchin thought "only new troops could accomplish such a wonderful feat." Perhaps the best evidence of the deadly nature of the fray was that when General Preston sent the flag of the 2nd Alabama battalion of Gracie's brigade to President Davis, who promoted Robert Y. Hiett, the standard-bearer "for conspicuous courage," the flag was found to have been pierced in eighty-three places by Federal balls.

The first volley fired at Gracie from behind the logs had opened wide gaps in his lines, but his men answered with a volley and a cheer and stormed up against the first salient in the Federal line. Then they settled down for the dogged combat, in which close to one half of the brigade was put out of action.

Archibald Gracie, thirty years old at Chicakamauga, was a native of New York City who had gone to Mobile, Alabama, in his father's mercantile business. Educated at Heidelberg, Germany, and at West Point, where he was graduated fourteenth in his class, Gracie became an excellent officer who later won the admiration of General Lee in the defense of Petersburg. He was killed there by a shell while observing the enemy lines through a telescope. His father and others of his family remained with the Union during the war but the son, who had become captain of a Mobile militia company, went with the South and soon commanded a regiment under Kirby Smith.[4]

The openhandedness of Governor Vance of North Carolina to other states could have been seen from an inspection of Kelly's brigade as it moved abreast Gracie's up the southern slope of Snodgrass Hill. The 58th North Carolina, led by Colonel John B. Palmer, had been recruited in the northwest mountain counties of the state, had moved to Johnson City, Tennessee, passed into the western armies of the Confederacy and lost connection with home. While Longstreet's corps was wearing new gray uniforms presented by the North Carolina governor, the 58th was wearing rags. Many had bare feet. The men had been ordered to refrain from cheering. As they passed their generals going into action they "took off their ragged old hats" and waved them silently around their heads. The officers were touched by the gesture.

Captain Isaac Bailey of Company B remembered the scene vividly: "The long shadows made by the declining sun that evening I shall never forget. . . ." He told of the loss of Ebbin Childs, Colonel Palmer's orderly, "whose smooth girlish face I see before me now, and whose bright sword flashed for the last time in the rays of the setting sun." He fell twenty paces from the Federal line, "his beardless face ablaze with the animation of battle, and his youthful figure transformed into a hero's statue. The dry parched earth of Snodgrass Hill never reddened with nobler blood." The regiment lost also its Lieutenant Colonel Edmund Kirby, killed, and Colonel Palmer and Major T. J. Dula, wounded.

But the attack here, like those of Longstreet's other brigades, was beaten off by the resolute and well-protected Federals. Still, if the position could not be carried, neither could Thomas hope to assume anything like an offensive. All he could hope for was that he would not be destroyed. Heavily outnumbered, all but surrounded, he held the precious road to McFarland's Gap. His task was to fight and hold and wait for darkness.

Preston's assault on Snodgrass Hill, like the earlier attack of Bushrod Johnson, was comparable in some respects to that of Pickett and Pettigrew on Cemetery Ridge at Gettysburg, especially in casualties. Gracie's Alabama brigade lost 698 men, approximately the loss of Kemper's brigade of 731 or Armistead's of 643 in Pickett's division. Pickett's third brigade, Garnett's, suffered the heavier loss of 941 at Gettysburg. Preston's other brigades, those of Trigg and Kelly, suffered fewer casualties than Gracie's.

J. H. Haynie of the 19th Illinois, Stanley's brigade—a part of Negley's division that had stayed on the field—said his regiment was engaged under "a most terrible fire." It exhausted its ammunition twice and used all it could find in the boxes of the killed and wounded. This was one of the regiments that met Gracie's furious assault. The Confederate colors were planted on the hill within 100 yards of those of the 19th Illinois and the two forces slugged it out until Gracie was finally driven back.

When he was recalling the battle in later years, Longstreet said he made twenty-five assaults in all on Snodgrass Hill. However he may have broken them down, they continued all afternoon and each seemed desperate and protracted. Instead of twenty-five, it was really one of sustained duration.[5]

CHAPTER THIRTY-ONE

Withdrawal and Retreat

GARFIELD returned to the battlefield by way of Rossville bearing orders from Rosecrans for Thomas to withdraw his part of the army immediately. That was what the conversation between the commanding general and his chief of staff had simmered down to, as interpreted by Garfield. Rosecrans confirmed the order by field telegraph at 4:15 P.M.

Garfield's ride to Snodgrass Hill, the last of it along the route that had been taken by Steedman down the La Fayette road and across the Mullis farm, has been described as "world famous," though it did not mean a great deal, for there was nothing Rosecrans could tell Thomas either about how to fight a battle or withdraw an army in safety in the face of a victorious enemy.

Garfield's ride has been graphically recounted as one of high drama and narrow escapes, of dashes through briar patches, over rugged, rocky land and across marshes, and it involved all this, even to passing the pesthouse the Confederates had used for their smallpox cases. He tossed money to the sufferers as he sped by. He stopped at times to make sure of his way. On nearing the battlefield he came under enemy fire. His two orderlies were killed and the horse of a captain who accompanied him was shot. Its fall broke the captain's leg, but Garfield plunged ahead, jumped his mount over a rail fence into a field of cotton, zigzagged across the field, and eventually came to Thomas in the clump north of the Snodgrass house. Garfield's horse had taken one wound during the ride. It was hit again just as he reached Thomas and dropped dead by the side of Thomas' mount. Garfield arrived at 4 P.M.

Garfield later told Major Frank S. Bond that when his party came under Confederate fire and he leaped the fence into the cotton field, he thought it was the tightest place he had ever been in and admonished himself, "Now is your time. Be a man, Jim Garfield."

Rosecrans was in error in directing Thomas to withdraw his force "immediately." Thomas explained this to Garfield when the chief of staff, in hurried, broken sentences, delivered Rosecrans' orders.

"It will ruin the army to withdraw it now," said Thomas. "This position must be held until night."

Garfield sent a message to Rosecrans, which contained the phase, "Thomas standing like a rock." It gave Thomas the sobriquet he carried into history. When the reassuring telegram from Garfield, sent over the telegraph wire from Rossville to Chattanooga, reached Rosecrans, Crittenden and McCook were with him. The message said Thomas had repulsed an attack in force, that he had seven divisions and could take care of himself.

A wave of elation passed through Rosecrans when he read Garfield's words. He waved the telegram over his head and shouted, "This is good enough. The day isn't lost yet." Then, trying to catch up the reins of command, he said to his two corps commanders, "Gentlemen, this is no place for you. Go at once to your commands at the front."[1]

At sunset Thomas began his withdrawal. While he has been justly acclaimed for his heroic stand on the battlefield for half a day after a considerable part of the army and the commanding general had fled from it, nothing in his generalship disclosed greater capacity than the manner in which he was able to extricate his divisions, locked in combat with superior forces all along the line, without any substantial loss of prisoners.

The battle on Thomas' left meantime had been renewed. Bragg had issued his orders at 2 P.M. for a resumption of Polk's attack and they had reached the different commands by three, but it was much later before the attack formations had been completed and the rattle of heavy musketry sounded from McDonald's farm to the Poe woods.

Thomas was not interested in entering into a new battle for the protection of his barricades, which had saved the army earlier in the day, but desired only to get his forces through McFarland's Gap. This was an actual gap through Missionary Ridge and not merely a road winding over the summit, such as so often bears the name of Gap or Pass. Once in it, it could easily be held.

The order of retreat set up for his left wing was for Reynolds to retire first, because he had the longest distance to travel. Palmer, Richard Johnson and Baird would follow in that order. Baird on the left would hold Polk's wing at bay until the divisions on his right had passed across his rear. Both Richard Johnson and Palmer feared the consequences of beginning their withdrawal while there was still daylight, and asked Thomas to postpone it, but their requests were lost somewhere in transmission. They were correct in their supposition that the withdrawal would not be permitted to proceed in routine fashion, but Thomas was equal to emergencies.

Just before Reynolds received his withdrawal orders and while the firing was being intensified along his front that extended across the southern end of Kelly field, his brigade commander Colonel Edward A. King was dropped by a Confederate sharpshooter. King fell at about 5 P.M. and Reynolds began his withdrawal at 5:30 P.M. King's men put his body on a caisson of the 19th Indiana battery and carried it off the field for burial at Rossville.

H. C. Woods of Knightstown, Indiana, who rode on the caisson with the body, said: "I well remember our men begging Colonel King to dismount and not expose himself needlessly, as several shots had been fired at him while sitting on his horse. He finally got off his horse and was shot in the head and killed instantly." It seemed a case where a bullet was intended for him and he dismounted to meet it.

King was a regular army officer and an adventurous spirit who at one time commanded the 6th United States Infantry, a celebrated regiment that had had on its rolls the names of Winfield Scott Hancock, Lewis A. Armistead and many others distinguished in both armies. King, born in Cambridge, Washington County, New York, began his military career under Sam Houston in Texas. He raised a company in New Orleans, reported to Houston

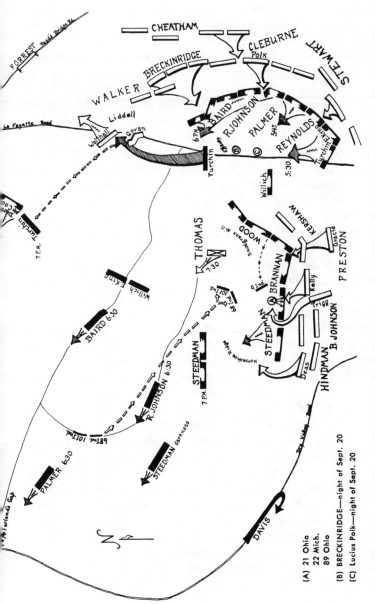

Thomas' withdrawal, 5:30 P.M. into darkness. Turchin is shown charging Liddell to clear Thomas' left flank. (A) Scene of the capture of three Federal regiments isolated and surrounded on Horseshoe Ridge. (B) and (C) indicate night positions of Breckinridge and elements of Cleburne. The two Indiana regiments, 68th and 101st, are shown as rearguards behind Snodgrass Hill. The brigades of E. King, Willich and Turchin cover retirement of Thomas' left.

(A) 21 Ohio
22 Mich.
89 Ohio

(B) BRECKINRIDGE—night of Sept. 20

(C) Lucius Polk—night of Sept. 20

and fought with him until Texas became a republic. As a captain in the 15th Infantry he served in Mexico and was critically wounded at Chapultepec.

King had been among the large bag of prisoners captured at Munfordville by Bragg on his invasion of Kentucky in 1862. He commanded the 68th Indiana, which possessed a beautiful silk flag. King concealed the flag by wrapping it around his body, which caused the Confederate General Buckner, who had charge of the surrender, to remark that the colonel had taken on weight since they were together earlier that year in Indianapolis after his surrender of Fort Donelson. The incident caused Edwin H. High, of the 68th Indiana, to say, "He saved our flag at Munfordville and we saved his body at Chickamauga, the only one brought off that bloody field." Early in 1864 the body was taken to Dayton, Ohio, where the funeral was described as the largest and most impressive in the city's history.[2]

When Bragg was able to get Polk's wing into energetic action, about 5 P.M., Breckinridge again, at his own request, was sent in co-operation with Walker against the Federal left. Cleburne, supported by two of Cheatham's brigades, was directed against the front of Thomas' barricades, while Generals Liddell and Gist of Walker's corps and Stewart of Buckner's renewed their efforts. Liddell's attack proved the most menacing. He reached the La Fayette road near the McDonald house north of Thomas and sent heavy waves of skirmishers across the road into the woods. They worked up to a position between Kelly's and the open Snodgrass fields, hauling two fieldpieces with them.

Dan McCook meantime had marched his brigade from McAfee's church following the route taken earlier by Granger and Steedman and had posted it on a companion elevation north of Snodgrass Hill, where it gave such security to Thomas that he allowed it to remain there and suggested that he could not have found a better place to post it. Dan McCook's artillery checked Liddell's skirmishers but they held their position in the woods to the left of Thomas' line and exchanged artillery fire with McCook.

Thomas' withdrawal orders reached Reynolds at 5:30 P.M., and

Turchin moved his brigade to the rear, followed by King's brigade, now under the command of Colonel Milton S. Robinson of the 75th Indiana, after the death of King. Thomas had ridden from Snodgrass Hill to the left of his line to guide Reynolds in beginning the withdrawal and came near the section of the woods held by Liddell's skirmishers. Some Federal soldiers who had been roaming about looking for water warned Thomas that Confederates were in the timber on his left, and had a battery with them. Not knowing the size of the force, what it signified or how strongly it might be supported, Thomas ordered Reynolds to form a line facing north so that the troops still east of the La Fayette road— the divisions of Baird, Richard Johnson and Palmer—could be retired under this protection. Reynolds gave the order to form the line to Turchin. Since Thomas was close by and Turchin was not sure where the Confederates were supposed to be, he went to Thomas, who pointed and said, "Right there in the woods." Then Thomas added, "There they are. Clear them out."

Turchin faced his brigade to the north, went into the woods, exchanged fire with the skirmishers, and then as a last dying gasp of Federal offensive power began one of the most audacious and spectacular actions of the battle. Under the eyes of their division and corps commanders, the men were stimulated to extraordinary effort. They drove the skirmishers to the east side of the La Fayette road, then fell on the flank of Govan's brigade and turned it, hit Walthall's brigade in the center and drove it back, captured 300 prisoners, seized the section of artillery Liddell's skirmishers had taken west of the road, captured Colonel Junius I. Scales of the 30th Mississippi, Walthall's brigade, and caused the retirement of Liddell's entire division.

The worsted Confederate brigades were soon re-formed but Turchin had cleared the Federal rear, had relieved Baird's left flank, which had been in danger of being surrounded, and restored order to Thomas' retirement.

An army unable to save its own guns was in no position to haul off captured pieces, so Turchin could not retain the enemy cannon. Among Turchin's thirty casualties in this attack was Captain

John Brown of Company D, 92nd Ohio. He had been with Have-
lock's famous brigade of the British army that had marched to the
pipes at Lucknow.

When a Nashville newspaper correspondent wrote of the heroic
roles at Chickamauga, he assigned one to Turchin for this attack,
saying it came when some were talking of surrender. Turchin's
opinion was requested.

"What, surrender?" he asked. "No sir; never. I shoost takes my
prigade, and *cuts* my way right out. When I tells my men to
sharge, de sharges right through. I tells, sir, we never surrender."

Turchin's vehemence silenced whatever talk there may have
been of surrender. According to the newspaper version, he ordered
his "prigade" from behind its barricades and led it forward. Someone shouted, "Huzza for General Thomas and victory!" and the
assault waves leaped ahead. As the observing correspondent described it, Turchin "burst through the closing lines of the enemy,
with an irresistibility equalled only by his energy and indomitable
will, amid one of the most terrific storms of shot and shell, and
whistling bullets, that has, perhaps, ever burst upon a moving
column of men without checking them." The correspondent went
on to say that while Turchin was not a Ulysses in council, he was
an Ajax in the "sharge."[3]

This account by a Nashville correspondent with Turchin, taken
with the long eyewitness account of the correspondent of the
Cincinnati *Gazette* describing the Snodgrass Hill defense, and with
Shanks's eyewitness report for the New York *Herald* of the arrival
of Steedman and Granger, goes far to refute the altogether unjust
remark of Rosecrans' staff officer, Horace Porter, that there
were no true accounts of the battle because, after the Confederate
break-through, "the first retrograde movement occurred among
that lying body of men, called 'the reportorial corps.' "[4] Turchin
thought that had the enemy's frontal attack been combined with
flank and rear attacks by Liddell's division supported by Gist after
the Federals had left their fortifications, Baird would probably
have been annihilated.

Thomas personally posted Reynolds' remaining brigade, King's
under Robinson, where it could guard the road leading to the rear,

the Mullis-McFarland Gap road over which much of Thomas'
left wing passed.

Palmer retired in good order. The general sat on a ridge 300
yards behind the line he had held so long east of the La Fayette
road and watched his men. "Cruft's troops left the field as if on
parade." Grose's, who went first, had difficulty and "did not maintain their character for steadiness." Not until Palmer reached
Rossville at 9 p.m. did he learn what had happened to the army's
right.

During the afternoon, after the right wing had been driven
from the field, Palmer, in front of Kelly field, knew nothing of it.
Everything in his front seemed safe and "I fully anticipated that
the day would close with a victory to our arms." He looked ahead
to the repulse of Bragg, then rapid pursuit. Now he was conducting the retreat of his two brigades, Cruft and Grose. His third,
Hazen, was on Snodgrass Hill.

As Grose retired he gave an example of courage by riding on the
left of his leading regiment with one of his aides carrying the
flag, occupying the position nearest the enemy, alongside the colors
that would draw heavy fire. Under a storm of bullets the brigade
made its way deliberately across Kelly field and the La Fayette
road. There Grose halted the 36th Indiana and 6th Ohio and faced
them toward the enemy to cover his retreat. Grose remembered
affectionately the 36th Indiana, which he had organized at Richmond, Indiana, and commanded in the Kentucky campaign and at
Shiloh.

"Brave old regiment!" he exclaimed. "Your country will remember you when these trying times are over."

A monument with crossed rifles and the Indiana seal, sur-
mounted by an acorn, stands in the Brotherton woods half a mile
east of the Brotherton house. That is mostly what survives of the
"brave old regiment," except the little share its sleeping members
have in a reunited nation.

Ebenezer Hannaford of the 6th Ohio gave a good picture of one
of the Confederate attacks during the withdrawal of Grose's brigade. His regiment had been under heavy artillery fire for an hour
when it saw the enemy coming through the woods four lines deep.

"The regulars were driven back pell mell, and we waited for the troops said to be in front of us to fall back, but in vain—*there were none there*. Tramp, tramp, tramp. We heard a heavy body of troops come marching through the underbrush and leaves, but nothing could be seen, until suddenly a gray line burst into view, and, before we were aware of it, fired into us a terrific volley." After that the two lines, fifty feet apart, fired rapidly at each other. The 6th then gave way. Every regiment suffered during the retirement, but only a few broke.

The breastworks along Richard Johnson's front consisted of a line of three big pine logs, two on the ground and one on top in the middle. Back and forth along the line brigade commander Willich had walked, "swearing in Dutch" and using his old, rolled-up hat for a stick. He would crack the men across the back with it and admonish them in clear enough English to "give 'em hell." Later he bent back his brigade to cover the gap between Thomas' wings.

In the attack on the 6th Indiana of Baldwin's brigade, a graycoat got near to Richard Johnson's line, jumped behind a tree and found he was too close to retreat. Everyone began to shoot at the tree. Finally the Confederate held out his hat, wigwagged it and Lieutenant Colonel Hagerman Tripp told the men to desist. A lanky Confederate, "the best tickled man I ever saw," stepped from behind the tree and came in a prisoner.

This regiment was dumfounded when ordered to take a position in the rear. It thought the battle was going well in its front. But retreat it was, and as they retired, Captain Rodarmel of Company E emitted an unearthly cry and "bounded through the briars like a Texas steer," his hand held to his rear.

When some of the men reached him he was near to tears. "Oh, my God, only think of it!" he exclaimed. "I am shot in the hind end."

What would the people back in Bean Blossom and Kokomo think of that! Some of his men examined him and discovered a spent ball inside his trousers that had not even broken the skin.

One of Thomas' captains, D. B. McConnell, who later served as chairman of the Indiana Chickamauga Commission, was at the

Kelly house when the withdrawal began. About him were dead and dying men, struggling horses, broken gun carriages, ambulances and litter-bearers, horror and desolation.

One of his men asked: "Captain, if this army is destroyed, what is there between this and the Ohio River to stay the enemy?"

"Nothing," the captain answered simply.

The man looked about and said that he would stay on the field rather than see Indiana invaded. He did, remained fighting, and died fourteen months later in Andersonville prison.[5]

Gradually the battle petered out on Snodgrass Hill and Horse-shoe Ridge. The right wing began to fall back toward McFarland's Gap. The larger part of the brigades of Whitaker and Mitchell on the extreme right were withdrawn first, in the face of Preston's attacks.

One advantage possessed by Preston was the presence of John Dyer by his side. This Confederate soldier, who had guided the division across his father's and the adjoining Snodgrass farm, knew every hill, hollow and pathway. When Preston brought up his reserve brigade, Trigg's, Dyer showed Trigg how to move his one Virginia and three Florida regiments around a wooded spur and up a ravine to the rear of three Federal regiments left on Horseshoe Ridge while Steedman was withdrawing on their right. While the three regiments were confronting Anderson and fighting a bloody battle with Kelly in their front, Trigg reached their rear and made prisoners of most of the survivors.

About the only order issued by Granger during that grisly afternoon was disastrous to these three stanch Federal regiments. When Thomas went to the left of his line to supervise the retirement of the divisions holding the barricades east of the La Fayette road, Granger became the ranking officer on Snodgrass Hill. The three regiments, exposed in front of the line after Steedman withdrew, had fought until their ammunition was exhausted. Unwilling to retreat without orders, they continued the battle with gun butts and bayonets. Few if any regiments in the army had performed more gallantly than these three—the 22nd Michigan and the 21st and 89th Ohio.

Observing that his condition was growing desperate, Colonel

Heber Le Favour of the 22nd Michigan sent a messenger to Granger requesting orders. Granger knew nothing of the situation on this part of the wooded ridge but he sent back word for Le Favour to use the bayonet and hold fast. Then Granger left the field without seeing the consequences.

The order might look well enough on the record books of the battle, where it would reflect an unyielding spirit, but it was scarcely practical when three enemy brigades were overrunning the hill and the Federal regiments were being left isolated, with supports falling back. They faithfully obeyed Granger. It has been held at times that they were left behind deliberately as a sacrifice so that the balance of the Snodgrass Hill force might retire safely. Instead, the loss appears to have been no more than Granger's carelessness. The gray tide quickly flowed past the flanks of the little force and engulfed it. Having no cartridges, their plight was hopeless. They surrendered.

Few if any isolated actions at Chickamauga evidenced greater gallantry than this resolute stand of the three regiments while the rest of the army was melting away behind them. Each regiment had its own heroic story. The 21st Ohio after its spectacular fighting with its Colt revolving rifles, had expended everything that could be gathered from the cartridge boxes of the near-by dead and wounded. The last round was fired just as darkness was shrouding the field. Confederates were on the right and rear. Lieutenant Colonel D. M. Stoughton, commanding the regiment, was mortally wounded. Major Arnold McMahan tried to cut his way out by ordering a bayonet charge, and did force the enemy back for a time. Part of the regiment managed to get away but Major McMahan and 115 officers and men were captured.

Colonel Caleb H. Carlton of the 89th Ohio surrendered with 13 officers and 158 men.

Colonel Le Favour's 22nd Michigan likewise fought to the last cartridge and still continued the battle. "Hand to hand in the dark woods, a deadly combat ensued . . . curses and commands . . . thousands of alert foes guarding every point . . . no avenue of escape." So ran the Michigan account. Then as the Confederates were about to exterminate them, they yielded and surrendered to parts of

Trigg's and Kelly's brigades. The 22nd Michigan surrendered 15 officers and 247 men.

When Kelly and Trigg were assailing the position on the ridge occupied by the three regiments, Brannan called for help to cover his right and Harker lent him the 9th Indiana, which had been lent to Harker in turn by Hazen. It was 5:30 P.M. when the regiment marched to Brannan's right and 8 P.M. when it retired, among the last regiments to leave the battlefield. During the two and a half hours, it stood as a sentinel while the right elements of Thomas' army withdrew behind it. After the three regiments had been captured, the 9th opened fire on Kelly and Trigg, who replied. The confusion resulting from this firing gave part of the 21st Ohio the opportunity to escape.[6]

This battle between the 9th Indiana and the two Confederate brigades was the last organized firing of the battle. There were as many claimants for the honor of firing the last shot at Chickamauga as for firing the first. The Confederate General Bate credited the Eufaula Battery of Stewart's division with firing both the first and last shots. Another claimant was the 35th Ohio of Van Derveer's brigade. As far as the Union army is concerned, the last volley undoubtedly was that of the 9th Indiana and the last troops to leave the field the 68th and 101st Indiana.

As these last two regiments were en route to McFarland's Gap they ran into a broken-down ammunition wagon from which they filled their cartridge boxes. Virtually the entire army was out of ammunition. When Thomas heard of the good fortune of these regiments, both of King's brigade of Reynolds' division, he ordered them back to Snodgrass Hill, where they acted as rear guard. After the 9th Indiana had fired the last volley and retired, the two regiments covered its retreat. The 68th Indiana was in the rear, the last element of Rosecrans' army to depart from the tragic field of Chickamauga.

As John Beatty described it, ". . . The fury of the battle gradually dies away, and finally we have a silence, broken only by a cheer here and there along the enemy's line."

The cavalry that had guarded the army's right at Crawfish Springs moved its trains at 5 P.M. into Chattanooga Valley and

behind the protection of Missionary Ridge rode north to Chattanooga, passing across the rear three miles west of the battlefield.

Sheridan has received unmerited applause on the mistaken impression that he returned to the battlefield by way of McFarland's
Gap and Rossville after being driven from the right flank at noon.
He marched from McFarland's Gap to Rossville, then moved with
obvious deliberation toward Thomas. He did not reach the Cloud
house on the La Fayette road until 7 P.M., after Thomas was withdrawing through McFarland Gap—by an entirely different road
from that on which the Cloud house stood. "Little Phil" took no
further part in the battle. But his march to the Cloud house from
Rossville did help save his military reputation, though there was
little in his conduct at Chickamauga to show that he possessed
tactical ability.

Perhaps at no other time in the war, even after the two Bull Runs,
was there a more melancholy march than that of Thomas' worn-
out soldiers dragging through the mountains and down the valley
to Rossville. John Beatty was struck by the gloom that pervaded
the army. Wounded men were lying for miles along the roadway.
Some had become so weak they could no longer crawl or call the
numbers of their regiments. "What must have been their agony,
mental and physical, as they lay in the dreary woods . . ." Beatty
thought the army was so mixed up and confused it was no more
than a mob, which a single enemy division could wipe out of
existence if it should attack before morning.

Captain Alfred Lacey Hough of Negley's division likened the
night march to the description of Washington's retreat from Long
Island in Irving's *Life of Washington*. The feature that impressed
him was the silence. As he passed along the column he heard not a
word spoken.

The stars served to guide. C. G. Briant of the 6th Indiana was
standing near by when an officer rode up to Colonel William W.
Berry, who commanded the brigade after the death of Colonel
Baldwin. "Do you see that star?" he inquired. He pointed north,
probably at the North Star, though Briant did not specify. "Let
your general course be toward that star. Move rapidly to the right

along the ridge till you strike a road. You will take to the left on this road toward Rossville."

The regiment made its way across rough, rocky hills and valleys, over logs and through brush and timber for about two miles. "Weary, worn, tired and hungry, we sullenly dragged ourselves along feeling a shame and disgrace that had never been experienced by the Old Sixth before."

Lieutenant Colonel Ward of the 37th Indiana awarded first place in coolness not to any masculine leadership, but to Mrs. Turchin, the general's wife, whom he encountered in the milling, agitated masses at Rossville. She was riding over the fields calmly and understood precisely what had happened to half the army. Ward talked with her and she apparently dropped some good suggestions. He ventured that if she had been in command of the right wing "she could have managed the emergency better" than the generals had there. It was not an excessive compliment. Surely she could not have managed worse!

One of the "cheerful" tragedies of the battle was that "Old Grant" had to be left behind. The name belonged to the mascot of Sergeant Gilbert Armstrong of Company C of the 58th Indiana, Buell's brigade of Wood's division. Old Grant was a rooster.

Not in all the army was there a better fighter. He could drive terror into the heart of any other cock, and terror also to the mare of Chaplain John J. Hight, which, according to the chaplain, "always passed him at the double-quick." Grant rode in the ambulance, where he often bullied the sick, but that appeared to be his privilege. Battle exhilarated him and his challenge had sounded amid the roar of Chickamauga. Sergeant Armstrong, his proprietor, was a famous sharpshooter who had served in the Mexican War, been a boatman on the western rivers, and was looked on as a man of parts in the regiment. He had received a Henry repeating rifle as a gift from fellow soldiers. Near the end of the battle he was severely wounded and had to be left behind. Old Grant disappeared. "Poor rooster, I fear—nay, hope—he was eaten by some hungry soldiers on that fatal frosty night."

When Thomas saw that the retirement of the army was under

way and proceeding as well as could be expected, he rode to Ross-ville to lay out a defensive line along which he might resist the enemy, who could be expected to advance in force in the early morning. The corps were brought together as much as possible after being dispersed during most of the fighting. Crittenden was formed on the left of Rossville gap, on Missionary Ridge. Thomas covered the gap with his own corps and extended it to the right to join McCook, who was posted across the valley between Missionary Ridge and Lookout Mountain, along the line of Chattanooga Creek. Mitchell's cavalry held the right flank.

An exceptional record was achieved by the 2nd Minnesota. In all the battle it did not have one man unaccounted for. The regiment went in with 384 and had 222 present for duty at the muster after the battle, the others being known casualties. No brigade in the army had performed more nobly than Van Derveer's. He saw the report and said: "It is a noticeable fact that the 2nd Minnesota Regiment had not a single man among the missing, or a straggler, during the two days' engagement."[7]

The battle was summed up succinctly by a Tennessee soldier: "The fight began at the Chickeymaugy River on Fri Sept 18th. Our boys went like a great Avalanche until we drove them to the forts at Chattanooga—and it is generally Believed that if gen. Pope [Polk] had obeyed orders we would have captured the whole army."

Another letter, from a private of the 47th Alabama, told his mother he had come through the battle safely and: "The boys had a fine time plundering the Yankes napsacks I got me a good nap-sack and too pare of socks and three packs of envelopes and several other tricks to teadios to mention. I got me the best blanket ofove [off of] the battle field that I ever saw so I am fix up for the winter."

At 10 A.M. on the twenty-first, Lieutenant Andrew Jackson Neal of Zebulon, Georgia, wrote to his father, then in Atlanta, about the closing phases of the battle: "Our fire was so demoraliz-ing on the enemy that they broke in utter rout throwing away their guns, knapsacks, etc. . . . The quantity of killed and wounded is immense on both sides. This is the hardest fighting unless Gettysburg beats it. Longstreet men say the New England Yankees do not fight as these men do."

Captain Wilson P. Howell of the 25th Alabama, Deas' brigade, lay that cold night with "an acre of wounded" around him, one of them "a fine looking, well dressed New York colonel" whom the litterbearers had brought in. The Confederates built fires among the rows of wounded of both armies to provide some comfort, but it was not until the next morning that anyone got a view of the field.

Howell, who became a minister in later life, went over the scene of slaughter. He said there had been no rain for a month. Fire had broken out early on Sunday. The clothing of many had been burned off the bodies. He told how the Confederate details had to begin the vast task of burying the dead of both armies.

Watkins of Company "Aytch," 1st Tennessee, told of a group of women looking over the battlefield with lanterns. They turned over several bodies and he heard a woman scream, "O, there he is! Poor fellow! Dead, dead, dead." She put the head in her lap and began kissing it, all the while saying, "O, O, they have killed my darling, my darling, my darling." The lament continued but he could stand no more. By that time his companion, William A. Hughes, was weeping.

Where the fire was burning close to the wounded, they would take sticks and desperately rake back the leaves and brush, hoping the flames could not travel over the clean ground. Some were seen scorched to death, still clinging to their sticks.

An unidentified Southern writer—and the Southern newspaper correspondents did not seek the rear any more than the Northern—told of the frightful battlefield that night: "I have never seen anything to compare with the horrors of the scene presented here. . . . The enemy had set fire to their works when forced to leave them, and the fire had communicated to the forests and lit up the scene far and wide. The dead and wounded lay in heaps, literally piled upon each other, and in many instances the fire had burned them to a cinder, and many of the wounded had their clothes burned off, and their bodies were a perfect blister."

Those who were spared the flames in this section begged for

water, the great need on the battlefield that night. The correspondent continued his description: "The groups of dead men and
horses, and writhing forms of the wounded, there in that dreary
forest, only seen by the scattered moonbeams as they stole through
the branches, and the flickering fire light, as it crept slowly but
steadily up to where they lay, and the fearful cries of those who
watched its advance, unable to drag their broken limbs beyond
the reach of the destroyer: and then the distorted and upturned
faces of those whose bodies were lying amidst the grim shadows
which fell around, conspicuous among which was the shadow of
death. All the pompous pageantry of the scene was gone, and
nought remained of all the glory lost and won upon that bloody
field save the wretched forms of those who no more will spring
forward at the call of arms."[8]

The Federal army was safe for a time in Rossville, but none
apparently had remembered Minty's cavalry brigade which had
been doing splendid service before, during and after the battle
trying to cope with Forrest's more numerous veteran horsemen.
Minty took up the flank guard at McAfee's church after the de-
partures of Granger and, a little later, Dan McCook, and there he
passed the night of the twentieth. Uncertain of what was happen-
ing in the rear at Rossville, Minty's men were alerted shortly before daylight when they heard cheering in their rear.

"Every man sprang to his feet," said Minty. "The blood coursing
through our veins warmed our chilled limbs and infused new life
into our bodies. More than one called out: 'There's Burnside, and
we'll whip them yet.' "

How vain a hope to rely on Burnside! Minty sent two orderlies
to get the news. They returned with the startling intelligence that
Rosecrans' entire army was at Rossville. Said Minty of his location
at McAfee's church: "A nice position to be in, truly. A little
brigade of cavalry (three regiments) and one section of artillery,
in all about 3,000 men, three miles in front of our army, and directly between it and the army we had been fighting for three
days."

Minty mounted, rode to Rossville and found Thomas "in the

famous grove of large trees" immediately beyond the gap. He told Thomas of his position.

Thomas looked at him inquiringly. "You should not be there, Colonel," he said.

"I know that, General, but I am there."

Thomas thought a minute. "Well, as you are there, delay the enemy as you can. Give me as much time as possible to get ready for them."

Minty performed that service. When he got back to McAfee's church his pickets already had reported enemy cavalry advancing on the roads from the battlefield and from Ringgold. He fought all the way back to Rossville and passed through the gap at one o'clock.[9]

Bragg's Dilatory Pursuit

AFTER the victory the Confederate army looked to its commander Bragg, and Bragg was not responsive.

The Southern triumph was well-nigh complete. Not an enemy soldier remained on the field. B. L. Ridley of Murfreesboro, Tennessee, a captain in Stewart's division, looked on as a number of Confederate generals gathered at Stewart's place in the line, shook hands with one another heartily and passed around their congratulations. "I felt like thanking God—I did thank Him," said the captain.

The generals who gathered included Longstreet, Stewart, Buckner, Bushrod Johnson, Law, Bate, Clayton and Brown. Their elation was indicated by the remarks of the observer Ridley: "The sun of Chickamauga was setting gloriously; the sable curtain of night was coming down. 'Hallelujah! 'tis done!' permeated the hearts of Bragg's army, when that old Rebel yell seemed really to shake the earth, peal over the hill tops, ring through the gorges, and hasten the footsteps of Rosecrans' stampeded army."

Here and there around the battlefield, civilians came from hiding. Colonel Watt W. Floyd of the 17th Tennessee passed along the Dry Valley road and was met by Hiram Vittetoe, who was on the watch at his house. He had gathered from the trend of the battle that the Southerners were victorious, but wanted to make sure. He told Colonel Floyd that the four women members of his family, his wife and three daughters, Samantha, Laura and Evada, were lying in a little hole under the kitchen floor, where they had been secreted from Federal soldiers for two days. The coming of Floyd's Tennesseans gave the family confidence. The women removed the planks and "came bounding out of the house with shouts of joy." They waved their aprons at the triumphant Southerners.

Most of the residents of the area had established a sort of refugee camp northwest of the Reed house. This house stood near the crossing of the Brotherton and Alexander's bridge roads, and when the battle neared the civilians moved farther into the woods and set up a new camp on the afternoon of the nineteenth. To it came members of several families—the Snodgrasses, Poes, Brothertons, Kellys, McDonalds, Brocks, Mullises and others. Without shelter, sleeping in the open through the chilly nights, without sufficient blankets, thirsty and hungry, they suffered in common with the soldiers, though less inured to hardships. In the early mornings the heads of the little children glistened white with a heavy coat of frost.

When the Federals were departing and the Sunday evening stillness settled over the field, the campers heard a band blare forth with a Southern battle song. That showed who commanded on the field. The music was a signal for wild rejoicing. The campers leaped and shouted. Women sang with joy. But those who tried to go home found their houses crowded with wounded. The Snodgrass house was too gory a shamble to be inhabited. The family moved to Elis Springs near Ringgold and camped there until the end of the war.[1]

Apparently the civilian residents of the battlefield area understood better than Bragg what had happened. Though Longstreet's criticism of the commanding general's ineptness seems excessive, Bragg quite clearly did not appreciate the completeness of his victory nor the opportunities it opened to the Confederate cause. Where Longstreet, Forrest, Bushrod Johnson and the better military intellects of the army were fired by the flight of their adversaries and the evidences of a splendid victory all about them— the prisoners, the abandoned cannon, thousands of Federal muskets and heaps of other equipment scattered over the field—Bragg gave no hint of an aggressive temperament or any ardor to complete the task which, as any great captain might have discerned, was only at the beginning.

Longstreet's view that Bragg did not realize on the afternoon and evening of the twentieth or even on the morning of the twenty-first that his army had won the battle seems well founded. Longstreet said: "It did not occur to me on the night of the 20th to send Bragg word of our complete success. I thought that the loud huzzas that spread over the field just at dark were a sufficient assurance and notice to anyone within five miles of us."

Brigadier General Frank C. Armstrong, commander of one of Forrest's cavalry divisions, saw Bragg that day, the twenty-first, engaged in his nervous habit of walking back and forth, excitedly, as Armstrong put it. The cavalryman dismounted and congratulated Bragg on his victory. Armstrong did not charge his commander with crudeness, but the incident brings to mind the frequent references to his lack of civility, even as early as his West Point days. He did not look at Armstrong or stop his nervous walking. He merely countered the congratulations with the words, "But the army is horribly disorganized." That would naturally be the case after such a battle. Would Stonewall Jackson have dwelt on this aspect? Everything about Bragg that day suggests that he was trying to justify a decision he doubted. He knew swift pursuit was the demand of the hour but he could parade through his mind every reason why it was impractical. His decision was akin to that in the days of the old army when as post quartermaster he rejected his own requisition.

Bragg went to Longstreet's bivouac in the morning for advice, and Longstreet suggested that the army cross the Tennessee River above Chattanooga, destroy Burnside in Knoxville and threaten Rosecrans' railroad communication with Nashville. Bragg pronounced such a movement utterly out of the question because of his lack of transportation. He did not recognize that however much he lacked, the enemy was still more destitute.

Certainly the broad Tennessee River imposed a major problem, but if Rosecrans had the resource to cross the bridgeless river in coming south, Bragg should have been able to improvise means to cross going north. It is not unlikely that the earnest threat of a crossing upstream would have led Rosecrans to evacuate the city.

Sorrel, accustomed to the celerity of the follow-up in Lee's army, expected speedy pursuit but soon saw that Bragg did not have a firm understanding of the realities of the situation. "He does not appear to have been closely present on the battlefield," said the able staff officer. Sorrel thought Rosecrans was not in control of the Federal army, either, and reckoned it "a unique instance of a great battle being fought out of the immediate presence of the respective commanders."

He quoted Old Peter's quick reply when Bragg asked for suggestions: "Move instantly against Rosecrans' rear and destroy him. Should we fail, we can put him in retreat, and then clear East Tennessee of Burnside and the Union forces."

This was so obviously the proper move that Longstreet did not need to reflect on it. As Rosecrans had maneuvered Bragg out of Chattanooga by passing the town and threatening the Confederate communications, so he might himself be dislodged by the same bold strategy. Manifestly the worst decision Bragg could make would be to invest Chattanooga. Any siege is likely to become protracted. The North possessed tremendous resources of manpower which, given two week's time, it could array against Bragg's army.

Longstreet opposed the idea of besieging Chattanooga. Bragg, nevertheless, adopted it in the belief that he could starve Rosecrans into abandoning the town by cutting his supply line at Bridgeport, down the Tennessee River. Starvation is a slow weapon. Speed was the prerequisite. If Rosecrans were not maneuvered out of the town and hit again or forced back to the Ohio, it might be expected that the numerous unemployed Northern soldiers would be coming from all directions to his relief. Even Polk, who had done so little to make pursuit possible, urged it! Bragg in his report said his army had no water on the morning of the twenty-first. He did not reflect that there was plenty of good water in the Tennessee River.

Sorrel's point that the armies were without commanders was made also by Colonel James Cooper Nisbet of the 66th Georgia, a new regiment assigned to Wilson's brigade of Walker's corps after the battle. The claim that Rosecrans in truth won the battle because after it he still held Chattanooga, the object of his campaign, was compared by Nisbet to the reply of the doctor when asked how the mother and baby were doing: "They are both dead but I have saved the old man." Continuing, Nisbet said: "A peculiar feature of this battle was the early ride of both commanders from the field, leaving the battle to their troops. Bragg did not know he had won a complete victory until the next morning, the 21st!"

Colonel William C. Oates said he never felt happier than on Sunday night, when he called at the campfire of every company in his regiment. The men were happy, too, despite the loss of comrades, because they believed they had been conspicuous in an outstanding victory. All expected quick pursuit.

"The next morning," said Oates, "to our surprise, the only order that came from General Bragg was to furnish details to gather up the arms scattered over the field." Then, about noon, the regiment was moved only a mile or two. All knew that Rosecrans was beaten and demoralized. "But the victory of Chickamauga, won at a fearful cost, was rendered barren by the inaction and lack of enterprise of the commanding general. I never did see or hear of any good excuse for it."[2]

Longstreet thought that Bragg was at first disposed to accept his advice and bypass Rosecrans in Chattanooga but was diverted by a message from Forrest.

On the morning of the twenty-first Forrest took up the pursuit. Accompanied by Brigadier General Frank C. Armstrong, he personally led his advance guard down the La Fayette road at a time when Minty with the Federal left-flank cavalry was drawing back on the Ringgold road from McAfee's church to Rossville.

Approaching Rossville, Forrest encountered the Federals. He and Armstrong charged with their 400 troopers and drove them toward Chattanooga, but the volley the Federals fired was aimed toward Forrest and a Minié ball cut the large artery in his horse's neck. Eager to pursue the fleeing bluecoats, but seeing the blood spouting from the wound, Forrest leaned over his mount, poked his finger into the artery, and so checked the bleeding. The noble animal continued to dash forward, but when the chase was over and Forrest had dismounted, the horse fell dead.

Forrest now noticed that he was near a clump of oaks on a spur of Missionary Ridge, where the Federals had built platforms among the branches and set up an observation station. He took the four Federal Signal Corps men in the trees by surprise. All they could do was to come down with their field glasses in obedience to his orders. The general climbed a tree himself and swept the country with a pair of the Federal glasses. When he descended he dictated to Major Charles W. Anderson what some, notably Longstreet, have regarded the most consequential and portentous dispatch in all the history of the Confederacy, though its full import could not have been appreciated by Forrest, or Bishop Polk or General Bragg who received it. It was directed to Polk and said:

"Genl We are in a mile of Rossville. Have been on the point of Missionary Ridge can see Chattanooga and everything around The Enemy's trains are leaving going around the Point of Lookout Mountain.

"The prisoners captured report two pontoons thrown across for the purpose of retreating. I think they are evacuating as hard as they can go. They are cutting timber down to obstruct our passage. I think we ought to push forward as rapidly as possible. Respectfully etc N. B. FORREST Brig Gen

"Lt. Gen L. Polk

Please forward to Gen Bragg."

The result of this dispatch was to send Bragg slowly against Chattanooga instead of quickly around it. Perhaps Bragg was justified in believing that Rosecrans was evacuating the town, as Forrest suggested. But even as Forrest was dictating he could hear Thomas' axes, the powerful arms which had given security to Rosecrans' left wing along the Chickamauga, ringing on the noonday air as his men felled trees to fortify their position at Rossville gap. That line in Forrest's message telling how the Federals were cutting timber might have caused Bragg to question whether Rosecrans meant to abandon the gap or the town, the focal point of his campaign, without another battle.

In later years Longstreet pointed to the high significance of Forrest's letter to Polk, saying: "It was that dispatch which fixed the fate of the Confederacy. General Bragg had decided to march around Rosecrans, leaving him in Chattanooga, when the dispatch was received which caused Bragg to think that the place would be abandoned on the night of the 22nd."

When he received it he decided to march through and not around Chattanooga.

Forrest could scarcely be blamed. He reported what he saw and believed. Bragg acted according to his best judgment, on the basis of his information. The play of chance entered. But did not Bragg's decision rest on unsound premises? If Rosecrans actually were evacuating, would not a brigade or division have been ample for pursuit immediately behind him, while the main army was being employed to interpose between him and Burnside, with whose army he would hope to unite, and overwhelm and capture Burnside and clear east Tennessee of Federal troops? Bragg was tardy and allowed his moves to be controlled by his adversary. Instead of striking out promptly on his own campaign like a victor, and compelling the enemy to conform to his movements, he advanced timidly, expecting to reply to theirs.

Unfortunately, and often unfairly, a commanding general's decision is judged correct only when it leads to victory. Bragg's Chattanooga campaign on which he was now entering was anything except victorious. But his main shortcoming was his tardiness. Either bypassing Chattanooga or following Rosecrans directly on his line of retreat would no doubt have proved advantageous to Bragg and difficult for Rosecrans had the Confederate commander acted with speed. It was not so much method as time. Later would not do. At Rossville Forrest with his clear military insight saw at once the opportunity and the means of seizing it. The word he sent back after he heard the Federal axes was that "every hour is worth 10,000 men."

When he received no reply from either Polk or Bragg, Forrest brought up guns and shelled Thomas' emplacements. The bombardment lasted several hours but accomplished nothing toward dislodging the batteries or driving Thomas back into Chattanooga. Forrest bivouacked that night on Missionary Ridge overlooking Rossville. When day broke on the twenty-second he found that

Thomas had withdrawn into Chattanooga under cover of darkness. By that time the town was well fortified, the morale of the Federal army was much improved, and whatever opportunities Bragg may have had for hot pursuit and delivering another blow while the Federal army was disorganized had passed. Forrest drew a line in front of Chattanooga reaching from the river above the town to the base of Lookout Mountain on his left. Bragg's infantry began to come up on the twenty-third, having made the twelve miles from the battlefield in two-and-a-half days.[3]

The battle of Chickamauga was followed by Bragg's siege of Chattanooga, and for weeks the high drama of conflict gave way to the humdrum of picket duty. The armies confronted each other much as they had around Murfreesboro and Tullahoma.

Things clicked back to normal. One of Longstreet's scouts on the outskirts of Chattanooga heard somebody cough. He stopped, then called out cautiously: "Who's there?"

"Yank," a voice replied. "Who are you?"

"Johnny Reb."

Then there were several moments of silence.

"Got any 'bacca, Johnny?" asked the sentry.

"Yaas. Got any coffee, Yank?"

"Yaas. Let's trade."

"You throw first, and look out for the tree or it will go in the water," cautioned the Southerner.

Something came whizzing through the air. The scout picked up from near his feet a little canvas bag and sniffed it eagerly. Then he threw over a sack of tobacco. They both said "Good night" but never saw each other. The battle was over, and the soldiers had settled down to routine.

When he was relieved by the infantry on September 23 Forrest was ordered to recuperate his command. He withdrew to rest and to reshoe the horses, then was directed against Burnside. This was his last association with Bragg. When Forrest was at Athens, Tennessee, the commanding general directed him to turn over his command to Wheeler, whose generalship Forrest had distrusted after being with him in February 1863 during the attack on Fort

Donelson, where Forrest's contingent lost heavily. The result of the order was Forrest's bitter and menacing denunciation of Bragg in the commanding general's own tent.

Perhaps never in the history of warfare has such a dressing down been given by a subordinate to his commanding general. It was a far cry from reasonable military conduct, however much the cavalryman may have felt himself goaded. But surely it is a reflection of Bragg's capacity as a commander that he did not recognize and utilize to the fullest in the interests of the Confederate cause Forrest's great talents as strategist, tactician and personal leader in combat. Spunk and rebelliousness are exciting qualities, and most opinion has tended to side with the temperamental genius Forrest over the lethargic servant of the regulations, Bragg. But if nations are to fight in armies instead of as individuals, Forrest's furious denunciation of his chief can scarcely be condoned, no matter how much it may be relished.[4]

Garfield carried Rosecrans' report on the battle of Chickamauga to Washington. He had been elected to Congress for the current term, the first session of which would convene in December.

Lincoln was at first disposed to retain Rosecrans in command of the Army of the Cumberland. Stanton, of course, wanted him out. But the descriptions of the battle given by Garfield and his critical accounts of his commander's conduct were the factors that weighed the scales against Rosecrans. In the end Lincoln compromised, appointed Grant to the over-all command in the West, and allowed him to decide whether Rosecrans should be continued or Thomas should replace him as commander of the Army of the Cumberland. Grant preferred Thomas.

It was an unhappy turn that the basis for the removal was that Rosecrans had fled from the field during the battle. Said Montgomery Blair: "This was the purport of the statement on which Rosecrans was removed—which was combatted by me and Chase —and which Lincoln told me had been verified by Garfield." The complaint was scarcely merited from Garfield, who had made the recommendation that prevented Rosecrans from returning to the field. Dana said it was another letter from Garfield to Chase "which finally broke the camel's back and made even Chase consent to Rosecrans' removal."

Rosecrans did have one distinction. He was, as Chase averred in his behalf, the only Northern general who fought all his battles against superior Confederate forces—a hard record for a Federal officer to establish in this war. Except for a period of ten minutes when he pulled Wood out of line at Chickamauga he did very well. He might be called the general of the one mistake. But it was a disastrous mistake.

Rosecrans told only once his own story of how he was relieved. He spoke at a reunion of the Army of the Cumberland in Washington in 1887 and broke a silence of twenty-five years:

"It was at night that I received the order, and I sent for General Thomas. He came alone to the tent and took his seat. I handed him the letter. He read it, and as he did so his breast began to swell and he turned pale. He did not want to accept the command, but we agreed on consideration that he must do so, and I told him that I could not bear to meet my old troops, afterwards. 'I want to leave,' said I, 'before the announcement is made, and I will start in the early morning.' I packed up that night, and the next morning about 7 o'clock I rode through the fog which then hung over the camp. The best of relations prevailed between General Thomas and myself, and as to the statement that he considered himself my superior and obeyed orders only from a sense of duty, I assure you it was not so."

The correspondent who reported the reunion added that Rosecrans was so greatly affected that his voice trembled. When he stepped from the platform there was none in the audience who did not feel sorry for him.

When Thomas became commander of the Army of the Cumberland, Major General John M. Palmer succeeded him as commander of the Fourteenth Corps.

Rosecrans relieved both Crittenden and McCook, both of whom he had preceded into Chattanooga. Certainly in the case of Crittenden the action was unjust. Both were absolved of any dereliction of duty and given later assignments.

Two or three post-bellum scenes are properly parts of the Chickamauga story—Thomas' meeting with Hood, who was almost a physical wreck after his Gettysburg and Chickamauga wounds; the affectionate reception of Rosecrans by veterans of both armies on the field of Chickamauga; Longstreet on the platform at the Rosecrans burial services, where the broken old Georgian, his reputation wounded by the political wars as severely as his body had been in the carnage of the Wilderness, paid homage to the Union general, whom he more than any other had defeated and sent into military obscurity.

Thomas and Hood happened to be in the same hotel, probably in New Orleans, though the chronicler of the incident, an unidentified Southern woman, does not specify. She arranged the meeting at Hood's request when he learned of Thomas' presence. She inquired of Thomas whether he would see the man against whom he had fought in three of his great battles, at Chickamauga, Atlanta and Nashville. Thomas answered, "Certainly, my dear madam."

Hood went to Thomas' room, clumping down the hall on his crutches, and when Thomas heard him he rushed out and threw his arms tenderly around his old foe. They talked for an hour. When Hood came back, the lady who had arranged the meeting said "the bravest fighter of all the Confederate forces had a trace of tears in his eyes and voice." What Hood said was: "Thomas is a grand man. He should have remained with us, where he would have been appreciated and loved."

Except possibly for a period immediately after the battle, Old Rosey never lost his popularity with his soldiers. The great occasion for him was when he attended the meeting of the Chickamauga Memorial Association on September 19 and 20, 1889, at Crawfish Springs, twenty-six years after the battle. John B. Gordon was then Governor of Georgia and though he had not been at Chickamauga, but with Lee in Virginia, he represented the Southern Army. The Grand Barbecue was held on the twentieth, attended by 10,000 veterans in blue and gray. Thirty tables were laid out, each 250 feet long, making 7,500 running feet of table space covering ten acres. Rosecrans and Gordon, on "full-blooded and magnificent horses," rode with the grand marshal and aides in the military procession. The 4th Artillery Band of the United States Army played "Dixie" and 10,000 voices joined in the Southern battle song, treasured in after years by both armies. Rosecrans and Gordon were seized by the veterans and lifted to the top of one of the barbecue tables. Gordon spoke and Rosecrans responded, addressing his "comrades on both sides." "Old veterans cried like infants" as they crowded around Rosecrans and clasped his hands.

Though he was constantly in demand to run for public office after the war, and did serve in Congress and in diplomatic office, Old Rosey probably had no greater moment than this, his return visit to the scene of his disaster.

Bragg was a more pitiful figure after the war, broken by poverty and pinched for companionship. All through his later life he seemed to be groping for a friendly hand. The Reconstructionists ejected him promptly from the job he obtained as superintendent of the New Orleans waterworks. He tried railroading, life insurance and other jobs. It was noticed that the one thing he retained was his unflinching integrity.

When he was walking down a Galveston, Texas, street thirteen years after the battle of Chickamauga, he fell over dead. He was a strange, unyielding man, who chanced to win one of the greatest victories ever scored by Anglo-Saxon arms. Perhaps there was no more peculiar figure among the many eccentrics in this Civil War, unless it was his adversary Rosecrans.[5]

CHAPTER THIRTY-THREE

An Abortive Victory

THE losses at Chickamauga were staggering. Bragg the assailant suffered more severely. While there are blanks in the reports and discrepancies in the estimates, the approximate losses of Bragg's army were 2,673 killed, 16,274 wounded and 2,003 missing, a total of 20,950 casualties. Longstreet's losses on Sunday afternoon, mainly in his assaults on Snodgrass Hill, were 1,856 killed, 6,506 wounded and 272 missing, a total of 8,634 of the 22,885 men he took into battle.

Bragg's army was probably the most representative of the South of any involved in a major engagement. He had troops from each of the eleven states of the Confederacy and from Kentucky and Missouri. Many Southerners who commented on the battle regarded it the most desperately fought of the Civil War, or any war. The same opinion was reflected frequently by Northern participants and writers. Compared with Chickamauga, "Bloody Shiloh" was looked on by some as little more than a skirmish. The general-historian Henry M. Cist said: "All things considered, the battle of Chickamauga, for the forces engaged, was the hardest fought and bloodiest battle of the rebellion." As Lieutenant Colonel Orrin D. Hurd of the 30th Indiana put it, "There is no record that will show harder fighting and better behavior of men than was displayed in this battle under the most trying circumstances." Indiana alone lost more in killed and wounded than were lost by American land and sea forces in the Spanish war. The Indiana casualties at Chickamauga, 3,926 killed and wounded, were one eighth of the state's losses in the entire four years of war.

The Federal army lost 1,656 killed, 9,749 wounded and 4,774 missing, a total of 16,179 casualties.

Thus the casualties of 37,129 for both armies at Chickamauga compare with total casualties of both armies of 23,582 on the single day at Antietam and 43,454 for the three days at Gettysburg.

Some reports and estimates put the Federal loss as high as 19,000 and some the percentage of Confederate loss as high as 40 per cent. Bragg said he lost two fifths of his force. Roughly, each side lost approximately one third its numbers.

Major General Joseph Wheeler made an analysis of the Confederate losses in major battles and showed that the percentage of loss at Chickamauga was substantially higher than at Gettysburg, Shiloh or Stone's River, and far ahead of that in such armies as Wellington's at Waterloo, Napoleon's at Wagram, Marengo or Austerlitz, or Marlborough's at Malplaquet or Ramillies.

Observing overseas, the Paris *Figaro* said of the battle: "These Americans are fighting on a military system inaugurated by the Kilkenny cats. The two armies meet and fight and slaughter each other with the utmost fury. Then they fell [sic] back and reorganize for another general massacre. Positively, the war will end when the last man is killed."

Rosecrans was unquestionably a gifted commander. He always had his school of defenders. John B. Gordon, as able a critic as could be found of the Civil War campaigns, thought the unfortunate opposition Rosecrans had in Washington should be taken into consideration in appraising him. "His ability as strategist, his skill in manoeuvre, and his vigor in delivering battle are universally recognized," Gordon said. "The high court of history will render its verdict in accordance with these facts."[1]

But events of the last day of Chickamauga established beyond doubt that Rosecrans had an erratic temperament incompatible with the high responsibilities of army leadership. His superior talents might carry him through nine times out of ten, but a great general cannot fail so utterly in the tenth emergency. His strategy, audacious and deceptive, became haphazard under the sway of good fortune. Nothing but imprudent self-satisfaction—not even his miserable intelligence about Bragg's dispositions—can explain the impetuous manner in which he plunged into Georgia with his army so widely dispersed after his splendid bloodless triumph in capturing Chattanooga. All of the blame cannot be placed on Halleck. Final responsibility for the reckless advance was Rosecrans'. This faulty movement set the stage for all his later misadventures. It forced him into a catch-as-catch-can battle, with his army still groping to get together when the fighting began.

His flight to Chattanooga while the battle was in progress was calamitous. Hindman's and Bushrod Johnson's failure or inability to pursue the fleeing right wing of the Federal army gave Rosecrans ample opportunity to re-form it wherever it could be halted behind McFarland's Gap or at Rossville and return to the field along the path of Steedman and Granger. He might have gained a drawn battle; it is remotely possible he could still have achieved a victory. Thomas, being on the defensive behind his breastworks, was almost able to gain a draw. If he had been given a little more help, he might not have been forced to retreat on the night of the twentieth and Bragg possibly would have judged further assaults against his well-protected lines altogether too costly.

A major cause of Rosecrans' defeat was failure to get the expected assistance from Burnside and Grant at a time when Bragg was being reinforced by Longstreet.

About the only advantage for the Northern side resulting from Chickamauga was that Bragg's staggering casualties left the South further enfeebled. The battle consequently might be looked on, like some of Grant's in Virginia, as a part of the process of attrition, or what Donn Piatt termed "warfare based on mutual slaughter." It helped to show that, in line with the thought expressed by Whitelaw Reid, the Confederacy was being conquered "by our Treasury rather than our generals."

From the Southern standpoint, the battle revived hopes despairing after Gettysburg and Vicksburg and allowed the South another year of war. Had Rosecrans won, Atlanta would have fallen and the Confederacy would have been reduced to little more than the Carolinas and a part of Virginia. After the battle the Richmond *Whig* was able to report, on October 11, 1863, under a heading "The Prospect" the following estimate:

"As the campaigning season of the third year of the war approaches its close, the principal army of the enemy [Rosecrans'], bruised, bleeding and alarmed, is engaged with all its might digging into the earth for safety. The second largest force, the once Grand Army of the Potomac, is fleeing before the advancing corps of Gen. Lee. The third, under Banks, a portion of which has just been severely chastised by a handful of men, is vaguely and feebly attempting some movement against Texas. The fourth, under Grant, has ceased to be an army of offense. The fifth, under Gilmore, with a number of ironclads to aid him, lays futile siege to Charleston. Nowhere else have they anything more than garrisons or raiding forces. At all points the Confederate forces are able to defy them."[2]

On the Southern side, the capable generalship was displayed by Longstreet and his subordinates, notably Bushrod Johnson and Hindman. For his brilliant work Johnson was promoted to major general. Bragg was unwilling to recognize Hindman's part in his victory and to let bygones be bygones. He placed Hindman under arrest for his failure to attack in McLemore's Cove, as he did Bishop Polk for his lack of enterprise on the morning of the twentieth. President Davis interceded, and neither case came to trial. Even toward the close of the battle Polk's contributions were so meager that some have attributed to him the failure of the Confederates to win at that stage an overwhelming victory. On this point Colonel William C. Oates said in an address years later on the battlefield:

"Why Polk's wing, during this last assault, lay still and failed to advance I do not understand. Had Polk thrown his wing forward and broken Thomas' single line of battle north of the Snodgrass range of hills, nothing could have saved Thomas from utter rout or the capture of a large part of his command."

Longstreet's conduct of his part of the field was so admirable compared with Polk's that criticisms are scarcely in order; still, there is inconsistency in his complaint that Bragg would not provide him with ample reinforcements to close the escape route behind Thomas. Longstreet asked for "a few troops that had not been so severely engaged as mine." The request was made when he saw Bragg at 3 P.M. on the twentieth, at a time when Bragg seemed to think the battle had been lost. Longstreet wanted the reinforcements "to allow me to go down the Dry Valley road, so as to interpose behind Thomas and cut off his retreat to Chattanooga."

But at the time Longstreet already had in Preston the only division on the battlefield that had not been engaged. He wanted to draw on the right wing and hold his own reserve intact. Surely he could not censure Bragg for the denial. Then, when he finally sent in Preston after his return from the conference with Bragg, it was not for Preston to go down the Dry Valley road and close the gap behind Thomas, but to continue the bloody, fruitless attacks on Snodgrass Hill and Horseshoe Ridge, after Thomas had been able to make his lines there almost impregnable.

Bragg expected to continue the battle on the twenty-first on the same field and seemed a little disappointed that the Federals had left him. One of the soldiers on duty with him listened to the generals:

"I heard Bragg discussing the proposition for a forward movement Monday. Some of his generals, Longstreet especially, wanted him to go ahead that day and attack Rosecrans . . . Bragg replied, 'How can I? Here is two-fifths of my army left on the field. My artillery is without horses.' "

He does not seem to have counted the number of good, eager soldiers he had, anxious to pursue.

There is no question but that the horse casualties had been abnormally heavy. The ease with which artillery could be approached in the woods allowed the infantry of both armies to draw close and shoot the horses and immobilize the batteries. Those going over the field after the battle were struck with the number of dead horses. Jim Brotherton said, "I walked over the field the morning after the battle. In one place down in the woods I counted sixteen big artillery horses lying in one heap. A little way off was another heap of twelve more. And that was the way it was all through there."

The soldier who overheard Bragg and Longstreet sympathized with the commanding general's position. When the matter was discussed at the reunions, he challenged the critics and said they overestimated the ability of the army to fight on the third day. Those who fought best on Sunday had not been engaged on Saturday. Though it might look different twenty-seven years after the battle, he doubted that Bragg "could have spurred his weary army to another assault on Monday."

Others who have studied the battle, among them the able Major General John B. Gordon, have defended Bragg, but it does seem that the desperate straits of the Confederacy in September 1863 called for desperate remedies. Oates felt that even Gordon had failed to make out a good case for Bragg, while Longstreet in his official report "was hard on Bragg but not unjust." But the Alabama colonel agreed that Bragg did not have the pontoons for crossing the Tennessee River, nor did the army have the necessary transportation for a march north through Cumberland Gap.[3]

Still, some good should have been found from such a tremendous victory. The Federal army was not destroyed but it was so badly routed that the highway to the Ohio was invitingly open. At this stage of the war, only venturesome leadership could save the Confederacy. None could be certain whether the curtain was descending or whether it was the Valley Forge before the sunshine. But it was surely the curtain if victory were followed by inaction. This of all times was the occasion for risk and boldness. Had Bragg possessed a hint of Stonewall Jackson's resolution and celerity, had Lee been in command with his clear strategic insight, the success might not have been altogether Pyrrhic. It could well be said, as was said after some of the battles in the eastern theater, that a few more such victories as Chickamauga and the Confederacy would be ruined.

ARMY OF TENNESSEE, C.S.A.
General Braxton Bragg

RIGHT WING
Lt. Gen. Leonidas Polk

POLK'S CORPS
Lt. Gen. Leonidas Polk

Cheatham's Division
Maj. Gen. Benjamin F. Cheatham
Jackson's Brigade: Brig. Gen.
John K. Jackson
Maney's Brigade: Brig. Gen.
George Maney
Smith's Brigade: Brig. Gen.
Preston Smith (k); Col. Alfred
J. Vaughan
Wright's Brigade: Brig. Gen.
Marcus J. Wright
Strahl's Brigade: Brig. Gen.
Otho F. Strahl

Hindman's Division
(Assigned to Longstreet)

HILL'S CORPS
Lt. Gen. Daniel H. Hill

Cleburne's Division
Maj. Gen. Patrick R. Cleburne
Wood's Brigade: Brig. Gen.
S. A. M. Wood
Polk's Brigade: Brig. Gen.
Lucius E. Polk
Deshler's Brigade: Brig. Gen.
James Deshler (k); Col.
Roger Q. Mills

Breckinridge's Division
Maj. Gen. John C. Breckinridge
Helm's Brigade: Brig. Gen. Benjamin H. Helm (k); Col.
Joseph H. Lewis
Adams' Brigade: Brig. Gen.
Daniel W. Adams (w)(c);
Col. Randall Lee Gibson
Stovall's Brigade: Brig. Gen.
Marcellus A. Stovall

WALKER'S RESERVE CORPS
Maj. Gen. William H. T. Walker

Walker's Division
Brig. Gen. States Rights Gist
Gist's Brigade: Col. P. H. Colquitt (k); Lt. Col. Leroy
Napier
Ector's Brigade: Brig. Gen.
Matthew D. Ector
Wilson's Brigade: Col. Claudius
C. Wilson

Liddell's Division
Brig. Gen. St. John R. Liddell
Liddell's Brigade: Col. Daniel
C. Govan
Walthall's Brigade: Brig. Gen.
Edward C. Walthall

LEFT WING
Lt. Gen. James Longstreet

BUCKNER'S CORPS
Maj. Gen. Simon B. Buckner

Stewart's Division
Maj. Gen. Alexander P. Stewart
Bates' Brigade: Brig. Gen. William B. Bate
Clayton's Brigade: Brig. Gen.
Henry D. Clayton
Brown's Brigade: Brig. Gen.
John C. Brown (w); Col.
Edmund C. Cook

Preston's Division
Brig. Gen. William Preston
Gracie's Brigade: Brig. Gen.
Archibald Gracie, Jr.
Kelly's Brigade: Col. John H.
Kelly
Trigg's Brigade: Col. Robert C.
Trigg

Hindman's Division
(detached from Polk's Corps)
Maj. Gen. Thomas C. Hindman
(w); Brig. Gen. Patton Anderson
Anderson's Brigade: Brig. Gen.
Patton Anderson; Col. Jacob
H. Sharp
Deas' Brigade: Brig. Gen.
Zachariah C. Deas
Manigault's Brigade: Brig. Gen.
Arthur M. Manigault

HOOD'S CORPS
Maj. Gen. John B. Hood

McLaws' Division
Brig. Gen. Joseph B. Kershaw
Kershaw's Brigade: Brig. Gen.
Joseph B. Kershaw (retained
brigade command)
Humphreys' Brigade: Brig. Gen.
Benjamin G. Humphreys

Johnson's Division
Brig. Gen. Bushrod R. Johnson
Johnson's Brigade: Col. John S.
Fulton
Gregg's Brigade: Brig. Gen.
John Gregg (w); Col. Cyrus
A. Sugg
McNair's Brigade: Brig. Gen.
Evander McNair (w); Col.
David Coleman

Hood's Division
Brig. Gen. E. McIver Law
Law's Brigade: Col. James L.
Sheffield; Col. William C.
Oates
Robertson's Brigade: Brig. Gen.
Jerome B. Robertson
Benning's Brigade: Brig. Gen.
Henry L. Benning

(c) captured   (k) killed   (w) wounded

ARMY OF THE CUMBERLAND, U.S.A.
Maj. Gen. William S. Rosecrans

FOURTEENTH CORPS
Maj. Gen. George H. Thomas

First Division
Brig. Gen. Absalom Baird

1st Brigade: Col. Benjamin F. Scribner

2nd Brigade: Brig. Gen. John C. Starkweather

3rd Brigade: Brig. Gen. John H. King

Second Division
Maj. Gen. James S. Negley

1st Brigade: Brig. Gen. John Beatty

2nd Brigade: Col. Timothy R. Stanley (w) ; Col. William L. Stoughton

3rd Brigade: Col. William Sirwell

Third Division
Brig. Gen. John M. Brannan

1st Brigade: Col. John M. Connell

2nd Brigade: Col. John T. Croxton (w) ; Col. William H. Hays

3rd Brigade: Col. Ferdinand Van Derveer

Fourth Division
Maj. Gen. Joseph J. Reynolds

1st Brigade: Col. John T. Wilder (mounted and detached)

2nd Brigade: Col. Edward A. King (k) ; Col. Milton S. Robinson

3rd Brigade: Brig. Gen. John B. Turchin

TWENTIETH CORPS
Maj. Gen. Alexander McD. McCook

First Division
Brig. Gen. Jefferson C. Davis

1st Brigade: Col. Sidney P. Post (guard duty)

2nd Brigade: Brig. Gen. William P. Carlin

3rd Brigade: Col. Hans C. Heg (k) ; Col. John A. Martin

Second Division
Brig. Gen. Richard W. Johnson

1st Brigade: Brig. Gen. August Willich

2nd Brigade: Col. Joseph B. Dodge

3rd Brigade: Col. Philemon P. Baldwin (k) ; Col. William W. Berry

Third Division
Maj. Gen. Philip H. Sheridan

1st Brigade: Brig. Gen. William H. Lytle (k) ; Col. Silas Miller

2nd Brigade: Col. Bernard Laiboldt

3rd Brigade: Col. Luther P. Bradley (w) ; Col. Nathan H. Walworth

TWENTY-FIRST CORPS
Maj. Gen. Thomas L. Crittenden

First Division
Brig. Gen. Thomas J. Wood

1st Brigade: Col. George P. Buell

2nd Brigade: Brig. Gen. George D. Wagner (on guard in rear)

3rd Brigade: Col. Charles G. Harker

Second Division
Maj. Gen. John M. Palmer

1st Brigade: Brig. Gen. Charles Cruft

2nd Brigade: Brig. Gen. William B. Hazen

3rd Brigade: Col. William Grose

Third Division
Brig. Gen. Horatio P. Van Cleve

1st Brigade: Brig. Gen. Samuel Beatty

2nd Brigade: Col. George F. Dick

3rd Brigade: Col. Sidney M. Barnes

RESERVE CORPS
Maj. Gen. Gordon Granger

First Division
Brig. Gen. James B. Steedman

1st Brigade: Brig. Gen. Walter C. Whitaker

2nd Brigade: Col. John G. Mitchell

Detached Brigade
Col. Daniel McCook, Jr.

(c) captured   (k) killed   (w) wounded

CAVALRY, FEDERAL
Brig. Gen. Robert B. Mitchell

FIRST DIVISION
Col. Edward M. McCook

1st Brigade
Col. Archibald P. Campbell

2nd Brigade
Col. Daniel M. Ray

3rd Brigade
Col. Louis D. Watkins

SECOND DIVISION
Brig. Gen. George Crook

1st Brigade
Col. Robert H. G. Minty

2nd Brigade
Col. Eli Long

CAVALRY, CONFEDERATE

WHEELER'S CORPS
Maj. Gen. Joseph Wheeler

Wharton's Division
Brig. Gen. John A. Wharton

Crews' Brigade
Col. C. C. Crews

Harrison's Brigade
Col. Thomas Harrison

Martin's Division
Brig. Gen. William T. Martin

Morgan's Brigade
Col. John T. Morgan

Russell's Brigade
Col. A. A. Russell

Roddey's Brigade
Brig. Gen. Philip D. Roddey

FORREST'S CORPS
Brig. Gen. Nathan B. Forrest

Armstrong's Division
Brig. Gen. Frank C. Armstrong

Armstrong's Brigade
Col. James T. Wheeler

Forrest's Brigade
Col. George G. Dibrell

Pegram's Division
Brig. Gen. John Pegram

Davidson's Brigade
Brig. Gen. Henry B. Davidson

Scott's Brigade
Col. John S. Scott

Notes, Bibliography and
Index

Notes

1. *Official Records*, Series I (hereafter *O. R.*), Volume XXX, Part I, 445-446. *Indiana at Chickamauga*, 299. On August 21 Rosecrans reported to Halleck "great commotion among the rebels" in Chattanooga and "clouds of dust arising." *O. R.*, XXX, Part III, 111.

Henry Cist, *The Army of the Cumberland* (hereafter Cist), 179, says the demonstrations extended 150 miles along the river. Cist was on Thomas' staff. Smith Atkins address, February 22, 1907, 4. (Hereafter Atkins.)

The Southern attitude about Chattanooga was reflected by the Confederate General William W. Loring, interviewed by W. S. Furay, a Cincinnati *Gazette* correspondent, after Loring's surrender. Loring said the confidence of the Confederacy weakened for the first time when Chattanooga fell, and added: "When your Dutch General Rosecrans commenced his forward movement for the capture of Chattanooga we laughed him to scorn; we believed that the black brow of Lookout Mountain would frown him out of existence; that he would dash himself to pieces against the many and vast natural barriers that rise all around Chattanooga; and that the Northern people and the government at Washington would perceive how hopeless were their efforts when they came to attack the real South." W. S. Furay, in Columbus, Ohio, *State Journal*, September 1888.

2. *O. R.*, XXX, Part I, 446. Atkins, 5-6. The Richmond *Sentinel* of August 24 said "the Yankees began shelling Chattanooga . . . without giving notice." *O. R.*, XXX, Part III, 161. Rosecrans reported, *O. R.*, XXX, Part III, 131, that Wilder had one man wounded and four horses killed in shelling Chattanooga and sinking the steamer. General T. J. Wood said, *O. R.*, XXX, Part I, 629, the colors of the 97th Ohio, Wagner's brigade, Wood's division, were the first planted on the Chattanooga works. He apparently did not know of Atkins' prior entry with mounted men. Alabama Archives, 33rd Regiment papers.

3. *O. R.*, XXX, Part I, 678-679. Atkins, 6. *Battles and Leaders of the Civil War* (hereafter *B. & L.*), III, 640. D. H. Hill says there was "perceptible diminution" in the congregation and that some women and children were killed by the bombing. Other references noticed credit

the congregation with steadfastness. A full account of the incident and the challenge is in one of the Robert Sparks Walker series of articles, "Pyramids of Chickamauga," published August 2, 1936, in the Chattanooga *Sunday Times*.

4. *O. R.*, XXX, Part I, 446 and 780.

Chapter Two—OVER THE RIVER AND RANGES

1. *O. R.*, XXX, Part III, 296. Rosecrans reported to Halleck that 700 feet of the span dropped into the water.
Michigan at Chickamauga, 41. Donn Piatt, *General George H. Thomas*, 376.

2. John Beatty, *Memoirs of a Volunteer*, 239.

3. *O. R.*, XXX, Part II, 23. *Annals of the War*, 460-466.

4. *B. & L.*, III, 640. Henry Fales Perry, *History of the Thirty-Eighth Regiment Indiana Volunteer Infantry*, 81-82. *O. R.*, XXX, Part I, 601-603.

5. *B. & L.*, III, 640. Bragg said, "A mountain is like the wall of a house full of rat-holes. The rat lies hidden at his hole, ready to pop out when no one is watching. Who can tell what lies hidden behind that wall?" He pointed to the range which concealed Rosecrans' army.

Bragg was not without cleverness in having his scouts pose as messengers and deserters, yet Rosecrans might have detected a ruse. The Confederate custom with couriers carrying important intelligence, or the mail from the trans-Mississippi department, was to equip them with small bottles of combustibles and matches. If they were about to be captured their documents could be destroyed. J. P. Austin, *The Blue and the Gray*, 105. Bragg had adopted the practice. When the supposed couriers began to allow their messages to be captured, Rosecrans might have noticed the change and wondered about the ease with which he was getting presumably good information about Bragg's dispositions and "flight."

Chapter Three—THE GENERAL RELISHES MIDNIGHT TALKFESTS

1. Frank A. Burr, *The Life of General Philip H. Sheridan*, 96.

2. John Fitch, *Annals of the Army of the Cumberland*, 39. Cist, 235

3. The Rosecrans family immigration from the Wyoming Valley to Delaware County, Ohio, was sizable, consisting of John Rosecrans and his four sons, and Daniel Rosecrans, a physician, and his four sons. Crandell Rosecrans, the general's father, was one of the sons in the

second group. Mrs. Luke G. Byrne, "Bishop Rosecrans" in *Old North-west Genealogical Quarterly*, IX, 311. Toledo, 1906, is followed on Rosecrans' descent from Governor Hopkins, on the governor's signature and John Adams' comments.

Henry Howe, *Historical Collections of Ohio*, II, 86. Fitch, 9-10. Fitch says Rosecrans had the recommendation of Representative Alexander Harper of Ohio, of whom Secretary of War Poinsett made inquiries. Whitelaw Reid, *Ohio in the War*, I, 312 is followed here. (Hereafter *Ohio in the War*.)

4. D. B. Sanger and T. R. Hay, *James Longstreet*, 8. *Ohio in the War*, I, 312-313. Fitch, 39. *Ibid.*, 12-15. Society of the Army of the Cumberland, *Burial of General Rosecrans*, . . . , 37. (Hereafter *Rosecrans Burial Services*.)

5. Howe, II, 87. Fitch appears in error, p. 36, when he says the family was Episcopalian. Joseph Taggart, *Biographical Sketches of Eminent American Patriots*, 296. *Dictionary of American Biography*.

During Rosecrans' Iuka campaign against General Sterling Price, someone at a dinner mentioned to Bishop Rosecrans that he and his brother seemed to be in different callings.

"Yes," said the Bishop, "he is fighting with Price and I am fighting without price." Frank Moore, *The Civil War in Song and Story*, 14. (Hereafter *Song and Story*.)

6. Jacob Dolson Cox, *Military Reminiscences of the Civil War*, 127-128. Fitch, 35. Donn Piatt, *General George H. Thomas*, 209. John M. Palmer, *Personal Recollections*, 147.

One of Rosecrans' privates, later Representative Washington Gardner of Michigan and commander in chief of the Grand Army of the Republic, said of the general's bravery that he "stood unmoved in the storm of lead," and: "If any criticism is due him from this standpoint of view, it is that, as a commander of an army, he took too many risks upon his life." *Rosecrans Burial Services*, 51.

7. Fitch, 35. Palmer's *Recollections*, 124. Philadelphia *Inquirer*, June 16, 1863. W. F. G. Shanks, *Personal Recollections of Distinguished Generals*, 258, 261. New York *Herald*, Sept. 20, 1863. W. D. Bickham, *Rosecrans' Campaign with the Fourteenth Army Corps*, 30.

Rosecrans emphasized his points by bringing down his right forefinger sharply, "rapier-like." When he passed Vallandigham through his lines to the Confederacy, he pointed in that manner and told the Ohioan that if he ever came back, "I'll be damned if I don't hang you!" Frazer Kirkland, *The Pictorial Book of Anecdotes of the Rebellion*, 138. (Hereafter *Anecdotes*.)

8. Beatty's *Memoirs*, 191, 201. Cox's *Reminiscences*, I, 111. Fitch, 259. Howard Swiggett, *The Rebel Raider*, 92-93. Bickham, 143ff.

9. Fitch, 261-262, 263. Bickham, 365. Howe, I, 560. Bickham, 144-145. Beatty, 177. Cox, I, 112.

Though he drove himself to the limit of his energies, some felt that Rosecrans was compassionate when others weakened. His overburdened aides would fall asleep often in their chairs. He would glance up, then proceed with his map work, without waking them. The officers were attentive to his wants. When Colonel James G. Jones sent Catawba wine and pawpaw brandy to John Beatty, half of it was to go to the commanding general. Despite the unmerciful reprimand Rosecrans had administered to him, Beatty retained a respect for the commanding general's ability and noted especially the hold he had on the private soldiers. "The general's popularity with the army is immense." Beatty, 186.

10. Fitch, 39. Cox, I, 111. Bickham, 143. Cox, I, 112n.

11. John Fiske, *The Mississippi Valley in the Civil War*, 253-254. Piatt, 79, 197, 329-330. *Ohio in the War*, 314. Cox, I, 477ff, gives a good analysis of the Halleck-Rosecrans correspondence. Cist, 151-152.

Chapter Four—POLITICIAN AND "BIRD OF ILL OMEN."

1. John Clark Ridpath, *Life and Work of James A. Garfield*, 120-122.

2. Beatty's *Memoirs*, 225. Palmer, 158. Ridpath, 129. Fitch, 37. Bickham, 143.

Garfield's letter is in the Society of Army of the Cumberland's pamphlet on *Rosecrans Burial Services*. Piatt, 330ff., discusses the Rosecrans-Garfield relationship. While Piatt's biography of Thomas was attacked when published because of its censure of some of the Northern generals, it is the candid offering of a well-informed army officer and newspaperman. The relationship is discussed also in *Rosecrans Burial Services*.

4. Cist, 173. *O. R.*, XXIII, Part II, 395-420 for answers of the generals. Ridpath, 137, gives Garfield credit for Rosecrans' advance. He quotes General Crittenden, 138, as saying it was "a rash and fatal move" and that Garfield was responsible.

5. C. A. Dana, *Recollections of the Civil War*, 104.

6. James H. Wilson, *Life of Charles A. Dana*, 171. *Dictionary of American Biography*. Wilson, 34ff. Lloyd Morris, *The Rebellious Puritan: Portrait of Mr. Hawthorne*, 129. Shanks, 261.

Chapter Five—BURNSIDE DALLIES AROUND KNOXVILLE

1. The best references noticed on Burnside's capture of Knoxville and Cumberland Gap are by Lieutenant Colonel G. C. Kniffin, W. S. Furay and G. C. Kniffin, article of Sept. 8, 1888; and the pamphlet by Lieutenant Colonel R. W. McFarland, *The Surrender of Cumberland Gap, September 9, 1863,* from which much of this chapter is taken. McFarland commanded the 86th Ohio at the capture of the Gap. *Anecdotes,* 565-566 and 318.

2. Raleigh *Weekly Standard* of Sept. 9, 1863. *Anecdotes,* 605.

3. McFarland, 7-26.

4. Furay and Kniffin, Sept. 8, 1888. Carl Sandburg, *Abraham Lincoln,* V, 369. Cox, I, 477.

Chapter Six—FRUSTRATION IN MCLEMORE'S COVE

1. *Pennsylvania at Chickamauga and Chattanooga* (Hereafter *Pa. at Chick.*), 217. Robert G. Athearn, editor, *Soldier in the West—The Civil War Letters of Alfred Lacey Hough* (hereafter *Hough Letters*), 137n. *Pa. at Chick,* 216-218.

2. Cox, I, 478. *O. R.,* XXIII, Part II, 384-386. Thomas B. Van Horne, *History of the Army of the Cumberland,* 105-106. Piatt, 381. *Pa. at Chick.,* 218.

On the subject of misinformation to Rosecrans, Lieutenant Colonel William P. Hepburn of the 2nd Iowa Cavalry, who served on Rosecrans' staff and later in Congress, explained Rosecrans' dispersal of his troops:

"It must be remembered that the advices from Washington to General Rosecrans persistently informed him that the Confederate troops were endeavoring to escape him. He was constantly urged to greater activity, lest Bragg would escape—advices making necessary the dispersion of troops to such points as, when the real facts were known, made concentration difficult and dangerous. No word of suggestion came to him that Longstreet and his veterans were being transferred from the Rappahannock to the Tennessee and that the forces of Bragg were augmented by twenty thousand troops that were the equals of any troops on earth." *Rosecrans Burial Services,* 42.

Contemporary writers tended to absolve Rosecrans of the initial blame for his wide-open pursuit, though the end responsibility was of course his. Reid, *Ohio in the War,* I, 340, gives what seems a conventional view. Rosecrans was deceived by his easy success into believing

Bragg was in full retreat and: "Certainly the General-in-Chief and the War Department did all they could to encourage such an idea; and even after Rosecrans (every nerve tense with the struggle to concentrate his corps) was striving to prepare for the onset of the re-enforced Rebel army, General Halleck informed him of reports that Bragg's army was re-enforcing Lee, and pleasantly added that, after he had captured Dalton it would be decided whether he should move still further southward!" Fitch, 263, said the notion that Bragg was in headlong flight was disseminated "in some unknown way," in Washington, which caused Rosecrans to receive the telegrams confirming his false impressions.

Some of Halleck's correspondence with Rosecrans is quoted in Note 6 of Chapter 8. It runs through Vol. XXX, Part III of *O. R.* Ser. I. Halleck's pressure did soften after the fall of Chickamauga and was more implied and cumulative from his earlier attitude, when it should have been a warning against an ill-prepared advance, based on the knowledge Washington should have had of the over-all picture.

3. *Pa. at Chick.*, 218-219. Bromfield L. Ridley, *Battles and Sketches of the Army of Tennessee*, 198. Bickham, 43. *Dictionary of American Biography. Hough Letters*, 139n. *O. R.*, XXX, Part I, 324f.

4. *Southern Historical Society Papers* (hereafter *S. H. S. P.*), IX, 396. *Ibid.*, XI, 203-205. John W. DuBose, *General Joseph Wheeler and the Army of Tennessee*, 191. Irving A. Buck, *Cleburne and His Men*, 139n. *B. & L.*, III, 641-642.

5. *Dictionary of American Biography. B & L.*, III, 445-455. Jay Monaghan, *The Civil War on the Western Border*, 255-256. Bragg to Major Sykes in William M. Polk, *Leonidas Polk: Bishop and General*, II, 309 (Hereafter *Polk*). Buck, 139-140.

6. Comte de Paris, *History of the Civil War in America*, IV, 80-81. 18th Alabama papers, Alabama Archives. *Pa. at Chick.*, 220.

7. Dana, *Recollections*, 109. Richard O'Connor, *Thomas: Rock of Chickamauga*, 21. Buck, 140. *S.H.S.P.*, XI, 203, 205. *Ibid.*, IX, 398. Polk to Bragg, *Polk*, II, 241.

Chapter Seven—SERVANT OF THE REGULATIONS

1. Dr. L. H. Stout, *Reminiscences of General Braxton Bragg*, 12-13. Mary Boykin Chesnut, *A Diary from Dixie*, 203. Seitz, 174. Alabama Archives, 25th Regiment papers.

2. Stout, 6-8. Seitz, 9. Lloyd Lewis, *Sherman, Fighting Prophet*, 132, gives two versions of the Buena Vista story, the second being that

Bragg was retiring to a ravine when met by Taylor who personally put his battery into action. The first account showing the good conduct of this battery and its leader seems to have sufficient authenticity. Thomas Robson Hay, *Braxton Bragg and the Southern Confederacy*, 267.

3. Seitz, 2-4. R. T. Bennison, "General Braxton Bragg," 600. Hay, 297n, cites Richmond College Historical Papers, I, 93. E. Merton Coulter, *The Confederate States of America*, 380, cites Richmond *Daily Examiner*, Feb. 24, 1864. *O. R.*, LII, Part II, 335. Hay, 300. Coulter, 379.

4. Hay, 295. Coulter, 458-459. Bragg to Major E. T. Sykes in *Polk*, II, 312-313.

5. Frank Moore, *Women of the War*, 170-175. Stout, 21.

6. Seitz, 271f. gives the correspondence and details of the controversy between Bragg and his generals.

7. *Ibid.*, 277f. Chesnut, *Diary*, 248. William Parker Snow, *Southern Generals*, 323.

Chapter Eight—"OLD PETE" HEARS DISTANT GUNS

1. G. Moxley Sorrel, *Recollections of a Confederate Staff Officer*, 179-180.

2. James Longstreet, *From Manassas to Appomattox* (Hereafter *Man. to App.*), 433f. J. B. Jones, *A Rebel War Clerk's Diary*, II, 28, 32, 36. *Man. to App.*, 435-436. *O. R.*, XXIX, Part II, 720. Lee transmitted the order.

3. Piatt's *Thomas*, 226. McLaws Papers, Southern Historical Collection, University of North Carolina. Sorrel, 185.

4. Sorrel, 186. Ezra J. Warner, *Generals in Gray*, 175-176. George Edgar Turner, *Victory Rode the Rails*, 283-285. Sanger and Hay, 198. E. P. Alexander, *Military Memoirs of a Confederate*. Du Bose, 190. Though none of Alexander's artillery arrived in time for the battle, rail transportation was secured for part of the command. Sorrel, 185.

5. *Man. to App.*, 437. *O. R.*, XXIX, Part II, 713. John B. Hood, *Advance and Retreat*, 55. Sorrel, 186-187. Chesnut, *Diary*, 241. Wilmington, N. C., *Daily Journal*, Sept. 11, 1863. Raleigh *Weekly Standard*, Oct. 14, 1863.

6. William C. Oates, *The War Between the Union and the Confederacy*, 253. Jones, *Dairy*, II, 42.

The story Major General William B. Franklin told Samuel L. Clemens, that he had witnessed Grant topple inebriated from his horse, Lloyd Lewis, *Sherman, Fighting Prophet*, 309, was countered by the explanation that the animal took fright from a streetcar. In any case,

Grant was out of action when the Confederate upsurge occurred in the late summer of 1863. The fault involved in the dispersal of his forces was of course not his, but that of Washington.

One of the mysteries of the war was how Longstreet was able to leave Virginia and reach Bragg without Rosecrans being informed about it and without the War Department knowing of it, or if it did, being willing to admit it. Rosecrans was sufficiently inquisitive to keep Halleck on the alert about the possibility of reinforcements reaching Bragg either from Johnston in Mississippi or Lee in Virginia. On August 24 he asked Halleck: "Would like to know if Grant is to do anything to occupy Johnston's attention." *O. R.*, XXX, Part III, 147. To this Halleck replied rather brusquely, "Grant's movements at present have no connection with yours." *Ibid.*, 162. Then on Sept. 3, when there were no evidences of co-operation, Rosecrans inquired: "Have you any news from Burnside? any reason to think forces will be sent from Virginia to East Tennessee? Any that Joe Johnston has sent any forces up this way?" *Ibid.*, 321. Halleck replied on Sept. 5: "There is no reason here to suppose that any of Lee's troops have been detached, except, perhaps, a small force to Charleston, S. C." *Ibid.*, 361.

Halleck had told Rosecrans on August 20 about rumors not that Lee was reinforcing Bragg, but that Bragg was sending troops to Lee. On Sept. 11, when Longstreet's movement was well under way, Halleck wrote in the same vein to Rosecrans: "It is reported here by deserters that a part of Bragg's army is reinforcing Lee." *Ibid.*, 530. Halleck told Rosecrans on Sept. 13 that most of Grant's army was on the west side of the Mississippi. Not until the late afternoon of Sept. 15 did he inform Rosecrans: "From information received here today it is very probable that three divisions of Lee's army have been sent to reinforce Bragg." By that time Rosecrans was picking up some news from scouts. He replied Sept. 16: "From information derived from various sources from my front, I have reason to believe what you assert in your dispatch of 4:30 P.M. of yesterday is true, and that they have arrived at Atlanta at last. Push Burnside down." The message as it was received by Halleck read, "Arrived at Atlanta. At least push Burnside down." That appears the correct wording. *Ibid.*, 666. Not until the battle was being fought was Rosecrans aware that Longstreet had reached Bragg, and he was even more certain that Burnside had not reached Rosecrans.

Confederate Veteran, June 1914, 264.

7. *B. & L.*, III, 638-639. *Ibid.*, IV, 6n. *South Carolina at Chickamauga*, 13-14.

Chapter Nine—ROSECRANS COLLECTS HIS SCATTERED FORCES

1. Bickham, 41. *B. & L.*, I, 526. *Dictionary of American Biography.* Lemark Duvall Ms.

2. *S.H.S.P.*, IX, 399. Henry E. Davies, *General Sheridan*, 64. *O. R.*, XXX, Part III, 644. Halleck's message gave no enlightening details and used the word "probable." There appeared a tendency to discount the reports. The New York *Tribune* on Sept. 18 said: "Departure of Gen. Longstreet for the West is disbelieved by most officers of the army and by the War Department. . . . The rumor of the weakening of [Lee's] forces by the departure of Longstreet was purposely spread by deserters and others in order to deceive the Unionist as to his real intentions and induce Gen. Meade to advance."

3. Comte de Paris, 95-96. Henry Villard, *Memoirs*, II, 106-107, refers to Rosecrans' concentration as a "bold manoeuvre."

4. Isaac H. C. Royse, *History of the 115th Illinois Volunteers*, 13, 94-97.

Chapter Ten—THE REPEATERS DELAY THE CROSSING

1. John Allen Wyeth, *Life of General Nathan Bedford Forrest*, 246. *Indiana at Chickamauga* (Hereafter *Ind. at Chick.*), 11.

2. *O. R.*, XXX, Part I, 464. John Watson Morton, *The Artillery of Nathan Bedford Forrest's Cavalry*, 115, 119.

3. Morton, 119. Wyeth, 249. Samuel C. Williams, *General John T. Wilder, Commander of the Lightning Brigade*, 1ff. Beatty, 226. Bell Irvin Wiley and Hirst D. Milhollen, *They Who Fought Here*, 114.

Chapter Eleven—MEETING ON THE "RIVER OF DEATH"

1. Perry's *38th Ind.*, 87. *O. R.*, XXX, Part I, 248-249. J. H. Hayme, editor, *The 19th Illinois*, 218.

2. Cox, II, 540. Jones, *Diary*, II, 45. The U. S. Naval Observatory gives the state of the moon as the first quarter, on Sept. 20. Some accounts, as Henry Coppee, *General Thomas*, 139, erroneously refer to the moon on the night of Sept. 18 as full. The night was clear and crisp. Ridley, 207. *Confederate Veteran*, March, 1919, 113. Ridley, 212. Wilbur F. Hinman, *The Story of the Sherman Brigade*, 417.

The name Thedford is often spelled Tedford in Chickamauga accounts. The writer has followed the spelling used for the name of the ford in the official U. S. Geological Survey map of the battlefield, used in *O. R.* and by the Chickamauga Park headquarters.

3. Undated news story in Chickamauga-Chattanooga National Military Park (hereafter Chick. Nat. Park) scrapbook of clippings. *Anecdotes*, 503. *Song and Story*, 224. Snow, 322. St. Louis *Globe Democrat* story in Chick. Nat. Park scrapbook.

Chapter Twelve—THOMAS STUMBLES INTO A BATTLE

1. *Ind. at Chick.*, 247. Thomas sent word to Palmer to attack the enemy in front while he did in flank and "I think we can use them up." Palmer, 175. *Ind. at Chick.*, 14-15. *O. R.*, XXX, Part I, 249-250. Thomas' report is in error in saying that Croxton became engaged at 10 A.M. Substantially all other accounts give around 7:30 A.M. Croxton's report indicates that he was not familiar with the names of the roads. Kellenberger Ms. letter of Nov. 15, 1863.

Dan McCook's message about the enemy brigade supposed to be isolated was addressed to "General Thomas or any other Union general." McCook later encountered Croxton to whom he gave the information orally. A brief sketch of General Brannan is included in Chapter 28, *Snodgrass Hill.* Kellenberger Ms. letter of Nov. 15, 1863.

2. *Ind. at Chick.*, 138. John M. Morgan, *Old Steady*, 84. Warner, *Generals in Gray*, 323-324. *Dictionary of American Biography.* At the time the battle opened Gist personally had not yet reached the field from Meridian, Mississippi.

3. Frank Moore, *Women of the War*, 172. Wyeth's *Forrest*, 250.

Brigadier General Absalom Baird, who commanded Thomas' first division, was a graduate of both Washington College (now Washington and Jefferson) in his home town of Washington, Pennsylvania, and of West Point. He might well claim original connection for his family with western Pennsylvania, because his great-grandfather, Lieutenant John Baird, had marched with the British General John Forbes in the expedition which wrested Fort Duquesne from the French and Indians. His grandfather had been a Revolutionary War surgeon. The son was in the West Point class of 1849, too late for the Mexican War, but he fought Seminoles and was at First Manassas and on the Peninsula as chief of staff to Brigadier General Erasmus Keyes, commander of the 4th Corps. When he was made a brigadier general in April 1862, he was transferred to the western theater. Thomas requested in August 1863 that he be assigned to the 14th (Thomas') Corps, to command the division that had been led by Major General Lovell H. Rousseau, a competent officer hard for anyone to follow. But Baird was capable, a tough fighter and a rigid disciplinarian, whose division would win fame throughout the North in later campaigning under Sherman. For a long period after the war he served as Inspector General of the Army.

4. Bratnober Ms. *S.H.S.P.*, IX, 494-495. *O. R.*, XXX, Part I, 250. *Ind. at Chick.*, 230.

5. Kellenberger Ms. *Ohio in the War*, II, 72. *Minnesota in the Civil and Indian Wars*, 95, 98. The question of the farthest advance by a North Carolina regiment at Chickamauga is discussed in Note 5 of Chapter 30.

Chapter Thirteen—"ROSEY" FOLLOWS THE BATTLE BY EAR

1. Dana, 112. *Song and Story*, 349.

2. James Alfred Sartain, *History of Walker County, Georgia*, 109. Shanks, 266. Atkins, 10. *Song and Story*, 343.

It is not clear just when Rosecrans was actually informed of the presence of Virginia troops in his front. His angry denial of the first information about Longstreet when Colonel Atkins brought in the prisoner from the Virginia army could not have been assumed. He appeared to recognize Longstreet's presence for the first time when he interviewed the captured officer of the Texas brigade. Garfield, who was almost continually in the commanding general's presence, knew about it the first day of the battle when a messenger dashed into headquarters and handed him an envelope. The contents as Garfield read them aloud were: "Longstreet has reinforced Bragg with seventeen thousand troops from Lee's Virginia army." Ridpath, 147. Where it came from was not stated. Evidence that Virginia troops were at hand was soon more persuasive than the contents of an envelope. Hood's battle rolled so near the Widow Glenn's that Garfield had to shout to Rosecrans to be heard. Ridpath, 149.

3. Piatt, 208. *Ind. at Chick.*, 129.

In the army before the war Richard Johnson had served on the staff of a fellow Kentuckian, Albert Sidney Johnston in Texas, but after Twiggs's surrender of his stores in Texas before the outbreak of the fighting, Johnson made his way to New York by ship. He served under Patterson in Pennsylvania, then as lieutenant colonel of the 3rd Kentucky Volunteers. In October 1862 he became a brigadier general in McCook's division, and later a division commander in McCook's corps. Fitch, 152-153. In the closing phases of the war he would share in the glory of Thomas' defeat of Hood at Nashville.

4. *Ind. at Chick.*, 157. *Ohio in the War*, I, 765-769. Fitch, 119. *Dictionary of American Biography*. Both Palmer and Rosecrans were great admirers of Stephen A. Douglas but Palmer became devoted to Lincoln while Rosecrans voted for Douglas. Palmer's influence on the election of McKinley came through his reaffiliation with the Democratic Party in disgust over Grant's first administration. He served in the Senate as a Democrat—after having been a Republican governor of Illinois—then ran for President as a Gold Democrat in 1896. He polled 130,000 votes of conservative Democrats.

Anecdotes, 270-271.

5. *Pa. at Chick.*, 196. *Ind. at Chick.*, 153.

Chapter Fourteen—THE "LITTLE GIANTS" DENT ROSECRANS' CENTER

1. *Ohio in the War*, I, 999. Adney Ms. *Ohio in the War*, 85-86. *Ibid.*, 502.

2. *B. & L.*, IV, 337.

An amusing story was told about Stewart's division. When Colonel L. T. Woodward of the 36th Alabama inspected the pickets, a private of Company A challenged him. This colloquy ensued:

Colonel—Suppose a body of men were to approach you, what would you do?

Picket—I would halt them and demand the countersign.

Colonel—Suppose they didn't halt or give the countersign?

Picket—I'd shoot them.

Colonel—Then what would you do?

Picket—I'd form a line.

Colonel—Line! What kind of line would you form?

Picket—A *beeline* for camp!

Whereupon the colonel made a beeline to inspect the next post. W. D. Brown's scrapbook, copied from Selma *Dispatch*. 36th Regiment papers, Alabama Archives. Ridley, 219. 39th Alabama papers, Alabama Archives.

3. Fitch, 174. *Ohio in the War*, I, 856. Comte de Paris, 117-119.

4. Palmer's *Recollections*, 176. *Ind. at Chick.*, 215.

5. *Confed. Veteran*, July 1894, 329. Ridley, 220. *Confed. Veteran*, July 1894, 330. Atkins, 10.

6. *Ind. at Chick.*, 301. Eli Lilly biography in *Encyclopedia of Biography of Indiana*, George Irving Reed, editor, 86. John S. C. Abbott, II, 423. *Song and Story*, 530.

Chapter Fifteen—VINIARD'S FARM

1. Oates, 253-254. John B. Hood, *Advance and Retreat*, 61-62. Buck, *Cleburne and His Men*, 58.

2. *B. & L.*, III, 623.

3. Heg, *Civil War Letters*. *Chattanooga Times*, July 12, 1936. St. Louis *Globe Democrat*, July 10, 1890.

4. *Ibid.* Hinman's *Sherman Brigade*, 422. *Confed. Veteran*, June 1914, 264. *Song and Story*, 169.

5. *Ibid.*, 345. Barnes. *86th Indiana*, 204. United Daughters of Confederacy collection, Vol. VII, Georgia Archives.

Chapter Sixteen—CLEBURNE'S SUNSET ASSAULT

1. Ms. of W. E. Preston of Dale County, Ala., in 33rd Ala. Regiment folder, Ala. Archives.

2. 16th Ala. papers, Ala. Archives.

3. Buck's *Cleburne*, 40. Coulter's *Confederate States*, 341. Ella Lonn, *Foreigners in the Confederacy*, 136. 45th Ala. papers, Ala. Archives.

4. 18th Ala. papers, Ala. Archives. Buck's *Cleburne*, 145. St. Louis *Globe Democrat*, July 10, 1890.

5. Briant's *6th Indiana*, 230-233. *Ind. at Chick.*, 31. *Song and Story*, 389. Perry's *38th Ind.*, 90.

Chapter Seventeen—DRIVING THIRST IN THE DEEP SHADOWS

1. *Ind. at Chick.*, 181. The term "the Sink" is quoted from inhabitants in St. Louis *Globe Democrat* battlefield reunion interviews, July 10, 1890. Chick. Nat. Park scrapbook. Duvall Ms. *Pa. at Chick.*, 221.

2. George Morgan Kirkpatrick, *Experiences of a Private Soldier*, 2.

Weather conditions were unusual in the autumn of 1863. Minnesota experienced freezing weather in August and the ice was one eighth inch thick. Corn was killed, and severe weather extended to Kansas, Missouri, Illinois and Indiana. A heat wave followed in the plains states in mid-September but temperature fell rapidly from the sixteenth to eighteenth. A general frost was experienced on Sept. 18, more destructive than that of late August. Winter came early, with a snow throughout the plains, from Utah to Minnesota and extending to Illinois and Indiana, on October 22. The snow was a foot deep in Wisconsin and three inches in Indiana. Thus battlefield reports of the cold weather during the Chickamauga and Chattanooga campaigns are sustained by the National Almanac for 1864, containing governmental and other reports for 1863.

Cunningham letter, 7. Ala. Archives. Hinman's *Sherman Brigade*, 426.

3. Ridley, 221. Shaver's *16th Ala.*, 14-15. Wyeth's *Forrest*, 250. Wyeth mentions that trees were crashing down "and the busy picks were playing a tattoo on the earth as the Union beavers toiled to strengthen their position." This is the only account noticed which says entrenching tools were employed, most references being only to log barricades. In *B. & L.*, III, 654n, the editors quote the New York *Herald* correspondent Shanks, who described the works as breast high and made of rails and logs. "The logs and rails ran at right angles to each other, the logs keeping parallel to the proposed line of battle and lying upon the rails until the proper height was reached. . . . The spade had not been used."

St. Louis *Globe Democrat* interview, Dec. 8, 1893.

4. Drake's *Annals of the Army of Tennessee*, 57 and 53. *Pa. at Chick.*, 236-237.

5. Clark, *N. C. Regiments*, III, 487-488. Hood's *Advance and Retreat*, 62.

Chapter Eighteen—ROSECRANS TALKS, MCCOOK SINGS

1. Ridpath, 151. Sartain's *Walker County*, 103-104. Dana, 113-114.

2. Van Horne's *Thomas*, 121. Van Horne says Thomas was "urgent" in his recommendation for pulling back the right wing.

3. Piatt's *Thomas*, 174. Beatty, 218. Leo Tolstoy's *War and Peace* (Heritage Press, New York, 1938), II, 270. Snow's *Southern Generals*, 331.

4. Palmer, 180.

Chapter Nineteen—ROSECRANS DELIVERS A COSTLY REBUKE

1. Letter to editor, St. Louis *Globe Democrat*, July 23 (no year) in Chick. Nat. Park scrapbook.

2. Ridpath, 152. Comte de Paris, 131. Chickamauga scrapbook. Hannaford's *6th Ohio*, 465.

3. Cist, 219-220. Shanks, 67. Freeman Cleaves, *Rock of Chickamauga*, 165.

4. O'Connor, 40.

5. E. V. Westrate, *Those Fatal Generals*, 222-223. *O. R.*, XXX, Part I, 634.

Chapter Twenty—OLD PETER REACHES THE BATTLEFIELD

1. *Man. to App.*, 437-438. *Polk*, II, 256. Hood's *Advance and Retreat*, 63. Chick. Nat. Park scrapbook.

Dr. Charles P. McIlvaine who converted Polk to an ecclesiastical career served for a time as Chaplain of the United States Senate, then as a professor at West Point. He acted as a special envoy of President Lincoln to Great Britain in the early days of the war.

Chapter Twenty-one—PARALYSIS ON BRAGG'S RIGHT

1. *Dictionary of American Biography. Anecdotes*, 260. Contemporary criticism of Polk's course is shown in Snow, *Southern Generals*, 420.

2. *B. & L.*, III, 608. Colonel Urquhart gave no date but the incident must have related to Polk's arrest after Chickamauga. Cist, 63. *Anecdotes*, 345. O'Connor, 271. Chesnut, *Diary*, 248.

3. *Polk*, II, 258. 253ff. tells in detail of Polk's activities. *B. & L.*, III, 653. *O. R.*, XXX, Part II, 140.

4. *B. & L.*, III, 653.

5. *O. R.*, XXX, Part II, 61. Captain Wheeless' account is given in detail in *Polk*, II, 260ff.

6. Watkins' "*Co. Aytch*," 195. *Polk*, II, 308-309. Pollard, 450.

7. St. Louis *Globe Democrat*, July 11, 1890.

8. *B. & L.*, III, 653 and 484. *Biog. Directory of the American Congress. Dictionary of American Biography*. Warner's *Generals in Gray*, 34-35.

Chapter Twenty-two—POLK'S FUTILE BRIGADE ASSAULTS

1. Gordon's *Reminiscences*, 205. 32nd Regt. Papers, Ala. Archives. Warner's *Generals in Gray*, 1-3.

2. Beatty's *Memoirs*, 196 and 173.

3. *Ibid.*, 251 and 246. *Confed. Veteran*, Sept. 1895, 279.

4. *Ind. at Chick.*, 262-263. "The Blood of Boone," American Press Association feature story, 1892. Chick. Nat. Park scrapbook. Gerald McMurtry, "Confederate General Ben Hardin Helm: Kentucky Brother-in-Law of Abraham Lincoln," Filson Club *History Quarterly*, Oct. 1958, XXXII, no. 4, 311ff. Ruth Painter Randall, *Mary Lincoln: Biography of a Marriage*, 294-296. William H. Townsend, *Lincoln and His Wife's Home Town*, 306-308. Katherine Helm, *The True Story of Mary, Wife of Lincoln*, 126-127, 187-188, 216. Other of Mrs.

Lincoln's brothers were killed: Samuel Todd at Shiloh and David Todd
mortally wounded at Vicksburg.

5. 41st Ala. Papers, Ala. Archives. Clark, *N. C. Regts.*, III, 488.

6. *Polk*, II, 307. Sorrel, 190.

7. Watkins, "*Co. Aytch*," 96. Dr. William J. Worsham, *The Old
Nineteenth Tennessee Regiment*, 88-89, quotes Polk as saying, "Give
them what Cheatham says, boys, we will pay off old chores today."
Only Jackson's brigade of Cheatham's division became seriously engaged. Walker's "Pyramids," Chattanooga *Sunday Times*, Aug. 23,
1936. St. Louis *Globe Democrat*, Chick. Nat. Park scrapbook.

8. *Ibid.* Comte de Paris, 144, contrasts Polk's and Stonewall Jackson's generalship. Walker's "Pyramids," Chattanooga *Sunday Times*,
Oct. 4, 1936. *South Carolina at Chickamauga*, 15. *Confed. Veteran*, Sept.
1913, 436.

9. *O. R.*, XXX, Part I, 252. Palmer's *Recollections*, 181-182. *S.H.S.P.*,
IX, 411.

Chapter Twenty-three—WOOD LEAVES A GAP

1. Beatty's *Memoirs*, 176. Stanley F. Horn, *The Decisive Battle of
Nashville*, 85-86. *Dictionary of American Biography*. Bickham, 42, says
that Wood "was regarded second to none in experience and cultured
intellect." *Anecdotes*, 125.

2. Wood's report, *O. R.*, XXX, Part I, 634-636. *B. & L.*, III, 663.

3. Ridpath's *Garfield*, 152, uses the term "chasm" to describe the
gap in the line. A contrary view that would apply to Garfield's orders
is expressed by Henry Villard, *Memoirs*, II, 132: "There must have
been carelessness or confusion at Rosecrans' headquarters in issuing
orders. . . ." This related to orders not to Wood, but to an earlier order
sent by Garfield to McCook.

O. R., XXX, Part I, 635. Bickham, 29. Ridpath in saying Garfield
wrote all other orders, which is followed in the text, is referring to those
of significance, for minor orders appear over Bond's name in *O. R. Ind.
at Chick.*, 18. Shanks, 258, says of Rosecrans, "I have known him when
merely directing an orderly to carry a dispatch from one point to
another, grow so excited, vehement and incoherent as to utterly con-
found the messenger."

4. Palmer's *Recollections*, 187. John B. Turchin, *Chickamauga*, 112-
114. Van Horne, 131. *Ohio in the War*, I, 350.

5. *O. R.*, XXX, Part I, 624. Coppee's *Thomas*, 146-147n. *O. R.*, XXX,
Part I, 635.

Chapter *Twenty-Four*—PIERCING THE FEDERAL CENTER

1. Turchin, 116. D. H. Hill said, *B. & L.*, III, 652, that Longstreet had 22,845 men in his left wing. Hill's number seems small, but by deducting the six brigades of Stewart's and Preston's divisions, which were not in the assaulting column, the estimate of 17,000 seems fair, although it is probably a minimum figure.

2. St. Louis *Globe Democrat*, no date. Chick. Nat. Park scrapbook. Meredith Nicholson, *The Hoosiers*, 199-200. *Confed. Veteran*, July 1894, 205.

3. *Man. to App.*, 440-441. Johnson in his report says the position where he formed was 600 yards east of the La Fayette road. Hindman formed abreast Johnson's front line. The battlefield marker shows that McNair formed only 200 yards east of the La Fayette road. Some of the participants including Longstreet give the distance as 300 yards, which is used here. Nothing remains in the forest to indicate the positions where McNair and Fulton formed their first line, except the battlefield markers. Sartain's *Walker County*, 102.

4. Turchin, 116. *Ohio in the War*, II, 124.

5. *Confed. Veteran*, June 1914, 265. The details of Johnson's advance are taken largely from *O. R.*, XXX, Part I, 458-463.

6. *Song and Story*, 441-442. Reference to the origin of "Tarheels" with Hoke's division is contained in this writer's *High Tide at Gettysburg*, 291, citing North Carolina *Folklore*, July 1957. Clark, *N. C. Regts.*, II, 713-714. Raleigh *Standard*, Oct. 14, 1863.

7. *Confed. Veteran*, May 1911, 211. Warner's *Generals in Gray*, 295. Clark, *N. C. Regts.*, II, 713.

8. Granger in his report referred to "a 'horse-shoe' ridge." In applying the term to the far western end of the elevation, the writer here is following the official Chickamauga Battlefield map of the U.S. Geological Survey, Department of the Interior. The name of Horseshoe Ridge is often applied in later literature to the entire elevation.

9. *Confed. Veteran*, Dec. 1908, 629. *Ibid.*, July 1911, 339. *Ibid.*, Oct. 1908, 490.

10. Warner, *Generals in Gray*, 157-158. *Dictionary of American Biography*.

11. The old epitaph, now obliterated, is given by R. D. Fletcher in *Confed. Veteran*, Dec. 1907, 551.

In few places did Longstreet receive greater recognition for the ability shown in his attack than from Charles H. Grosvenor, lieutenant colonel of the 18th Ohio, Negley's division, long a member of Congress and later chairman of the Chickamauga National Park Commission. Speaking at the Rosecrans burial services conducted by the Society of the Army of the Cumberland, Grosvenor said that the Federals had no trouble at Chickamauga with Bragg's old force, "but there came like a scourge upon a battlefield a great body of tried soldiers from the Army of Northern Virginia under the command of the intrepid Longstreet." Calling attention to Longstreet's reference to numerous assaults, he said they seemed to him only one, which began around noon and lasted till dark. Then: "It came like a thunderbolt. It struck the battlefield at the river . . . and it crossed the battlefield, assailing at every point our lines, until its right was at Dry Valley Road, and wherever Union forces were found it struck with the mailed hand of a trained soldier." *Rosecrans Burial Services*, 44.

Sketches of Longstreet, Hood, Law, Robertson, Benning and a few lines about Humphreys and Kershaw, all of Longstreet's corps, are given by this writer in *High Tide at Gettysburg* and therefore omitted here.

Chapter Twenty-five—POE'S FIELD TO SNODGRASS HILL

1. Hood, *Advance and Retreat*, 63-65. Wilmington, N. C., *Journal*, Nov. 19, 1863. *Confed. Veteran*, Dec. 1912, 563. Chesnut, *Diary*, 248.
2. *Confed. Veteran*, Dec. 1912, 564. *Man. to App.*, 448. Ms. Reminiscences, Georgia Archives. Oates, 255. Oates, Speech, 4. Oates, 256-257.
3. *Man. to App.*, 448-449. Duvall Ms., 13-14. Turchin, 120-121.
4. *Ind. at Chick.*, 21 and 231-235. Piatt's *Thomas*, 213.

Chapter Twenty-six—ROUT OF DAVIS AND SHERIDAN

1. Hindman's report, *O. R.*, XXX, Part I, 303. Turchin, 116. *Ind. at Chick.*, 110.
2. Palmer, *Recollections*, 198, described Jefferson C. Davis as "an Indiana copperhead . . . but he was a soldier" who loved his country and was "the bravest of the brave." Atkins, 11. Wilder in St. Louis *Globe Democrat* interview, July 15, 1890.
3. E. O. Randall and D. J. Ryan, *History of Ohio*, V, 72. Reid, in *Ohio in the War*, 883, gives the six stanzas of "Antony and Cleopatra." *Michigan at Chick.*, 135. Howe, I, 835. Walker's "Pyramids," Chattanooga *Sunday Times*, Sept. 13, 1936. *Michigan at Chick.*, 136.

4. *Ohio in the War*, 880-883. Walker's "Pyramids," Sept. 13, 1936. *Song and Story*, 221.

5. Seitz, *Bragg*, 305, quotes in full the sonnet Lytle had in his pocket. Oates, 258. Walker, "Pyramids," Sept. 13, 1936, quotes the verses of "Company K."

6. *Ind. at Chick.*, 206. Wilder's report, *O. R.*, XXX, Part III, 448. *Ibid.*, I, 303.

7. Matthew F. Steele, I, 444, points out that Sheridan and Davis might have rallied and returned to the field as have others. *Confed. Veteran*, July 1914, 307-308.

8. *Song and Story*, 297. 39th Ala. papers, Ala. Archives. Wilson P. Howell Ms., Ala. Archives. Cunningham Letter, Ala. Archives.

9. *Confed. Veteran*, Nov. 1895, 329. *Man. to App.*, 452. *B. & L.*, III, 659.

Chapter Twenty-seven—THE PANIC OVERWHELMS ROSECRANS

1. Sartain's *Walker County*, 104. Theodore A. Dodge, *Hannibal*, Boston, 1896, 53. William D. Ward, *The Storm Breaks*, Ms. in DePauw University Archives. Hannaford, 464. Ted Gronert, *Sugar Creek Saga*, 173.

2. Gates P. Thruston, "The Crisis at Chickamauga," in *B. & L.*, III, 663-665. Surgeons F. H. Gross and J. Perkins, medical directors of McCook's Corps, also made their way to Thomas with Thruston. Van. Horne, 140.

3. Major Frank S. Bond's account was in a news feature story of the McClure syndicate in 1895. Chick. Nat. Park scrapbook. The Rose-crans-Garfield colloquy is from "The Relief of Rosecrans," in the booklet *Rosecrans Burial Services*, 88-89. Russell H. Conwell, *Life of James A. Garfield*, 170, says Garfield's influence over Rosecrans had become "almost supreme."

4. *Hough Letters*, 151n. Cist, 226. Cox, II, 10. Cox, who was not present, gave a graphic account of the rout of the right wing which he obtained shortly after the battle from Garfield in Cincinnati. His description of Rosecrans' return to Chattanooga was from an unidentified "eyewitness."

5. Dana, *Recollections*, 115-116. Wilder's account of his meeting with Dana is from his address to the Ohio Commandery, Loyal Legion, Nov. 4, 1908, 7-8. Atkins, 11.

6. Wilder address. Madison is quoted from this writer's *Poltroons and Patriots*, II, 533. Williams' *Wilder*, 34. Dana in *McClure's Magazine*, Feb. 1898, 352.

Chapter Twenty-eight—SNODGRASS HILL

1. Thomas Robson Hay, "The Campaign and Battle of Chicka-mauga," *Georgia Historical Quarterly*, VII, 299. Bragg spoke affectionately of "Old Tom" in the Mexican War days, *B. & L.*, III, 658n, but declined to receive a message from him during the Chattanooga campaign on the ground he had been unfaithful to his native state. Bickham, 33. Piatt, 212, 170 and 61. O'Connor, 358. Turchin, 165. Piatt, 180, 347. Bickham, 32. Coppee, 21. Horace Porter, *Campaigning with Grant*, 295. Richard Johnson, *Memoir of Major General George H. Thomas*, 83. Thomas was severed from his three sisters and one of his two brothers. He never saw his sisters after he remained with the Federal service, but was in contact with one brother, Benjamin, in Tennessee after the war. Two of his sisters were still living in the old Thomas home property in southern Virginia when Coppee wrote in 1893. Coppee's *General Thomas*, 3.

2. Piatt, 50, 334. *S.H.S.P.*, I, 426. Sorrel, 191. Cist, 237. O'Connor, 367. Piatt, 77, 342-343, 347.

3. Morton C. Hunter address reported in Bloomington, Ind., *Telephone*, Oct. 7, 1887. The number Brannan rallied on Snodgrass Hill has been estimated as high as 4,000, many of them men who returned without their officers and refused to be driven off the field. Turchin, 132. *Ohio in the War*, I, 955. Beatty, 253.

4. *Minnesota in the Civil and Indian Wars*, 100. *S.H.S.P.*, IX, 415. *Man. to App.*, 451. Oates, 259-260. Hinman, 429. St. Louis *Globe Democrat* story from Chick. Nat. Park scrapbook. *Ohio in the War*, I, 643; II, 838. Opdycke was breveted major general for his gallant service in the battle of Franklin, Tenn.

5. Turchin, 136. Hindman does not recognize in his report any leadership by Bushrod Johnson but Longstreet, *Man. to App.*, 450, said Johnson was ordered around noon to reorganize "his own brigades and those of Hindman for renewed work." Hindman was listed as wounded in the returns. He said, *O. R.*, XXX, Part I, 305, that he did not turn over command of his division to General Anderson until 11 P.M. but Longstreet apparently looked to Johnson much earlier for leadership of both divisions, after Hood had been taken from the field.

Chapter Twenty-nine—MARCH OF GRANGER AND STEEDMAN

1. John M. Morgan's *Old Steady*, etc., 85. Much of the detail about the march of Granger and Steedman is from Isaac H. C. Royse, *History of the 115th Illinois Volunteers*, 120-131.

2. Morton, *Forrest's Artillery*, 121. J. T. Woods, *Steedman and His Men*, 44.

3. Abbott, II, 426, gives the account of the observer Shanks. Woods, *Steedman*, 48.

Chapter Thirty—HORSESHOE RIDGE

1. *Anecdotes*, 317. *Song and Story*, 389. *Pa. at Chick.*, 238.

2. St. Louis *Globe Democrat*, Chick. Nat. Park scrapbook. *Ibid.*, July 11, 1890. Ridley, 226.

3. Frank A. Burr interview, Cincinnati *Enquirer*, Chick. Nat. Park scrapbook. *Ohio in the War*, II, 151. Edward Anderson paper, Chick. Nat. Park scrapbook. Bloomington, Ind. *Telephone*, Chick. scrapbook.

4. Oates, 264. *B. & L.*, III, 602. 28th Ala. Papers, Ala. Archives.

5. Clark, *N. C. Regts.*, III, 447. There appears no stronger case that the 58th N. C. here made the farthest advance at Chickamauga than that the 60th did in Breckinridge's earlier attack. Captain Clinton C. Cilley of Van Derveer's brigade (Federal) is quoted in *N. C. Regts.*, V, 172, as saying the North Carolina commissioners marking the field agreed that the 58th N. C. reached the "point where the topmost wave of Southern battle broke nearer than any other to the unbroken lines of Thomas' defense," a rather uncertain claim in such a fluid battle. With the lines so vague, it would be difficult to establish what regiment or brigade made the farthest advance.

Neither Brigade Commander Kelly nor Colonel Palmer, commanding the 58th North Carolina, made the claim of farthest advance. *O. R.*, XXX, Part II, 441 and 445. Kelly said the regiment was exposed to a galling fire in front and flank and "after losing about half its numbers was compelled to fall back." The regiment was shifted in the brigade line for a second attack an hour and a half later but in this action did not advance as far as Trigg's brigade.

Gracie in his report, *O. R.*, XXX, Part II, 421 gave his loss as 705. Others have placed it still higher.

Chapter Thirty-one—WITHDRAWAL AND RETREAT

1. Ridpath's *Garfield*, 155. Bond account in McClure Syndicate article, 1895, Chick. Nat. Park scrapbook. Van Horne, 140. Cist, 226.

2. *Ind. at Chick.*, 199-200, gives details of King's death, contained in a letter by General T. J. Wood, whose wife was King's niece. High's *68th Ind.*, 95-96. *Ibid.*, 280.

3. Turchin, 147ff. *Ohio in the War*, II, 514. *Song and Story*, 367.

4. Horace Porter's statement reflecting on the courage and veracity of the newspaper correspondents is quoted in Kenneth P. Williams, *Lincoln Finds a General*, V, 263, from a letter from Porter to his sister.

5. Palmer's *Recollections*, 184 and 182. *Ind. at Chick.*, 172. Hannaford, 467. Briant's *6th Ind.*, 238-239. *Ind. at Chick.*, 88-89.

6. St. Louis *Globe Democrat*, Chick. Nat. Park scrapbook. Morgan's *Old Steady*, 91. *Ohio in the War*, II, 150-151. Belknap's *Michigan Organizations*, 150-151.

7. *Ind. at Chick.*, 129, 196. Beatty, 251-252. *Hough Letters*, 152. Ward, *The Storm Breaks*. High's *58th Ind.*, 185. Van Horne, 147.

8. Ms. letter, Emory University Special Collections. 25th Ala. papers, Ala. Archives. Watkins, "*Co. Aytch*," 98.

. Lack of water was as pressing a problem on Snodgrass Hill as was the enemy. Scarcely was there a canteen that was not empty. Thirst was fully as acute on Thomas' old lines east of the La Fayette road. A correspondent ran across 17 or 18 wounded soldiers in an old house, forgotten by their commands. They were members of two Ohio and one Indiana regiment and all were moaning for water.

N. J. Hampton, *An Eyewitness*, 34. *Song and Story*, 297 and 374.

9. *Mich. at Chick.*, 94-95. Before the battlefield was well marked, direction boards were nailed to trees. One was intended to show the road followed by some of Thomas' divisions leaving the field. It read "Route of Baird's and Johnson's Divisions on evening of the 20th." Some wag climbed the tree and knocked off the "e," making the sign read "Rout of Baird's and Johnson's divisions, etc." St. Louis *Globe Democrat* clipping in Chick. Nat. Park scrapbook.

Chapter Thirty-two—BRAGG'S DILATORY PURSUIT

1. *Confed. Veteran*, Oct. 1896, 358. *Tennessee Monuments and Markers*, 32. Sartain's *Walker County*, 101-102 and 108.

2. *B. & L.*, III, 659n. Du Bose's *Wheeler*, 196. Pollard, 453. Sorrel, 192. Van Horne, 149. *Polk*, II, 280. James C. Nisbet, *Four Years on the Firing Line*, 206-214. Oates, 264.

3. Wyeth's *Forrest*, 259-263. Morton, *Forrest's Artillery*, 127-128. *B. & L.*, III, 662.

4. St. Louis *Globe Democrat*, July 11, 1890.
Morton, 130, tells the story of Forrest's denunciation of Bragg, as related by Dr. J. B. Cowan, who accompanied Forrest.

5. *Rosecrans Burial Services*, 96. The case that Garfield was a factor

in the removal of Rosecrans seems well established. Henry Howe, I, 562-563. Piatt, 51. *Proceedings of Chickamauga Memorial Association,* 27-31. L. H. Stout, *Reminiscences of General Braxton Bragg,* 19.

Chapter Thirty-three—AN ABORTIVE VICTORY

1. *Ind. at Chick.,* 135. Cist, 227. *Ind. at Chick.,* 103. *Polk,* II, 287. Piatt, 229. Gordon's *Reminiscences,* 212.

2. *Ohio in the War,* I, 1030.

3. Oates address, 4. St. Louis *Globe Democrat,* July 11, 1890. *Ibid.,* July 10, 1890. Oates, 264-265.

Bibliography

Abbott, John S. C. *The History of the Civil War in America.* 2 vols. New York, 1863 and 1866.

Adamson, A. P. *Brief History of the 30th Georgia Regiment.* Griffin, Georgia. No date.

Adney, Robert. Ms. Account of the Battle of Chickamauga. Oakley, Kansas.

Alabama Archives. Folders of Ms. letters, diaries, memoirs, etc., relating to Alabama regiments in brigades of S. A. M. Wood, Helm, Adams, Deas, Manigault, Bate, Clayton, Gracie, and Law.

Alexander, E. P. *Military Memoirs of a Confederate.* New York, 1907.

Anderson, Archer. *Campaign and Battle of Chickamauga.* Southern Historical Society Papers. IX. 1881.

Anderson, Edward L. (Capt. 52nd Ohio Vol. Inf.). "Colonel Archibald Gracie's *The Truth About Chickamauga.*" Ohio Commandry, the Loyal Legion, Feb. 7, 1912.

Annals of the War. Philadelphia, 1879.

Athearn, Robert G., editor. *Soldier in the West—The Civil War Letters of Alfred Lacey Hough.* Philadelphia, 1957.

Atkins, Smith D. *Chickamauga: Useless, Disastrous Battle.* Address. Freeport, Ill. 1907.

Austin, J. P. *The Blue and the Gray.* Atlanta, 1899.

Barnes, James A., James R. Carnahan and Thomas H. B. McCain. *The Eighty-sixth Regiment Indiana Volunteer Infantry.* Crawfordsville, Indiana. 1895.

Battles and Leaders of the Civil War. 4 vols. New York, 1884.

Beatty, John. *Memoirs of a Volunteer.* Edited by Henry S. Ford. New York, 1946. Also earlier edition: *The Citizen Soldier, or Memoirs of a Volunteer.* Cincinnati, 1879.

Belknap, C. E. *History of the Michigan Organizations at Chickamauga, Chattanooga and Missionary Ridge.* Lansing, 1899.

Bennison, R. T. "General Braxton Bragg." *The Field Artillery Journal,* November—December, 1931, page 601. Field Artillery Assn., 1918 Harford Avenue, Baltimore.

Bickham, W. D. *Rosecrans' Campaign with the Fourteenth Army Corps.* Cincinnati, 1863.

Bloomington, Indiana, *Telephone.* Newspaper. Address by General Morton C. Hunter at Columbus, Indiana. Oct. 7, 1887.

Boynton, H. V., compiler. Dedication of the Chickamauga-Chattanooga National Military Park, Sept. 18 to 20, 1895. "Report of Joint Committee . . ." Government Printing Office, Washington, 1896.

Bratnober, August. Ms. diary of member of Scribner's Brigade, owned by his grandson Carl Bratnober, St. Paul, Minn.

Briant, C. G. *History of the 6th Indiana Regiment.* Indianapolis, 1891.

Buck, Irving S. *Cleburne and His Men.* Thomas Robson Hay, editor. Jackson, Tenn., 1959 (reprinted).

Burr, Frank A. *The Life of General Philip H. Sheridan.* Providence, Rhode Island, 1888.

Byrne, Mrs. Luke G. "Bishop Rosecrans." *Old Northwest Genealogy Quarterly,* vol. 9 (1906), Toledo. P. 311.

Canfield, S. S. *History of the 21st Ohio Regiment.* Toledo, 1893.

Chattanooga *Times.* Newspaper.

Chesnut, Mary Boykin. *A Diary from Dixie.* Edited by Isabella D. Martin and Myrta Lockett Avary. London, 1905.

Chickamauga and Chattanooga National Park Commission. "The Campaign for Chattanooga." 1896.

Chickamauga and Chattanooga National Military Park. Troop position maps. Also miscellaneous letters and manuscripts.

———. Scrapbooks of clippings from random newspapers.

Chickamauga Memorial Association. Proceedings at Chattanooga, Tennessee and Crawfish Springs, Georgia, Sept. 19-20, 1889. Chattanooga, 1889.

Cincinnati *Enquirer.* Newspaper. Clippings, including undated interview with Colonel Frank A. Burr, 21st Ohio Infantry.

Cist, Henry M. *The Army of the Cumberland.* New York, 1882.

Clark, Walter. *Histories of the Several Regiments and Battalions from North Carolina in the Great War, 1861-1865.* 5 vols. Vols. II and III. Raleigh, 1901.

Cleaves, Freeman. *Rock of Chickamauga—The Life of General George H. Thomas.* Norman, Oklahoma, 1948.

Commager, Henry Steele, editor. *The Blue and the Gray.* Indianapolis, 1950.

Confederate Veteran.

Connolly, James A. *Three Years in the Army of the Cumberland.* (Edited by Paul M. Angle.) Republished, Bloomington, Indiana, 1959.

Conwell, Russell H. *The Life, Speeches and Public Service of James A. Garfield.* Boston, 1881.

Coppee, Henry. *General Thomas.* New York, 1893.

Coulter, E. Merton. *The Confederate States of America, 1861-1865.* Baton Rouge, 1950.

Cox, Jacob Dolson. *Military Reminiscences of the Civil War.* 2 vols. New York, 1900.

Cummings, Kate. *Journals of Hospital Life.* Louisville, 1866.

Cunningham, John. "A letter Written by My Brother W. H. Cunningham Immediately after the Battle of Chickamauga." No date. Evergreen, Ala. (Letter dated Sept. 27, 1863.)

Dana, Charles A. *Recollections of the Civil War.* New York, 1898.

———. "Reminiscences of Men and Events." *McClure's Magazine,* Vol. 10, Nov. 1897.

Davies, Henry E. *General Sheridan.* New York, 1897.

Dickert, D. Augustus. *History of Kershaw's Brigade.* Newberry, S. C. 1899.

Dictionary of American Biography.

Drake, Edwin L., editor. *Annals of the Army of Tennessee.* Nashville, 1878.

DuBose, John Witherspoon. *General Joseph Wheeler and the Army of Tennessee.* New York, 1912.

Duvall, Captain Lemark. "Description of the Battle of Chickamauga." Ms. at New York Public Library copied May 25, 1923, by Harry G. Gager from Ms. letter to his father, George W. Gager of Cincinnati.

Eckenrode, H. J., and Bryan Conrad. *James Longstreet, Lee's War Horse.* Chapel Hill, N. C., 1936.

Emory University. Soldiers' letters in Special Collections Department.

Fiske, John. *The Mississippi Valley in the Civil War.* Boston, 1902.

Fitch, John. *Annals of the Army of the Cumberland.* Philadelphia, 1863.

Freeman, Douglas Southall. *Lee's Lieutenants.* 3 vols. New York, 1942. Vol. 3.

Furay, W. S. (War correspondent of Cincinnati *Gazette*), and Colonel G. C. Kniffin (Chief Commissary 21st Corps). "The Real Chickamauga." Articles in *State Journal,* Columbus, Ohio, September 1888.

Georgia—Soldiers' Letters in Historical and Archives Department, State of Georgia.

Globe Democrat. Series of news stories from Washington and Chickamauga, in Scrap Book at Chickamauga National Military Park. No dates or city specified but apparently St. Louis *Globe Democrat* articles of 1890-1893.

Gordon, John B. *Reminiscences of the Civil War*. New York and Atlanta, 1904. (Memorial edition.)

Gracie, Archibald. *The Truth about Chickamauga*. Boston, 1911.

Greeley, Horace. *The American Conflict*. 2 vols. Hartford, 1867. Vol. 2.

Gronert, Ted. *Sugar Creek Saga*. Crawfordsville, Ind., 1958.

Hampton, N. J. *An Eyewitness to the Dark Days of 1861-1865*. Nashville, 1898.

Hannaford, E. *The Story of a Regiment*. (Sixth Ohio Volunteers.) Cincinnati, 1868.

Hartpence, William R. *The 51st Indiana Volunteers*. Cincinnati, 1894.

Hay, Thomas Robson. *Braxton Bragg and the Southern Confederacy*. (Pamphlet.) Reprinted from *Georgia Historical Quarterly*.

———. "The Campaign and Battle of Chickamauga," *Georgia Historical Quarterly*, vol. 7.

———, editor; Buck Irving S., author. *Cleburne and His Men*. Jackson, Tennessee (reprinted), 1959.

Haynie, J. H., editor. *The 19th Illinois*. Chicago, 1912.

Heg, Hans Christian. *Civil War Letters of Colonel Heg*. Norwegian-American Historical Association, Northfield, Minn., 1936.

Helm, Katherine. *The True Story of Mary, Wife of Lincoln*. New York, 1920.

Henry, Robert Selph. *"First with the Most" Forrest*. Indianapolis, 1944.

Herr, John. Ms. Letter to his brother Shirl Herr of Crawfordsville, Indiana, after visit to Chickamauga battlefield in 1913.

High, Edwin W. *The 68th Indiana*. Metamora, Ind., 1902.

High, John J. *History of the 58th Regiment of Indiana Volunteer Infantry*. Princeton, Indiana, 1895.

Hinman, Wilbur F. *The Story of the Sherman Brigade*. 1897.

Hood, John B. *Advance and Retreat*. New Orleans, 1880.

Horn, Stanley F. *The Army of Tennessee. A Military History*. Indianapolis, 1942.

———. *The Decisive Battle of Nashville*. Baton Rouge, 1956.

Howe, Henry. *Historical Collections of Ohio*. 2 vols. Cincinnati, 1889-1891.

Indiana at Chickamauga. Report of Indiana Commission, Chickamauga National Park. 1901.

Johnson, Richard W. *Memoir of Major General George H. Thomas*. Philadelphia, 1881.

Jones, J. B. *A Rebel War Clerk's Diary.* 2 vols. Philadelphia, 1866.

Kellenberger, T. B. Ms. Letter, Indiana State Library. Nov. 15, 1863. Also Ms. diary of 6th Indiana Volunteer Infantry, 1861-1864.

Kirkpatrick, George Morgan. The experiences of a Private Soldier of the Civil War. No date or place.

Kirkland, Frazer. *The Pictorial Book of Anecdotes of the Rebellion, etc.* Hillsdale, Michigan, 1887.

Lewis, Lloyd. *Sherman, Fighting Prophet.* New York, 1932.

Longstreet, James. *From Manassas to Appomattox.* Philadelphia, 1896.

Lonn, Ella. *Foreigners in the Confederacy.* Chapel Hill, 1940.

Lossing, Benson J. *Pictorial History of the Civil War.* Hartford, 1874.

Martin, W. T. *A Defense of General Bragg's Conduct at Chickamauga.* Natchez, Miss., Feb. 3, 1883. Southern Historical Society Papers, XI, 1883.

McFarland, R. W. (Late Lt. Col. 86th Ohio Vol. Inf.) *The Surrender of Cumberland Gap, September 9, 1863.* Columbus, O., 1898.

McLaws, Lafayette, Papers. Southern Historical Collection. University of North Carolina Library. Chapel Hill, N. C.

McMurtry, R. Gerald. *Confederate General Ben Hardin Helm: Kentucky Brother-in-Law of Abraham Lincoln.* The Filson Club Historical Quarterly. Louisville, Ky., October 1958.

Minnesota in the Civil and Indian Wars. St. Paul, 1890.

Monaghan, Jay. *The Civil War on the Western Border, 1854-1865.* Boston, 1955.

Moore, Frank, editor. *The Civil War in Song and Story.* New York, 1889.

————. *Women of the War.* Hartford, 1866.

Morgan, John M. *Old Steady: The Role of General James Blair Steedman at the Battle of Chickamauga.* Northwest Ohio Quarterly, Spring 1950.

Morris, Lloyd. *The Rebellious Puritan: Portrait of Mr. Hawthorne.* New York, 1927.

Morton, John Watson. *The Artillery of Nathan Bedford Forrest's Cavalry.* Nashville, 1909.

Nash, C. E. *Biographical Sketches of Generals Pat Cleburne and T. C. Hindman.* 1898.

National Military Park, Chickamauga—Chattanooga. An Historical Guide. Cincinnati, 1895.

New York *Herald.* Newspaper. Files of 1863.

New York *Times.* Newspaper. Files of 1863.

New York *Tribune.* Newspaper. Files of 1863.

Nicholson, Meredith. *The Hoosiers.* 1900.

Nisbet, James Cooper. *Four Years on the Firing Line.* Chattanooga.

Oates, William C. *The War Between the Union and the Confederacy.* New York, 1905.

———. Speech on Battle of Chickamauga at Dedication of Chickamauga-Chattanooga National Park, Sept. 20, 1895.

O'Connor, Richard. *Thomas: Rock of Chickamauga.* New York, 1948.

Official Records of the Union and Confederate Armies. Washington, 1882-1900.

Ohio Archeological and Historical Society Papers.

Palmer, John M. *Personal Recollections of John M. Palmer.* Cincinnati, 1901.

Paris, Comte de. *History of the Civil War in America.* 4 vols. Philadelphia, 1888. Vol. IV.

Peele, W. J. *Lives of Distinguished North Carolinians.* 1898.

Pennsylvania at Chickamauga and Chattanooga. Captain George W. Skinner, Editor and Compiler. 1897.

Perry, Henry F. *History of the 38th Indiana Regiment.* Palo Alto, 1906.

Philadelphia *Inquirer.* Newspaper.

Piatt, Donn. *General George H. Thomas.* A Critical Biography, with Concluding Chapters by Henry V. Boynton. Cincinnati, 1893.

———. *Memoirs of the Men Who Saved the Union.* New York, 1887.

Polk, William M. *Leonidas Polk: Bishop and General.* 2 vols. New York, 1915. Also edition of 1893.

Pollard, Edward A. *The Lost Cause.* New York, 1866.

Polley, Joseph Benjamin. *Hood's Texas Brigade.* New York, 1910.

Porter, General Horace. *Campaigning with Grant.* New York, 1907.

Raleigh *Weekly Standard.* Newspaper.

Randall, E. O., and D. J. Ryan. *History of Ohio.* 1912. Vol. V.

Randall, Ruth Painter. *Mary Lincoln: Biography of a Marriage.* Boston, 1953.

Reid, Whitelaw. *Ohio in the War—Her Statesmen, Generals and Soldiers.* 2 vols. Columbus, Ohio, 1893.

Richmond *Examiner.* Newspaper. Files of 1863.

Richmond *Inquirer.* Newspaper. Files of 1863.

Richmond *Whig.* Newspaper. Files of 1863.

Ridley, Bromfield L. *Battles and Sketches of the Army of Tennessee.* Mexico, Missouri, 1906.

Ridpath, John Clark, *The Life and Work of James A. Garfield.* Cincinnati, 1881.

Royse, Isaac H. C. *History of the 115th Illinois Volunteers*. Terre Haute, Ind., 1900.

Rustling, James F. *Men and Things I Saw in Civil War Days*. New York, 1899.

Sandburg, Carl. *Abraham Lincoln: The War Years*. New York, 1939.

Sanger, D. B., and Thomas Robson Hay. *James Longstreet*. Baton Rouge, 1952.

St. Louis *Globe Democrat*. Newspaper.

Sartain, James Alfred. *History of Walker County, Georgia*, Vol. I. Dalton, Georgia, 1932.

Seitz, Don C. *Braxton Bragg*. Columbia, S. C., 1924.

Seventy-third Illinois Volunteer Infantry. *Proceedings of various regimental reunions held at Springfield, 1887 to 1898*. Illinois State Library.

Shanks, W. F. G. *Personal Recollections of Distinguished Generals*. New York, 1886.

Shaver, Lewellyn A. *A History of the Sixteenth Alabama Regiment, Gracie's Alabama Brigade*. Montgomery, 1867.

Sheridan, Philip H. *Memoirs*. New York, 1892.

Smith, J. C. "Oration at the Unveiling of the Monument Erected to the Memory of Major General James B. Steedman." 1887.

Snow, William Parker. *Southern Generals, Their Lives and Campaigns*. New York, 1866.

Society of the Army of the Cumberland. *Burial of General Rosecrans, Arlington National Cemetery, May 17, 1902*. Cincinnati, 1903.

———. Proceedings at reunion of Chickamauga battlefield, Sept. 15-16, 1892.

Sorrel, G. Moxley. *Recollections of a Confederate Staff Officer*. New York, 1905. Reprinted, Jackson, Tennessee, 1958.

South Carolina at Chickamauga. No date or place.

Southern Bivouac.

Southern Historical Society Papers.

Steele, Matthew Forney. *American Campaigns*. 2 vols. Washington, 1909.

Stout, Dr. L. H. *Reminiscences of General Braxton Bragg*. Roswell, Georgia, 1876. Hattiesburg, Mississippi, 1942.

Sullivan, James R. *Chickamauga and Chattanooga Battlefields*. Washington, 1956.

Swiggett, Howard. *The Rebel Raider. A Life of John Hunt Morgan*. Indianapolis, 1934.

Sykes, E. T. "A Cursory Sketch of General Bragg's Campaigns." Serially in *Southern Historical Society Papers*, XII, 1884.

Taggart, Joseph, *Biographical Sketches of Eminent American Patriots*, Kansas City, 1907.

Taylor, Richard. *Destruction and Reconstruction*. New York, 1879.

Tennessee Monuments and Markers. Report of the Tennessee Commission for Chickamauga.

Thompson, E. P. *History of the First Kentucky Brigade*. 1868.

Townsend, William H. *Lincoln and His Wife's Home Town*. Indianapolis, 1929.

Turchin, John B. *Chickamauga*. Chicago, 1888.

Turner, George Edgar. *Victory Rode the Rails: The Strategic Place of the Railroads in the Civil War*. Indianapolis, 1953.

United Daughters of the Confederacy, Georgia Division. Bound typewritten copies of letters and reminiscences of Confederate soldiers, Vols. I and VII. Georgia State Archives.

Van Horne, Thomas B. *History of the Army of the Cumberland*. Cincinnati, 1873.

———. *Life of Major General George H. Thomas*. New York, 1882.

Villard, Henry. *Memoirs of Henry Villard, Journalist and Financier, 1855-1900*. Vol. II. New York, 1904.

Walker, Robert Sparks. "Pyramids of Chickamauga." Series in Chattanooga *Sunday Times*. 1936.

Ward, William D. *The Storm Breaks*. MS. in DePauw University Archives.

Warner, Ezra J. *Generals in Gray*. Baton Rouge, 1959.

Warner, J. H., *Personal Glimpses of the Civil War. Nineteenth Tennessee*. Chattanooga, 1914.

Watkins, Sam R. *"Co. Aytch." Maury Grays First Tennessee Regiment*, or, A Side Show of the Big Show. Nashville, 1882.

Welles, Col. E. T. "The Campaign of Chickamauga." *U. S. Service Journal*, Vol. XVI (Sept. 1896). Pp. 217-227.

Western Pennsylvania History Magazine, April, 1931. Article by A. P. James on "General James Scott Negley."

Westrate, Edwin V. *Those Fatal Generals*. New York, 1936.

Wilder, John C. Paper of John C. Wilder, Colonel 17th Indiana Volunteers, of Knoxville, Tenn. Read before the Ohio Commandery of the Loyal Legion, Nov. 4, 1908.

Wiley, Bell, and Hirst D. Milhollen. *They Who Fought Here*. New York, 1959.

Williams, Kenneth P. *Lincoln Finds a General.* 5 vols. New York, 1959. Vol. V.

Williams, Samuel C. *General John T. Wilder, Commander of the Lightning Brigade.* Bloomington, Ind., 1936.

Wilmington, N. C., *Daily Journal.* Newspaper.

Wilson, James H. *Life of Charles A. Dana.* New York, 1907.

Wolfe, Thomas. Battle of Chickamauga, in *The Hills Beyond.* New York, 1958.

Woods, J. T. *Steedman and His Men at Chickamauga.* Toledo, 1876.

Worsham, Dr. William Johnson. *The Old Nineteenth Tennessee Regiment, C. S. A., June 1861-April 1865.* Knoxville, 1902.

Wyeth, John Allen, M. D., *Life of General Nathan Bedford Forrest.* New York and London, 1899.

Young, J. P., *The Seventh Tennessee Cavalry (Confederate), A History.* Nashville, 1890.

Index

444   CHICKAMAUGA

Scales, Col. Junius I., 363
Scammon, Eliakim Parker, 35
Schofield, Maj. Gen. John M., 142, 146, 323
Schueler, Lt. Gustavus, 270
Scituate, R. I., 32
Scott, Gen. Winfield, 106, 123
Scribner, Col. Benjamin F., 133-34
2nd Alabama, 351
2nd Arkansas, 247
2nd Georgia, 171
2nd Kentucky, 238, 242, 310
2nd Indiana Cavalry, 245
Second Manassas, 35, 46
"Second Methodist Regiment," 106
2nd Minnesota Infantry, 134, 136-37, 155, 242-43, 333, 372
Seddon, Sec. James A., 83, 86-87
Sedgwick, Maj. Gen. John, 78
Seibles, Major, 335
Seminary Ridge, 29, 125
Seminole Indians, 131
Senate of Carthage, 52
Sevastapol, Battle of, 148
7th South Carolina, 335-36
7th Texas, 172-73
17th Indiana Infantry, 115-16, 298, 308
17th Kentucky, 155-56, 332
17th Ohio, 266
17th Tennessee, 264-65, 376
72nd Indiana Mounted, 113, 162
73rd Illinois, 106, 324
74th Indiana, 130
75th Indiana, 157-58, 363
77th Pennsylvania, 146, 189
78th Pennsylvania Infantry, 60, 64, 146, 188
79th Illinois, 189
79th Indiana, 155-56
79th Pennsylvania, 192, 348
Shackelford, Brig. Gen. James M., 57
Shanks, W. F., 37-38, 139-40, 205, 344, 364
Shaver, Lewellyn A., 190
Shawnee Indians, 122
Sheffield, Col. James L., 261, 282-83
Shelby, Gov. Isaac, 103
Shellmound, 21, 23, 28
Shenandoah Valley, 65, 92, 231
Sheridan, Maj. Gen. Philip H., 23, 104
05, 115, 166, 174, 204-05, 207, 216-17, 266-70, 288-90, 292-93,

299-300, 302-03, 309-12, 315-16, 321, 335, 344, 370
Sherman, William T., 77-78, 116, 120, 146, 152, 167, 252, 265, 276, 341
"Sherman's Hairpins," 116
Shiloh, Battle of, 20, 22, 69, 75-76, 79, 102-04, 116, 142, 144-45, 152, 156, 179, 234, 276, 355, 365, 388-89
Shurtleff College, 146
Sickles, Gen. Daniel E., 211, 285
Sill, Gen. Joshua W., 294
Sirwell, Col. William, 64, 68, 234, 333, 351
6th Indiana, 144, 164, 366, 370
6th Kentucky, 238-39, 242
6th Ohio Battery, 122, 204, 365
6th Texas, 77, 245
16th Alabama, 179, 190
16th U.S. Infantry, 134, 360
60th North Carolina, 192, 243
63rd Virginia, 353
65th Georgia, 353
66th Georgia, 379
68th Indiana, 361-62, 369
Skinner, Capt. George W., 147
Skipper, Bryant, 335
Slavens, Lt. James W. L., 5
Sloan, John N., 302-03
Slocum, Henry W., 229
Smith, Caleb B., 55
Smith, Lt. Frank G., 134
Smith, Col. John T., 5
Smith, Kirby, 90, 220, 235, 354, 356
Smith, Brig. Gen. Preston, 20, 142, 145 46, 185, 189
Smith, Col. Thomas Benton, 160
Snodgrass, George Washington, 202-03
Snodgrass Farm, 197, 268, 330, 333, 335-36, 362, 367
Snodgrass Hill, 7, 109, 270, 272-73, 275, 279, 288-89, 299-300, 303-04, 311, 317-19, 321, 339, 341-42, 344, 346, 348-49, 351-53, 356-58, 361-65, 367-69, 388, 391-92
Snowden, Lt. Col. Bogardus, 7, 271, 276
Society of the Army of the Cumberland, 32
Somerville, Tennessee, 271
Sorrel, Lt. Col. G. Moxley, 85-86, 91, 93, 95, 211-14, 244, 326, 378-79